STUDIES IN IMPERIALISM

D1111505

general editor John M. MacKenzie

Established in the belief that imperialism as a cultural
phenomenon had as significant an effect on the dominant
as on the subordinate societies, Studies in Imperialism
seeks to develop the new socio-cultural approach which
has emerged through cross-disciplinary work on popular
culture, media studies, art history, the study of education
and religion, sports history and children's literature.
The cultural emphasis embraces studies of migration and
race, while the older political, and constitutional,
economic and military concerns will never be far away.
It will incorporate comparative work on European and
American empire-building, with the chronological focus
primarily, though not exclusively, on the nineteenth and
twentieth centuries, when these cultural exchanges were
most powerfully at work.

STUDIES IN
IMPERIALISM

Empire
and sexuality
THE BRITISH EXPERIENCE

Ronald Hyam

**MANCHESTER
UNIVERSITY PRESS**
Manchester and New York

Distributed exclusively in the USA and Canada
by ST. MARTIN'S PRESS

Copyright © Ronald Hyam 1990, 1991, 1992

Published by **MANCHESTER UNIVERSITY PRESS**
OXFORD ROAD, MANCHESTER M13 9PL, UK
and ROOM 400, 175 FIFTH AVENUE, NEW YORK, NY 10010, USA

Distributed exclusively in the USA and Canada by
ST. MARTIN'S PRESS, INC.
175 FIFTH AVENUE, NEW YORK, NY 10010, USA

Reprinted in paperback 1991, 1992

British Library cataloguing in publication data
Hyam, Ronald
　　Empire and sexuality : the British experience. – (Studies in imperialism)
　　1. British imperialism, Sexual aspects, history. I. Title
　　325.320941

Library of Congress cataloging in publication data
Hyam, Ronald.
　　　　Empire and sexuality : the British experience. — Ronald Hyam.
　　　　　　p.　　cm. — (Studies in imperialism)
　　　　Includes bibliographical references.
　　　　ISBN 0-7190-2505-2 paperback
　　　　　　1. Sex—Great Britain—Colonies. 2. Imperialism. 3. Prostitution—Great Britain—
　　　　Colonies. I. Title. II. Series: Studies in imperialism (Manchester, England)
　　　　HQ18.G7H93　　1990
　　　　306.7'0941—dc20　　89-77936

ISBN 0-7190-2505-2 *paperback*

Typeset in Trump Mediaeval by
Koinonia Limited, Manchester

Printed in Great Britain by
Bell & Bain Limited, Glasgow

CONTENTS

LIST OF FIGURES

PREFACE

I am indebted to the editors of the *Journal of Imperial and Commonwealth History* for permission to reproduce material which first appeared as articles in vols. XIV (January and May 1986) and XVII (October 1988) and to those readers who wrote to share their insights with me. I am especially grateful for the help and suggestions I have received from Christopher Bradbury Robinson, Eamon Duffy, Vic Gatrell, Anthony Kirk-Greene, John MacKenzie, Ged Martin and Andrew Porter. I also wish to thank Timothy d'Arch Smith, John Lonsdale, Peter J. Marshall, Anthony Milner, Doug Munro, David Throup and Charles van Onselen for guidance on particular issues; together with Mary Coleman, who did most of the typing. The extract from 'Annus Mirabilis' in *High Windows* by Philip Larkin is reprinted by permission of Faber and Faber Ltd and Farrar, Straus and Giroux, Inc.

A wise reviewer once said that there are too many books about sex, and the only way to reduce their number would be to make it mandatory for a full frontal nude photograph of the author to appear on the dust-jacket. I hope it will not seem unduly evasive if I describe this book as primarily a study of British imperial history; although it has rather a lot to say about sex, it is addressed first and foremost to those who are interested in exploring the underlying realities of British expansion on the world stage. If it seems Eurocentric, that is in part the inevitable result of concentrating on the attitudes and activities of the men who ran the empire; but it is in part, I believe, an illusion, for my ways of looking at sex have become decidedly more Asian than European, and this gives its own perspective to my evaluation of British experience as a whole. If it also seems at times slightly elegiac, that is no doubt the subconscious effect of its being written during the upsurge of AIDS, which may mark the end of a sexual era in the history of mankind. Whether the imperatives are medical or political, however, a return to late-Victorian sexual values is the last thing the world needs.

R.H.
Magdalene College, Cambridge

PREFACE
TO THE PAPERBACK EDITION

Not unnaturally, I have been scanning the recent literature to see if the hypotheses of this book are being sustained. On points of detail, one of my speculations seems to be wrong. The suggested close relationship between anal intercourse, clitoridectomy and AIDS (p. 197) already seems unconvincing. As far as the larger issues of interpretation are concerned, the importance of sex in the racial policies of empire is confirmed by Ann L. Stoler, 'Making empire respectable: politics of race and sexual morality in twentieth-century colonial cultures', *American Ethnologist*, XVI, 1989, pp. 634-60. And I am more convinced than ever that scholarship is demolishing the notion of a single, privileged, universally 'correct' code of sexual behaviour, least of all one constructed in western Christendom. Fundamentally different (essentially more pragmatic and relaxed) views exist in Africa and Asia, which represent the conclusions of alternative civilisations, not to be dismissed as morally backsliding versions of the European construct. Two very important new articles on this theme are: J. C. Caldwell *et al.*, 'The social context of AIDS in sub-Saharan Africa', in *Population and Development Review*, XV, 1989, pp. 185-234, and D. L. Davis and R. G. Whitten, 'The cross-cultural study of human sexuality', *Annual Review of Anthropology*, XVI, 1987, pp. 69-78. The extraordinary hypocrisy and cruelty of British sexual politics has been demonstrated by Richard Davenport-Hines, *Sex, death and punishment: attitudes to sex and sexuality in Britain since the Renaissance*, 1990; while the tendentious machinations of inaccurate biblical translators have been exposed by the Revd Dr Jeffrey John in 'The Bible and homosexuality', *Christian Action Journal*, Summer 1990, pp. 12-23. All of these recent writings powerfully support my contention that official British attitudes towards sexuality have been fundamentally flawed and peculiar.

R.H.
Spring 1991

CHAPTER ONE

Introduction:
problems and approaches

Historiographical context

The Master read a letter from Professor Kinsey asking if it were possible for him to see the unpublished parts of the Pepys Diary as a part of his study of human sexual behaviour. It was agreed that the Master should write to say that . . . the College was not prepared to make available any passages that were not already published. [Magdalene College Governing Body minute, 1952.[1]]

I propose to try to show how sexual attitudes and activities influenced the lives of the imperial elite as well as the subjects of empire. Also, and perhaps more significantly, I shall argue that sexual dynamics crucially underpinned the whole operation of British empire and Victorian expansion. Without the easy range of sexual opportunities which imperial systems provided, the long-term administration and exploitation of tropical territories, in nineteenth-century conditions, might well have been impossible. This, however, was far from being an uncontested proposition in late-Victorian Britain itself, when it was increasingly urged that, if the British empire was to survive, the imperial race must exercise sexual restraint, and government must intervene to enforce it. Through a fanatical Purity Campaign, sexual opportunity was from the mid-1880s gradually reduced, first at home, and then, in Edwardian times, overseas. The result was that in the British empire after 1914, outside the fighting services, almost no sexual interaction between rulers and ruled occurred. In this it differed not only from its own nine-teenth-century practice, but also from every other European imperial system.

It will not be argued that the formation of empires can be explained by sex drives. It would indeed be nonsense to suggest that more than a minority of men initially went overseas in order to find sexual satisfaction. The minority included explorers, perhaps, though even with them it was not a primary consideration. For most of the nineteenth century there was no shortage of sexual opportunity in the British home base,

[1]

and most of those who went overseas went for the adventure and the possibility of making money. As far as expansionist enterprise is concerned – leaving exploration aside – a 'surplus sexual energy' theory will not explain its causes, although a simple 'surplus energy' theory remains a real explanatory possibility. But if sex cannot explain the fundamental motives behind expansion, it may nevertheless explain how such enterprises were sustained. It is relevant not so much to the question why empires were set up as to how they were run. Empire provided ample opportunities for sexual indulgence throughout the nineteenth century, though it was more obvious in frontier situations and the fighting services than in settler communities. Sexual conscious-ness was heightened among soldiers and traders alike. Sexual relation-ships soldered together the invisible bonds of Victorian empire. In the erotic field, as in administration and commerce, some degree of 'col-laboration' from the indigenous communities was helpful to the main-tenance of imperial systems. The empire-builder was exposed to more relaxed attitudes and alternative life styles; even some evangelical missionaries took advantage of these exotic opportunities.

Historians of empire have to come to grips with sex if only because it is there. The sex drive, even in its weakest manifestations, has repercus-sions on how men relate to other people and how they go about their work. An understanding of individual sexual desire is thus important for interpreting a career. In a broader sense too, assessment of the true nature of British empire and expansion needs an examination of its soft underbelly. The expansion of Europe was not only a matter of 'Christi-anity and commerce', it was also a matter of copulation and con-cubinage. Sexual opportunities were often seized with imperious confi-dence.

The explorer H. St J. B. Philby (father of the traitor Kim Philby) became a Muslim and exercised to the full his privileged access to con-cubines and slave girls at the court of Ibn Saud; from 1945 he had a 'second family' in Mecca. Gustave Flaubert spoke for all those who regarded visits to oriental lands, especially at government expense, as providing additional sexual education even for the experienced woman-iser. In 1850 he wrote from Cairo, 'Here . . . one admits one's sodomy. . . . We have considered it our duty to indulge in this form of ejaculation.'[2] Such behaviour was not always popular. Rumours of sexual molestation of Chinese women precipitated the San-yüan-li incident near Canton at the start of the First Anglo-Chinese War (1841), while the deep-seated hostility of the Afghan people towards the British may well have been due to their resentment of the undisciplined lust with which British soldiers fell upon the women of Kabul in the same year. Major-General Roberts (as he then was) was determined to have no repetition in 1879,

[2]

and the return of the troops to Peshawar as a result created an exceptional demand for sex, disrupting the routine services of Indian army
prostitutes for several months.[3] In Africa the Ndebele rebels in 1896 and
the Zulus in 1906 also had grievances about the British treatment of
their women. The Nandi and the Maasai in Kenya resented the demand
for women generated by the building of the Uganda railway. From
Bechuanaland in 1933 came news of the predatory seduction over a
period of years of young Mongwato girls in Serowe by Phinehas McIntosh and two equally wild and unsavoury companions (all mechanics in
their late teens and early twenties). They had made a series of brutal
assaults on local men in retaliation for insults, and incurred punishment
by the Bangwato Regent Tshekedi. The result was an extraordinary
imperial incident in which Tshekedi was suspended for 'exceeding his
authority', despite the fact that the conduct of the young white men was
wholly indefensible, involving the abandonment of several girls as soon
as they became pregnant, leaving them to fend alone for their bastards.[4]

In general, however, despite such occasional protests, the Afro-Asian
world was remarkably accommodating to the sexual demands placed
upon it, even despite the sometimes unfortunate results. Britain has
spread venereal disease around the globe along with its racecourses and
botanical gardens, barracks and jails, steam engines and law books.[5]
Britain did not merely sell cotton clothes to all the world: it also exported
nude erotic photographs. George Cannon, William Dugdale and Henry
Hayler were world leaders among the entrepreneurs of pornography.
There was a flourishing free trade in prostitution.[6] But alongside this
often insensitive activity, paradoxically the British had another export
too, and a very influential counterbalancing one: its official prudery.
Practice and theory diverged. Britain had 'an ultra-squeamishness and
hyper-prudery peculiar to itself':[7] narrow, blinkered, defective and intolerant attitudes towards sex which it all too successfully imposed on the
rest of the world. One of the worst results of the expansion of Britain was
the introduction of its guilty inhibitions about sex into societies previously much better sexually adjusted than perhaps any in the West.

When in 1960 I began research into the British empire, to write about
its sexual aspects seemed so chimerical a project that I then put aside
such evidence as I came across. There was almost nothing in the way of
secondary sources. (My own college was still refusing to reveal to
scholars the sexual passages in the Pepys Diary, until persuaded out of
this policy by C. S. Lewis. The diary was not published unexpurgated
until the 1970s; the new material proved to be essentially innocuous,
although none the less valuable to historians of seventeenth-century
sexual attitudes.)[8] Since 1960 the whole position has, however, been
entirely transformed by modified sexual attitudes, and by the resultant

[3]

successful reconstruction of the history of sex in British society,[9] together with the progressive removal of reticence from biography, including political biography.[10] Historians of empire cannot claim to have played much part in this process. Although most imperial historians have long accepted that W. E. B. Du Bois was right to point to the problem of the colour line, the relations of Europe with the rest of the world, as the major problem for twentieth-century resolution, there has been widespread reluctance to take up the challenge of his related observation that he could forgive the West almost everything, including slavery, but not the way the white man took sexual advantage of black women. (He was writing for an American audience, but his words have a wider application.)

> I shall forgive the white South much in its final judgement day: I shall forgive its slavery, for slavery is a world-old habit; I shall forgive its fighting for a well-lost cause, and for remembering that struggle with tender tears; I shall forgive its so-called 'pride of race', the passion of its hot blood, and even its dear, old, laughable strutting and posing; but one thing I shall never forgive, neither in this world nor the world to come: its wanton and continued and persistent insulting of the black womanhood which it sought and seeks to prostitute to its lust.[11]

My own modest attempt to discuss sexuality in *Britain's Imperial Century* (admittedly done partly tongue-in-cheek and rather naively) was greeted in 1976 with little enthusiasm and some embarrassment.[12] With the important subsequent exceptions of Ballhatchet for India, and of van Onselen and Gann and Duignan for Africa,[13] historians writing about the empire remain extremely shy about putting sex on to their agenda. Many years ago Sir William Tarn felt a squeamish reluctance to discuss the sex life of Alexander the Great, and relegated it to an appendix, but at least he did confront the problem.[14] By contrast, of the seven principal biographies of Robert Clive published in the mid-1970s, only that by Bence-Jones has any significant discussion of Clive's private life, despite the fact that vivid speculation has always surrounded it. Spear's otherwise authoritative book was especially chaste.[15] A major recent biography (1976) of Cecil Rhodes by John Flint has less than a sentence about Rhodes's sex life, despite ample evidence.[16] It was left to Thomas Pakenham, a military historian, to bring Milner's mistresses into the light of the day.[17] In his pioneering studies of the Colonial Service, Heussler barely applied himself to European sexual relationships in the rich field of Malaya, still less in Nigeria, though the latter, it is true, would provide much less evidence.[18] It is perhaps understandable that the Church of Scotland Mission's official history should skirt the issue of clitoridectomy in Kenya which had been its *cause célèbre*, but there is much less excuse for accounts of the Baganda martyrs which play down or even obscure the sexual basis of the persecution.[19] Social histories of the British in India remain remarkably reticent. References to, let alone studies of, the Eurasian community are rare. Even a popular work like *Plain Tales from the Raj* resolutely refuses to name the 'unmentionable' plainly. It is still possible to produce serious histories of the army overseas without mentioning 'regimental brothels' and, as late as 1981, to produce a biography of Field Marshal Auchinleck almost hysterically denying that his interest in Indian boys had an active sexual side.[20]

While the Oxford Movement and Victorian Anglo-Catholicism have been ransacked for homo-erotic undertones,[21] the early Victorian Punjab administration has surprisingly escaped comparable scrutiny – I refer to the triangular friendship of Henry Lawrence, Herbert Edwardes and John Nicholson, with their communal households and young protégés.[22] Historians have thus until very recently been dangerously pursuing a picture of European expansion which was both bowdlerised and incomplete: and, in comparison with metropolitan domestic history, suddenly out of date.

In this situation, the pre-existing research base on which to rest a synthesis of the kind this book attempts is, not surprisingly, rather small. For the domestic British scene the available materials are now adequate. On a considerable number of imperial problems, however, systematic research remains to be done, and I have had to make some pioneering forays into the archives. My approach is accordingly broad and selective. Chronologically, material is included from the late-eighteenth to the mid-twentieth centuries, but the focus is upon the period from the 1860s to 1914. Such shape as my account may have derives mainly from an emphasis on the late-Victorian and Edwardian rewriting of the 'rules of engagement'. In 1880, going overseas to work as an official almost invariably meant an enlargement of sexual experience. Within thirty years or so, this had in most places ceased to be the case. How this came about is one of the main themes of this study.

The evidence uncovered in the investigation is patchy. It is necessarily impressionistic. The effect at times is rather like peering only into the relatively clear surface layer of the waters of a particularly deep and opaque pool, since most sexual activity is simply not observable, still less recorded. The issues discussed and the sources used here were in the main generated because something went wrong. Private behaviour became officially or publicly scandalous, and therefore the subject of enquiry and record. The surviving evidence is thus biased towards the sensational and the discreditable. Similarly, there is a built-in tilt towards same-sex activity, because the empire was often an ideal arena for the practice of sexual variation, and there were many scandals of this sort; but it is well to remember that the vast majority of sexual relationships, even in the British empire, were between men and women. Overall, too, the truth is probably more ordinary and more benign than the rather lurid and perfervid picture that follows. Sexual preoccupation may well be even more pervasive than we can document (one of the major assumptions of this work), but its expression is likely to have been generally less exploitative than the record might suggest. At any rate, this is one of the main propositions suggested below.

Before any coherent account of sexual activity in the empire can be presented it is necessary to establish the context and the perspectives of the British experience overseas. The book therefore begins with an examination of the nature of sexuality and of its influence on individuals, taking as examples those with some connection with the empire. There follows a brief account of the forms and extent of sexual opportunity in Britain itself in mid-Victorian times. The core of the book describes the situation overseas and changes within it – a description that reaches its climax in the main dramas of sexual confrontation between the British and their subjects, which were all experienced in the mission field. Finally, some attempt is made to assess the extent to which an understanding of sexual issues may enhance our perception of race relations in the British empire.

The psycho-sexual dimension

The sexual impulse is a force, to some extent an incalculable force, and the struggle of the man to direct that force, when he and it are both constantly changing, is inevitably attended with peril, even when the impulse is normal or at all events seeking to be normal. [Havelock Ellis, *Psychology of Sex*, 1933, p. 305]

What, socially speaking, are the facts of life as they are now understood by sexologists and psychiatrists? Sexual attitudes, and conventions as to what is normal and permissible, differ widely between human societies in time and space, perhaps astonishingly so. The striking variation that anthropologists have shown to exist can be explained only by differences of cultural learning and not by genetic variation. Heterosexual coitus is in any society the most prevalent form of sexual relationship, but it is never the only type of activity.[23] The most performed act is auto-masturbation. Sexual function is deeply embedded biologically in human behaviour. As Freud put it: 'children bring germs of sexual activity with them into the world'. Boys are sometimes born with an erection, and their genitals are usually the first parts of the body to reach adult size.

[6]

Nature ensures that reproduction of the race can begin from about thirteen or fourteen years of age. The sexual organs are so tough that almost no amount of ordinary use, prolonged even for sixty years, is of itself capable of injuring them. Individuals do, however, vary significantly in the level of their sexual appetite and performance, just as they vary in every other attribute. Some people are highly sexed, while others have a low sex drive. Not all women are equally orgasmic. The ejaculatory mechanism varies greatly – some males spurt, others dribble. Nutritional factors have a bearing too. There are differences between the sexes which have major implications for the adjustment of sexual relationships. Male and female needs are to a degree dysfunctional. Males are at the height of their sexual potency by their late teens; females do not reach their peak until they are into their thirties, and probably lose interest earlier as well. Sexual desire fluctuates in women more than it does in men. Moreover, whereas only about two per cent of men are not much interested in sex, the proportion of women with a weak response is nearer thirty per cent.[24]

These variations are one reason for the wide differences of judgement which exist between otherwise equally sensible people, and perhaps between the sexes themselves, as to the importance of sex in life as a whole. Those for whom it is not important are not well placed to understand the problems of the highly sexed. The young have a tendency to promiscuity, which is only brought under control through the achievement of sexual satisfaction and a stable and transforming love relationship. Perfect love casteth out promiscuity. That is its sociological function. It is necessary to the smooth functioning of society that most of its members find something, however briefly, of that private perfection. Many never do, even in marriage. It ill becomes those for whom sex is not – or is no longer – a problem to castigate, still less to stigmatise, those for whom it is. The need to love, the tendency to hate, the persistence of contradictions, inner conflicts and unresolved infantile anxieties are the common lot of all, and they are not in themselves abnormal. Therefore, I shall not make simplistic value judgements about people's sexual interests, unless they have demonstrably adverse behavioural consequences, and often not even then. If occasionally I use the terms 'promiscuity' and 'pornography', I do so without pejorative intent.

Nor shall I employ a separate category of 'homosexual'. Examples of so-called homosexual and heterosexual conduct will be intermingled and treated indifferently within the same chapters. 'Homosexuality' is a concept ripe for contest and deconstruction. It is an imprecise and dangerous word for historians, since it has become associated with a supposedly exclusive identity and with the 'gay' cultural groups of our own day. Some writers within this culture have a tendentious desire to extend its roots backward in time in a way that is wholly unhistorical. It is an inappropriate term for application to ancient Greece or traditional Melanesia. It is equally anachronistic when applied to medieval monks or seventeenth-century Caribbean pirates – in fact, to any society before that of twentieth-century Europe and America.[25] Even within these parameters, the term 'homosexual' remains a false and vulgar label when applied to individuals such as Kitchener and Montgomery. They are both easily acquitted of any actual physical contact with other males. But in Montgomery's case there is a confusion: he was not in the least attracted by men but he was emotionally involved with small boys. Either way, much ink has been spilled on trying to find an answer to the question why some people are attracted to members of the same sex. The relative importance of inherited and learned behaviour, of maternal and paternal contributions, of initial sexual experiences and enforced circumstances, and so forth, has been much disputed. No theory of homosexuality ever constructed is entirely satisfactory, and I shall not bother with any of them. It is something that defies all explanations, perhaps for the very good reason that there is nothing much to explain. As Freud observed, the real mystery is not why some people remain 'homosexual' but why most become 'heterosexual': 'from the perspective of psychoanalysis the exclusive sexual interest of man for woman is a problem requiring elucidation and not a foregone conclusion'.[26] Though it will still seem to some controversial to say so, in many ways same-sex attraction does appear to be – or can be shown historically to have been – a matter of circumstance, even of taste: and as well enquire why some people prefer Byrd to Beethoven or Rembrandt to Bridget Riley. In any case, the categorisation of people into rigid sexual compartments is to employ distinctions as misleading as they are potentially harmful ('labels are more lethal than libels'), not to say counterproductive of a right ordering of society. It is, moreover, quite unnecessary. We are all more or less bisexuals nowadays,[27] though it has taken Western mankind a long time to realise it. Human beings are naturally capable, at least in some stages of life and in certain circumstances, of responding to the same sex. Any attempt to restrict oneself exclusively to one sex (whether the same sex or the opposite sex) is likely to be at some cost to the wholeness of personality. Leaving aside all questions of traditional Christian morality, and whatever we may think about mid-twentieth-century gay life styles, sexual behaviour between males as we encounter it in this book need not be a problem for us.

In general, human sexual behaviour provides us with *variation* rather than *deviation*. What is 'perversion'? To employ one of the most right-wing anti-libertarian philosophical definitions currently available, it is the sexual urge reduced to impersonal terms, becoming in the process indifferent to evoking a pleasurable response in a partner. Intention is all-important. As Scruton puts it, 'The sadist, like the necrophiliac, the paedophile, and the rapist, can accept the other only in terms that are dictated by himself. . . The other's body is the means to accomplish a private ceremony.' Thus, he argues, homosexuality is not inherently a perversion, but bestiality with animals most certainly is, while necrophilia is its *reductio ad absurdum*.[28] We shall need to pause over paedophilia, but first let us agree that an act is perverted if its primary aim is domination rather than mutual enjoyment: if it becomes an expression of power rather than sensuality, and is thus so to speak plundering rather than worshipping. Rape is its commonest form. Most other perversions are peripheral phenomena, of almost no interest to anybody, and require no comment here.

The one exception is, of course, paedophilia, which, in one form or another, crops up rather often in the British experience, both at home and overseas. It also happens to be a highly problematic matter of contemporary debate. There are those who would argue that the problem (like 'homosexuality' in general) is in fact an artificial one, that 'a paedophile is a person like you and me'. As a Dutch expert writes, 'Paedophilia is, above all, the problem of people who are not paedophiles: that is, of society in general. As long as society continues to make a problem out of sexuality, no solution to the problem it has created is possible'; if society would accept child sexuality as a fact, 'the label paedophile will fall into disuse. . .'.[29] Unfortunately, it is not quite as simple as that, and paedophilia has more than one manifestation, not all of them benign. Whilst no doubt the British could be said to exaggerate the dimensions of their 'child sexual abuse' problem in the 1990s, it remains a fact – however incredible it may seem – that some men do force phallic entry into very young children of both sexes.[30] This is a serious matter, and it can only fall within the definition of perversion adopted above. There remain, however, the crucial issues of intention, attitude and consent. A loving relationship between a man and a consenting boy, usually at or past the age of puberty – and such alone was the classical Greek version – might become for later generations incomprehensible, misguided or illegal, but it is not from a theoretical point of view a perversion.

The point is that it is not so much the sexual desire itself which is the source of trouble as the problems to which it gives rise, especially when it is repressed. Theoretically, most sexual acts that spring from love are psychologically harmless, though they may have medical and legal consequences, which are at best unwanted (such as pregnancy), and at worst positively catastrophic (such as AIDS). The aftermath even of loving acts, especially the effect of the obligatory guilt which society may demand, *can* be damaging. Repression, however, almost certainly *will* lead to some degree of maladjustment, to eccentricity and even mental illness.

Repression of the sexual instincts is closely linked to 'sublimation', the psychoanalytic concept most commonly employed by historians. Great explanatory power is attributed to this ill-defined idea. Sublimation is said to have been an animating force behind empire-building: 'love's loss is empire's gain', in Wayland Young's famous phrase. Ensor suggested in 1936 (and all credit to him for raising the issue at that time) that the late-Victorian elite and professional business classes 'spent, there can be little doubt, far less of their time and thought on sex interests than either their continental contemporaries or their twentieth-century successors; and to this saving their extraordinary surplus of energy in other spheres must reasonably be in part ascribed'.[31] Some forty years on, Lawrence Stone has a similar conclusion for a broader period: 'The sublimation of sex among young male adults may well account for the extraordinary military aggressiveness, the thrift, the passion for hard work, and the entrepreneurial and intellectual enterprise of modern Western man.'[32] Gann and Duignan, in an aside, hint at empire-building as possibly 'a sublimation or alternative to sex'.[33] There are innumerable biographers and historians too who talk loosely about their subjects' 'sublimating themselves in hard work'. (This is explicitly done by Magnus on Kitchener, Sinclair on Sir George Grey, Wraith on Guggisberg, Montgomery on Montgomery, Yarwood on the Rev. Samuel Marsden, Higgins on Rider Haggard, and Jeal on Baden-Powell).[34] Other writers are looking for connections between private vision and public policy: it will be interesting to see how Keynes is reassessed in this connection.[35]

It is clearly high time to scrutinise rigorously these explanatory tendencies and speculations, and pay more attention to the various experts. What is sublimation? Freud (from 1905) thought that apparently non-sexual activities (and especially artistic creation and intellectual enquiry) could be an expression of the sexual instinct, by a deflection from sexuality. He considered that the price of (Western) civilisation was sexual restraint. These may well have been important insights, but his concept of sublimation has not, until very recently, been properly investigated. It is by no means sure that he remained convinced of its viability: he certainly seems to have equivocated about the source of a sublimating instinct. His idea was actually a simple one, using a hydraulic, conversion-of-energy model, conceived within a rather mechanistic nineteenth-century neurophysiological frame of reference.[36] Twentieth-century thought, however, has to take account, for example, of the theories of relativity and psychology, and today's post-Kleinian psychoanalytic theory has shifted the emphasis on to a subtle and highly sophisticated concern with the internal ordering of the mind and its relation to the external world. As a result, Freud's original idea has become largely redundant.[37] Nevertheless, many people feel that Freud pointed to something of which they are vaguely aware. However difficult it is to be precise, there does seem to be a deep but obscure relation here, a gap perhaps between spirituality and sensuality which 'sublimation' may bridge conceptually. Did not Renoir say he painted with his cock? Do not the nudes of the Sistine Chapel disturb us because they tell us something about Michelangelo's sexual interests – and, perhaps, our own? One of the last of the imperial *roués* in India used to urge visiting novelists, 'Don't write about it: do it!' Many of us may wonder whether we are not 'sublimating' something through our fantasies, dreams and visual enjoyments. If, however, we are to keep sublimation as a serviceable concept for historians, three qualifications insistently suggest themselves. One, we must recognised that sublimation (in Freud's sense) is difficult to achieve and therefore uncommon. Two, we must not confuse it with stratagems which are not sublimation at all. Three, we should regard it more as an internal thought process than as a quasi-physiological transfer mechanism.

Freud himself soon warned that 'not every neurotic has a high talent for sublimation'. This seems to have gone unheeded, for, as Havelock Ellis observed, it was 'usually offered too easily and too cheaply' as a remedy. How much the more that applies to historians who take it (and distort it) as an explanatory mechanism! If physical impulses are transformed into some impulse of higher psychic activity (so that they cease to be urgent as physical needs), it should be obvious that such a transformation is, as Ellis put it, 'not easy or swift of attainment, and perhaps only possible at all for those natures which are of finer than average nervous texture', such as those of artists and priests.[38] For if this Freudian sublimation is to retain meaning, its principal operation must be seen as involving a change into a higher cultural or spiritual realm. According to Meltzer, true artistic achievement represents a successful projection of internal driving forces into external productivity. This can occur only when the artist's inner world has been positively integrated and stabilised through an acceptance of responsibility for psychic reality, which places concern for others above selfish gratification.[39] Simple displacement of unchanged sexual activity into another (less dangerous) channel is not sublimation. Those who are revolted by sex, or who seek to repress it, are not truly sublimating their desires.

Kinsey's opinion also needs to be pondered. Sublimation, he argued, is not a scientific concept. We cannot switch or divert sexual energy as if it were an electrical current; it is not enough to say that busy and successful people are 'sublimated' merely because they are energetic in non-sexual pursuits. Kinsey identified perhaps two per cent of men as apathetic about sex. (These may be called 'a-sexuals'.) The sexual inactivity of such men is, he considered, no more sublimation of the sex drive than blindness and deafness are sublimations of the perceptive capacities. Kinsey could not find in his sample (5,300 men) *any* clear-cut case of sublimation. He concluded, 'sublimation is so subtle, or so rare, as to constitute an academic possibility rather than a demonstrated actuality.'[40] This is not conclusive in itself. It would be a philosophical solecism to suppose that the concepts of disciplines which do not obey the scientific procedural models of theoretical physics or the taxonomy of bees are somehow invalidated. Fundamentally illuminating though they undoubtedly are, Kinsey's conclusions based on clinical question-naires cannot of themselves 'disprove' the theoretical constructs of psychoanalysis, which are in any case being constantly refined. How-ever, in that process of refining, psychoanalysts have come to a point where they no longer use sublimation as a central working concept. (Perhaps this is partly because of the way the term has slipped through their esoteric fingers into common parlance.) They retain it to deal with those aspects of behaviour where sexual aim and objective are obscure without the aid of psychoanalytic investigation of the unconscious: and in this context it emerges as describing a fraud or deceit perpetrated on one part of the mind by another. Sublimation thus appears more evasive than admirable, illuminating not so much high cultural achievement as everyday personal adjustment or maladjustment – perhaps in ways which yet remain to be closely defined. Nor is it now thought necessary to regard the pleasures of work as 'desexualised' in any sense, since 'all work is sexual in its meaning' (Meltzer).[41] The fact that people work hard and creatively tells us nothing about their sex lives, which may just as well be fulfilled as not. Successful careers and high achievement often tend to *increase* sexual confidence and desire.

So where does all this leave us? Quite certainly as historians we should make less use of 'sublimation' than more, having already done more than enough violence to the concept. But, even if largely redundant in psychoanalysis, it is likely to remain an honoured term. Perhaps therefore we should accept that sublimation seems to have some explanatory value when applied to 'artistic creation and intellectual enquiry' among a few highly gifted individuals (as Freud intended its use to be restricted, or as he mostly used it himself). We can see that it may have a continuing validity in psychoanalysis to describe the more puzzling sexual states of mind; but we should accept that the term has far less point when applied to ordinary people's lives, or to political, economic and imperial activities. It certainly seems useful to distinguish between sublimation and a-sexuality (following Kinsey). As far as expansionist enterprise is concerned, even if a simple 'surplus energy' theory remains a possibility, the formation of empires cannot be explained specifically by the sex drive, whether sublimated or not. If 'sublimation' (in its original sense, implying transfer) is inapplicable to most ordinary individuals, it is certainly inapplicable to the activities of whole societies.

Very often, then, what the historian is looking at is not sublimation at all, but a-sexuality. 'A-sexuals' are men who are fundamentally apathetic about sex: they are unresponsive to erotic stimulus, attach little importance to sex and find little hardship in abstinence. A tentative list of high achievers in public life belonging to this a-sexual category might include Benjamin Jowett and A. C. Benson (dons), Speke and Thesiger (explorers), Gordon, Kitchener and possibly Montgomery (soldiers), Sir Matthew Nathan and Sir Edward Twining (governors), and Winston Churchill and Harold Macmillan (politicians). Some of these men never married; those who did seldom worried about being parted from their wives (for example, Churchill and Twining).[42] Let Dean Inge, A. C. Benson and Thesiger be the spokesmen for all a-sexuals. Inge wrote in his diary, 'in a decent, well-ordered life, sex does *not* play a very important part'. In his diary Benson wrote, '. . . for me the real sexual problem does not exist. . . I don't want to claim or to be claimed. . . and thus a whole range of problems means nothing to me'.[43] Thesiger wrote in his autobiography, 'Sex has been of no great consequence to me, and the celibacy of the desert left me untroubled. . . with no sense of deprivation.'[44] For several of these men, disenchantment with sex was directly caused by an unhappy, possibly even traumatic, adolescent experience. Jowett had 'a deeply laid antipathy to the very idea of carnal knowledge', induced by a youthful event.[45] Gordon 'wished I was a eunuch at fourteen'; 'I never had a sorrow like it in all my life, therefore I love children so very much.'[46] Macmillan's sustained innocence and detachment (refusing all overtures at Eton, and from Ronald Knox at Oxford) left him ill-equipped to deal either with the protracted adultery between his wife and Robert Boothby or with the Profumo affair, which haunted the twilight of his premiership. ('I had no idea of [this] strange underworld. . . all this kind of thing was not only distasteful but unthinkable.')[47] It must not be supposed that a-sexuals, those who by and large opt out, pose no problems for others by their abstinence. All too often, they lose touch with reality. Benson represented more than one generation of schoolmasters unable to come to terms with adolescent sexuality ('the dread possibility', 'the dark shadow on the life of a schoolmaster, his most anxious and saddest preoccupation'). Baden-

Powell influentially transmuted his own rejection of sex (especially masturbation) into a Scout law.[48] Such men gratuitously attempted to stamp out teenage masturbation. General Gordon was quite happy provided he could give the occasional bath to a dirty urchin and talk to him of God. But Gordon was probably unsuited to high responsibilities by the very fact of his not really caring about anything in life except his 'Gravesend laddies', or 'kings' as he revealingly called them. Kitchener, whose private life focused on merely sentimental relationships with a few young officers, and who became involved in the Purity Movement, caused havoc in the First World War by his reluctance to introduce venereal disease prophylaxis for the army in Europe.[49]

Above all, there is the classic case of Montgomery, a man incontestably fitted for high command if not for anything else. Sex was something he largely repudiated, even during his ten years of marriage, and despite (or more likely because of) his deep-rooted tenderness towards boys. Montgomery was sometimes said to be able to derive an almost unfair advantage by his 'sublimated' ability to concentrate on his career, especially after his wife's early death in 1937; but clearly he was lonely, and there were repressed drives and tensions which fundamentally affected for the worse his behaviour and judgement. Behind a relentless generosity to his pre-pubertal protégés, Montgomery was equally unforgiving of his mother for the Farrar genetic inheritance, and of his son's divorce. Nor could he, also for reasons of sexually-based moral revulsion, get on with Auchinleck. He issued wholly unrealistic orders to his men about restricting access to wives in wartime. His crack-down upon excesses among the fleshpots of Egypt in 1931-33 and novel measures against venereal disease in the war got him into serious trouble. Of all public figures he was the most absurdly virulent and flippantly irrational in 1965 in attacking the Wolfenden proposals for reforming the laws concerning homosexuality; in a speech to the House of Lords, he even suggested an age of consent fixed at eighty. This is a clear example of *reaction formation*, a psychological stratagem designed to cover impermissible erotic wishes by exaggerated reaction against them in an opposite direction. Having so deeply repressed his sexual instincts, Montgomery's residual requirements were to be allowed to entertain young friends to tea and a bath, to provide camping facilities for Boy Scouts, and to give occasional treats, for example to the choristers of Westminster Abbey. (On one occasion, he put the entire juvenile cast of the musical *Oliver!* on parade.) He met his wife by first becoming friendly with her two sons.[50] He had a succession of young friends as a widower after the war, beginning with Lucien Trueb, whom he met in Switzerland in 1945 when the boy was eleven. He was genuinely in love with Lucien, but there were half a dozen more who followed in strict succession, all of whom were set aside on reaching puberty. Montgomery, like all who cannot integrate their fantasies, was doomed to repeat them in an endless vicious circle of need and frustration. One of these friends, staying with him for a weekend at the age of nine, recalls that he was puzzled and frightened by his host's demand to 'have a look at him', making him perform naked drill after his pre-dinner bath. Later that evening the Field Marshal was 'extremely affectionate, as if a test had been passed'. As a result of this experience, the boy began to behave 'subversively' at school – his fees were being paid by Montgomery. He had had revealed to him the inner weakness of authority figures.[51]

Montgomery's official biographer does not mince his words. There were two sides to him: professional excellence and emotional retardation (an 'insatiable need' to swagger before 'impressionable schoolboys', lording it over them). What is one to make of a man who wrote letters to boys which ended 'With my fond love, Montgomery of Alamein, F.M.'? Or indeed who told a superannuated sixteen-year-old, 'I often wish you were twelve again'? It is clear that Montgomery was not a happy man and that he suffered from grotesque vanity. Seeing the naked body of a boy seems to have been the limit of 'sexual aim' for him, as it had also been for General Gordon. But this a-sexual limitation is not sublimation; it is closer to what Freud called scopophilia. It is also likely that Gordon and Montgomery were restrained by the legal and moral codes of their day. But if so, that is not sublimation, either; it is enforced repression. And, as we have already observed, the repression of sexual urges can have serious implications for an individual's total well-being and behaviour; and, if he is in a position of leadership, it can have important repercussions not only on those around him but also on public policy itself.

Extended speculation as to why Montgomery (or anyone else) had the interests he did is futile. There have been more than enough biographical examples of supposedly applied Freudianism to show that it all too often ends up in crude jargon-ridden assertions about 'Oedipus complexes' or 'infantile regressions', largely empty of real content where they are not actually comic. The preceding pages have, moreover, explained why the concept of 'sublimation' will not be used in this study. The calls sometimes made for the application of 'psychoanalytic' insights to historical personages seem based on a misunderstanding as to the result. It is far from clear that the development of a fully fledged psychoanalytic history would have much to offer in terms of furnishing ready-made explanations of the conduct of individuals, for the business of modern psychoanalysis is description pure and complex. Its aim is to improve a person's present state of mind rather than to elucidate its roots in past experiences, too often regarded (mistakenly, as it now seems) as in some way unchangeably 'formative'. What greater insight into private life and the psyche can do is to provide a salutary reminder of the complexity of all human beings and the fragility of the integration of personality. It will enable us to approach historical characters with a more compassionate understanding. It will perhaps both diminish and increase our admiration for those who, like Montgomery, had unexpected flaws (in his case, the trouble was not loving children but loving them childishly) yet were able to achieve so much on such a slender basis of personal integration. It will curb any tendency to make simplistic and moralising value judgements.[52]

Feminist studies and literary evidence

> Women famed for their valour, their skill in politics, or their learning, leave the duties of their own sex, in order to invade the privileges of ours. . . The modest virgin, the prudent wife, or the careful matron, are much more serviceable in life, than petticoated philosophers, blustering heroines, or virago queens. [Oliver Goldsmith, *The Citizen of the World*, LXII]

In order to understand the sexual aspects of the history of the British empire, it is essential that the historian should have some grasp, however basic, of the dynamics of human sexuality as revealed in the work of sexologists and psychoanalysts. In order to understand the range of sexual attitudes and activities in the world as a whole, and to provide a context for the British experience, it is equally necessary that he should be aware of the findings of anthropologists and sociologists. Today this is accepted as self-evident. We have now to consider briefly what use, if any, he can make of feminist studies and literary evidence.

One of the most publicised historiographical developments of recent years has been the development of women's studies from a feminist viewpoint. Much work has been done, but not much of it has direct relevance to the theme of this book, which focuses upon the attitudes and activities of the men who ran the empire. A large body of material is now accumulating on the role of women in traditional societies, which is in its own right a genuine augmentation of previous anthropological work. Some studies have also been made of overseas prostitution. The role of memsahibs and colonial women is also being reassessed. I have not, however, found much help in specifically feminist constructs and approaches. More generally, feminist studies seem to be stuck in a specialised sub-branch of historical explanation. The feminism which we have at present is, no doubt, a fairly primitive and exploratory version. It may well become more sophisticated in future. At the moment, however, feminist studies remain of limited value to the general historian.[53]

How is the poverty of feminism to be explained? Its self-imposed parameters are artificial and constricting. A conceptual framework which is itself so fundamentally hostile to sex is, of course, the very last tool likely to be found useful for understanding the history of sexuality. As a matter of fact, feminists are more interested in gender than in sex, whereas it is sex – what people did – not gender which is the subject of this book. Moreover, many of the leading works in the feminist canon arise out of contemporary American experience, which limits their historical value. Some of them are hugely over-preoccupied with rape, ludicrously defined in an influential book by Susan Brownmiller as 'nothing more or less than a conscious process of intimidation by which *all men* keep *all women* in a state of fear' (her emphases).[54] Almost all of them are suffused with the original feminist dogma about the supposedly 'pervasive violence against women by men'.[55] The London Feminist History Group sees the missing dynamic of history as 'men's powers and women's resistance',[56] while other groups talk of 'women's silence, men's violence', or the 'sexual colonisation of our bodies'.[57] These sour and immature views deny the very essence of adult sexual behaviour as understood by all right-thinking people: namely that we combine with, but also grant autonomy to, the beloved partner. It is, accordingly, hard to see how these feminist hysterics can advance our understanding of the past. Their quintessential historical assumption and tendency are to represent women as mere victims ('in many cases unwilling and exploited victims of circumstances beyond their control'). This is in itself a form of the 'patriarchal condescension' which feminists complain of in traditional male historians. In the same way, too ready an acceptance of the feminist thesis that rape is a monstrous destruction of female bodily integrity connives at the worst male exaggerations of phallic power. We ought, surely, to take (as I believe I do) a more favourable view of the *resilience* of 'exploited' women, and of their ability to turn circumstances to their advantage.[58]

The truth is that the construction of a convincing feminist history of sex can be written only by renouncing the crude, angry and militant presuppositions that all forms of sex (except lesbianism) are unequal and that all male sexual activity is aggression. This renunciation will undoubtedly have to be made if feminist history is to 'come of age'. Meanwhile, the search for a revised historiographical framework not unnaturally fumbles. Even Martha Vicinus is doubtful whether the 'new history of sexuality' can be feminist-defined rather than male-dominated. The current 'dominant paradigm' and 'male bias' of the 'energy-control model' (the sexual force, seeking release), especially as adumbrated by Lawrence Stone and others, is plainly unsatisfactory, but it hardly seems likely to be exceeded in explanatory power by a 'feminist affirmative model' of sexuality, based on what? Passive internalisation?[59] A better balance of *yin* and *yang* in our history would no doubt be a good thing, but that is not what the feminists have so far offered us. Far from it.

Militant feminism operates to humourless rules, and likes to see a heavy dose of moral outrage in all historical reconstructions. If Victorian men found beauty and sensuous appeal in a seemingly exotic East, especially in comparison with the plainness and dourness of Africa, feminists will not allow it to be recorded without complaining that it perpetuates 'the male myth about Asian women'.[60] Of course we must beware of glamorising the past, and take account of the sordid aspects of Asian prostitution, but the plain fact is that Victorian men did feel this oriental attraction strongly. And it was well understood at the time to be insidious. Consider the following reflections by Sir Hugh Clifford about 'the glamour which will always hang about the rags of the East while our world lasts':

> Viewed at the right time, and seen in this deceptive light, all manner of things in themselves hopelessly evil and unlovely have the power to fascinate as far more attractive objects too often fail to do. . . The atmosphere is apt to destroy a man's ability to scale things accurately; it deprives him of his sense of proportion.[61]

That is a far more powerful insight into the white man's behaviour and mistakes than anything the feminists have come up with.

Because of the paucity of historical research and the poverty of feminism, we are entering a field where, partly for want of anything better, there is a danger of relying unduly on seductively attractive literary evidence. Novels such as *Heart of Darkness*, *A Passage to India* and the Raj Quartet are almost too well known in this context to require comment. The perceptions of the best 'colonial' novels about race and power, misery and personal humiliation have in a general way much to tell us, if only because they may reflect something of the attitudes of the time in which they were written.[62] Nevertheless, novels seldom tell true stories. No boy convicts in Australia ever entered into a suicide pact, as happens in Marcus Clarke's *For the Term of his Natural Life*. J. M. Stuart-Young's *The Soul-Slayer* may be a welcome release from the slushy sentiment of the typical Victorian novel about adolescence – though it frightened six publishers off – but the sufferings of the half-caste 'Ibra' were never endured by his real-life model Ibrahim.[63] Hugh Clifford may well have dallied with Malayan women, but he never got into the catastrophes afflicting Frank Austen, hero of *Since the Beginning, a Tale of an Eastern Land* (1898). Similarly, the tales in Gerald Hanley's *The Consul at Sunset* (1951) and David Caute's *At Fever Pitch*

(1959) are given a heightened narrative and a sharper moral than ordinary experience could provide. These examples – drawn from Liberia and Nigeria to Somaliland and points east – may remind us that any novel must have conflict and climax. Goodness and ordinariness are unpropitious material. (Did not Tolstoy say something to that effect?) Also, novels give us larger-than-life characters. The literary stereotype of the memsahib is one particularly potent and influential example of this. Historical perceptions of the memsahib have been strongly influenced by literary presentations. It is a negative and unfavourable image, both for India and for Malaya. The fact, however, that the principal authors who propagated it, E. M. Forster and W. Somerset Maugham, were both misogynists ought, at least, to put us on our guard, and it is almost certainly in need of revision.[64] Novels give us symbolic meanings and character stereotypes. They may be ways of conveying a truth, but they are not the truth as it actually happened. Their insights are not easily converted into strictly historical evidence. Nor is it particularly necessary, since firmer evidence can in fact be tracked down. Accordingly, I shall not rely on literary evidence in any central way.

The objective, in short, of this book is to get methodologically beyond an inadequate historiography, made up largely of evasion and reticence, or of pseudo-Freudian speculation, feminist dogma and literary criticism, by returning to a technique of more definite historical reconstruction using the written records of the past. I aim to make this essentially traditional kind of historical exploration armed with as little as possible in the way of conceptual baggage, relying instead on a humane sensitivity to the complexity of all things, and the relativity of western value systems, especially where sexual matters are concerned.

Investigation must start with the individual impulse.

Notes

1 Magdalene College Archives, Group B, 609, Minute Book IX, f. 12, 1 May 1952, no. 9, quoted by kind permission of the Master and Fellows.

2 E. Monroe, *Philby of Arabia*, London, 1973, pp. 150-3, 271; F. Steegmuller, (ed.), *The Letters of Gustave Flaubert, 1830-57*, London, 1980, pp. 111, 121 (ch. 5 of this work, and the more popular *Flaubert in Egypt: a Sensibility on Tour*, London, 1972, provide insight into sexual opportunity in Egypt and Constantinople at mid-century: the Nubian girls, the dancing youths and the young bath boys).

3 F. Wakeman, *Strangers at the Gate: Social Disorder in South China, 1839-61*, London, 1966, p. 56; F.-M. Lord Roberts of Kandahar, *Forty-One Years in India*, London, 1898 ed., p. 397; W. H. Hannah, *'Bobs': Kipling's General: the Life of Field Marshal Earl Roberts of Kandahar*, London, 1972, p. 33; C. Deveureux, *Vénus in India: or Love Adventures in Hindustan*, Brussels, 1889, I, pp. 23-4.

4 P. Mason, *Birth of a Dilemma: Conquest and Settlement of Rhodesia*, London, 1958,

pp. 183, 241-2; *Annual Register for 1907*, pp. 411-12; S. Marks, *Reluctant Rebellion: the 1906-8 Disturbances in Natal*, Oxford, 1970, p. 47; J. Lord, *Duty, Honour, Empire: Life and Times of Colonel Richard Meinertzhagen*, London, 1971, p. 145; M. Crowder, *The Flogging of Phinehas McIntosh: a Tale of Colonial Folly and Injustice, Bechuanaland 1933*, Yale NH,1988, esp. pp. 34-45; C. Knapman, *White Women in Fiji, 1835-1930: the Ruin of Empire? . . .*, Sydney, 1986, p. 173, shows that independent-minded Fijians came to object to increasing loss of control over their women.

5 L. Doyal and I. Pennell, '"Pox Britannica": health, medicine, and underdevelopment', *Race and Class*, XVIII, 1970. For the catastrophic effects of venereal disease upon the Maoris, see A. W. Crosby, *Ecological Imperialism: the Biological Expansion of Europe, 900-1900*, Cambridge, 1986, pp. 231, 242-4, 257.

6 I. McCalman, 'Unrespectable radicalism: infidels and pornography in early nineteenth-century London', *Past and Present*, 104, 1984; *idem*, *Radical Underworld: Prophets, Revolutionaries and Pornographers in London, 1795-1840*, Cambridge, 1988; 'Pisanus Fraxi' [H. S. Ashbee], I, *Index Librorum Prohibitorum*, 1877, p. xix, n. 17; I. Bloch, *Sexual Life in England, Past and Present*, 1903, trans. W. H. Forstern, London, [n.d.], pp. 659-60. Dugdale was convicted ten times. Cannon was imprisoned three times; he used to employ agents, posing as laundrymen, to throw his publicity products over the walls of girls' boarding schools. Hayler was even better organised: when raiding him in 1874, the police found 130,248 'obscene' photographs and 5,000 slides, many depicting himself, his wife and his two sons. Alfred Dyer, the Purity fanatic, spent much time in India, 1888-1911, because he feared British obscene photographs would set off another Mutiny, in which all white women would be ravished (see E. J. Bristow, *Vice and Vigilance: Purity Movements in Britain since 1700*, Dublin, 1977, p. 87). The word 'pornography' was not used before 1864.

7 [Ashbee], I, *Index Librorum Prohibitorum*, p. xvii.

8 R. Latham and W. Matthews, (eds.), *The Diary of Samuel Pepys*, 11 vols, London, 1970-83; L. Stone, *The Family, Sex and Marriage in England, 1500-1800*, London, 1977.

9 The pioneering articles are: K. Thomas, 'The Double Standard', *Journal of History of Ideas*, XX, 1959; P. T. Cominos, 'Late-Victorian respectability and the social system', *International Review of Social History*, VIII, 1963; B. Harrison, 'Underneath the Victorians', *Victorian Studies*, X, 1967; F. B. Smith, 'Sexuality in Britain, 1800-1900', *University of Newcastle Historical Journal*, II (New South Wales), 1974; J. Weeks, '"Sins and diseases": some notes on homosexuality in the nineteenth century', *History Workshop Journal*, I, 1976; T. C. Smout, 'Aspects of sexual behaviour in nineteenth-century Scotland', in A. A. MacLaren (ed.), *Social Class in Scotland*, London, 1976; R. Trumbach, 'London's sodomites: homosexual behaviour and western culture in the eighteenth century', *Journal of Social History*, XI, 1977; R. Porter, '"Mixed feelings": the Enlightenment and sexuality in eighteenth-century Britain', in P.-G. Boucé (ed.), *Sexuality in Eighteenth-Century Britain*, Manchester 1982.

The pioneering books are: S. Marcus, *The Other Victorians: a Study of Sexuality and Pornography in Mid-Nineteeth-Century England*, London, 1966; E. Trudgill, *Madonnas and Magdalens: Origins and Development of Victorian Sexual Attitudes*, London, 1971; J. Weeks, *Coming Out: Homosexual Politics in Britain*, London, 1977; Stone, *Family, Sex and Marriage*; Bristow, *Vice and Vigilance*; G. R. Quaife, *Wanton Wenches and Wayward Wives: Peasants and Illicit Sex in Early Seventeenth-Century England*, London, 1979; M. Foucault, *The History of Sexuality*, I: *An Introduction*, 1976, trans. R. Hurley, London, 1979; J. Weeks, *Sex, Politics and Society: the Regulation of Sexuality since 1800*, London, 1981; A. Bray, *Homosexuality in Renaissance England*, London, 1982; P. Gay, *The Bourgeois Experience: Victoria to Freud*, I: *The Education of the Senses*, London, 1984.

Also important was the publication of [('Walter'], *My Secret Life*, 2 vols, ed. G. Legman, New York, 1966. The author of these autobiographical confessions remains unknown, but from internal evidence it is deduced that he was a gentleman, born *c.* 1822; the manuscript was first privately printed, *c.* 1890, in eleven volumes; even if in part a literary invention, the work contains vital evidence of Victorian sexual life: see M. Spilka in *Victorian Studies*, X, 1967, p. 295; and M. Charney, *Sexual Fiction*, London, 1981.

10 Among the more revealing biographies of politicians and other 'establishment' figures
    are: E. Longford, *Wellington*, 2 vols, London, 1969, 1972; I. Butler, *The Eldest Brother:
    Richard Wellesley*, London, 1973; B. Donoughue and G. W. Jones, *Herbert Morrison:
    Portrait of a Politician*, London, 1973; S. Chitty, *The Beast and the Monk: a Life of
    Charles Kingsley*, London, 1974; S. Roskill, *Admiral of the Fleet Earl Beatty, the Last
    Naval Hero: an Intimate Biography*, London, 1980; M. Egremont, *Balfour: a Life of
    Arthur James Balfour*, London, 1980; R. T. Shannon, *Gladstone*, I: *1809-65*, London,
    1982; K. Bourne, *Palmerston*, I: *Early Years, 1784-1841*, London, 1982; R. Skidelsky,
    John Maynard Keynes: a Biography, I: *1883-1920*, London, 1983; B. Pimlott, *Hugh
    Dalton*, London, 1985.
11 W. E. B. Du Bois, 'The damnation of women', *Writings* (Library of America, ed. N.
    Huggins, New York, 1986), p. 958, reprinted from *Darkwater: Voices from Within*,
    New York, 1920.
12 R. Hyam, *Britain's Imperial Century, 1815-1914: a Study of Empire and Expansion*,
    London, 1976, ch. 5. According to one commentator this book 'offers a bizarre Freudian
    explanation of imperial expansion'! (J. P. Halstead, *The Second British Empire: Trade,
    Philanthropy and Good Government, 1820-90*, Westport, Conn., 1983, p. 244). Its
    significance was much more readily appreciated by historians of sex, such as Jeffrey
    Weeks.
13 K. Ballhatchet, *Race, Sex and Class under the Raj: Imperial Attitudes and Policies and
    their Critics, 1793-1905*, London, 1980; C. van Onselen, *Studies in the Social and
    Economic History of the Witwatersrand, 1886-1914*, 2 vols, London, 1982; idem,
    '*Chibaro': African Mine Labour in Southern Rhodesia, 1900-33*, London, 1976; L. H.
    Gann and P. Duignan, *The Rulers of British Africa, 1870-1914*, London, 1978, esp. pp.
    239-43. See also A. H. M. Kirk-Greene, 'Colonial administration and race relations:
    some research reflections and directions', *Ethnic and Racial Studies*, IX, 1986, pp. 275-
    87.
14 W. W. Tarn, *Alexander the Great*, II, London, 1948, Appendix 18; 'Alexander's attitude
    to sex', pp. 319-26.
15 M. Bence-Jones, *Clive of India*, London, 1974; J. Watney, *Clive of India*, London, 1974;
    P. Spear, *Master of Bengal: Clive and his India*, London, 1975; N. C. Chaudhuri, *Clive
    of India: a Political and Psychological Essay*, London, 1975; J. P. Lawford, *Clive,
    Proconsul of India: a Biography*, London, 1976; R. Garrett, *Robert Clive*, London,
    1976; M. Edwardes, *Clive: the Heaven-Born General*, London, 1977. See also C.
    Carraccioli, *Life of Robert, Lord Clive*, 4 vols, [n.d.] (late eighteenth century). The
    balance is over-corrected in A. Edwardes, *The Rape of India: a Biography of Robert
    Clive and a Sexual History of the Conquest of Hindustan*, New York, 1966; see below,
    ch. 2 n. 22.
16 J. E. Flint, *Cecil Rhodes*, London, 1976.
17 T. Pakenham, *The Boer War*, London, 1979, pp. 32-4.
18 R. Heussler, *British Rule in Malaya: the Malayan Civil Service and its Predecessors,
    1867-1942*, Oxford, 1981; idem, *The British in Northern Nigeria*, Oxford, 1968.
19 E. G. K. Hewat, *Vision and Achievement, 1796-1956: a History of the Foreign Missions
    of the Churches united in the Church of Scotland*, London, 1960; H. B. Hansen,
    Mission, Church and State in a Colonial Setting: Uganda, 1890-1925, London, 1984,
    p. 14. J. V. Taylor, *Growth of the Church in Buganda*, London, 1958, p. 57, not only fails
    to mention sodomy but also gives the wrong reasons for the martyrdom of Joseph
    Balikuddembe: see ch. 8 below.
20 D. Kincaid, *British Social Life in India, 1608-1937*, 2nd ed., London, 1973; F. Anthony,
    Britain's Betrayal: Story of the Anglo-Indian Community, Bombay, 1969; P. Barr, *The
    Memsahibs: the Women of Victorian India*, London, 1976; C. Allen (ed.), *Plain Tales
    from the Raj: Images of British India in the Twentieth Century*, London, 1975; T. A.
    Heathcote, *Indian Army: the Garrison of British Imperial India, 1822-1922*, London,
    1974; P. Warner, *Auchinleck: the Lonely Soldier*, London, 1981, pp. 262-4.
21 The connection is classically demonstrated by Tom Driberg: see his autobiography,
    Ruling Passions, London, 1977; and it prevented his ever attaining ministerial office;
    Dictionary of National Biography, 1971-80, 1986. See also D. Hilliard, 'UnEnglish and

unmanly: Anglo-Catholicism and homosexuality', *Victorian Studies*, XXV, 1982. The Oxford Movement remains more problematic: see P. G. R. Brendon, *Hurrell Froude and the Oxford Movement*, London, 1974, pp. 60-74. For the way in which the 'unmentionable' has now become integral, see E. T. Williams (ed.), *Dictionary of National Biography, 1961-70*, London, 1981, p. vi: 'Less reticence today about homosexuality may make more intelligible the career of E. M. Forster or W. Somerset Maugham.'

22 See below, pp. 29-30.
23 C. S. Ford and F. A. Beach, *Patterns of Sexual Behaviour*, London, 1952, 1965, is the essential work. For exemplary use of anthropological material to give historical context, see R. Trumbach, 'London's sodomites: homosexual behaviour and western culture in the eighteenth century', *Journal of Social History*, XI, 1977, esp. pp. 1-10.
24 A. C. Kinsey, W. B. Pomeroy and C. E. Martin, *Sexual Behaviour in the Human Male*, Philadelphia, 1948; and *Sexual Behaviour in the Human Female*, Philadelphia, 1953.
25 B. R. Burg, *Sodomy and the Perception of Evil: English Sea-Rovers in the Seventeenth-Century Caribbean*, New York, 1983, is – despite its reissue under a revamped title in 1988 – the most absurd, inadequate and pretentious attempt to project backwards the gay life styles of the present day, and contains only minimalist historical evidence. Very much more scholarly is J. Boswell, *Christianity, Social Tolerance and Homosexuality: Gay People in Western Europe from the Beginning of the Christian Era to the Beginning of the Fourteenth Century*, Chicago, 1980. For a salutary discussion of the problems of homosexual labelling see G. Chauncey, Jr, 'Christian brotherhood or sexual perversion? Homosexual identities and the construction of sexual boundaries in the World War One era', *Journal of Social History*, XIX, 1985, pp. 189-211.
26 N. L. Thompson and B. R. McCandless, 'Homosexual orientation and its antecedents' in A. Davids (ed.), *Child Personality and Psychotherapy*, III, New York, 1976, is the best available short statement. Freud quoted in P. Gay, *The Bourgeois Experience, Victoria to Freud*, II: *The Tender Passion*, New York, 1986, p. 243.
27 To adapt Oscar Wilde's dictum on Socialism. Instead of dividing people into heterosexual and homosexual, I believe it might be more in tune with reality to divide them into a-sexual and bisexual: that is, those who are not keen on sexual activity and those who are. For a-sexuality see discussion on pp. 12-13. For 'lethal' labelling, see Fr. Rolfe, *The Desire and Pursuit of the Whole*, London, 1934, p. 186.
28 R. Scruton, *Sexual Desire: a Philosophical Investigation*, London, 1986, pp. 284-311.
29 F. Bernard, *Paedophilia: a Factual Report*, Rotterdam, 1985, pp. 14-15, 86.
30 For the historical context of child sex abuse, see L. de Mause (ed.), *The History of Childhood*, London, 1976, ch. 1, pp. 43-52; P. Ariès, *Centuries of Childhood*, London, 1979 ed., ch. 5, p. 98 ff. It is difficult to penetrate anyone anally without their co-operation. That at any rate is the inference to be drawn from *The Glory of the Perfumed Garden; the 'Missing Flowers': an English translation from the Arabic of the second and hitherto unpublished part of Shaykh Nafzawi's Perfumed Garden*, London, 1975, ch. 2. 'On sodomy and the tricks of sodomites'. In such a matter, sixteenth-century North African pederasts are much more likely to be right than twentieth-century paediatricians in the North of England. The *scale* of the problem there cannot, prima facie, be as large as has been maintained.
31 Wayland Young, *Eros Denied*, London, 1965, ch. 20: unfortunately the author does not develop his theme with enough evidence. R. C. K. Ensor, *England, 1870-1914*, Oxford, 1936, p. 170. In the succeeding volume of the Oxford History, A. J. P. Taylor observes that the historian 'has his hands on a [sexually] frustrated people. The restraint exercised in their private lives may well have contributed to their lack of enterprise elsewhere': *English History, 1914-45*, Oxford, 1965, p. 166. See also J. D. Unwin, *Sex and Culture*, Oxford, 1934; and *idem, Hopousia: or the Sexual and Economic Foundations of a New Society*, London, 1940. The 'sublimation' idea informed the 'British theory' held by the superintendent of the temple of Jaganath at Puri near Calcutta: 'your whole material prosperity is based on sex-control, which drives you to conquer new worlds, partly in compensation for what has been denied, and partly to enable you to gain the object of your desire... and unless you do have natural sex lives,

either your civilisation will perish or your women will revolt': see F. Yeats-Brown, *Bengal Lancer*, London, 1930, p. 235. Both predictions appear to have come true.

32 Stone, *Family, Sex and Marriage*, pp. 54, 579-80, 490-1, 652.

33 Gann and Duignan, *Rulers of British Africa*, p. 240.

34 K. Sinclair, *A History of New Zealand*, London, 1969 ed., p. 81; J. Rutherford, *Sir George Grey, 1812-98*, London, 1961, pp. 63-6, 428, 573; R. E. Wraith, *Guggisberg*, London, 1967, pp. 247-9; B. Montgomery, *A Field Marshal in the Family*, London, 1973, pp. 236-8; A. T. Yarword, *Samuel Marsden: the Great Survivor*, Melbourne, 1977; D. S. Higgins, *Rider Haggard: the Great Storyteller*, London, 1981, p. 90; T. Jeal, *Baden-Powell*, London, 1989, p. 109.

35 Skidelsky, *Keynes*, p. xvii, referring to his 'childless vision' (Schumpeter).

36 S. Freud, *Three Essays on the Theory of Sexuality*, trans. J. Strachey, London, rev. ed. 1962, pp. 104-5. There are earlier literary expressions of what is sometimes called 'proto-sublimation', for example in Henry Thoreau's *Walden*, 1854: 'generative energy, which when we are loose, dissipates and makes us unclean, when we are continent invigorates and inspires us'. Diderot is blunter: 'There is a bit of bollock at the bottom of our most sublime sentiments and most refined tenderness', quoted in P. Gay, *The Bourgeois Experience*, II, p. 48. H. W. Loewald, *Sublimation: Inquiries into Theoretical Psychoanalysis*, Yale, was published too late for me to use here.

37 D. Meltzer, *Sexual States of Mind*, Perthshire, 1973, ch. 17: 'Work, play and sublimation', pp. 122-31.

38 Havelock Ellis, *Psychology of Sex*, New York, 1933, p. 307.

39 A. Stokes, *Painting and the Inner World: including a Dialogue with Donald Meltzer, MD*, London, 1963, pp. 23-39.

40 Kinsey *et al*, *Sexual behaviour in the Human Male*, pp. 205-13; I use 'a-sexual' here to distinguish the psychological from the biological condition, 'asexual' (= lacking sex).

41 Meltzer, *Sexual States of Mind*, pp. 128-31.

42 D. Bates, *A Gust of Plumes: a Biography of Lord Twining of Godalming and Tanganyika*, London, 1972; H. Pelling, *Winston Churchill*, London, 1974.

43 Magdalene College Archives, Group F: W. R. Inge Diary, 37, 31 January 1940, with reference to the novels of Somerset Maugham; A. C. Benson Diary, 179, f. 44, 21 March 1925; quotations from the two diaries by kind permission of the Master and Fellows of Magdalene College. For Benson see D. Newsome, *On the Edge of Paradise: A. C. Benson the Diarist*, London, 1980; R. Hyam, 'A. C. Benson: on the edge of hell?' *Cambridge Review*, CII, 1980, pp. 56-9.

44 W. Thesiger, *The Life of my Choice*, London, 1987; see also *idem*, *Desert, Marsh and Mountain: the World of a Nomad*, London, 1979.

45 G. Faber, *Jowett: a Portrait with Background*, London, 1957, pp. 83-100.

46 C. Chenevix Trench, *Charley Gordon: an Eminent Victorian Reassessed*, London, 1978, pp. 3-4.

47 H. Macmillan, *Memoirs*, VI: *At the End of the Day, 1961-63*, London, 1933, pp. 437-44; N. Fisher, *Harold Macmillan: a Biography*, London 1982, pp. 327, 350; A. Horne, *Macmillan, 1894-1956* (Official biography, I), London, 1988, pp. 85-90, 98, 115, 178, 296, 341. Macmillan's lifelong friend, Harry Crookshank (Leader of the House of Commons, 1951-55), had no sex life at all, because of war wounds to the genitals: see *Dictionary of National Biography, 1961-70*, London, 1981, p. 248-9.

48 A. C. Benson, *The Schoolmaster: a Commentary upon the Aims and Methods of an Assistant Master in a Public School*, London, 1908, pp. 148-9; Jeal, *Baden-Powell*, ch. 3.

49 P. Magnus, *Kitchener: Portrait of an Imperialist*, London, 1958; Bristow, *Vice and Vigilance*, p. 148. For the more relaxed French attitude see V. Purcell, *Memoirs of a Malayan Official*, London, 1965, p. 32.

50 N. Hamilton, *Monty*, I: *The Making of a General, 1887-1942*, London, 1981, pp. xv-xvi, 5-6, 22-3, 52, 210, 406-7; and II, p. 619; and III: *The Field Marshal, 1944-76*, 1986, pp. 617-20; B. Montgomery, *A Field Marshal in the Family*, London, 1973, pp. 73-5, 196-7, 215, 236-8; A. Chalfont, *Montgomery of Alamein*, London, 1976, pp. 30-1, 82-8; *House of Lords Debates*, 5th series, 266, cc. 645-8 (24 May 1965), and 267, c. 342 (21

June 1965); E. Pine, *The Westminster Abbey Singers*, London, 1963, p. 251 (I owe this reference to Dr C. S. Knighton). Montgomery was the grandson of Dean Farrar (author of *Eric: or, Little by Little*), and two of his uncles were involved in homoerotic scandals.

51 T. E. B. Howarth (ed.), *Monty at Close Quarters: Recollections of the Man*, London, 1985, esp. the contributions of Dr R. Luckett (albeit expurgated) and Dr L. F. Trueb, chs. 9 and 10.

52 P. Gay, *Freud for Historians*, New York, 1985. For comic psychobiography, see n. 45 in ch. 2.

53 M. Strobel, 'African women: a review essay', *Signs: a Journal of Women in Culture and Society*, VIII, 1987. None of the leading feminist academic journals has much to offer the historian of empire, while *History Workshop: a Journal of Socialist and Feminist Historians* equally concentrates on European and North American issues.

54 S. Brownmiller, *Against our Will: Men, Women, and Rape*, London, 1975, p. 15.

55 C. Enloe, *Does Khaki become you? The Militarisation of Women's Lives*, London, 1983, p. 209.

56 London Feminist History Group, *The Sexual Dynamics of History*, London, 1983.

57 M. Jackson, in L. Coveney *et al.*, *The Sexuality Papers: Male Sexuality and the Social Control of Women*, London, 1984, p. 46.

58 M. T. Berger, 'Imperialism and sexual exploitation: a review article'; and R. Hyam, 'A reply', *Journal of Imperial and Commonwealth History*, XVII, 1988. The observation of Vern and Bonnie Bullough is pertinent here: prostitution is 'an outstanding example of the perverse resilience of human beings, since women, including prostitutes, have turned their sexual subordination into a weapon that allows them in turn to victimise men': *Women and Prostitution: a Social History*, New York, 1987, p. 292.

59 M. Vicinus, 'Sexuality and power: a review of current work in the history of sexuality', *Feminist Studies*, VIII, 1982.

60 Berger, 'Imperialism and sexual exploitation', p. 87.

61 Hugh Clifford, *Since the Beginning: a Tale of an Eastern Land*, London, 1898, p. 3.

62 A. P. A. Busia, 'Miscegenation as metonymy: sexuality and power in the colonial novel', *Ethnic and Racial Studies*, IX, 1986, pp. 360-72; G. D. Killam, *Africa in English Fiction, 1874-1939*, Ibadan, 1968; E. Ingram, 'The "Raj" as daydream: the Pukka Sahib as Henty hero in Simla, Chandrapore, and Kyauktada', in G. Martel (ed.), *Studies in Imperial History: Essays in Honour of A. P. Thornton*, London, 1986, pp. 159-77.

63 R. Hughes, *The Fatal Shore: a History of Transportation of Convicts to Australia, 1787-1868*, London, 1987, pp. xiii-xiv, 602; T. d'Arch Smith, *Love in Earnest: Some Notes on the Lives and Writings of English 'Uranian' Poets from 1889 to 1930*, London, 1970, Appendix (a): 'John Moray Stuart-Young', pp. 202-19.

64 H. Callan and S. Ardener (eds.), *The Incorporated Wife*, London, 1984; H. Callaway, *Gender, Culture and Empire: European Women in Colonial Nigeria*, London, 1987.

CHAPTER TWO

Sexual imperatives

Private lives and public responsibilities

Perhaps it doesn't matter how hair-pins are related to balloons, perhaps there is no relation worth mentioning, but in this business of human sex and its relation to life and work, it is obvious that the relation is both real and important. It must, obviously, make a lot of difference to men and women whether they live lives of puzzledom and repression, false valuations and romantic sentiment, untruth and bad conscience, or whether they escape all such troubles and go through life clear-headed and happy; and it is obvious that, among all the things that are influential in our lives to mar or make our happiness, the instinct of mating is one of the most important. [Eric Gill, *Autobiography*, 1940, 52-3.]

Ideally, no doubt, historians should leave the sex lives of public figures in decent obscurity, as they are frequently urged to do, on the argument that such private matters are no part of the historian's business. However, British official attitudes make this unrealistic. Since the private lives of public figures, if they go wrong, are considered a matter of public concern, all private lives are potentially liable to get into the public domain.[1] The historian therefore cannot confine himself merely to those that do.

Sex matters to most people, and has a direct bearing on their relationships. Innumerable autobiographies testify to this. Here, two quotations from members of the Colonial Service will have to suffice. Sir Frederick Lugard wrote, 'The real key to the study of a life lies in a knowledge of the emotions and passions. . . Of these the sexual instinct is recognised as the most potent for good or ill, and it has certainly been so in my life.'[2] Dr Victor Purcell (Malayan official turned historian) did not regard himself as particularly promiscuous, but 'I have never been able to distinguish the sexual urge and the urge to live.'[3]

Sexual needs can be imperative, and people will go to extraordinary lengths to satisfy them. There was an eighteenth-century senior Resident of Calcutta who had himself circumcised in order to improve his relations with Muslim women. Margery Perham observed in 1932 francophone African migrant labourers in Kano queuing up to be circumcised in order to be able to visit the Muslim prostitutes of the town.[4] Many men have pursued the illusion of sexual satisfaction (most wanted when it is least obtainable, least needed when it is most available) to the point of obsession. Some men took risks with their careers at which the historian can only marvel. Roger Casement sought out rent boys for more than twenty years. For ten years (1891-1901) Sir Alfred Milner maintained a secret mistress called Cécile in a 'seedy back street in Brixton'. Even on a working holiday in England at the end of the crucial year 1898 he vanished on a six-day bicycling trip with her on the South Downs.[5] Lord Rosebery as Prime Minister may also have had something to hide: we simply do not know for sure, but he refused to let the private secretary he inherited from Gladstone open his letters; he behaved oddly during the Wilde trials, and maintained a villa in Naples, which looks suspiciously like a typical ploy of late-Victorian upper-class married men who were attracted to other males.[6] Eldon Gorst (1861-1911) as a young man in Egypt had such an obvious succession of women friends that he was reprimanded by Cromer in 1898 for being too conciliatory with the opposite sex (and not conciliatory enough with his colleagues).[7] But there were many others whose private life became disastrously public.

Two early Victorian governors in Australia ran into trouble. Sir John Eardley-Wilmot went out as Lieutenant-Governor of Van Diemen's Land in 1843, his wife remaining in England. Tales of his licentious behaviour and amours were published in the press in 1845. A committee of inquiry (set up by himself) concluded the charges were so vague as to be beyond investigation. Their validity remains doubtful. However, Gladstone — Secretary of State for the Colonies at the time – insisted on his recall, mainly because Eardley-Wilmot had got into dispute with the Anglican episcopacy and failed to check the sodomitical propensities of the convicts.[8] Then there was Sir Charles Fitzroy, Governor of New South Wales 1846-55. His wife was killed in a driving accident at Parramatta in 1847. Within a year he and his sons were accused of 'undue partiality for women'. The attacks increased, reaching a truly embarrassing climax in 1854, when a hostile amendment to his farewell address in the Legislative Council alleged that his influence on the morals of society, and the example set from Government House, Sydney, were 'deleterious and baneful in the highest degree'. This was not the usual stuff even of cut-and-thrust colonial politics, so there was almost certainly a real fire behind the smoke. (Indeed, there usually is).[9]

Sir Henry Pottinger was dismissed within a year as Governor of Cape Colony in 1847. (Theal wrote: 'no other Governor of the colony ever lived in such open licentiousness as he. His amours would have been inexcusable in a young man; in one approaching his sixtieth year they were scandalous.')[10] Valentine Baker, brother of Samuel the explorer, wrecked his army career by assaulting a lady in a railway carriage in 1875, and had to transfer to the Turkish army.[11] Divorce scandals ruined the careers not only of C. S. Parnell in 1890, but also of Sir Charles Dilke, rising hope of the progressive Liberals until 1886. Boy lovers took particularly horrendous chances.[12] General Sir Eyre Coote (1762-1823) (a former Member of Parliament and Lieutenant-Governor of Jamaica) in 1815 made regular Saturday excursions into Christ's Hospital school, and was eventually caught with his trousers down in a flogging and groping session with six boys aged fourteen and fifteen.[13] Even more dangerous was the life style of Sir Hector Macdonald, who shot himself in 1903. Lewis Harcourt (ex-Colonial Secretary) in 1922 exposed his erection (or 'stalagmite' as the old satyr called it) once too often to a teenage house guest, on this occasion an Eton boy of thirteen, Edward James, who complained to his mother.[14] For 'Loulou', also, suicide was the sequel, exactly a hundred years after Lord Castlereagh had killed himself, apparently acutely depressed by the sodomy scandal centring on the Bishop of Clogher, arrested with a Guardsman in a Haymarket public house.[15]

We can thus demonstrate the scandalous collapse of a number of 'imperial' careers. More generally, it is helpful for the historian to know who or what sustains leaders in a crisis, or officials in their routines; to whom they turn to make the strain endurable, to whom they write in their loneliness, what inner image is the lynchpin of their lives. Asquith was certainly not the only Prime Minister, or even First World War leader, to be kept (more or less, in his case) on an even keel by exchanging letters with a lady love.[16] Others also had their 'pole stars', their Venetia Stanleys. Asquith was not even alone in endangering security by indiscreet disclosures. Contemporaneously, Field Marshal Sir John French, despite what one would have thought more than adequate experience in these matters, was ridiculously swept off his feet by Winifred Bennett, writing to her almost daily in 1915 and signing himself 'Peter Pan' to her 'Wendy'. His battle cry before Neuve Chapelle was 'Winifred'.[17] Admiral Beatty's appointment as Commander-in-Chief practically coincided with the inauguration of his affair with Eugené Godfrey-Faussett, his 'fairy queen'; it was essential compensation for a lunatic wife.[18] Lloyd George had his mistress-secretary, Frances Stevenson, whose unwanted pregnancy obtruded itself at the height of the war leadership crisis. Contemplating an earlier war, Milner found crucial relaxation in Cape Town (in the fateful autumn of 1899) with Lady Edward Cecil, his 'godsend'. When at last she was free, he married her in 1921. Earlier still, Nelson (whose flagrantly happy adultery long embarrassed naval hagiographers) truly observed that if there were more Emma Hamiltons there would have been more Nelsons.[19]

However, not all life, even in the empire, takes place on the battlefield, and routine may be just as hard to get through, especially overseas. Palmerston livened up those long years behind a desk at the War Office and Foreign Office with sexual relaxations: he successfully fitted intercourse into the interstices of the working day. The words 'fine day' in his diary in fact recorded successful propositions; sometimes there were five such entries a week, some of them on the same day, though he also failed quite often with his overtures. For twenty-eight years he maintained a mistress before they were free to marry.[20] Even Gladstone had extra-marital emotional support in Mrs Thistlethwaite, a high-class ex-courtesan. Though he was a faithful husband (and thus almost unique among nineteenth-century prime ministers), his nocturnal perambulations seeking out (beautiful) prostitutes for 'rescue' carried its own special risks of misinterpretation and catastrophe. (His success rate was under one per cent.) More seriously, perhaps, Gladstone was himself deeply perplexed by his own mixed motives, and for several years flagellated himself as a punishment, an act which must surely only have reinforced the cycle of excitement and doubt.[21]

Turning overseas, and looking for the moment no farther than India: Clive probably should not be described as fornicating his way across the subcontinent – at least, not after he was married – and, in view of the temptations in his path, was probably 'astonished at his own moderation'. However, he made the most of his early opportunities. A revealing letter survives from John Dalton, his bachelor-days chum, which not only refers to their both having been 'clapped' more than once but looks forward to a joint exploration of the brothels of Covent Garden, expressing relief that in spite of rumours about marriage 'you fuck as usual'.[22] Wellesley notoriously lived a life of sexual tempestuousness; his brother Wellington (certainly no abstainer himself: 'Publish and be damned!') was so shocked as to wish him castrated. Metcalfe (acting Governor-General 1835-36) took an Indian mistress and had three Eurasian sons between 1809 and 1817; they brought him little happiness. Lord Auckland, who was Viceroy 1836-42, was unmarried, his sisters acting as hostesses for him.There were a good many raised eyebrows about the consistently handsome looks of their chosen aides-de-camp. As Viceroy 1872-76, Lord Northbrook was unpopular for reasons directly related to his private misfortunes: the double bereavement of both wife and son made him taciturn. He took dubious consolation from 'a notorious white woman' called Mrs Searle at Ranikhet in 1875, while at the same time becoming over-lyrical about children. His successor, Lord Lytton, had a strong flirtatious streak.[23]

Of great interest are the private relationships of the Punjabi administrators of the 1830s and 1840s, who were long regarded as heroes among 'the guardians of India'. Henry Lawrence went to India in 1822 and often felt acutely lonely. He met his future wife, Honoria Marshall, in 1827, but it was ten years before he was ready to marry her. His lack of interest at one point seemed so great that she was briefly engaged to someone else. Meanwhile, Henry Lawrence 'buried himself in ferocious hard work', and, in and around Gorakhpur, collected 'poor Christian boys' to live with him. These he trained in his survey office. Some were so little they were known as 'Lawrence's offsets'. He married Honoria in 1837. She went to India with him, immediately throwing herself with some enthusiasm into running a house constantly filled with her husband's lame ducks to be helped and protégés to be guided. In 1839, after a marked lack of consideration for his wife's pregnancy, at the news of the coming Afghan war he rushed back to the Artillery Brigade with Honoria and their three-week-old infant, which made both of them seriously ill. Within five years Honoria was more or less an invalid, and thereafter she was repeatedly dangerously ill. She died in 1854. She had gone home in 1846 for her fourth pregnancy, and did not return for two years. In the meantime, Lawrence had become very friendly with John Nicholson from 1842, and with Herbert Edwardes, who became his assistant Resident and private secretary at Lahore from 1846. The three men bound themselves in an extraordinarily close friendship. Lawrence and Edwardes even slept in the same room for three months. The love of Nicholson and Edwardes made them (as Edwardes's wife later described it) 'more than brothers in the tenderness of their whole lives . . . the fame and interests of each other were dearer to them both than their own'. Moreover, Honoria said she loved John Nicholson like a son. Nicholson never married. When Henry Lawrence left the Punjab in 1852, Nicholson was deeply upset and talked of going with him. Outside this trio of friends, Nicholson found himself at ease only with small boys. In 1848 a dying Pathan chief left a seven-year-old son in his care, and John became the boy's affectionate second father. A letter to Edwardes of 1854 finds him much preoccupied with finding suitable toys which might appeal to Waziri boys – perhaps humming-tops or Jew's harps: 'I don't ask for peg-tops, as I suppose I should have to teach how to use them, which would be an undignified proceeding on the art of a district officer.'[24]

Both Nicholson and Lawrence died in the Mutiny. At Nicholson's death, Edwardes wrote the following panegyric:

> I feel as if all happiness had gone out of my career . . . never, never again can
> I hope for such a friend. How grand, how glorious a piece of handiwork he

was! It was a pleasure to behold him even. And to have had him for almost a brother, and now to have lost him in the prime of life – it's an inexpressible and irreparable grief . . . Henry Lawrence was the father and John Nicholson the brother of my public life.

These Punjabi administrators led intense emotional lives. They were apt to quote biblical texts at one another. Nicholson frequently burst into tears when he had to order executions, although he seemed rather to enjoy administering floggings. Lawrence set up three schools for 'deserving boys'; so close was his involvement that he and Honoria lived on the premises of one of them for three months in 1851. A fourth school was founded as a memorial to him. All three men had a cordial dislike of John Lawrence, Henry's brother, who had little time for these beautiful and perfervid relationships – which, however, underpinned a comparatively effective administrative machine. Time and time again the historian registers surprise at the disjunction between sober and sensible public achievement and chaotic or peculiar private life. The management of public affairs, it seems, is altogether less demanding than are personal relationships.[25]

The adjustment of public responsibilities and private lives is always a delicate business. Most people muddle through, without their sexual imperatives actually wrecking their careers. But some there were who suffered major calamities as a direct or indirect result of their sexual activities, notably Parnell, Macdonald and Casement. All these indulged in private behaviour that could have wrecked their careers at any time.

Three tragedies: Parnell, Macdonald, Casement

Politicians who put themselves into the public arena should have, or at least appear to observe, a higher standard of behaviour than citizens at large. . . It may be seen as one of the responsibilities and burdens entailed in thrusting oneself into public life, and a part of the heat that those who will not stay out of the political kitchen are often exhorted to endure. But . . . there are many senior civil servants, police officers and soldiers to whom the two-tier doctrine of public morality is sadly unfair, and the heavens will sometimes fall on them without justice being done. [G. Marshall, *Constitutional Conventions*, 1984, pp. 109-10]

As leader of the Irish Parliamentary Party after 1880, Charles Stewart Parnell towered over late nineteenth-century British politics in a way surpassed only by Gladstone himself. And Gladstone described Parnell as the most remarkable man he had ever met. To the Irish people he was their 'uncrowned king', the dominating, mesmerising, even messianic hero, directing a national movement on an international scale, and giving them back their self-respect. His personality was undoubtedly a commanding one. His definitive biographer, Professor Lyons, writes of 'the courage, the pride, the tenacity, the ruthlessness, the obstinacy, the resilience, the concentrated passion which . . . in his prime made him an almost elemental force in British and Irish affairs'. He propelled Home Rule to the centre of the Westminster stage. It was a glittering achievement. In doing so, he virtually invented the modern political opposition party: his Irish party, with its tactical plans, tight discipline, unifying pledges and payment of members, was not only his most striking personal achievement but the prototype of all subsequent innovations in British political parties, and the model for every emergent nationalist movement in the British empire.[26]

Parnell conducted a long-standing, extremely reckless and ultimately fateful liaison with Katharine O'Shea, who had been effectively living apart from her husband for five years before it began. The lovers had two children together. Katharine was an important political intermediary for Parnell, carrying letters for him, and so forth, but above all else she made a home for him in England, at Eltham. All the while her husband, Captain William O'Shea, hovered in the background. He was willing to be 'squared', but, knowing that his wife was due to inherit from an aunt, he was asking £20,000. The affair shows Parnell's complete indifference to the sexual and social conventions of his time. This indifference was, of course, the reverse side of the coin of his contempt for political and parliamentary convention – not least in his notorious obstruction of Commons procedure – which made him the great nationalist leader he was. But even his most sympathetic supporters found his affair hard to forgive, for it seemed to put a vital political cause entirely at the mercy of Mrs O'Shea's unscrupulous husband. When in 1890 O'Shea at last sued for divorce, Parnell was doomed. Gladstone withdrew his tentative support, and Parnell's career was shattered. He died only a year later, married now to 'Kitty', but a broken man. And he was only forty-five.[27]

Parnell is an enigma. There were many sides to him. On the one hand he was a traditional, unassuming, rather ordinary country gentleman; on the other a political genius with a gift for charismatic leadership. At one moment he seemed just a casual private man – charming as a companion, endearingly eccentric (he was hag-ridden with superstition, and searched for gold as a hobby), frequently wallowing in lazy domesticity – and at another, intermittently, a man of dark, elemental passion, 'driven by a demonic pride and self-will to prodigies of concentrated energy'. It is to his 'domestic' mode that Parnell the lover properly belongs. Like all embattled love affairs, however, Parnell's liaison with Kitty was 'star-crossed' and sentimental to the point of soppiness. But it also had its demonic side, and tragic consequences. There is no convincing answer to the charge that for the sake of love, and a legacy which conveniently went with it, he 'subordinated his judgment to that of his mistress and in so doing had recklessly jeopardised the important national interests committed to his charge'. This was not a brief liaison into which he drifted willy-nilly in his declining years. The affair began in the very year he became party leader. It was conducted with the wife of one of his chief supporters, and went on for ten dangerous years, compelling Parnell into humiliating subterfuges. If it did not involve quite such lunatic episodes as folklore sometimes suggested (such as scrambling on to fire escapes), it nevertheless reduced him to using false names and disguises and flitting from one rented house to another. In the end, the trouble was not simply that he sacrificed his career for love – manifestly he wanted both and could not see their incompatibility – but that he misjudged the safe balance between them . Almost certainly, natural arrogance as well as deteriorating health was crucially involved. As a result he allowed the affair to absorb too much time and energy. From 1882 he was so often in Eltham that his party management can only be described as fitful. Contact with his followers became neglected. His sublime indifference to them by the end of the 1880s was matched by parliamentary absenteeism: he voted in only fifty out of 250 divisions in the 1890 session. So magnetic was the attraction of Mrs O'Shea that on one occasion he could scarcely bring himself to spend as long as two hours in Cork, at a banquet given by his constituents, before hurrying back to England. Thus Parnell had by neglect thoroughly undermined his own leadership and let it pass into inferior hands, long before the divorce scandal broke and finally destroyed him.[28]

Enoch Powell once observed, 'there is no important political figure for understanding whose career and actions his secret emotional life is so crucial as Parnell'. In his case, as Powell said, we happen to know the secret, but this is exceptional, and it should 'make us wonder whether in other lives we have the necessary materials for a true judgment'. Parnell's was not the only career to be heavily determined by the exigencies of private emotion, but he was unlucky. As the third Earl of Durham wrote privately to a friend, 'Parnell's *amours* were undignified, but not nearly so discreditable as some of mine! But he has been exposed, so must pay the penalty in this most hypocritical and *virtuous* land'.[29]

There are two reasons why the tragedy of Sir Hector Macdonald (1853-1903) looms large. One is the magnitude of the disaster: a national hero committing suicide after indulging in pederasty on a scale usually associated only with major sex criminals, running a big 'vice ring'. The other is the fact that he was shown no mercy by the 'establishment'. It has long been argued that this was because he was an outsider, a 'ranker', a Scottish working-class lad made good.[30] I used to think this a fairly daft piece of special pleading: now, I am not so sure. Macdonald was, after all, far from being the only prominent British soldier who liked small boys. There was General Gordon a little while before him, and in the mid-twentieth century there were two field marshals in the same case; and all three of them were protected by the absolute loyalty of their staff. Whereas Macdonald was probably told by the king that the best thing he could do was to shoot himself, Auchinleck was let off with a high-level warning. Moreover, shortly before Macdonald's fall, two establishment figures guilty of similar offences, Robert Eyton (canon of Westminster), and the seventh Earl Beauchamp, both escaped prosecution: Eyton was allowed to slip quietly off to Australia, while Beauchamp (having already been Governor of New South Wales) was allowed to remain and get married, although deprived of public office for nearly ten years.[31] Macdonald was, of course, actually caught more or less *in flagrante delicto*, but it is still hard to see that he must necessarily have been required to face a court martial.

Macdonald was a crofter's son who became a draper's apprentice and then enlisted in the ranks in 1870, serving eight or nine years in India, and becoming a captain in the Egyptian army by 1887. At Edinburgh in 1884 he went through a declaratory form of marriage with a girl barely sixteen, Christina Duncan. They had a son, but within less than ten years they had parted. Macdonald never informed the War Office of his marriage. He became the hero of the hour at Omdurman, and went on to have a good war in South Africa. By now he was a Scottish national hero, one of the most popular generals of his day. Yet his principal friend was a Glenalmond schoolboy from Aberdeen called Alaister Robertson, to whom he wrote letters which strangely prefigure those Montgomery would write to his boy friends half a century later. ('I am sending you a tin of the Queen's chocolate, which you can eat with your best friends, and think of me. You should keep the box as a memento.') Before the battle of Paardeburg it was Alaister's photograph he had beside him as he wrote demanding 'more news about your dear self'.[32]

In 1902 he was appointed Commander-in-Chief, Ceylon. Accusations about his behaviour were laid before the Governor, Sir Joseph West Ridgeway, in mid-February 1903. Ridgeway suggested he should go to England on six months' leave in order to think things over and discuss the problem, and to avert an immediate public scandal. He informed Field Marshal Roberts, who admitted he already knew that Macdonald in South Africa had been 'given to quaint practices . . . love-making to quite young girls – but this must be something much worse'. Indeed it was. There was even the possibility that Macdonald had earlier used the services of a procurer of males who was convicted of murder in 1902. In London, Roberts told Macdonald that he could not remain in the army unless he cleared his name. Although no offence had been committed under the laws of Ceylon (which had not adopted the mother country's 1885 legislation), he must go back there and answer to a court-martial.[33] Macdonald then saw the king. On 20 March 1903 he left England to return to Ceylon, staying for a few days at the Hotel Regina in Paris. Meanwhile Ridgeway, under pressure in the Ceylon legislature, revealed that 'serious charges' had been laid against Macdonald, who was returning to be court-martialled. The story broke in the European edition of the *New York Herald*, whereupon Macdonald immediately shot himself. The relief of the authorities was enormous. If he had come to trial, the dimensions of the scandal might have been revealed as the largest ever known in the history of the empire. We shall never know its precise dimensions. Macdonald's case file was almost certainly destroyed as a precaution immediately after his suicide.

Ceylon furnished Macdonald with a lethal combination of a military command which was inactive and uninteresting and a community of boys who were interesting and very active. He soon became aware of the bonzes' catamites at the temples, the obliging waiters of the Grand Oriental Hotel, the up-country rest-house dancing boys, the ubiquitous nude-bathing boys on the beaches, perhaps even of the Tamil boy prostitutes in the Colombo docks. He became friendly with a Burgher family called de Saran, and it became his undoing.[34] White planter society (which he shunned) disliked the friendship, and noted that he seemed to spend too much time with the two de Saran boys, with whom, it was suspected, he was having a sexual relationship. There seems also to have been a dubious club attended by both British and Sinhalese youths, which Macdonald patronised.

And then came the famous denouement in a railway carriage at Kandy. Macdonald was discovered in a compartment (with the blinds down) in company with four Sinhalese boys. He was (more or less) wearing civilian clothes, but was recognised by the startled intruder, a tea-planter, as ill luck would have it. The planter, who had probably interrupted a communal masturbation session, spread the gossip in such a way that a number of schoolmasters and two clergymen were induced to lay charges before the governor. There were seven or eight cases thus alleged, but the governor was assured that more would follow if the scandal became public knowledge. Macdonald denied the charges. There was enough evidence, however, to convince Ridgeway that Macdonald was involved in 'a habitual crime of misbehaviour with several schoolboys'. Up to seventy witnesses could have been called. Apparently Macdonald was engaged in a systematic pattern of serious sexual activities with possibly scores of boys aged twelve and upwards. 'Some, indeed most of his victims, whose cases were dealt with,' wrote Ridgeway, 'are the sons of the best known men in the colony, English and Native.' One boy, the son of a doctor, had already 'gone off his head' with anxiety. It was rumoured that Ridgeway's own son was one of Macdonald's circle. At any rate, the governor was desperately anxious to conceal all the details, hoping 'no more mud would be stirred up'.[35]

People accused Ridgeway of hounding Macdonald to death. He defended his action in sending Macdonald home:

> If he had remained a few days the clergy and planters and others who had practically formed a Vigilance Committee in Colombo would have taken action and a warrant would have issued for his arrest. What would he have gained by staying? He knew his case to be helpless. There was just the chance he might be allowed to retire. If not, suicide remained the only alternative. My action has been so far successful that the revolting details of the case have not transpired and need not transpire unless the poor man's friends are very indiscreet. The danger is that they provoke revelations. However I shall continue to try to ensure silence.

Silence appears to have been his main thought throughout, fearing such revelations regarding Macdonald's life not only in Ceylon but in earlier years as would produce a 'terrible scandal' prejudicial and demoralising both to Ceylon and to the army.[36] It is perhaps hard to see how Ridgeway could have acted otherwise. He successfully muzzled the Ceylon press, and ensured discretion from those who made the original allegations. The real villain of the piece would seem to have been Roberts, who insisted on a court martial.

For none, perhaps, was the Macdonald tragedy more poignant than for Sir Roger Casement (1864-1916). Of Macdonald's 'terrible end', Casement wrote in his diary, 'The reasons given are pitiably sad. The most distressing case this surely of its kind, and one that may awake the national mind to saner methods of curing a terrible disease.'[37]

Casement spent a third of his life in Africa, beginning in 1884. By 1895 he was in the consular service at Lourenço Marques, transferring to Luanda (Angola) in 1897. He then served in the Congo Free State, and in Brazil from 1906, becoming Consul-General at Rio. He achieved internationally important successes in two great anti-slavery campaigns, in Leopold's Congo and in Putumayo (Peru), reporting upon and exposing to the world the 'red rubber' scandals.He raised the British consular service to an unprecedentedly high prestige. Yet at the same time he was insatiably and surreptitiously pursuing sexual satisfaction with young men. Casement seems to have known his way around urban sexual undergrounds, British and Portuguese, very well indeed. Once again we are confronted with a personality prepared to jeopardise all his public work by sexual escapades, because discovery would assuredly have undermined the credibility and authority of his reports on 'red rubber'. There are those indeed who would further argue that whilst exposing one kind of exploitation Casement himself was almost equally guilty of exploiting people sexually. This is, however, to confuse real evil with mere peccadillo. Casement's task was to expose appalling abuses of power: flogging, starving, torturing, mutilating and shooting plantation workers or, in the case of the overseers of the Peruvian Amazon Company, raping little girls and turning them into concubines. Even assuming that Casement had casual sexual relations with youths among these exploited people – and it is a big assumption – it would hardly be of the same order of exploitation. In fact it is extremely unlikely that he ever used his official position to obtain sexual services, despite the temptations which faced him. His investigations meant examining abused bodies, and they took place in remote communities where it was commonplace to see nude bathing, juvenile masturbation and sexual display. Casement's desires were often aroused by what he saw (and perhaps by native policemen), but he behaved with propriety. His sexual contacts were thus strictly off-duty activities, in situations where partners mostly would not know who he was. Mainly they were pursued with professional rent boys in towns: in London, Dublin, Lisbon, Las Palmas, Buenos Aires.[38]

The notorious 'black diaries' which reveal all this did not begin until 1903, by which time his sexual career was well advanced. It is possible he may have been introduced to male sex by Europeans in Oil Rivers, where he was in the survey department in the early 1890s. When one of the first European traders in Kano early this century was convicted of sodomy, his excuse was that it had been condoned in Oil Rivers, where he had spent many years.[39]

The recording of sexual life in journals or diaries tends to be either purely notational (as in the case of Palmerston and Gorst), or more literary in form – in Pepys's case coy, in Corvo's 'Venice letters' lyrical, in Joe Orton's diaries arch, in Edmund Backhouse's accounts fantastic.[40] Searight, whom we shall meet in India, used both methods in parallel, one version in tabulated shorthand, another in poetry recollected in some degree of tranquillity. Casement's method was much more of an instant compromise. His diaries are in note form, often cryptically recorded with a breathless immediacy. They still have the power to shock, where more explicit but finished accounts do not. Often he did no more than jot down sightings of beautiful youths with prominent bulges in their left/right trouser legs. Here are two extracts from 1910, the first written in February in Rio, the second in May in the United

Kingdom. (X stands for intercourse):

> Deep screw and to hilt X 'poquino'. Mario in Rio 8½ x 6" 40$. Hospeclaria, Rua do Hospicio. 3$ only FINE room shut window lovely, young, 18 and glorious. Biggest since Lisbon July 1904 and as big. Perfectly huge. 'Nunca veio maior.' Nunca.

> To Belfast, John McGonegal, huge and curved up by Cregagh Road, met by chance near clock tower and off on tram. It was huge and curved and he awfully keen. X 4/6.

Like Frederick the Great, Casement liked very tall young men, and he wanted them well hung, keen to take the active role in anal coition. A fairly typical payment made was ten shillings, but Irish and Jamaicans appear to have got less. Apart from a few regular partners, he never revealed his proclivities to any of his friends. But it was decidedly a double life. On an occasion in June 1910, for example, he records two rent-boy payments (10s and 6s 6d) at 1.00 a.m. in the morning – after dining with Sir Arthur Conan Doyle and watching his play *The Speckled Band*, in company with the Congo Reform Association organiser E. D. Morel.[41] The strain of concealment, especially when everyone regarded him as a person of unimpeachable integrity, was severe enough to produce a gradual disintegration of personality. By his forties, Casement was probably a manic-depressive and prone to sporadic breakdown. The extraordinary Irish episode which led to his arrest and execution in 1916 as a traitor – or Irish patriot, depending on your point of view – scarcely looks the action of a rational man.

For a long time, many people chose to believe that the sexual entries in his diaries were forgeries engineered by an unscrupulous British government bent on blackening his name yet further in the interests of getting a popular conviction. The entries are not interpolations by another hand, however, and all historians now accept them as genuine.

It has been argued that Casement's sexual needs were a determinant, even a positive one, of his public conduct – that they made unusual loyalties possible, and explain his commitment to helping the weak, the vulnerable and the politically oppressed. It is possible there is something in this. Also , it has been argued that he set a grand precedent for the 'Homintern' of the 1930s, the Soviet moles who began as Cambridge 'Apostles' and went on to combine homosexuality with treachery. The link between treachery and homosexuality is, however, tenuous. At Bletchley Park during the Second World War, two of the key figures in the ULTRA intelligence secret, Professor F. E. Adcock, the Cambridge recruiter, and Alan Turing, the mathematical genius, were both sexually inclined toward males, as were H. O. Evenett and doubtless others; but there were no spies at Bletchley and unbroken secrecy was maintained.

In Casement's case, it was not his sexual preferences as such which turned him into a traitor, but his excessive conceit. Miraculously, he had always got away with his secret sexual life. He had done so much by brilliant powers of diplomacy that, once he courted the idea of an independent Ireland, he deceived himself into thinking he could bring it about almost of his own volition. Casement was a 'mad prophet', hopelessly carried away by his apocalyptic vanity, disorientated by his realisation of society's cruel intolerance of his brand of sexuality.[42]

Marriage, celibacy, women and the service of the empire

What wickedness and what folly to under-value and to be insensible to the affection of a wife. [Sir Robert Peel, c. 1827, on the Duke of Wellington]

At this point I shall consider the behaviour of members of the imperial ruling elite, and examine their attitude to marriage and the relationship between their private lives and service of the empire. Some never married, some married late, and some married disastrously. One way or another there was a remarkably high incidence of unhappiness and hardheartedness. The nineteenth-century empire was a distinctly masculine affair.

There were some conspicuously inveterate bachelors or a-sexuals among the famous and successful, men such as General Gordon, Lord Kitchener, Cecil Rhodes and Sir Matthew Nathan. 'Charley' Gordon, hero of campaigns in China and the Sudan, never showed the remotest interest in women, but spent six years of his life (1865-71) trying to create in London his own little land where the child might be prince, housing and improving ragged urchins (turning 'scuttlers' into 'kings'), until they were packed off to sea with the onset of puberty. 'How far better', he wrote, 'to be allowed to be kind to a little scrub than to govern the greatest kingdoms.' Whilst in Basutoland, he confessed to a sympathetic missionary that his one real desire in life was to retire into Mount Carmel monastery and establish there a small refuge or school for poor Syrian boys, to whom he would teach the Christian faith and 'something useful to them in the world'.[43] Horatio Kitchener admitted few personal distractions to his army career, and 'thereby reaped an incalculable advantage in competition with his fellows'. There is no evidence that he ever loved a woman. His male friendships were few but fervent: from 1907 until his death at sea in 1916 his constant and inseparable companion was Captain O. A. FitzGerald, who devoted his entire life to Kitchener. Kitchener had no use for married men on his staff. Only young officers were admitted to his house – 'my happy family

of boys', he called them. He avoided interviews with women, wor-
shipped General Gordon, cultivated great interest in the Boy Scout
movement, took a passing fancy to General Botha's son and the sons of
Lord Desborough, and embellished his rose garden with four pairs of
sculptured bronze boys.[44]

The most intimate relationship Cecil Rhodes ever had was his friendship with Neville Pickering, four years his junior, with whom he shared
house in Kimberley from 1881 until Pickering's death in 1886. For
Rhodes, Pickering was the incarnation of the masculine ideal and, in the
opinion of a recent biographer, 'probably the only person whom Rhodes
ever really loved'. In his second will, Rhodes named Pickering as the sole
beneficiary. On his deathbed, Pickering is said to have whispered to
Rhodes, 'You have been father, mother, brother and sister to me.' For the
remainder of his short life, Rhodes was probably a lonely man, despite
his friendships with Alfred Beit (the mining magnate) and Dr L. Jameson
(an attachment which another friend described as 'fervent'). Described
by Bramwell Booth as 'a great human heart hungering for love', he found
little happiness at the peak of his career in the 1890s. When asked if he
was happy, Rhodes replied, 'Happy? I, happy? Good God, no.' And this
was the confession of a man who added two provinces to the empire,
became Prime Minister of the Cape, a millionaire in the City of London,
the virtual dictator of a chartered company and two mining firms, as
well as the owner of several newspapers. He once said he could not get
married because he had too much work on his hands. It may have been
true; but it is also the case that he wanted only unmarried male
secretaries in his household – as soon as they married, he transferred
them to one of his companies; he considered their marriage an act of dis-
loyalty, and he told at least one bride that he was jealous of her. Rumours
about his inclinations always pursued him. Although he may have had
relations with Coloured and Zulu women, there is 'modest circumstan-
tial evidence' (Rotberg) that his hearty horseplay with blue-eyed valets
(his 'lambs') may have been expressed sexually on occasion. More likely,
though, he was an a-sexual. His dislike of English female company and
servants was notorious; his high-pitched, effeminate voice did not help
matters, nor did his openly displayed collection of phallic cult carvings.[45]

An altogether less colourful figure was Sir Matthew Nathan (1862-
1939), successively Governor of the Gold Coast, Hong Kong, and Natal.
His was a very successful run in the *cursus honorum* of colonial
governorships. Though he may have had a romance while at Woolwich,
there is no other comment in his letters or papers which suggests
involvement with a woman until he was over fifty. He had no close men
friends, so that alternative can be ruled out. He enjoyed the company of
a number of female friends, provided they did not try to get emotionally

involved. These included notably Mary Chomondeley, a confidante for twenty-eight years, and Mrs Amber Blanco-White for ten years, but also (more briefly) Violet Asquith and Constance Spry (as she later became). Mary Kingsley was quickly dropped when she tried to bring affection into their relationship. Nathan was a dedicated careerist, determined to have no distractions. He had made a conscious decision to avoid the retarding risks of family ties, and set himself sustained and successful campaigns not to be held back either by his Jewishness or by marriage (or perhaps by his intellectual limitations). He became simply a dutiful and good public servant of empire. His reward was to be regarded by the Colonial Office as a governor superior to the great Lord Lugard himself.[46]

Then there were those who married late: Lord Milner at sixty-seven, Lord Baden-Powell at fifty-five, H. M. Stanley at fifty-one, Lord Lugard at forty-four, and Lord Curzon at thirty-six. The explorer Henry Stanley (1841-1904) found most relationships difficult, owing to his illegitimate, workhouse background and an unsatisfied youthful search for affection after his rejection by his Welsh mother. He wanted a wife, but he also needed the company of deprived boys. He became attached to fifteen-year-old Lewis Noe, and then to thirteen-year-old Edwin Balch. He tried to take Balch on his expedition to find Livingstone, but the boy's parents not unnaturally refused permission; he then almost literally picked up three working-class companions. On another occasion he tried to find a workhouse boy to live with him, but failed. In Africa, he was presented with little Kalulu in 1871, and became extremely fond of him; but the boy died in 1877 towards the end of Stanley's Nile expedition. Stanley celebrated the relationship in a novel *My Kalulu: Prince, King and Slave*. Meanwhile, in 1874 he had fallen in love with a rich American girl called Alice Pike, but she jilted him in 1876 during his absence on the Nile. Subsequently, he was also turned down by Kate Gough-Roberts and, at the first time of asking, by Dolly Tennant. Dolly, however, eventually accepted him, by which time he was over fifty, recognised as the leading explorer in the world and the chief discoverer of central Africa, albeit a gun-addicted one. During a critical part of his career, he had deliberately steeled himself against all but platonic love, turning himself into an utterly ruthless conquistador.[47]

Robert Baden-Powell (1857-1941), founder of the Boy Scouts, had idolised his mother. In India, he attached himself to Kenneth McLaren (known as 'The Boy' on account of his youthful looks) as his closest friend, and for life. While besieged at Mafeking, Baden-Powell wrote to him every day, and on his return to England the first thing he did was to visit McLaren. 'The Boy' became chief administrator of the Boy Scouts. Baden-Powell's eventual wife was expected to spend her honeymoon in a Scout tent and then run the Girl Guides. His relations with McLaren were not physical, those with his wife scarcely more so. Discovering that performing conjugal duties gave him severe headaches, he moved his bed on to the balcony. In effect, Baden-Powell was an a-sexual, deeply fearful of sexuality. He mitigated his sexual repression only by a life-long interest in the male sex, especially in men and boys nude for bathing, whether in the flesh or in photographs. The Scout Movement was the creative offspring, at once cathartic and narcissistic, of these sexual tensions. [48]

After his rejection of his proposal by Margot Tennant on the Nile at Luxor, Sir Alfred Milner (High Commissioner in South Africa 1897-1905) nursed a bundle of love letters. He did not marry until his retirement from the Colonial Office in 1921. This, however, was because he had fallen in love with a married woman, Lady Edward Cecil. Until she became free to marry him, he had consoled himself with a mistress.[49]

Lord Curzon (Viceroy of India 1899-1905) in early life deliberately forced celibacy upon himself in order to complete the twelve-year programme of oriental study and travel which he hoped would qualify him to become Viceroy. After a hearty friendship with the four Tennant sisters (and how they keep cropping up!), he somewhat callously kept his future wife, Mary Leiter, waiting an unconscionably long time. He fell in love with Mary in 1890, took two years to propose, and three years more to redeem his promise. He took himself off on his travels again, leaving her to fend off another suitor. In 1893 he wrote to her that by her faithfulness, 'I am spared all the anxieties of what is called a great courtship, and I have merely, when the hour strikes, to enter into possession of my own.'[50]

The famous theorist of Indirect Rule, Frederick Lugard (1858-1945), admitted that the sexual instinct was the most powerful influence on his life. At the age of twenty-nine he abandoned an extremely promising military career and set sail as a deck passenger to an unknown African destination, all the while contemplating suicide. Three years earlier, in India, he had fallen in love with a woman who subsequently rejected him, establishing herself in a pleasure-seeking circle in London that was utterly uncongenial to him. Emotional desperation, together with the depressant effects of fever, led him to want danger and, if possible, death in some distant place and among strangers – perhaps in Ethiopia. Britain, he felt, must remain barred to him because it contained his unrequited love. He struggled with the longing for self-destruction all the way to Zanzibar, where he recovered himself a little; and in 1888 he entered the service of the African Lakes Company at Blantyre. Years of constructive effort in Nyasaland, Uganda, Nigeria, and ultimately Hong Kong followed. When at last, in his mid-forties, he met and married Flora Shaw (a *Times* journalist) in 1902, his desire to make up for lost time and remain with his wife led him to devise a preposterous scheme for the 'continuous administration' of tropical colonies (that is, the governor continuing to run them for part of the year from London) – a scheme scornfully rejected by the Colonial Office.[51]

It cannot be said that the incidence of marital happiness was notably high among those servants of empire who did marry. There were some exceptions, such as Warren Hastings and Lord William Bentinck in India, Sir Reginald Wingate in the Sudan, and R. T. Coryndon in Africa, but for all too many marriage meant almost literally living out the proverbial lifetime of repentance: among them Lord Wellesley, Lord Wellington, Viceroy Lord Ellenborough, Sir George Goldie, Sir Eldon Gorst, the novelist Rider Haggard, Governors Sir Donald Cameron and Sir Gordon Guggisberg, and any number of politicians. Joseph Chamberlain was twice widowed, with six children.[52]

A classic case of a man whose promising career fizzled out because of private dissipation is provided by Richard, Marquis Wellesley, who, as Governor-General of India 1798-1805, made the most crucial conquests for the Raj but who, unlike his younger brother, the Duke of Wellington, failed to get to the top in British politics.He met Hyacinthe Roland (daughter of a French actress and a Parisian Irishman) in 1786. She became his mistress and bore him five children before he married her. In 1797 he went to India as Governor of Madras, but his wife refused to accompany him. He made meticulous provision for his family, and then, 'torn with sorrow', lived alone for seven years. For the first two he was faithful, hoping his wife would join him. He never forgave her failure to do so. Fundamentally, however, he appears to have been relieved to be free of domestic responsibility, and eventually abandoned himself to the brothels. Bitter hatred developed between husband and wife. In 1801 Hyacinthe complained furiously that for eighteen months he had written her not 'one affectionate or comforting letter', not one that had not been full of selfishness, vanity and ambition. She mocked the lack of philosophic courage which might have enabled him to be indifferent to decorations and titles: he, 'before whom all the rulers of Asia tremble', was 'devoured by fury' over baubles. He replied by commenting on the 'unbearable silliness' of her letters. The rift grew, and in 1810 they were legally separated. He then had other mistresses, among them Sally Douglas and Miss Leslie. In Spain during the Peninsular War, he flaunted his women. His second marriage, to a Catholic, Marianne Paterson, was an almost immediate disaster, and a political liability when he was at Dublin Castle as Lord-Lieutenant of Ireland. His youngest son was threatened by the cut-throat associate of one of his whores at Covent Garden (the young man was reputed to be living the life of an effeminate 'Asiatic debauchee' in Ramsgate). The conqueror of India was not, in short, a stable family man, but lived a life of sexual tempestuousness and frustration. His brother, the Duke of Wellington, was appalled at the way he threw his career away upon whoring until 'he had entirely worn out his constitution by the profligate habits of his life'.[53]

As for the Iron Duke himself, he dithered too long over whether or not to marry Kitty Pakenham, and when he did so in 1806 she was already grown old and ugly. It was a quite unsuitable match. She was a boring, gossipy, motherly little Irishwoman. He would not abandon her; he just ignored her, and flirted with more intelligent women.[54]

Lord Ellenborough, Viceroy of India 1842-44, lost his first wife after six years. He divorced his second wife, also after six years, on the grounds of her adultery, in 1838. Thereafter, he had three illegitimate children.[55]

Sir George Grey (Governor of New Zealand 1845-53 and 1861-6, and of the Cape in South Africa 1854-61) was completely estranged from his wife for thirty-seven years. In the words of Professor Sinclair, in the latter part of his career, as a lonely party politician, Grey 'compensated for the absence of wife and friends by seeking, through his skill as a popular orator, the approval of the masses'.[56]

Sir George Goldie (1846-1925), the creator of Nigeria, left Britain in 1877 for West Africa largely in order to escape from personal entanglements. As a young man, he lived for three years idyllically with an Arab girl in the Egyptian Sudan. He returned to a life of dissipation in Britain, shocked everybody by eloping with the family governess, and then hopelessly compromised himself as a result of getting caught up with her in the Paris siege in 1870. He married her in 1871, but it was what the Victorians called an 'unfortunate marriage', and he was not a faithful husband.[57]

Often the service of empire required long and sometimes painful separation from families. Livingstone furnishes a particularly sad example. The disruption of his family life drove his eldest son to death and turned his wife into a terminally ill alcoholic; but the alternative was further accusations from his mother-in-law of dragging his wife 'cruelly and indecorously' about the bush. Sir William MacGregor's family relationships suffered a melancholy breakdown (with his daughters alienated) consequent on successive postings to Fiji, Papua, and Nigeria in the late nineteenth century.[58]

Then there was the enhanced risk of bereavement. Service of empire brought tragedy to many families. The climate of Java and Sumatra killed Sir Stamford Raffles's first wife in 1814. He remarried in 1817, and then four of the children of this marriage died in 1821-22. In 1824 on his return home, he lost in a fire at sea most of his possessions (worth at least £25,000), quite apart from his official and anthropological documents and two thousand drawings on natural history. Raffles, famous as the founder of Singapore, was only forty-four when he died.

Similar misfortune struck distinguished families throughout the century. Lord Charles Somerset (Governor of the Cape 1814-26) was widowed in 1815: his wife never really recovered from the voyage out to South Africa.[59] Lord Dalhousie, whose wife died half-way through his viceroyalty in 1853 when he was forty-one, was as poignant a widower as any ('almost too hard to bear . . . my whole future is shivered by it'). In 1861 his successor Lord Canning's wife also died in India, from 'jungle fever'. Such men were tough and they kept going: but the strain not infrequently made them harder to work with. In fact, Canning was so stricken that he suffered a complete breakdown in spirits and health only three months after retiring to Britain. The eighth Earl of Elgin's first wife died in Jamaica after a shipwreck; his son (Viceroy of India 1894-9) lost *his* first wife after years of ill health made irreparable by residence in India. Lord Curzon's first wife died prematurely, shortly after his viceroyalty was over: it had hastened her end. Viceroy Lord Hardinge's wife died in the middle of his term, in 1914.[60] Examples could be multiplied. Those who wanted greater assurance of domestic bliss and stability were best advised to stay at home. Not all did so. The sense of public duty was sometimes strong – as with the Elgins, or the Brookes of Sarawak.

The white rajas of Sarawak provide an interesting illustration of contrasting attitudes to marriage through three generations. The first raja, James Brooke (1803-68), devoted his entire life to the interests of Sarawak and its peoples. He never married, although there was an early broken engagement and an illegitimate son, Reuben George Brooke. James had been wounded in the Burma War in 1825. Opinions differ as to whether the wound was in the lung or the testicles. In view of the acknowledgement in his will of a son born after this event, it would certainly seem that Brooke was not rendered impotent. The existence of the son was kept secret for many years. It is possible that the story of James Brooke's emasculation may have been given currency to explain his embarrassingly total lack of physical interest in women. For it is indeed indisputable that he was not of the marrying kind.[61] He showed, however, great affection for his nephews, one of whom he took with him to Sarawak in 1840. The younger nephew (who eventually succeeded him) he doted upon for some years: a letter from 'this great pet' ('full of his boyish pranks and thoughts') was a major emotional joy for James Brooke. He acquired other boy protégés all over the place. He was compulsively drawn to thirteen-year-old midshipmen, describing how they 'would skylark over his body as if he were one of themselves'. In 1843 he befriended the thirteen-year-old great-nephew of the Bishop of Calcutta, and wrote of this 'fine little fellow':

I have got quite fond of him since he has been here; and somehow there is something in the position of a young volunteer of thirteen years of age, which rouses one's kind feelings; so young, yet forced into manhood, to share privations and fatigues, when yet a boy. Since my nephew, Charlie, has embarked in the same line, I feel doubly inclined to be friendly with all the mids;. . . I was delighted with a letter I have just received from the youngster.[62]

Brooke also had a close attachment with Badrudin, a Sarawak prince ('my love for him was deeper than anyone I knew'). After Badrudin's death, and above all others, Brooke loved Charles ('Doddy') Grant (grandson of the seventh Earl of Elgin), who was recruited in 1848 when he was sixteen. Their affection was mutual.[63]

Turning now to Brooke's nephews, the eldest, Captain John Brooke Brooke,lost two wives and a son in rapid succession. He was then disinherited – for 'disobedience' – by his uncle, who made no allowance for his nephew's emotional state after the tragedy. Charles Johnson Brooke (1829-1917), the second white raja (succeeding in 1868), was potent enough with women, but remarkably cold and indifferent towards his wife, Margaret, whom he married when he was forty. Their first three children died of cholera, but there were three surviving sons. The marriage ended when he destroyed his wife's pet doves and served them in a pie for supper. He reckoned that marriage lost an officer ninety-nine per cent of his efficiency; compliant local mistresses (such as he himself had taken as a young man), not burdensome European wives, was his prescription. Only five women were present when he entertained the entire European community of Sarawak to a jubilee dinner in 1887. The third raja, Vyner Brooke (1874-1963), was a compulsive womaniser and, significantly perhaps, much the least efficient of the three white rajas, thus giving point to his father's dictum. He too had his marital troubles. He lived apart from his wife for the second half of their marriage, although maintaining friendly discussions with her about his endless stream of mistresses. And we have his wife's testimony that he was 'not good in bed'; to quote her own devastating words, 'he made love just as he played golf – in a nervous unimaginative flurry'.[64]

The marital record of the higher echelons of the imperial elite is thus depressing. Why should this be so? In the first place it has to be recognised that sexual compatibility is central to marriage (even if it means no more than agreement to dispense with love-making). Moreover, successful sex demands optimum conditions, which seldom applied before the twentieth century, least of all in the overseas empire. It requires privacy, time, soap, effective and aesthetic birth control, warm bedrooms (or cool ones in the tropics), uninhibited attitudes and a modicum of erotic education. Then again, the misery of separation, the awesome uncertainties of childbirth, and recurrent ill health in tropical lands put fearful strains on marriage. The problems were further compounded by the often rather juvenile attitudes of Victorian men towards women, although it has to be said that there were also some silly and sickly wives about, incapable of giving the expected support to their husbands in their work. Old-school-tie loyalties, clubland fellowship and gang fraternities seem to have been almost a more important emotional prop than marriage for many servants of empire: such groups as 'Howe's boys' (including Metcalfe) in Calcutta, the Lawrence commune in the Punjab, Wolseley's 'Staff Ring' (a select band of favourite officers), Rhodes's 'lambs', Kitchener's 'cubs' or 'family of boys', Sir Robert Hart's Canton 'kindergarten' in Chinese customs administration, or Lord Milner's better-known South African 'kindergarten'; or, to take a striking foreign example, Marshal Lyautey's 'Zaouia' (the Chapel of the Faithful, or favourite young collaborators) in Morocco.[65]

The misogyny in all this must not be misunderstood. They were men's men all right, but they were not well-adjusted personalities. So many members of the ruling elite seem to have suffered degrees of emotional retardation – those who never got over being head prefect at school, or for whom everything in life after membership of the elite society 'Pop' at Eton was an anticlimax. St John Brodrick (1856-1942), one-time Secretary of State for War, at the end of his life reflected that no responsibility could ever compare with that youthful one. Alfred Lyttelton (Secretary of State for the Colonies 1903-05) agreed: 'No position in after life, however great, could be as complete as that of a swell at Eton.'[66] Baden-Powell never got his Charterhouse days out of his system. Here we could elaborate what Cyril Connolly once called 'the theory of permanent adolescence' – an intensity of school experience so deep as to cause arrested development. It is remarkable, for example, that Lord Curzon always kept a room at Kedleston Hall as a replica of his Eton room; he also kept a photograph album of his Eton contemporaries, mostly with the names, details and dates of death meticulously recorded. He was devoted to his wife, yet Lord Ampthill thought him 'as variable and neurotic as a woman'. Curzon's sense of isolation as Viceroy reduced him to tearful self-pity, all the more intense since it meant rupture with one of his closest school friends, St John Brodrick. At school, Curzon and Brodrick, together with Alfred and Edward Lyttelton (who became headmaster of Eton), all older than himself, had formed a quartet. And yet Curzon has been described as 'less Eton-orientated than many of his generation'.[67]

There was a 'persistent streak of puerility' in Rudyard Kipling, whose love life from the age of fourteen seems to have been based on a search for a mother substitute to provide him with the kind of affection he was denied in his early years. After several affairs, including one with an overt mother surrogate, he married Caroline Balestier, but only after the death of his friend, her brother Wolcott, to whom he was intensely devoted. Thereafter, he always felt more at ease with his son than his authoritarian wife.[68]

'Boyishness' was actually an admired quality, and it has been pointed out that 'many of the great men of the Empire were essentially boy-men' who had 'never been able to outgrow their boyhood ideals'.[69] Many of them enjoyed escapades, and escapes from families, none more so than the explorers. The exception who proves the rule was Sir Samuel Baker (1821-93), but no other explorer had such an intrepid wife. She always travelled with him, although, perhaps significantly, she was Hungarian and not English. Edward Eyre (1815-1901) began his heroic exploration along the Great Australian Bight with three Aborigine boys, one of whom had been with him for four years; he formed repeated close associations with such boys before his (unsatisfactory) marriage, and brought two of them to Britain in 1844 to be educated at his expense.[70] Deprivation in desert conditions and close contact with sexually rather sophisticated African and Arabian peoples often led to intense male interracial friendships. Heinrich Barth (1821-65) joined the British government expedition to 'Central Africa' in 1849 and spent the next five years of his short life swooning over the beauty and affectionateness of Nigerian teenagers, two of whom he brought back to Britain with him in 1855. H. M. Stanley, as we have seen, was also fond of African boys; Speke may have been, but this is much less certain.[71] Wilfrid Thesiger enjoyed the company of Arabian youths, while the intrepid canoeist, Major Raven-Hart, was on equally close terms with Egyptian, Sudanese, Burmese and Sinhalese boys, writing up (in the 1930s) his adventures with an incidental candour about his relationships which would have rendered them unpublishable had they concerned British boys.[72]

The masculine nature of the imperial enterprise has been emphasised. The handful of women who contributed something notable to it seems also to confirm the thesis of emotional deprivation: equally incompetent and a-sexual in their love lives as the men. Mrs Caroline Chisholm (1808-77) has an important place in the history of Australia in the first half of the 1840s on account of her efforts to promote the immigration of women and children, whom she quaintly described as 'God's police', because they were the only hope of improving the moral tone of the colonies. Her first venture was running a Female Immigrants' Home. Her efforts right through to 1857 (when her health failed) made her one of the most famous women of her time, and an inspiration to Florence Nightingale. When she married Captain Archibald Chisholm, it had been on condition that she should be free to do any philanthropic work she wished. Her husband loyally and self-effacingly kept to that commitment, taking an active, if sometimes grumbling, part in the advancement of her schemes. She assisted the settlement of some 11,000 immigrants in New South Wales in the 1840s, and then spent some years in England founding the Family Colonisation Loan Society, the most important private agency of its kind in the 1850s. Meanwhile, her own family of six children had to take decidedly second place to her efforts to promote the domestic happiness of other families. (Even the dedicated career woman of this date could not limit her pregnancies properly.) In 1851 her husband went back to Australia three years ahead of her to act as colonial agent for her society, which sent out more than 3,000 emigrants by 1854. Caroline Chisholm was never a fanatical crusader for women's rights, and the sacrifice of her own family life was probably a real sadness to her, but it underlines the point that constructive achievement for the empire inevitably involved personal sacrifice.[73]

Miss Angela Burdett-Coutts (1814-1906) was a very different kind of woman. Capricious, she certainly did not arrive early at sexual adjustment. Famous as the richest heiress in England (her family was in banking), she declined many proposals of marriage (even, it was rumoured, from Wellington and Louis Napoleon), preferring to devote herself to philanthropy – and to her inseparable friend Hannah, her former governess. This attachment survived even Hannah's eleven years of marriage. Hannah Brown, however, outlived her husband by twenty-three years, and it was not until Hannah herself had been dead for three years that Baroness Burdett-Coutts (as she had become) eventually married, at the age of sixty-seven. Meanwhile, she endowed the bishoprics of Cape Town, Adelaide and British Columbia, introduced cotton gins into Abeokuta in Nigeria, tried to rescue the fishing industry of south-west Ireland, and organised help for the wounded in the Zulu War of 1879. She became the friend of men who were congenitally hardhearted towards women: men like General Gordon (to whom she gave a letter case), James Brooke, Livingstone, Stanley, and John Moffat. She gave vital support to the Sarawak enterprise, making a gunboat and a £5,000 loan available, and taking interest in a model farm on her estate there at Quop. Brooke was impressed with her, and from 1863 to 1865 she was his heir. In their remarkable correspondence in the 1860s they exchanged pressed flowers and accounts of their patronage of boys and young men. In the course of her life she placed hundreds of destitute boys in training ships for the navy and merchant service. James Brooke often wrote jointly to her and Hannah, and, regarding them at one time as his only friends, was anxious for the health and welfare of those 'in whose society I have [the] only hope of peace and quiet in this world'. In 1863 he took one of Angela's young friends, Charles La Touche, back to

Sarawak with him. Brooke sent her fond reports of 'your Charlie'.[74]

Mary Kingsley (1862-1900), a naturalist and anthropologist who travelled in remote parts of West Africa in the mid-1890s, denied ever having had any love affairs: 'I make the confession humbly,' she wrote, 'quite as I would make the confession of being deaf or blind. I know nothing myself of love.' But she knew a lot about West Africa and did much to help its peoples; her efforts to make the world understand Africa better remain of almost unequalled importance.[75] The famous Middle East expert Gertrude Bell (1868-1926), Oriental Secretary to the High Commission in Iraq from 1920, also said her life was devoid of sex. This was more from bad luck than want of trying. She was engaged to Henry Cadogan of the diplomatic service in Persia in the mid-1890s, but he died. Then, when she was about forty, she fell in love with a soldier, Doughty-White, who was already married and would not divorce; he was killed in the First World War in 1915.[76]

The positive influence of women on the development of the empire was probably greatest in twentieth-century mission work, especially in Africa. Most of these female missionaries were unmarried. A steady stream of able women founded major schools and hospitals throughout Africa. Lady Cook, wife of a famous Church Missionary Society doctor, Sir Albert Cook, pioneered African women's nursing in Uganda. Mother Kevin (born Teresa Kearney in Ireland in 1875), a Franciscan nun, spent fifty-one years in Uganda, opening fifteen convents (each complete with chapel, school and hospital), together with a model leprosarium, a senior girls' secondary school and a training school for secondary school-teachers.[77] A handful of governor's wives, such as Lady Twining in Tanganyika and Lady Coryndon in Swaziland and Uganda, also did sterling work in nursing and medical care.[78]

Thus there existed among the British elite a whole spectrum of behaviour ranging from extreme indulgence to total sexual inactivity (a-sexuality it has been called here). As far as the imperial elite is concerned, the number of those who for shorter or longer periods sacrificed their private lives, ruthlessly rejecting romantic entanglements in pursuit of their careers, is impressive. It includes James Brooke and Rhodes, Livingstone and Stanley, Curzon and Nathan, Henry Lawrence and F. D. Lugard, Kitchener and Montgomery. The rulers of empire as a group display a high degree of emotional deprivation. Without resorting to vague assertions about sublimation, it is possible to see a basic truth in the contention that 'love's loss was empire's gain'. Having examined the private lives of some key individuals, it is time to turn to the overall structure of British sexual attitudes and practices which conditioned the background of the rank-and-file servants of empire.

Notes

1 G. Marshall, *Constitutional Conventions: the Rules and Forms of Political Accountability*, Oxford, 1984, ch. 6: 'The morality of public office'.
2 M. Perham, *Lugard*, I: *The Years of Adventure, 1858-98*, London, 1956, pp. 59-73.
3 V. Purcell, *Memoirs of a Malayan official*, London, 1965, p. 251.
4 C. Bayly, *Imperial Meridian: The British Empire and the World 1780-1830*, London, 1989, p. 115. M. Perham, *West African Passage: A Journey through Nigeria, Chad, and the Cameroons, 1931-2*, ed. A. H. M. Kirk-Greene, London, 1983, pp. 75-6.
5 T. Pakenham, *The Boer War*, London, 1979, pp. 32-4.
6 R. Ellmann, *Oscar Wilde*, London, 1987, pp. 38, 423; J. Lees-Milne, *The Enigmatic Edwardian: the Life of Reginald, 2nd Viscount Esher*, London, 1986, p. 99; H. R. Trevor-Roper, *A Hidden Life: the Enigma of Sir Edmund Backhouse*, London, 1976, pp. 261-2. For sexual opportunity in Italy, see M. Holloway, *Norman Douglas: a Biography* London, 1976; and C. Woolf (ed.), *Fr Rolfe, Baron Corvo: the Venice Letters*, London, 1974.
7 P. Mellini, *Sir Eldon Gorst: the Overshadowed Proconsul*, Stanford, 1977, p. 67. Gorst kept a diary, with references to many affairs in the fourteen years before his marriage, using symbols x and o for sex; for example, 1890, 'x=132, o=18'; and 1891, 'x=96, o=21' (see p. 26); 'x' usually means intercourse in this sort of notation, and 'o' presumably means oral sex.
8 M. Roe, 'Sir John Eardley-Wilmot', *Australian Dictionary of Biography, 1788-1850*, I, pp. 345-8; *idem, Quest for Authority in Eastern Australia, 1835-51*, Melbourne, 1965; R. T. Shannon, *Gladstone*, I: *1809-65*, London, 1982, p. 191; R. Hughes, *The Fatal Shore: a History of Transportation of Convicts to Australia, 1787-1868*, London, 1987, pp. 529-38.
9 J. M. Ward, 'Sir Charles A. Fitzroy', *Australian Dictionary of Biography, 1788-1850*, I, pp. 384-9.
10 G. M. Theal, *History of South Africa since 1795*, III: *Cape Colony, 1840-60*, London, 1908, pp. 50-2. At about the same time, the conduct of Colonel Henry Somerset, Commander of the Cape Mounted Rifles (son of a former Governor-General) with Hottentot women was also common knowledge: A. J. Smithers, *The Kaffir Wars, 1779-1877*, London, 1973, pp. 323; L. King-Hall (ed), *Sea Saga:being the Naval Diaries of Four Generations of the King-Hall Family*, London, 1935, pp. 186-7. *Generations of the King-hall Family*, London, 1935, pp. 186-7. John Dunn as Cetewayo's adviser had 48 Zulu wives *(Dictionary of South African Biography)*.
11 L. H. Gann & P. Duignan, *The Rulers of British Africa, 1870-1914*, London, 1978 p. 94. S. M. Edwards, *Female Sexuality and the Law*, Oxford, 1981, pp. 126-9 notes a moral panic over the 'rape in a railway carriage' syndrome – a rapid increase from 1870 in allegations of assault in railway compartments.
12 F.S. L. Lyons, *Charles Stewart Parnell*, London, 1977; R. H. Jenkins, *Sir Charles Dilke: a Victorian Tragedy*, London, 1958, 1965.
13 *A plain statement of facts relative to Sir Eyre Coote, containing the official correspondence and documents concerned with his case and the proceedings of the Military Board appointed for its investigation*, 1816. See also H. M. Stephens, in *Dictionary of National Biography*, XII, pp. 161-2. This Sir Eyre Coote is not to be confused with the earlier Sir Eyre Coote (1726-83) of India, to whom he was nephew and heir. One of the many features of the affair which seems strange today is that Coote pleaded: 'I am doing no harm, upon my honour, – I was only flogging these boys'.
14 Edward James, *Swans reflecting Elephants: my Early Years*, ed. G. Melly, London, 1982, pp. 26-8; Lees-Milne, *The Enigmatic Edwardian*, pp. 112, 176, 337-38.
15 W. Hinde, *Castlereagh*, London, 1981, p. 277; L. Crompton, *Byron and Greek Love*, California, 1985, pp. 300-6.
16 M. & E. Brock (eds), *H. H. Asquith: Letters to Venetia Stanley*, London, 1982; R. Blake, 'Prime ministers' pets', *London Review of Books*, V, 1983, I, p. 9.
17 R. Holmes, *The Little Field Marshal: Sir John French*, London, 1981.
18 S. Roskill, *Admiral of the Fleet Earl Beatty*, London, 1980, pp. 33-56, 202, 367.

19 J.Grigg, *Lloyd George: from Peace to War, 1912-16*, London, 1985, pp. 223-5; Pakenham, *Boer War*, pp. 90, 116-17; Roskill, *Beatty*, p. 367; C. I. Hamilton, 'Naval hagiography and the Victorian hero', *Historical Journal*, XXIII, 1980.

20 K. Bourne, *Palmerston*, I; *The Early Years, 1784-1841*, London, 1982, pp. 191-4, 201-4, 213.

21 Shannon, *Gladstone*, I. pp. 21-3, 94-5, 198, 235-6, 255, 274.

22 M. Bence-Jones, *Clive of India*, p. 27. A. Edwardes, *The Rape of India: a Biography of Robert Clive and a Sexual History of the conquest of Hindustan*, New York, 1966 – with its claims that Clive was circumcised for phimosis on 22 January 1743, had an erection of twelve cms, and occasionally asked his servants to fellate him – is an elaborate hoax: see Bence-Jones, p. 309, n. 19. (By extension, A. Edwardes, *The Jewel in the Lotus: a Historical Survey of the Sexual Culture of the East*, New York, 1961, is, as they say, only to be used with caution.) Edwardes's hoax over Clive is clever enough to have fooled university library cataloguers, but it is not quite clever enough. He is careful to keep things within the bounds of a normative probability; he presents Clive as a compulsive masturbator, heterosexually promiscuous, but homoerotic ventures are strictly limited. His 'Sources', he concedes, are 'often fragmented' and sometimes of doubtful authorship, but often enough they 'seem trustworthy'. But he makes three crucial mistakes: (1) He purports to rely on the evidence of two medical officers, Dr Ives and Dr Rae, but it can be shown that no such persons served in India, since the names of all European doctors associated with the East India Company have been listed: see D. G. Crawford, *Roll of the Indian Medical Service, 1615-1930* London, 1930. (2) He overlooks the one piece of really hard documentary evidence about Clive's pre-marital promiscuity (Orme MSS 288, John Dalton to Clive, 21 October 1752), as quoted in my text, and taken from Bence-Jones; it is also picked up by Michael Edwardes, *Clive: the Heaven-Born General*, London, 1977, p. 72. (3) Like all the best erotic literature it leaves little to the imagination in its over-precise detail; the carefully cultivated archaic style of quotations is too uniform; and the evidence is persistently reported as being in 'postscripts' to versions 'missing in the Clive Papers'. The survival of private collections from the eighteenth century in India is almost unknown, yet Edwardes purports to use the 'Col. Mark Wilks collection' in the possession of Mirza 'Abdul-Aziz Khan of East Pakistan, which contains an 'unexpurgated Persian copy of Sayd Ghulam Husayn Khan's *History*, and an 'anonymous unexpurgated copy of the chronicle *Tarikh-i-Mansuri*'. *Rape of India* also draws on C. Carraccioli, *Life of Robert, Lord Clive*. Here too Bence-Jones has largely removed Carraccioli finally from the realm of serious evidence. Some of Carraccioli is pure invention, not least the allegations of promiscuity in France, when in fact Clive was accompanied by his wife; they went everywhere together, mostly sightseeing, entertaining guests to curry, riding, shooting, fishing, playing cards and chess, and keeping up with the official mail.

23 I. Butler, *The Eldest Brother: Richard Wellesley*, London, 1973, pp. 50-2, 96-9, 257-9; E. Ingram, *Commitment to Empire: Prophecies of the Great Game in Asia, 1797-1800*, London, 1981, pp. 119-20; E. Longford, *Wellington*, I, London 1969, pp. 214; E. Thompson, *Life of Charles, Lord Metcalfe*, London, 1937, pp. 2, 101-2; P. Barr, *The Memsahibs: the Women of Victorian India*, London, 1976, pp. 7-18, 47. For Northbrook, see E. C. Moulton, *Lord Northbrook's Administration, 1872-76*, London, 1968; M. Bence-Jones, *The Viceroys of India*, London, 1982, p. 82; C. Deveureux, *Vénus in India*, Brussels, 1889, I, pp. 84-5, and II, p. 40. See M. E. Yapp, *Strategies of British India: Britain, Iran and Afghanistan, 1798-1850*, London, 1980, p. 220, for Auckland, and *passim* for relationship between private lives and public ambitions lower down the scale. For Lytton see D. Hudson, *Munby: Man of Two Worlds*, London, 1972, p. 23.

24 J. W. Kaye, *Lives of Indian officers*, 2 vols, London, 1889; Lady [E. S.] Edwardes, *Memorials of the Life and Letters of Herbert B. Edwardes*, 2 vols, London, 1886; L. J. Trotter, *Life of John Nicholson*, 9th ed, 1904; J. L. Morison, *Lawrence of Lucknow, 1806-57: Life of Sir Henry Lawrence*, London, 1934; H. Pearson, *Hero of Delhi: Life of John Nicholson*, London, 1939; M. Diver, *Honoria Lawrence: a Fragment of Indian History*, London, 1936; M. Edwardes, *The Necessary Hell: John and Henry Lawrence* *and the Indian Empire*, New York, 1957.

25 Trotter, *Life of John Nicholson*, p. 311; Edwardes, *Memorials . . . Herbert B. Edwardes*, II, p. 50; Kaye, *Lives of Indian Officers*, II, p. 688. A particularly striking contrast between official effectiveness and personal oddity is afforded by the example of Lord Esher, the Edwardian courtier, trusted adviser to two kings, and architect of imperial defence policies, who had an overpowering and decidedly prurient passion for his own son Maurice ('Molly'), simultaneously rejecting his other three children (one of whom became the Ranee of Sarawak): see Lees-Milne, *The Enigmatic Edwardian*, esp. pp 110-12, 136-9, 335.

26 F. S. L. Lyons, *Charles Steward Parnell*, London, 1977. If the ensuing references on Parnell appear rather thin, this is because all previous work and interpretation has been superseded by this definitive biography. See also Lyons's *Fall of Parnell, 1890-91*, London, 1960. On constitutional issues see also C. C. O'Brien, *Parnell and his Party*, Oxford, 1957, esp. pp. 352-5.

27 P. Bew, *C. S. Parnell*, Dublin, 1980, pp. 42-3, 110-13.

28 Lyons, *Charles Stewart Parnell, passim*. See also S. Leslie, *Studies in Sublime Failure*, London, 1932; and E. Norman in *Times Literary Supplement*, 3 June 1977, pp. 666-7.

29 J. Enoch Powell in *Historical Journal*, XXI, 1978, pp. 197-8. Jack Durham quoted in Lees-Milne, *The Enigmatic Edwardian*, p. 83.

30 K. I. E. Macleod, *The Ranker: the Story of Sir Hector Macdonald's Death*, London, 1976. Macleod discusses the possibility of a plot against Macdonald's reputation and argues that even now he cannot be proved guilty.

31 Earl Beauchamp was Governor of New South Wales, 1899-1901, and his career restarted as First Commissioner of Works, 1910-14. He inspired H. Belloc's poem *Lord Lundy* (*Oxford book of Satirical Verse*, 1980, p. 366):

> Towards the age of twenty-six,
> They shoved him into politics; . . .
> In turn as Secretary for
> India, the Colonies, and War.
> But very soon his friends began
> To doubt if he were quite the man: . . .
> A Hint at harmless little jobs
> Would shake him with convulsive sobs.
> While as to Revelations, these
> Would simply bring him to his knees, . . .
> 'Sir! you have disappointed us!
> We had intended you to be
> The next Prime Minister but three: . . .
> But as it is! . . . My language fails!
> Go out and govern New South Wales!'

32 J. Montgomery, *Toll for the Brave: the Tragedy of Major-General Sir Hector Macdonald*, London, 1963, esp. p. 115.

33 National Army Museum, Roberts Papers, 7101/23/122/5, ff. 108-9, Roberts to Kitchener, 20 February, 1903; 7101/23/122/5, f. 150, Roberts to Kitchener, 19 March 1903; 7101/23/46, f. 114, Ridgeway to Roberts, 17 May 1903.

34 T. Royle, *Death before Dishonour: the True Story of 'Fighting Mac'*, London, 1982, pp. 119-32. For the temptations of Ceylon see: R. Raven-Hart, *Ceylon: a History in Stone*, Colombo, 2nd ed., 1973, pp. 56, 157-8, etc; A. W. E. Holden, *Ceylon*, London 1939; Edward Carpenter, *From Adam's Peak to Elephanta: Sketches in Ceylon and India*, 2nd ed., London, 1910, pp. 14-15; G. Tillett, *The Elder Brother: Biography of Charles W. Leadbeater, 1854-1934*, London, 1982; R. Peyrefitte, *Exile of Capri*, translated 1961; C. Green & A. D. Maclean (eds), *A Skilled Hand: a Collection of Stories and Writings by G. F. Green, with Memoirs and Criticism*, London, 1980, pp. 106-9.

35 PRO, CO 537/410/6835, CO 537/411/41391 (Supplementary secret correspondence). There are no significant references in CO 54 (Ceylon, original correspondence).

36 Roberts Papers, 7101/23/46, f. 113, Ridgeway to Roberts, 20 April 1903.

37 P. Singleton-Gates & M. Girodias (eds), *The Black Diaries: an Account of Roger*

Casement's Life and Times, Paris, 1959, pp. 121-2 (17 & 19 April 1903).

38 B. Inglis, *Roger Casement*, London, 1973, pp. 64-5, 175-80, 380-8; R. Sawyer, *Casement: the Flawed Hero*, London, 1984; J. B. Ure, *Trespassers on the Amazon*, London 1986, pp. 80-5; J. Meyers, *A Fever at the Core: the Idealist in Politics*, London, 1976, pp. 59-88.

39 Stanhope White, *'Dan Bana': the Memoirs of a Nigerian Official*, London, 1966, pp. 166-7.

40 C. Woolf (ed.), *Fr Rolfe, Baron Corvo: the Venice letters*, London, 1974; J. Lahr (ed.), *The Orton Diaries*, London, 1986; H. R. Trevor-Roper, *A Hidden Life: the Enigma of Sir Edmund Backhouse*, London, 1976, esp. pp. 243-79.

41 Singleton-Gates and Girodias (eds), *The Black Diaries*, 28 February 1910, p. 207; and 26 May & 24 June 1910.

42 O. D. Edwards, 'Divided treasons and divided loyalties: Roger Casement and others', *Transactions of the Royal Historical Society*, 5th series, 32, 1982, pp. 153-74; W. R. Louis, 'Roger Casement and the Congo', *Journal of African History*, V, 1964, pp. 99-120. For Bletchley see T. E. B. Howarth, *Cambridge between Two Wars*, London, 1978, p. 240.

43 J. Widdicombe, *Fourteen Years in Basutoland*, London, [1891], p. 210; *Dictionary of National Biography*, XXII, pp. 169-76; R. Maugham, *The Last Encounter*, London, 1972.

44 P. Magnus, *Kitchener: Portrait of an Imperialist*, London, 1958; D. Dilks, *Curzon in India*, London, 1970, II, p. 24; R. Storrs, *Orientations*, London, 1943, p. 105; T. Royle, *The Kitchener Enigma*, London, 1985, p. 391.

45 J. G. Lockhart & C. M. Woodhouse, *Rhodes*, London, 1963; J. Marlowe, *Cecil Rhodes: the Anatomy of Empire*, London, 1972, pp. 94, 212; M. F. Shore, 'Cecil Rhodes and the ego ideal', *Journal of Interdisciplinary History*, X, 1979, pp. 249-65; G. Shepperson, 'C. J. Rhodes: some biographical problems', *South African Historical Journal*, XV, 1983. F. Gross, *Rhodes of Africa*, London, 1956, pp. 63, 247-50, quaintly ascribes all Rhodes's 'strange imperialism', juvenile romanticism and 'chronic homosexuality' to a 're-tarded puberty' during which he was unable to sweat out his 'glandular troubles' and 'secretory overflow' in either sport or poetry. R. I. Rotberg (with M. F. Shore), *The Founder: Cecil Rhodes and the Pursuit of Power*, Oxford & New York, 1988, pp. 148, 404-8, 680, 690, is much more sophisticated.

46 A. P. Haydon, *Sir Matthew Nathan: British Colonial Governor and Civil Servant*, Queensland, 1976.

47 R. Hall, *Stanley: an Adventurer Explored*, London, 1974. See also n. 71 below.

48 W. Hillcourt, *Baden-Powell: the Two Lives of a Hero*, London, 1964; W. S. Adams, *Edwardian Portraits*, London, 1957; P. Brendon, *Eminent Edwardians*, London, 1979; B. Gardner, *Mafeking: a Victorian Legend*, London, 1966, pp. 19, 163, 226. T. Jeal, *Baden-Powell*, London, 1989, ch. 3, 'Men's man', pp. 74-109, is now far and away the best discussion of Baden-Powell's sexuality and can be taken as definitive.

49 T. Pakenham, *The Boer War*, London, 1979, pp. 32-4; see also letter from C. Quigley to *Times Literary Supplement*, 23 July 1976, p. 924.

50 K. Rose, *Superior Person: a Portrait of Curzon and his Circle in late Victorian England*, London, 1969, pp. 277-90.

51 M. Perham, *Lugard*, I: *The Years of Adventure, 1858-98*, London, 1956, pp. 59-73; R. Hyam, *Elgin and Churchill at the Colonial Office, 1905-08*, London, 1968, pp. 203 ff.

52 M. Edwardes, *Warren Hastings. King of the Nabobs*, London, 1976; J. Roselli, *Lord William Bentinck: the Making of a Liberal Imperialist, 1774-1839*, London, 1974, pp. 56-7; C. P. Youé, *Robert Thorne Coryndon: Proconsular Imperialism in Southern and Eastern Africa, 1897-1925*, Gerrards Cross, 1986, p. 47; R. Wingate, *Wingate of the Sudan*, London, 1955, p. 257; P. Mellini, *Sir Eldon Gorst: the Overshadowed Proconsul*, Stanford, 1977; D. S. Higgins, *Rider Haggard: the Great Storyteller*, London, 1981; H. A. Gailey, *Sir Donald Cameron, Colonial Governor*, Stanford, 1974; R. E. Wraith, *Guggisberg*, London, 1967. Sir Gordon Guggisberg made two unsatisfactory marriages: (1) to a seventeen-year-old daughter of a colonel, (2) to an actress. Wraith stresses his insensitivity as a husband, and comments, 'one can only assume that the qualities

needed to govern a colony are less exacting than those required to be a successful family man' (p. 20). Just so.

53   I. Butler, *The Eldest brother: Richard Wellesley*, London, 1973, pp. 50-2, 96-9, 257-9; E. Longford, *Wellington*, I, London, 1969, pp. 162, 203, 214, 361; and II, 1972, pp. 114-22; E. Ingram, *Commitment to Empire: Prophecies of the Great Game in Asia, 1797-1800*, Oxford, 1981, pp. 119-20.

54   Longford, *Wellington*, I, pp. 100-27; and II, pp. 74-87; Joan Wilson, *Wellington's Marriage: a Soldier's Wife*, London, 1987.

55   A. H. Imlah, *Lord Ellenborough: a Biography of Edward Law*, Harvard, 1939, pp. 14-15, 26-30, 54-5.

56   J. Rutherford, *Sir George Grey, 1812-98: a Study in Colonial Government*, London, 1961, pp. 63-6, 428, 439, 573; K. Sinclair, *A History of New Zealand*, 1969, ed., p. 81.

57   J. E. Flint, *Sir George Goldie: the Making of Nigeria*, London, 1956, pp. 4-5. Those ever-perceptive writers, R. E. Robinson and J. Gallagher, note that Goldie was unusual among empire-builders in having no fear of women (*Africa and the Victorians*, London, 1961, p. 167).

58   J. Listowel, *The Other Livingstone*, London, 1974, pp. 45-56, 200-2; R. B. Joyce, *Sir William MacGregor*, Melbourne, 1971.

59   D. C. Boulger, *Life of Sir Stamford Raffles*, ed. A. Johnson, London, 1973, pp. xiv-xxviii, 176-7; A. K. Millar, *Plantagenet in South Africa: Lord Charles Somerset*, London, 1965, pp. 74, 134.

60   J. G. Baird (ed.), *Private Letters of the Marquess of Dalhousie* (1910), Shannon, 1972, pp. 257-8; M. MacLagan, *'Clemency' Canning*, London, 1962, p. 305; V. Surtees, *Charlotte Canning, 1817-61*, London, 1975, p. 296; Hyam, *Elgin and Churchill at the Colonial Office*, pp. 12-13; B. C. Busch, *Hardinge of Penshurst*, London, 1980; S. Checkland, *The Elgins, 1766-1917: a Tale of Aristocrats, Proconsuls and their Wives*, Aberdeen, 1988.

61   E. Hahn, *James Brooke of Sarawak*, London, 1953, pp. 16, 26-9, 223.

62   J. C. Templer (ed.) *Private Letters of Sir James Brooke*, 3 vols, London, 1853, I, p. 283, but also pp. 253, 257, 273, 286-7; and II p. 113; O. Rutter (ed.), *Rajah Brooke and Baroness Burdett Coutts: consisting of the Letters. . .*, London, 1935, pp. 131-2, 154, 160, 214, 269, 284-5.

63   N. Tarling, *The Burthen, the Risk and the Glory: a Biography of Sir James Brooke*, Kuala Lumpur, 1982, pp. 7-9, 66, 102, 112, 430; M. Saint, *A Flourish for the Bishop; and Brooke's Friend Grant: Two Stories in Sarawak History*, Braunton, 1985, pp. 174, 181, 247; Sylvia Brooke, Ranee of Sarawak, *The Three White Rajahs*, London, 1939, pp. 16, 36-40.

64   Sylvia Brooke, *Queen of the Headhunters: an Autobiography of the Ranee*, London, 1970, pp. 28, 81, 134-5; J. Morris, *Pax Britannica: the Climax of an Empire*, London, 1968, p. 311; R. Pringle, *Rajas and Rebels: the Ibans of Sarawak under Brooke Rule, 1841-1941*, London, 1970, pp. 333-6.

65   A. P. Thornton, *The Imperial Idea and its Enemies*, London, 1959, pp. 89-93; Thompson, *Life of Charles, Lord Metcalfe*, vii, pp. 25-6; A Maurois, *Marshal Lyautey*, trans. H. Miles, London, 1931, pp. 117-18; A. Scham, *Lyautey in Morocco*, Berkeley, 1970, pp. 6-8.

66   Thornton, *Imperial Idea and its Enemies*, pp. 90-2; E. Lyttelton, *Alfred Lyttelton: an Account of his Life*, London, 1917, p. 46.

67   Dilks, *Curzon in India*, II, p. 24; S. Leslie, *Studies in Sublime Failure*, London, 1932, p. 186; Rose, *Superior Person*, pp. 34-5, 333-4; R. R. James (ed.), *'Chips': the Diaries of Sir Henry Channon*, London, 1967, p. 7.

68   J. I. M. Stewart, *Rudyard Kipling*, London, 1966, p. 170; E. T. Stokes, 'The voice of the hooligan: Kipling and the Commonwealth experience', in N. McKenrick (ed.), *Historical Perspectives: Studies in . . . Honour of J. H. Plumb*, London, 1974, p. 295; Lord Birkenhead, *Rudyard Kipling*, London, 1978, pp. 133-4; E. L. Gilbert (ed.), *'O beloved kids': Rudyard Kipling's Letters to his children*, London, 1983; Angus Wilson, *The Strange Ride of Rudyard Kipling: his Life and his Works*, London, 1979, pp. 214, 367-8; H. Brogan, *Mowgli's Sons: Kipling and Baden-Powell's Scouts*, London, 1987.

69 J. Richards, '"Passing the love of women": manly love and Victorian society', in J. A. Mangan & J. Walvin (eds), *Manliness and Morality: Middle-Class Masculinity in Britain and America, 1800-1940*, Manchester, 1987; H. Arendt, *Origins of Totalitarianism*, 1967 ed., p. 211. The British 'boyish master' syndrome was first suggested by G. Santayana, *Soliloquies in England*, London, 1922, p. 32: 'the sweet, just, boyish master of the world'.

70 G. Dutton, *The Hero as Murderer: the Life of E. J. Eyre, Australian Explorer and Governor of Jamaica, 1815-1901*, London, 1967, pp. 13-14, 134.

71 A. H. M. Kirk-Greene (ed), *Barth's Travels in Nigeria*, London, 1962, intro.; F. M. Brodie, *The Devil Drives: a Life of Sir Richard Burton*, London, 1967 and 1971, pp. 174, 188. F. McLynn, *Stanley, making of an African explorer*, London, 1989.

72 W. Thesiger, *Desert, Marsh and Mountain: the World of a Nomad*, London, 1979, pp. 23, 39-40, 177; R. Raven-Hart, *Canoe errant on the Nile*, London, 1936, pp. 7, 17, 76, 96-7, 228; idem, *Ceylon: History in Stone*, 2nd ed., Colombo, 1973, *passim*; idem, *Canoe to Mandalay*, London, 1939, pp. 31, 81, 158, 186, 215; and other works.

73 M. Kiddle, *Caroline Chisholm*, abridged ed., 1969.

74 Rutter, *Rajah Brooke and Baroness Burdett Coutts*, pp. 17-22, 197, 214; *Dictionary of National Biography, 2nd Supplement*, London, 1912, I, pp. 259-66.

75 R. Glynn Grylls (ed.) *Mary Kingsley's Travels in West Africa*, London, 1972, p. xvi; W. K. Hancock, *Survey of British Commonwealth Affairs, 1919-39*, II/2, Oxford, 1942, appendix A; 'Note on Mary Kingsley', pp. 303-4; Caroline Oliver, *Western Women in Colonial Africa*, Westport, Conn. 1982, pp. 79-89.

76 H. V. F. Winstone, *Gertrude Bell*, London, 1978.

77 Oliver, *Western Women in Colonial Africa*, esp. pp. 166-85, 190-2.

78 P. Duignan, 'Sir R. Coryndon (1870-1925)', in L. H. Gann and P. Duignan (eds), *African Proconsuls: European Governors in Africa*, Stanford, 1978, p. 330; Youé *R. T. Coryndon*, p. 158.

c

CHAPTER THREE

The British home base

Victorian sexuality

'England has always been disinclined to accept human nature.' [E. M. Forster, *Maurice*, p. 196]

During the eighteenth century two contradictory developments took place in British attitudes towards sexuality. On the one hand, and partly as a reflection of Enlightenment doctrines, sexuality for the leisured and affluent classes became more relaxed. Public figures kept mistresses and walked out with them, as the Duke of Grafton did with Nancy Parsons. Erasmus Darwin (grandfather of Charles) openly brought up two illegitimate daughters. According to him, sex was 'the purest source of human felicity, the cordial drop in the otherwise vapid cup of life'. John Wilkes, not surprisingly, put it more bluntly:

Life can little else supply
But a few good fucks and then we die.

An eighteenth-century gentleman was nothing if not a man of the world. In 1769 in Polynesia, when Captain James Cook saw a 'young fellow' lying with a girl of ten or twelve, who was being instructed in her part by women, he readily understood that 'it appeared to be done more from Custom than Lewdness'.[1] Erotic literature sold well and was freely available. *Fanny Hill, or the Memoirs of a Woman of Pleasure* (1749) sold twenty editions before 1848.[2] Prostitution increased considerably. On the other hand, child sexuality evoked a new nervousness, and an anti-masturbation campaign was launched. This began with *Onania* (c. 1707-17) which sold perhaps 138,000 copies by mid-century. It was by a clergyman turned quack. His ideas were taken up by S. A. D. Tissot, a reputable physician. His *Dissertatio de febrique bibliosis... tentamen de morbis ex manusturpatione* was published in Switzerland in 1758 and translated into English by A. Hume in 1766. This gave a new, supposedly scientific, basis of hostility to sex, based on a 'wastage of energy' theory. By 1800 the anti-masturbatory hypothesis was widely accepted, while the idea of a 'spermatic economy' had resonance for an industrialising society.[3]

More generally, too, the reasonably relaxed and open eighteenth-century attitudes fell victim to the Evangelical Revival, with its fresh emphasis on sin and decorum. (John Wesley urged his congregations not to urinate in the streets.) The cult of Romanticism at the same time led to an increasing idealisation both of love and of women. Nevertheless, many relatively unrepressed eighteenth-century attitudes survived long into Victoria's reign. What, above all, the study of nineteenth-century sexuality requires today is chronological refinement and sharpening. It is impossible to generalise about Victorian attitudes over the period as a whole.[4] I shall give much emphasis to profound shifts and changes taking place from the 1880s. Whereas an eighteenth-century soldier might take a copy of *Fanny Hill* with him to the French wars, a hundred years later it would be *Three Men in a Boat* which was found in the knapsack at Spion Kop.

Historically, the sexual practices and attitudes of the British have several peculiarities compared with the rest of the non-European world. First, the age of marriage has been set unusually high: it was deferred to the average age of thirty for men in the eighteenth century, and in the mid-nineteenth century it was twenty-nine. Perhaps 10 per cent of men never married; the figure was 25 per cent for the eighteenth-century elite.[5] Various premarital 'intermediate technologies' were devised to offset this situation, and it helps to explain a high incidence of prostitution. Second, under the influence of Judaeo-Christian teaching and fear of dissent, the British have long had a general abhorrence of overt sex between males which, from the late nineteenth century, culminated in a hostility which was almost pathological. It was accompanied by an insistent commitment thereafter to monosexuality of whatever tendency.[6] Third, during the nineteenth century there was a widespread cultivation of the pretence that women and children are incapable of a sexual response. 'Suffer and be still' was the classic admonition to women in bed. Female orgasm was certainly not 'respectable', while juvenile masturbation was increasingly a matter for pious eradication. An extraordinary narrowing-down occurred of the polymorphous bisexual impulse. All was reduced to the exclusive promotion of reproductive adult marital sexuality. Divorce was made reprehensible, and fatal to a political career. Fellatio was often viewed with intense disgust among the middle classes, if it was even known about at all.[7] Fourth, the British became ever more interested in a 'discourse of sex' as a scientific problem than in its practice as a pleasurable art. Foucault indeed suggests that the truly original feature of Western culture is the specification of notions of 'perversity', and the creation of corrective psychiatric mechanisms, which stigmatised a large number of unorthodox sexual practices. Some of these 'deviant' categories were spurious, notably 'homosexuality'; sex between males is, however, so widespread in the world as not to be at all unorthodox. For the rest, the new stigmatised categories were mostly of wholly peripheral significance, almost less than fringe phenomena (zoophilia, gerontophilia, coprophilia, coprolalia, urolagnia).[8] In the twentieth century the cumulative result of these four peculiar features was a society with too many frigid wives (or at least 'porcelain where pottery is wanted', as Burton put it),[9] too many terrorised and desexualised children, and too many outcast men, stigmatised whenever they strayed into any variations from the supposed 'norm'. In short, there resulted a generalised proliferation of needless anxiety and sexual starvation, with a diversion into outright eccentricities, such as flagellation (the 'English vice') and sympneumata.[10]

Of course, this 'model of sexual politics', derived from Foucault, represents a strategy or programme of the middle class, an image of its self-affirmation. There are plenty of qualifications to be made in practice. The working class for a long time managed to escape some or all of these limitations (though not the taboo on sex between men). The lower classes had a long tradition of promiscuity and pre-marital sex. Religious imperatives were not always heeded (for the seventeenth century, Quaife noted that 'God does not loom large as a damper on lower-class sexual activity').[11] Some Victorian bourgeois couples clearly did transcend – within their own privacy, at any rate – the limits and restraints prescribed for them. For such couples the disjunction between sex and love was not total: they could in general enjoy eroticism more richly than they could express it, and a few of them even committed their raptures to paper.[12] The Rev. Charles Kingsley wrote to his wife in 1843 about his belief that heaven would allow uninterrupted sexual bliss:

> a more perfect delight when we lie naked in each other's arms, clasped together toying with each other's limbs, buried in each other's bodies, struggling, panting, dying for a moment. Shall we not feel then, even then, that there is more in store for us, that those thrilling writhings are but dim shadows of a union which shall be perfect?[13]

America reproduced all the British ambivalences, and some American women, at least, were perfectly aware of their orgasmic capacity, as the Mosher survey showed in the 1890s.[14] Moreover, sex between young males obstinately and quietly refused to succumb to a generalised sense of interdiction: Bray believes it was traditionally practised upon a 'massive and ineradicable' scale.[15] And there was a large escape clause: according to Renier, the empire demonstrated 'at least a subtle modification of the canons of sexual behaviour, a latitudinarian tendency which is not less real for being kept in the background'.[16]

Nevertheless, the repressive, joyless, Pauline prescriptions of the Church, the old anti-sodomy statutes of the State (with their frightening penalties, even if these were seldom invoked before their repeal in 1861), the absence of any erogenous education, and the pervasive conspiracy of silence: all these features placed cultural barriers between Britons and non-Europeans. The magnitude of the gulf can be seen, for example, in the facts that Taoism prescribed two ejaculations a day for fourteen-year olds,[17] that prostitutes were attached to Hindu temples, that Melanesian converts thought it right to place phallic images on the Christian altar,[18] that the Japanese regarded it as effeminate to refuse sodomy, and scornfully laughed at St Francis Xavier in the streets for believing its practice to be wrong,[19] that Sambian men in New Guinea were connoisseurs of semen-tasting much as some westerners are of wine-tasting.[20]

To describe sexual opportunity in Britain during the first half of the nineteenth century means looking first at the three principal sources of initiation for young males: home, school and brothel. The evidence is overwhelming that for many boys the first experience of the opposite sex was with a female servant living in the family home. (Even Freud was seduced by his nurse.) In Wales in the 1860s it was said that among Welsh farmhouse servants 'bastardy was commonplace and unchastity the rule'. At that time, eighteen per cent of all households in England and Wales had at least one living-in servant, and the percentage increased in the next few years. By 1881 the servant population was 1.3 million. Subordinate and sexually accessible women (almost literally so: knickers came into use only after about 1850) thus surrounded the future servant of empire from his boyhood.[21] Alternatively, or in addition, his cousins and chums would be another source of early stimulation. Boys in boarding schools frequently shared beds before the 1850s, and we cannot automatically assume that one thing did not lead to another. On arrival at Charterhouse in 1817, Thackeray found the first order he received from a schoolmate was 'come and frig me'.[22] Harrow in 1854 was recalled thus by J. A. Symonds:

> Every boy of good looks had a female name, and was recognised either as a public prostitute or as some bigger fellow's 'bitch'. Bitch was the word in common usage to indicate a boy who yielded his person to a lover. The talk in the dormitories and the studies was incredibly obscene. Here and there one could not avoid seeing acts of onanism, mutual masturbation, the sports of naked boys in bed together.[23]

Such graphic glimpses are rare for the nineteenth century, even in erotic literature, and they do not necessarily represent continuing traditions within a school. Even more elusive is the reconstruction of individual experience. However, there are strong suspicions that Curzon was kissed at Eton in the 1870s by a teacher, Oscar Browning (who was sacked but remained a lifelong friend); that he was loved by Alfred Lyttelton (a future Colonial Secretary), his senior, and was 'guilty of immorality with R. E. Macnaghten'. When Curzon discussed sexual problems of Indian empire with his Secretary of State, Lord George Hamilton, the latter claimed enough experience of schools, seminaries and colleges to know that 'few of these institutions escape being infected with some immorality or other'.[24] Even before leaving public school, some Victorian boys would have been to a brothel, perhaps especially if they were at Eton, where the existence of a sixth-form brothel was alleged in 1798, while proximity to the military presence at Windsor brought its own further possibilities.[25] This form of initiation was, however, never so central as it was for French schoolboys. (According to Zeldin, it was practically an institutionalised *rite de passage* for a French sixteen-year old to make his first visit to a brothel. France's brothels from the 1880s swarmed with schoolboys on holidays and Thursday afternoons, and it was rare indeed for a French boy of eighteen to be sexually inexperienced.)[26]

And so we come to that pervasive and protean problem of Victorian prostitution.[27] Clearly it was practised on a large scale. No one of any region who wanted a prostitute would have had any difficulty in finding one. At mid-century there were almost certainly more brothels in London than there were schools and charities put together. To get an accurate statistical measure of the extent of prostitution, however, remains impossible, 'an exercise comparable in futility with attempts by theologians to estimate the number of angels who could be accommodated on the head of a pin'.[28] The problem is that nobody knows how many clandestine prostitutes there were over and above those 'known' to the police. It is possible that for every known prostitute there were three or four more clandestines, but the size of the statistical multiplier to be used could reasonably range between two and ten. Police estimates of known prostitutes in London ranged from about 5,500 to 7,100 between 1858 and 1868, and, for England and Wales, 24,300 to 29,500. Using a high multiplier to include the clandestines, the total estimate of 80,000 prostitutes for London, which was advanced by some contemporaries and mechanically repeated, is by no means totally implausible. Independent investigators came up with total figures (including clandestines) in the 1840s of 800 prostitutes for Edinburgh, and an amazing 888 for Norwich (one for every twenty-three adult men). In 1817 there were about 2,000 prostitutes in 360 houses in the City of London parishes with a population of 59,000. There were some French prostitutes in London, together with a few West Indians, although no all-black brothel appears to have survived into the nineteenth century.[29]

As far as the causes of prostitution are concerned, the tendency of recent discussion (mostly by female if not feminist historians) has been to stress prostitution as a social necessity, a 'strategy for survival'. Women, it is argued, were driven into short-term ventures of prostitution because of poverty. Where good stable traditional employment was available for women, prostitution was uncommon: Dundee, with its jute factories, is said to have been an example. But clearly this is not the whole answer. As Havelock Ellis pointed out, many prostitutes came from domestic service, 'the group of workers most free from economic anxieties'. Several different surveys indeed suggest that up to forty or fifty per cent of prostitutes were drawn from the servant classes. It is therefore unlikely that economic necessity was the most fundamental cause, and we today are not likely to be any more impressed than Ellis was by the argument of 'biological disposition' to deviance (prostitution as the 'female form of criminality'). Instead, Ellis stressed the 'moral advantage' and 'civilisational value' of a potentially beneficial escape from the monotony of routine life: 'the effort to supplement the imperfect opportunities for self-development offered by our restrained, mechanical, and laborious civilisation'. For perhaps a third of prostitutes this deliberate rejection of drabness and drudgery in favour of a supposed life of colour and pleasure could have been a major inducement. Many came from broken homes. Although the hopes of many of them must have been dashed, few of them ever returned home again.[30] An analysis of over 3,700 prostitutes undertaken in the early 1880s by the chaplain of Clerkenwell Prison suggests that for more than half these women the 'immediate cause' of turning to prostitution was being led astray by other girls into 'choosing the streets', and that for only 1.5 per cent of them was an urgent necessity to support a family involved. The noted Purity campaigner Miss Ellice Hopkins also recognised that the most extensive cause of the increase in prostitution was 'getting entangled with girls who are already lost . . . the sight of finery and luxury' – a view strongly endorsed in the Select Committee's report of 1882 on the *Protection of Young Girls*.[31]

Whilst in some ways these contemporary explanations might be conscience-salving devices to shift blame from structural sociological causes to personal factors for which the State could not be held responsible, we still need to take account of what Peter Gay aptly calls 'the lure of prostitution'.[32] The demand factor must also have been important – the shortage of willing sex partners. After all, prostitution declined from about 1918 as 'demand' gradually found its natural alternative outlet in increasingly complaisant girlfriends, protected by contraception.

Four principal features of Victorian prostitution may be delineated. 1. It was in many ways the obverse of the Victorian notion of the family, with the prostitute acting as its 'most efficient guardian of virtue' (Lecky). Ideals of the virgin bride and chaste wife could be sustained only by the services of the prostitute. To say that all women were either angels or whores is an obvious simplification; nor can it really be true that if a married man 'wanted sexual enjoyment he went to a brothel' (Henriques). Nevertheless it does seem to be the case that for many men the erotic impulse was projected on to prostitutes. This was because of the taboo on pre-marital intercourse, the sexual anaesthetisation and trivialisation of wives, and because the taking of mistresses never really caught on in Britain (though there were some remarkable exceptions). In other words, Ellis's view that prostitution was 'an essential part of the whole system' does seem to be sustained.[33]

2. It was of an extremely degraded character: at least the observable bit of it was, drawn from the deprived working class; but there were also high-class prostitutes and 'kept' women. Lecky said that in no other European country was prostitution so 'hopelessly vicious'. Commentators from abroad agreed in the 1850s that the forms of London prostitution (street-walking, group parading, window exhibitionism, impudent solicitation and alley intercourse) were more shocking than anything to be seen in Europe or America. Down to the 1830s several brothels accepted boys as young as ten as clients, and there were even special nursing homes for pre-teens infected with venereal disease. Another unpleasant aspect was that many prostitutes robbed their clients. Finally we may remark the damaging evidence that British prostitutes were unexportable on account of their degraded character, 'independent-mindedness' and ignorance of the refinements of their trade (that is, oral and anal gratification). Irish prostitutes were considered by 'Walter' to be the worst of eighty nationalities: the 'lowest, bawdiest, foulest-tongued ... dirtiest ... ' and the most given to cheating. Even as late as 1954, the Home Secretary believed that the 'deplorable' soliciting which went on in Soho was 'probably without parallel in the capital cities of other civilised countries'.[34]

3. It was characterised also by the large number of juvenile participants. This is difficult to quantify, because most juveniles were likely to be clandestine prostitutes. But the high proportion of youngsters was probably not typical of prostitution world-wide, and all contemporary observers (Ryan, Mayhew, Tait, Acton, Bloch, Beatrice Webb) commented on the sexual promiscuity of the pre-pubertal children of the British lower classes, to say nothing of the completely commonplace nature of their involvement in incest. The age of consent for girls was twelve until 1875 (when it was raised to thirteen), and did not apply to

boys. In London there were brothels which specialised in supplying girls under thirteen, and girls as young as eight or nine were on the streets, particularly in the early nineteenth century. Two hundred child prostitutes under twelve were recorded in Liverpool in 1857. Child labour in factories was a major source of recruitment.[35]

4. It was parallelled by male prostitution, although this was seldom discussed. Flexner in 1914 described this as a phenomenon which existed throughout European cities on a considerable scale, and it is possible that London was not so much a centre of male prostitution as Berlin or Paris. It is most unlikely that more than half a dozen men's brothels were operating after mid-century, plus a hammam in Jermyn Street. Brothels specialising in small boys existed in London during the 1830s, but did not survive the purges which took place in 1837, when David Romaine of Mile End and William Sheen of Spitalfields were both arrested for running well-established boy brothels. Thereafter boy prostitutes took to Piccadilly, the parks and the railway stations. The problem was visible enough in the early twentieth century for the White Cross League to establish a shelter home for 'boy sodomites', run by an ex-police constable and his wife in Clapham Common. They dealt with sixty-five boys between 1912 and 1915, many of whom combined sex with hop-picking; the failure rate of 'rehabilitation' was at least 50 percent. The Catholics had a similar establishment in St George's House, Westminster Bridge Road.[36] Otherwise, the predominant form of male prostitution was military. This was casual and traditional. J. A. Symonds was accosted in 1865 by a young grenadier off Leicester Square, and in 1877 was taken to a male brothel near the military barracks in Regent's Park: 'it was a far more decent place than I expected'. The 'nice' young soldier he encountered there seemed to find in it all 'nothing unusual, nothing shameful'. Symonds was also told by a corporal in the 2nd Life Guards that some men enlisted on purpose to indulge their propensities. When in 1881 the Bishop of London asked the Director of Criminal Investigations 'Is it a fact that there are boys and youths soliciting in the streets?', the answer he got was: 'It is the fact, and it is an undisputable fact', with Eton boys, cadets and subalterns most exposed to it.[37]

The Victorian State made a definite experiment with licensed and regulated prostitution – a system of tolerated 'reglementation', not legalisation – through the enactment of the Contagious Diseases Acts. Essentially these arose out of alarm about venereal disease in the army, which in 1860 reached the rate of 369 per thousand. Certain dockyards and garrison towns were accordingly designated as areas wherein prostitutes were to be registered and compulsorily examined. This was preeminently an imperial system devised by the military-medico establishment to protect the soldiers of the empire, but Oxbridge dons also expressed interest in it. The pilot scheme began in 1864. The original towns covered were Portsmouth, Plymouth, Woolwich, Chatham, Sheerness, Aldershot, Colchester, Shorncliffe, the Curragh, Cork and Queenstown. In 1866 Windsor was added; and in 1869 Canterbury, Dover, Gravesend, Maidstone, Winchester and Southampton – making eighteen towns in all. The radius covered was in each case extended to ten miles from the town centre. But these measures were ineffective because the application remained so localised, and it was therefore proposed to extend the system to the whole country. This seemed reasonable, since those towns which had the system rather liked it, because the State paid for controlling a local nuisance.

But a national campaign, led by Josephine Butler, was launched against the Contagious Diseases Acts. Although the campaign was slow at first to attract attention, its inauguration in 1869 was a portentous event. The objections to the compulsory examination system were that it legalised the 'double standard' and assumed prostitution was necessary and ineradicable, that it tended to professionalise it, making it harder for the amateur to escape, that it increased the power and interference of the State, that it gave powers of arrest to special plainclothes 'morals police', and that it inspected only prostitutes and not their clients. Compulsory and painful examination by vaginal speculum was held to constitute 'instrumental rape by a steel penis', and the campaign harped upon 'medical lust in handling and dominating and degrading women'. A Royal Commission was appointed in 1871. Some 766 public meetings were held in the 1870s and petitions were collected with 2.6 million signatures. The government was led in 1883 to suspend its experiment with regulated prostitution ('reglementation'), a decision which was slowly to reverberate around the world.[38]

The reduction of opportunity

Sexual intercourse began
In nineteen sixty-three
(Which was rather late for me) –
Between the end of the *Chatterley* ban
And the Beatles' first L.P.

Up till then there'd only been
A sort of bargaining,
A wrangle for a ring,
A shame that started at sixteen
And spread to everything.

[Philip Larkin, 'Annus mirabilis']

The campaign against regulated and licensed prostitution spear-headed the way for a multiple assault on sexual life in the 1880s: an attack on the easy-going attitudes of the working class, and a concerted effort to eliminate adolescent sexuality. This important Purity Campaign represented an outburst of neurotic puritanism. It resulted in a repressive new sex code, and the reduction of sexual opportunity. The 'canonisation of sexual respectability' was, suggests Annan, the most prized achievement of the Victorians. The imperial historian will naturally wish to relate this Purity Campaign to fears of imperial decline and alarm about the degeneration of the imperial race. As Barry Smith puts it, 'This grand fear directly linked sexual pollution with the threat of social chaos and the fall of the Empire.'[39] Its architects were William Coote and the National Vigilance Association, W. T. Stead and the *Pall Mall Gazette*, Alfred Dyer (a fanatical Quaker journalist), Mrs Josephine Butler and Miss Ellice Hopkins (Christian feminists) – a 'bourgeois Anglo-Saxon pack of Jesuits' as Symonds witheringly described them.[40] They co-opted Archbishop E. W. Benson, Cardinal Manning, Kitchener, Baden-Powell and other assorted a-sexuals, together with the entire cohorts of the Headmasters' Conference. The climax came in 1885 (the '*annus mirabilis* of sexual politics') with the Criminal Law Amendment Act, 'to make further provision for the protection of women and girls, and the suppression of brothels, and other purposes'. The Act introduced a summary (and effective) procedure for action against brothels. It was the end of an era in the history of prostitution: 'in the whole Victorian underworld no other important field of activity underwent so clear-cut a change'.[41]

The age of female consent, raised in 1875 from twelve to thirteen, despite a good deal of grumbling in the House of Lords, now went up to sixteen. In order to make it easier to obtain a conviction it was no longer necessary to prove that a child understood a court oath. All this put a stop to the traffic in young girls to Belgium. The 'other purpose' was met by the ineffably awful clause XI, the 'Labouchere amendment', which made illegal *all* types of sexual activity between males (not just sodomy, as hitherto), and irrespective of either age or consent. It is not clear whether this was a genuine attempt to deal with male prostitution, or a 'Purity' measure, opportunistically and irrelevantly tacked on to the Bill, or whether it was Labouchere's way of trying to overturn a Bill he disliked by a ridiculously extravagant amendment. Whatever the intention, the effect of its enactment is clear: Britain ended up with a proscription going far beyond anything else in any other country at the time. Italy and the Netherlands actually *abolished* punishment for consenting adults in private in the late 1880s, while it took the advent of Hitler to make Germany follow the new British model.[42]

In this ferocious Purity Campaign there were eight targets.

1. *The Contagious Diseases Acts.* As symbols of 'state-regulated prostitution', the Acts were repealed in Britain in 1886, having been suspended in 1883. But they were also in force in Jamaica, Trinidad, Hong Kong, Fiji, Gibraltar, Malta, India, Burma, Ceylon, the Australian colonies, Malaya and the Cape (where they were re-enacted in 1885). They were established in Cairo twenty-four hours after the troops arrived from the battle of Tel-el-Kebir. Josephine Butler launched the campaign against the empire Contagious Diseases Acts in May 1887 at Exeter Hall. They were suspended in India in 1888, resulting in a disastrous and immediate increase in venereal disease (see fig. 2, p. 127). Consequently there was much argument there and elsewhere and several modifications were introduced.[43]

2. *The age of consent.* Raising this to sixteen gave British girls the maximum protection then available anywhere in the world. Even so, the Purity people wanted it fixed at eighteen. By comparison, we should note that in the United States, ten had been the usual age of consent, though in Delaware it was seven, and in some states non-existent. Several American states now followed Britain, and some even went to twenty-one. Among European states only Belgium, Iceland, Holland and Norway increased the age as high as sixteen. In 1927 the age of consent, both male and female, still remained thirteen in France and Japan, and twelve in Italy; even in New Zealand it remained at twelve for girls and silent as to boys (nor was any protection for boys then thought necessary in India, Ceylon, Western Australia, Tasmania, China, Japan, Holland, Spain, Denmark, Sweden or Uruguay).[44]

3. *Masturbation and schoolboy sex.* Although there had been since the early eighteenth century periodic scares about the supposedly deleterious effects of masturbation, much of the earlier emphasis had been upon the undesirability of adult masturbation. The young Gladstone was worried about it from 1829 to 1831 ('beast, fool, blackguard, puppy, reptile'), but not apparently because of its supposed *physical* effects.[45] The drive against masturbation was renewed in the 1860s with specific attention to juveniles and a fresh terrorising catalogue of physical consequences: there was a raising of the stakes to include the risks of blindness and insanity, as well as the old bugbears of indigestion and pimples.Dr Acton advised cold baths and quoits as suitable alternative exercise, but felt horse riding to be contra-indicated. The drive was implemented with ever increasing publicity from the 1880s. Thring was expelling boys from Uppingham for 'solitary vice' from 1879. Masturbation became a symbol of catastrophe, because it was believed to be a cause of degeneration in the next generation. It was denounced in sermons and pamphlets as dangerous, cowardly, selfish and very bad for

team spirit. Baden-Powell carried the message strongly into the Boy Scout movement.[46] Simultaneously there was an entirely original effort to eradicate all forms of sex from public schools. A watershed was clearly reached in 1872 at Wellington when the governors disputed, but failed to overturn, what several of them regarded as headmaster E. W. Benson's over-reaction in insisting on the expulsion or withdrawal of three boys who had sexual intercourse with a fourteen-year-old serving-maid in the home of one of them during the Christmas holidays – the eldest got venereal disease. There was also an end to the traditional presumption of innocence in friendships between boys of different ages. Benson ran barbed wire along the tops of dormitory cubicles. And masters had to be more circumspect too. William (Johnson) Cory had to leave Eton in 1872. Oscar Browning was dismissed in 1875, taking refuge in King's College, Cambridge, where he was left undisturbed to make friends with an extraordinary set of choristers, boy sailors and school-leaver servants. Some schools banned bare knees at football. Mrs Warre-Cornish, wife of a former Vice-Provost of Eton, is said to have complained that sex between boys, 'the old hereditary vice of Eton', was 'unknown in these modern, sanitary, linoleum schools'.[47] It was an increasingly eccentric attitude. Such a remark would not have amused Kipling, who was much more in tune with contemporary opinion when he wrote to his son John at Wellington in 1912:

> I wanted to tell you a lot of things about keeping clear of any chap who is even suspected of beastliness. There is no limit to the trouble possible if one goes about (however innocently) with swine of that type. Give them the widest of berths. Whatever their merits may be in the athletic line they are at heart only sweeps and scum and all friendship or acquaintance with them ends in sorrow and disgrace. More on this subject when we meet.[48]

4. *Homosexuality*. There was a most significant and unpleasant attack on homosexuality in general, a concept now becoming articulated: what Weeks calls the 'construction of homosexuality', the invention of an interdicted category. Whereas in the past one particular act (anal intercourse) had been unlawful, henceforth the criminality of sexual behaviour between males was extended to take in fellatio and even mutual masturbation, and it was turned into an *identifiable condition* as well, a disease as well as a crime. A state of mind became suspect. A traditional derision of (rather than hostility to) sodomy now switched to a broader hostility towards a supposedly generalised homosexual disposition. Bentham's 'innoxious' or 'imaginary offence' now became problematic for society as a whole.[49] All this may fairly be represented as a disaster. By banishing male affection from 'normal' life and experience, men in general were impoverished, even diminished.

More particularly, male-oriented sex became ever more cultic and romantic. The tendency to effeminacy (by no means an inevitable feature) was reinforced. The new laws forced a polarisation of personal position, a rigid self-labelling of an inherently harmful kind, and may even have increased the incidence of 'homosexuality'. They opened a route to blackmail, and drove homosexual groups underground, whence they later emerged both militant and promiscuous.[50] In 1889 flogging was introduced for homosexual solicitation. There were a number of unsavoury scandals. These involved high Dublin Castle officials (1884), London telegraph boys and aristocrats (Cleveland Street, 1889-90), Piccadilly rent boys, street vendors, valets and unemployed stable lads in the scandal concerning Oscar Wilde and Lord Alfred Douglas (1895). A. C. Benson privately bemoaned the 'sickening ... conventionality that smashed Wilde', who was not a vicious man. W. T. Stead feared a wholesale exodus from public schools if the purges continued.[51] No. 19 Cleveland Street was a male brothel attracting soldiers and people like Lord Arthur Somerset (an extra-equerry to the Prince of Wales, just back from army service in Egypt), the Earl of Euston and Prince Albert Victor of Wales (though the latter almost certainly went there under a misapprehension). The Wilde trials revealed the dangers of blackmail in 'feasting with panthers', the avaricious and adenoidal late adolescent 'rough trade' of the metropolis.[52]

5. *Soliciting*. The late nineteenth century saw a big effort to clean up the streets. It was not successful, because the closure of brothels under the 1885 Act only forced more prostitutes into outdoor soliciting. (The annual average of prosecutions against brothels went up from eighty-six per annum, 1875-85, to over 1,200 per annum, 1885-1914.) The four-year crusade against street prostitution launched in 1883 was unpopular, and a public relations disaster for the police, which they were reluctant to repeat. Action against specific targets like saloons, pleasure gardens and theatres was more effective than trying to control soliciting in the streets. Soliciting in theatres was also reduced by the simple device of disallowing the building of promenades in new theatres constructed after 1889. Winston Churchill made his first public speech in 1893 protesting about 'prudes on the prowl' in theatres, and the futility of trying to abolish sin by Act of Parliament. There were further attempts to check soliciting in 1901-06 and 1919-23, but there was no substantive change in the law until 1959.[53]

6. *Pornography*. The Metropolitan Police Obscene Publications Squad was formed in 1863. Lord Chief Justice Cockburn produced a famous working definition of obscenity in 1868 as that which had 'the tendency. . .to deprave and corrupt'. But the 1876 Customs Consolidation Act went much further and empowered officials to seize prints, books

and photographs, etc., which were 'indecent or obscene'. The Vice Society seized a quarter of a million photographs between 1868 and 1880. By the 1890s London as the centre of the international erotic picture trade was under serious threat, and the great age of British pornography was over. An epoch-making prosecution of Emile Zola's publisher, Henry Vizetelly, in 1888 for a translation of *La Terre* (in which the climax, strongly described, is a bull servicing a cow) gratuitously turned 'obscenity' laws against serious literature. Vizetelly, unrepentantly defiant, was sent to prison in 1889 for three months for further offences. Prudery in this field was an establishment defence against the enormous increase in literacy consequent upon the 1870 Education Act. There was a further effective crack-down on erotic pictures in the 1900s, and a new law in 1908 against sending 'obscene wares' through the post. The following works were added to the 'index' of British banned books: Havelock Ellis, *Sexual Inversion* (1898), D. H. Lawrence, *The rainbow* (1915), James Joyce, *Ulysses* (1923), and *The Satyricon* of Petronius; the full publication of *Lady Chatterley's Lover* (1928) was, of course, not even attempted.[54]

7. *Incest*. 'Incestuous crime,' declared Lord Shaftesbury in 1861, 'is frightfully common in various parts of London.' Thirty years later, in Charles Booth's 'darkest England', incest was 'so familiar as hardly to call for remark'. The Victorians shied away from the problem, because it was clearly a structural product of their social organisation: the result of inadequate and overcrowded housing – 'the crowded couch of incest in the warrens of the poor', as Tennyson put it. When Queen Victoria died, London had 56,000 one-room and 55,000 two-room flats. In 1911 three-quarters of a million Londoners were classed as living in overcrowded dwellings. The Punishment of Incest Act (1908) arose out of years of lobbying by the National Society for the Prevention of Cruelty to Children after its foundation in 1889. There were draft Bills from 1893. The need for legislation was hotly debated. Lord Chancellor Halsbury was against it. So was Lord Crewe (Lord President of the Council). They argued that ninety per cent of cases could be dealt with under the 1885 Act and the Cruelty to Children Acts. No major scandal preceded the 1908 Act, which arose simply out of the Purity Movement. It was important to Purity-mongers as a symbolic public affirmation of society's commitment to Purity: 'less an act of rational social policy than a manifestation of the strength and status of the Social Purity Movement'. Only males could be prosecuted under it.[55] The Incest Act has often been justified on the grounds that the taboo against incest is universal. This is very far from being certain. For example, a Gilbertese Islander told Sir Arthur Grimble, 'how wonderful are white folk! So kind and wise in many ways, so ignorant and cruel about love within the family.'[56]

[69]

8. *Nude bathing.* Bathing costumes (bathing in 'the French style') began to appear in the 1850s and 1860s, but the campaign to get the populace to abandon nude swimming took a full half-century and more to achieve. Municipal swimming pools did not necessarily require costumes even in the 1870s, though the sexes were segregated. (At first, swimming pools merely replicated the conditions of river bathing, and dogs were admitted.) Local practice in seaside towns was also very variable by the 1870s: the Rev. Francis Kilvert could mostly sea-bathe naked when he wanted to but no longer felt able to rely on it: Weston-super-Mare and Ilfracombe were all right, but it was already frowned on at Seaton and Shanklin. Frank Sutcliffe's famous prize-winning photograph of Whitby harbour, 'Water rats', shows nude boys bathing in 1886, but some residents were complaining about it. Not until 1890 did the Amateur Swimming Association rule that bathing-drawers must be worn in competitive schoolboy racing.[57] Cambridge and (even more successfully) Oxford were among the last pockets of resistance to swimming costumes. Gwen Raverat's rhapsodies about nude swimming in the River Cam reflected a dying practice. It was frowned on by the city fathers after 1894 and finally banned from the town bathing sheds in 1910, although screened and segregated nude sunbathing survived until (ironically) the mid-1960s.[58]

Thus the Purity Campaign was extremely comprehensive in its scope, and changed the visible face of British life as well as many of its inner attitudes. But how effective was it? Undoubtedly there was thereafter more decorum, more chastity, less opportunity and less fun. But presumably not all aunts cut their nephews out of their wills if they so much as visited Paris, as happened to the aspiring diplomat Vansittart, trying to learn French.[59] Weeks believes there was 'no final victory' for Purity, only a continuing battle. Masturbation among the middle class seems likely to have been reduced but not eradicated, though the working class was largely deprived of this taboo, as of so much else. (Canadian foster-parents of working-class immigrant apprentices frequently complained of their masturbatory habits.)[60] The attack on sex between males did not entirely intimidate the elite, as is evident from the ethos of certain Cambridge colleges, the 'Apostles' (with their 'higher sodomy' doctrines), Bloomsbury and all that. Hugh Dalton took it in his stride when, after his father's death in 1931 , he discovered that the venerable Canon of Windsor had hoarded an enormous affectionate correspondence with young men: 'a strong homosexual strain is very clear'. (He was also amused to discover at Le Havre in 1916 that two of the inmates of the venereal disease hospital were English army chaplains.)[61]Some male-orientated men found outlets overseas. Casement continued to combine secret sodomy with consular and diplomatic assignments in Africa and Latin America. The empire provided an occasional bolt hole for those who fell from grace, like Canon Robert Eyton, Rector of St Margaret's, Westminster, exiled to a remote rectory in Queensland in 1900 after a scandal. Paedophiles were not yet singled out for persecution, and popular culture continued to validate a strong emotional interest in boyhood until well into the 1920s. Dreadful 'Uranian' poets quaintly flourished in Edwardian times.[62] It was only in the 1930s that the Archbishop of Canterbury – something of an expert in these matters – noticed that the commonest form of immoral charge against Church of England vicars was 'misconduct' with their choirboys and servers.[63] Meanwhile, although sexual opportunity was generally reduced in Britain, the empire continued to provide for traditional expectations, at least where white wives had not penetrated in significant numbers. However, by 1908 or thereabouts the Purity establishment was ready to tackle the problem of sexual licence in the empire as well.

The worst result of the late-Victorian campaign was the silence which descended over all aspects of sex, producing the most appalling ignorance. This was not just confined to couples embarking on marriage. Wilfrid Blunt, brother of Anthony, the traitor, was at Marlborough just before the First World War. The facts of life were never explained to him, not even masturbation. Confirmation classes merely 'went through the motions' of giving explanations. The chaplain's vague references were not understood; if 'homosexuality' was hinted at, young Blunt failed to get the reference. For many years yet he remained in ignorance of this taboo subject, though it was where his fundamental interests lay. Even when he was twenty-seven, he failed to realise precisely what it was Arab boys were offering tourists in Algeria and Tunisia. Presumably he had not read his Gide.[64] By 1914 the whole British concept of masculinity – not least in the public schools – had been redefined, partly in the name of empire, to mean not sexual prowess and maturity but sexual restraint and 'cleanness'. Real sexual activity receded so far into the background that according to Larkin's famous poem it was not rediscovered again 'until 1963'.

Empire and concepts of masculinity

There is no point on which my convictions are stronger than on the power of boarding schools in forming national character. . . The learning to be responsible and independent, to bear pain, to play the game, to drop rank, and wealth, and home luxury, is a priceless boon. I think myself that it is this which has made the English such an adventurous race; and that with all their faults . . . the public schools are the cause of this 'manliness'. [Rev. Edward Thring, headmaster of Uppingham School]

Intimately connected with the process I have called 'the reduction of opportunity', and indeed a key instrument of the Purity campaign, was the growth of the public schools dedicated to the doctrines of late-Victorian manliness. Early-Victorian men were fairly sentimental in their friendships. They walked about arm-in-arm (as much of the rest of the world outside the Anglo-Saxon nations still does); they described themselves in their letters as 'loving friends'; they accepted romantic, non-sexual attachments with each other in youth as part of the natural order of things – see, for example, the novels of the time and the memoirs of those involved in the Oxford Movement. (Disraeli wrote in *Coningsby*, 'At school friendship is a passion. It entrances the being; it tears the soul.')[65] Overseas, they often lived together on an intimate collegiate basis, sometimes sharing in small groups nicely called 'chummeries' (as Henry Lawrence, Herbert Edwardes and John Nicholson did in the Punjab), rejoicing in the unalloyed love they thought possible only between men. (No late-Victorian would have written to his sister, as Charles Metcalfe did in 1824, of 'joys . . . in the pure love which exists between man and man, which cannot, I think, be surpassed in that more alloyed attachment between the opposite sexes, to which the name of love is in general exclusively applied'.)[66] They were not much given to competitive sport, but preferred country pursuits, rambling, shuttle-cock and board games. They had no fear of tears.

During the course of the century, however, there was a marked shift in the meaning of 'manliness': a shift from the ideals of moral strenuous-ness, a Christian manliness, to a cult of the emphatically physical (what later generations would call 'machismo'); a shift from serious earnest-ness to robust virility, from integrity to hardness, from the ideals of godliness and good learning to those of clean manliness and good form. Manliness, it has been said, moved first from chapel to changing-room, into an 'overpowering phil-athleticism' (an over-valuation of games), and then into almost a militarisation of the public schools after 1901.[67] Newsome describes the manly virtues of the late nineteenth century thus:

> the duty of patriotism; the moral and physical beauty of athleticism; the salutary effects of Spartan habits and discipline; the cultivation of all that is masculine and the expulsion of all that is effeminate, unEnglish and excessively intellectual.[68]

The qualities most unsparingly disparaged by the late-Victorians were sentimentalism and lack of sexual control. They had a horror of sex for the unmarried. The late nineteenth-century cult of manliness became a powerful and pervasive middle-class moral code.

The golden age of athleticism was from about 1860 to 1914. Public schools' playing-fields were often better equipped than their class-rooms. Harrow had thirty-four football pitches. Organised games were a means of artificially providing adversity.The need to experience pain was held to be a necessary preparation for the self-reliance and wretch-edness of the imperial frontier. Edward Lyttelton, headmaster of Eton (1882-90), complained that the development of smooth pitches made cricket 'comparatively worthless' because it removed the pain from the game. Games were not only seen as a good start to a military or empire career, they were also advocated as the best possible antidote to 'immor-ality' such as had been more or less cheerfully ignored by earlier generations. There was to be no 'French schoolboy depravity' in Ed-wardian Britain. As Mangan points out, other factors may also help to account for the emphasis on games, such as a boring curriculum, an admiration for Greek aestheticism, or the natural extension of the rural and estate pursuits of parents and pupils; but it was essentially the imperial destiny that tipped the balance decisively towards public school athleticism. The games ethic was a frontiersman's code, empha-sising stamina and grit and team spirit. It helped to produce useful colonists, uncomplaining soldiers and resourceful missionaries.[69]

This educational revolution, the cult of games and the pervading concern with imperial destiny mutually reinforced one another. Foot-ball, cricket and boxing were seen as 'moral agents' in running the empire, capable of weaning subject peoples from unhealthy sexual preoccupations, intertribal warfare and cattle raiding – even from petty theft. J. E. C. Welldon, Bishop of Calcutta and headmaster of Harrow (1885-98), believed that 'in the history of the British Empire it is written that England has owed her sovereignty to her sports'.[70]

Almost equally important, and certainly affecting larger numbers of young people, was the inauguration of the Boy Scout movement c. 1908, much preoccupied not only with masculinity but with Purity and empire as well. British boys, declared its founder, Sir Robert Baden-Pow-ell, must not be disgraced like young Romans of old, who lost the empire of their forefathers by being 'wishy-washy slackers without any go or patriotism in them'. His aim was to make the rising generation 'into good citizens or useful colonists'. Here indeed was an attempt to incul-cate some sort of demotic manly 'warrior tradition' into British youth. Despite a recent abortive challenge to the orthodox view of the origins of Scouting – the revisionism that failed – its fundamental purpose still seems to have been that of providing a militaristic insurance against a recurrence of the political and military incompetence of the Boer War. Marksmanship was stressed.[71] In seeking ways of raising 'moral tone',

Baden-Powell was impressed by the *bushido* ideals of the Japanese samurai, and by the bush training of the Zulu and Swazi. 'Images of frontier manliness were fed back into the metropolis' (MacKenzie).[72]

Worries about educational ideals, masculinity and patriotism were parallelled by concern over the evidence of 'physical deterioration' revealed by recruitment for South Africa. Alarming symptoms showed a clear danger to the continued existence of Britain as a world power. In 1900 recruitment medicals showed that 565 men per thousand were below the standard army height of 5 ft 6 in., compared with only 105 per thousand in 1845. Forty-four men in every thousand weighed under 7 st. 2 lb. At the Manchester recruiting depot in 1899, 8,000 out of 12,000 men were rejected as virtual invalids; only 1,200 of them were found after service in the army to be physically fit in all respects. Three thousand men had to be sent home from South Africa on account of bad teeth. Baden-Powell considered that half the British losses in war from sickness could have been avoided by better personal hygiene. A committee of the Privy Council prepared a report on 'Physical Deterioration'. The *British Medical Journal* commented in July 1903 on the symptoms of physical decline coming to light, just at the very time when Britain required 'stalwart sons to people the colonies and to uphold the prestige of the nation'.[73] The birth rate was falling, while infant mortality in the 1890s was believed to be rising. There was therefore a concerted drive to try to reduce it. There was widespread demand for 'education for motherhood' and 'eugenicist' breeding.[74] As Rosebery declared in 1900:

> An empire such as ours requires as its first condition an Imperial Race – a race vigorous and industrious and intrepid. Health of mind and body exalt a nation in the competition of the universe. The survival of the fittest is an absolute truth in the conditions of the modern world.

For the sake of the empire, he concluded, there must be social reform in Britain itself. This theme was widely accepted. Earl Grey (Governor-General of Canada, 1904-11) expressed fears that 'our successors will not be able to bear the burden of empire'. Between 1906 and 1911 Winston Churchill became a social reformer from anxiety about the stability of society and the empire: 'to keep our empire we must have a free people, an educated and well-fed people'. That, he said, was why the Liberal government was in favour of social reform; the degraded condition of the poor contained 'the seeds of imperial ruin and national decay' and it was, he argued, 'a serious hindrance to recruiting for the army and navy'; the essential foundation of security was 'a healthy family life for all'. The introduction of subsidised school meals in 1906 and of compulsory school medical inspection in 1907 were in effect, writes the historian of the Welfare State, Bentley B. Gilbert, 'an institutionalised legacy of the anxieties of the Boer War period'; anxieties which were a potent means of focusing attention on physical fitness, reinforcing the tough image of masculinity, and forcing it lower down the social scale.[75]

One symbolic, and far from insignificant, new development in this process was the introduction of routine infant circumcision of boys among the upper and professional middle classes of Britain (and America). We know less about this practice than we do about the rituals of some of the most obscure African peoples. Before another generation has elapsed, no one in Britain will even remember it ever happened or, if they do, will regard it as a quaint post-Victorian fad, on a par with antimacassars and aspidistras. The first and most difficult problem is to establish when it began. Circumcision was for centuries unthinkable to a Christian. 'Christendom', wrote Richard Burton, 'practically holds circumcision in horror', a point only underlined by the eccentric attempt of some millenarian false prophets to reintroduce it as 'the baptism of blood' in the 1820s.[76] Christian iconography has always refused to be honest on this point. Michelangelo's 'David', for all his realism, is not circumcised as he should be. The infant Jesus, even when patently well past the eighth day, is never depicted as circumcised.[77] In 1810, when Byron wanted to draw out the main differences between the 'Turks and ourselves', he seized upon the fact that 'we have a foreskin and they have none' (adding that 'we talk much and they little. . . We prefer a girl and a bottle, they a pipe and a pathic').[78]

'Walter' (born early 1820s), with his insatiable curiosity about all aspects of sex, wrote two essays on the physiognomy of the penis. Both assume the presence of a foreskin. Circumcision is not even mentioned in them. His 'sample' was pretty good. His field observations were based on his recollections of exhibitionism and swimming-bath scenes during his school-days, on what he saw of fellow participants in orgies, and during a great many voyeuristic episodes in brothels. He also gathered oral evidence from prostitutes, whom he found well informed about their clients' genitals. Those who had been maidservants described their employers' sons' organs as well. He knew a good deal about the variable retraction of the foreskin in its natural adult state, so he may probably be accounted an accurate observer. The only two circumcised organs he ever saw belonged to Muslims, the first probably in Egypt about 1870 ('at once surprised, as I was for a moment, it occurred to me that he must be circumcised. Such a prick I'd never seen. . .').[79] Walter's evidence is supported by the entire corpus of mid-Victorian erotica. The first mention of circumcision in the genre appears to be in the 1880s; the first didactic reference c. 1907, in the anonymous *Memoirs of a Voluptuary*, (The dating must be more or less right, even if it is a fudged imprint, because two of the villains are schoolboy characters called 'Elgar' and

'Benson' – in real life the authors of 'Land of Hope and Glory', 1902 – and the joke would fall flat unless it were topical.) 'Elgar' is described as having 'an awfully funny cock', the skin being 'cut off like a Jew'. It was the first time the narrator had seen such a member. He was not impressed, although he discovered later 'it was not confined to Jews and Muslims', and 'a number of modern medical men approve of it'.[80]

Discussion about the possible benefits of circumcision began about 1890. One of the most enthusiastic publicists was Dr Remondino, who considered that evolution might eventually remove the foreskin. Meanwhile, outright war must be waged on this 'debatable appendage':

> Circumcision is like a substantial and well-secured life annuity; . . . parents cannot make a better saving investment for their little boys, as it ensures them better health, greater capacity for labour, longer life, less nervousness, sickness, loss of time, and less doctor bills, as well as it increases their chance for an euthanasian death.

The *British Medical Journal* reviewer welcomed Remondino's book as focusing attention on an important subject insufficiently ventilated hitherto. Not surprisingly, he found some of the arguments 'excessive and strained', but concluded that many of Remondino's views were of 'undoubted value'.[81] A more sophisticated advocate was the eminent surgeon, Sir Jonathan Hutchinson, who stressed that the operation 'must necessarily tend to cleanliness' and almost certainly help to reduce cancer.[82] Some doctors thought it would reduce liability to hernia. On the other side, Herbert Snow denounced circumcision as barbarous and unnecessary. Army doctors now joined in the debate, perhaps decisively. Captain F. J. W. Porter in 1892 said he had performed a hundred circumcisions (using cocaine) in India on his last tour and twenty-five in six months back in the station hospital at Colchester; in fact, he operated 'whenever there is a sore on the prepuce'. Dr R. E. Foott, a former army surgeon, recalled how frequently he had been appalled by the 'filth collected' under the prepuces of the uncircumcised, and how soldiers often had to be made to wash the smegmatic accumulation away before he could examine them properly. This unhygienic state, he believed, 'assisted the absorption of the syphilitic virus'. Doctors as a group were now rapidly becoming convinced of the benefits of circumcision. There was a lot of discussion as to how they could persuade mothers to accept the operation. By the mid-1890s, however, they were alarmed by the number of 'specialist operators' who were sending circulars to parents who announced in *The Times* the birth of a son – circulars which laid much stress on a suggestion that this was an ideal moment for fathers to put themselves in good genital standing too. In 1899 a Hertfordshire 'country doctor' reported from Welwyn that 'of recent years most parents' in his private practice were asking for infant circumcision of boys.[83]

The answer to the first problem therefore seems fairly definite: British circumcision began in the 1890s – at a time when a great deal of public interest was focused on the empire. The debate was over by about 1903. By 1907 it was reported to be 'very common in children's hospitals'; 874 operations were performed in 1906 at Great Ormond Street. At the Middlesex Hospital in 1906, fifty-four children and twelve adults were circumcised. In the main, however, it was an operation left to general practitioners.[84]

The second question we have to consider is why it was adopted. Two motivating strands can readily be identified: Jewish and Indian-imperial.As far as Jewish influences are concerned, there was at this time a good deal of reluctant admiration for Jewish methods of child care. Time and time again, doctors testified to the low incidence of infant mortality among Jews, to the sturdiness of Jewish children, to their supposedly low rates of masturbation, and to the rarity of venereal disease and cancer of the penis. The report of the interdepartmental Committee on Physical Deterioration (1904) accepted Jewish family life as an ideal to which the rest of the nation had to move if they were really to improve the health of British children. General Sir Frederick Maurice felt that 'it does not follow that a stereotyped copying of the habits of the Jews would be desirable', but he accepted that the British evidently had much to learn from them.[85] As far as Indian experience is concerned, it is clear that circumcision had long been used as a treatment in the Indian army, possibly well back into the eighteenth century. Hot, humid climates are not good for sensitive foreskins, any more than sandy ones are (as the Jews and Muslims of the Middle East had always known). There can be little doubt that British Indian medical authorities strongly favoured the introduction of infant circumcision in Britain as a procedure which would eliminate a tiresome cause of later trouble for future servants of empire.[86] Together these Jewish and imperial strands are a sufficient explanation for the adoption of circumcision by the British elite. (Sadly, however, the finesse of the Jewish *mohel* was not assimilated, and the crudity of the British form of circumcision had to be seen to be believed. This fact deprives the whole discussion of any elegiac quality it might otherwise have had.) It is not necessary to invoke its supposed properties as an anti-masturbation device; anyone who advocated it for that reason was indulging in pure quackery.[87]

Lastly, we have to establish the significance of the late-Victorian adoption of circumcision. Symbolically, the anthropologist (to whom we must turn for guidance) would regard circumcision as a change 'from a state of infantile filthiness to a state of clean maturity', of rebirth into 'masculinity and personality'. In some societies it serves as a public demonstration of loyalty to the group (since the father risks the future basis of his power as a man with descendants); it is a ritual of kinship unity, an act of obedience to ancestral custom and thus a legitimation of those in authority. But, most fundamentally and broadly, circumcision is the establishment of a strong male identity: an assertion of maleness, a conquest of feminine elements. Among the Merina of Madagascar, for example, it is sometimes called *mahasoa* (making sweet and clean); it is making a boy properly male, achieving a correct sexual differentiation, and perhaps even regarded as ensuring sexual potency.[88] Viewed in the light of these anthropological insights, we can see how British circumcision was meant to contribute to the general improvement of the physical and self-confident manliness of the future custodians of empire. It was a dramatic reassertion of masculinity, in accordance with the lessons of practical experience of working in hot climates. Perhaps also it had an appeal as satisfying the symbolic requirements of ruling an empire of seventy million Muslims. It was widely adopted in the white dominions.[89]

That British circumcision is to be seen primarily as an imperial phenomenon is, finally, demonstrated statistically by its differential adoption among various social groups. It was chiefly characteristic of the upper and professional classes, pioneered by doctors and army officers. In the 1930s – there are unfortunately no earlier statistics – it seems to have been carried out on about two-thirds of boys in the leading public schools. At the highest level of the social scale the proportion may even have exceeded four-fifths, whereas in some 'deprived' working-class areas, rural and urban, it may never have got beyond one-tenth. Overall, by the 1930s almost exactly one-third of the total British male population was being circumcised. A survey of soldiers, mostly National Servicemen, in 1953 found thirty-four per cent of them to be circumcised (reflecting, of course, its incidence c. 1935). Its decline began as one of the casualties of war. In the national sample of 2,428 boys born on 4 March 1946, only twenty-four per cent were circumcised, but the class differential was still highly significant: 38.8 per cent among professional and salaried groups, and 21.9 per cent among manual and unskilled workers.[90] By 1946 the whole business was under sentence of death, precipitately killed off by the end of the Indian Civil Service and by the economies of the National Health Service. Today less than one per cent of the population is circumcised in infancy, and only in the main for religious reasons.[91]

We began the analysis of sexual imperatives and British attitudes by noting that a senior Resident in eighteenth-century Calcutta had himself circumcised in order to promote his sexual relations with Muslim women. Occasionally other British men overseas were reported as being 'converted to Islam', which was sometimes a euphemism for the same thing. It is a symbolic irony that by the twentieth century things had so changed that circumcision was being actively advocated by the imperial authorities for an entirely opposite reason: the promotion of a more effective rule over an empire of Muslims and others. With this observation our brief analysis of the dynamics of Victorian British sexuality, in individuals and in society as a whole, can be regarded as complete. The sharply contrasting situation in the Victorian empire will now be delineated in the next chapter.

Notes

1 R. Porter, *English Society in the Eighteenth Century*, London, 1982, pp. 161-4, 278-82; 'Mixed feelings: the Enlightenment and sexuality in eighteenth-century Britain', in P.- G. Boucé (ed.), *Sexuality in Eighteenth-Century Britain*, Manchester, 1982, pp. 2-21; J. C. Beaglehole (ed.), *The Journals of Capt. James Cook on his Voyages of Discovery*, Cambridge, 1955, I. p. 86.

2 P. J. Kearney, *The Private Case: an Annotated Bibliography of the Erotica Collection in the British (Museum) Library*, London, 1981, pp. 136-42.

3 E. H. Hare, 'Masturbatory insanity: the history of an idea', *Journal of Mental Science*, 108, 1962, 1-25; R. H. MacDonald, 'The frightful consequences of onanism', *Journal of History of Ideas*, XXVIII, 1967, pp. 423-8; G. Barker-Benfield, 'The spermatic economy: a nineteenth-century view of sexuality', in M. Gordon (ed.), *The American Family in Social-Historical Perspective*, New York, 1973; L. DeMause, 'The evolution of childhood', in L. DeMause (ed.), *The History of Childhood*, London, 1976, pp. 1-74; V. Bullough, *Sexual Variance in Society and History*, New York, 1976, pp. 496-9; J. H. Plumb, 'The new world of children in eighteenth-century England', *Past and Present*, 67, 1975, pp. 64-93, esp. pp. 92-3. Tissot, by employing the word *manusturpatione*, focused on 'abuse', whereas *turbare* means 'to agitate'.

4 E. J. Bristow, *Vice and Vigilance: Purity Movements in Britain since 1700*, Dublin, 1977, p. 22 (for Wesley); R. Pearsall, *The Worm in the Bud: the World of Victorian Sexuality*, London, 1969; C. Z. & P. W. Stearns, 'Victorian sexuality: can historians do it better?', *Journal of Social History*, XVIII, 1985. The failure to construct a convincing nineteenth-century chronology is a frequent defect, and one of the major flaws in the work of Lawrence Stone: see 'Sexuality', in *The Past and the Present Revisited*, London, 1987, ch. 19.

5 L. Stone, *Family, Sex and Marriage in England, 1500-1800*, London, 1977, pp. 50, 217, 490-1; J. Weeks, *Sex, Politics and Society; the Regulation of Sexuality since 1800*, London, 1981, p. 30.

6 J. Boswell, *Christianity, Social Tolerance and Homosexuality: Gay People in Western Europe from the Beginning of the Christian Era to the Fourteenth Century*, Chicago, 1980, pp. 92-117, for an argument that the biblical texts may have been misread; but see also P. Ariès & A. Béjin (eds), *Western Sexuality: Practice and Precept in Past and Present*, trans. A Forster, London, 1985; I. Bloch, *Sexual Life in England, Past and Present*, London, [1903] pp. 388-9; Bullough, *Sexual Variance, passim*; A. D. Harvey, 'Prosecutions for sodomy in England at the beginning of the nineteenth century', *Historical Journal*, XXI, 1978.

7 Stone, *Family, Sex and Marriage*, pp. 511-16; Plumb, 'New world of children'. For middle-class aversion to fellatio, see [Ashbee] III, *Catena Librorum Tacendorum*,

London, 1885, p. 458; 'Walter', *My Secret Life*, II, New York, 1966, p. 2149; Michael Ramsey, Archbishop of Canterbury, in *House of Lords Debates, 5th series*, 267, c. 302 (21 June 1965) – 'every whit as disgusting and horrible as sodomy. . .'

8 Foucault, *History of Sexuality*, London, 1978, I, pp. 103-5, 114-18; W. Stekel, *Patterns of Psychosexual Infantilism*, London , 1953; F. S. Caprio, *Variations in Sexual Behaviour: a Psychodynamic Study of Deviations*, New York, 1957; T. S. Szasz, *Manufacture of Madness: a Comparative Study of the Inquisition and the Mental Health Movement*, London, 1971, pp. 170-4, 242-3.

9 F. M. Brodie, *The Devil drives: Life of Sir Richard Burton*, London, 1957, p. 253. (Burton was comparing white wives with Amerindian women in Salt Lake City.)

10 [Ashbee], I, *Index Librorum Prohibitorum*, pp. xxxix-xlvii; T. Gibson, *The 'English Vice': Beating, Sex and Shame*, London, 1978. 'Sympneumata' was the limitation of sexual activity, even in marriage, merely to prolonged mutual masturbation in bed: see P. Henderson, *The Life of Laurence Oliphant*, London, 1956, p. 236; 'karezza' was a variant: prolonged body-contact without orgasm, advocated by Mrs A. B. Stockham and Edward Carpenter (see J. Weeks, *Coming Out*, London, 1977, p. 61).

11 K. Thomas, 'Double standard', *Journal of History of Ideas*, XX, 1959, p. 206; Foucault, *History of Sexuality*, I, p. 121; G. R. Quaife, *Wanton Wenches and Wayward Wives*, London, 1979, p. 177. Equally, working-class sexuality should not be idealised: despite a good deal of premarital latitude, there was little sophistication and plenty of prudery, dirt, inhibition, brutality and inadequacy: see R. Roberts, *The Classic Slum: Salford life in the First Quarter of this century*, London, 1971, pp. 37-40.

12 P. Gay, *The Bourgeois Experience*, I: *Education of the Senses*, London, 1984.

13 S. Chitty, *The Beast and the Monk: a Life of Charles Kingsley*, London, 1974, pp. 76-81. In 1844 Kingsley wrote that the begetting of their first baby was 'the most delicious moment of my life up to that time. Since then, what greater bliss!' Kingsley also had an eye for male beauty: see p. 53 (imagining a butcher's boy in the Resurrection).

14 C. N. Degler, 'What ought to be and what was: women's sexuality in the nineteenth century', *American Historical Review*, 79, 1974; G. J. Barker-Benfield, *The Horrors of the Half-Known Life: Male Attitudes towards Women and Sexuality in Nineteenth-Century America*, New York, 1976; C. E. Rosenberg, 'Sexuality, class and role in nineteenth-century America', *American Quarterly*, XXV, 1973.

15 A. Bray, *Homosexuality in Renaissance England*, London, 1982, p. 79; T. Vanggaard, *Phallós: a Symbol and its History in the Male World*, London, 1972 transl., pp. 175-84.

16 G. J. Renier, *The English: are they Human?*, London, 4th ed., 1956, p. 208; Bullough, *Sexual Variance in Society and History*, p. 576; Roy Porter makes the point well: 'For many English travellers, exotic parts and peoples were realisations of fantasies, sources of sexual or mystical discovery, havens for scoundrels and screwballs, ways of jumping the rails of Western Classical-Christian civilisation': see *History*, 69, 1984, p. 102, review of P. J. Marshall and G. Williams, *The Great Map of Mankind*.

17 M. Beurdeley *et al.*, *The Clouds and the Rain: the Art of Love in China*, Fribourg, 1969, p. 8.

18 N. Gunson, *Messengers of Grace: Evangelical Missionaries in the South Seas, 1797-1860*, Melbourne, 1978, p. 305.

19 G. Schurhammer, *Francis Xavier: his Life and Times*, IV: *Japan and China, 1549-52*, trans. M. J. Costelloe, Rome, 1982, pp. 77, 84-5, 144, 154-5, 160-1; see also C. S. Ford and F. A. Beach, *Patterns of Sexual Behaviour*, London, 1952, 1965, pp. 136-40.

20 G. H. Herdt (ed.), *Ritualised Homosexuality in Melanesia*, California, 1984, p. 210, n. 7. In many parts of Melanesia, the insemination of boys (anally or orally) was held to be essential for their proper growth and maturity.

21 Stekel, *Patterns of Psychosexual Infantilism*, p. 60-1; P. Horn, *Rise and Fall of the Victorian Servant*, London, 1975, pp. 135-6; T. M. McBride, *The Domestic Revolution: Modernisation of Household Service in England and France, 1820-1920*, London, 1976, pp. 100-4; Deveureux, *Vénus in India*, Brussels, 1889, II, p. 31; DeMause (ed.), *History of Childhood*, 1976, pp. 48-9. For knickers, see 'Walter', *My Secret Life*, I, pp. 334, 726.

22 G. N. Ray, *Thackeray: the Uses of Adversity, 1811-46*, London, 1955, p. 452, n. 39.
23 P. Grosskurth (ed.) *The Memoirs of John Addington Symonds*, London, 1984, pp. 94-5; see also J. R. de Honey, *Tom Brown's Universe: Development of the Victorian Public School*, London, 1977, pp. 167-203; J. Chandos, *Boys together: English Public Schools, 1800-64*, London, 1984, pp. 286-339. In the House of Lords debate on the Wolfenden proposals, the Earl of Arran declared that at his public school (Eton) some twenty to thirty boys 'regularly and actively engaged in minor homosexual practices, though it did not last' (*House of Lords Debates, 5th series*, 266, c. 74, 12 May 1965). For twentieth-century literary revelations, see *inter alia*: R. Maugham, *Escape from the Shadows: his Autobiography*, London, 1972, pp. 56-68 (Eton again); J.R. Ackerley, *My Father and Myself*, London, 1971 ed., pp. 70-2 (Rossall); and [Anon.] *Memoirs of a Voluptuary: the Secret Life of an English Boarding School*, 2 vols, London, 1908.
24 Benson Diary, 179, f. 22 (21 March 1925); I. Anstruther, *Oscar Browning: a Biography*, London, 1983, p. 63; K. Rose, *Superior Person: a Portrait of Curzon and his Circle in late-Victorian England*, London, 1969, p. 35; Honey, *Tom Brown's Universe*, p. 190; K. Ballhatchet, *Race, Sex and Class Under the Raj*, London 1980, p. 120. As Viceroy, Curzon viewed all Indian princes as lecherous schoolboys, and discouraged their travelling abroad; he drew up a list of those with homoerotic tastes (*ibid.*, pp. 118-21).
25 C. Hollis, *Eton: a History*, London, 1960, p. 178; *Gentleman's Magazine*, LXVIII, 1798, i, pp. 95, and 383-4.
26 T. Zeldin, *France, 1848-1945*, I: *Ambition, Love and Politics*, Oxford, 1973, pp. 305-9.
27 The classic studies of British prostitution include: M. Ryan, *Prostitution in London, with a Comparative View of that in Paris and New York*, London, 1839; H. Mayhew, *London Labour and the London poor*, IV, London, 1862, pp. 32-269; W. Acton, *Prostitution, considered in its Moral, Social, and Sanitary Aspects*, London, 2nd ed., 1870, 1972 (but see criticisms of Acton, for example, M. J. Peterson, 'Dr Acton's enemy' *Victorian Studies*, XXIX, 1986, p. 569-90); Havelock Ellis, *Studies in the Psychology of Sex*, VI; *Sex in Relation to Society*, Philadelphia, 1910, 1921, ch. 7; A. Flexner, *Prostitution in Europe*, London, 1914; see also K. Nield (ed.), *Prostitution in the Victorian Age: Debates on the Issue from Nineteenth-Century Critical Journals*, London, 1973. The modern reappraisals include: F. Henriques, *Prostitution and Society*, III: *Modern Sexuality*, London, 1968; E. M. Sigsworth and T. J. Wyke, 'A study of Victorian prostitution and venereal disease', in M. Vicinus (ed.), *'Suffer and be still': Women in the Victorian Age*, Bloomington, Ind., 1972, pp. 77-99; E. Trudgill, 'Prostitution and paterfamilias', in H. J. Dyos and M. Wolff (eds), *The Victorian City: Images and Reality*, II, London, 1973; F. Finnegan, *Poverty and Prostitution: a Study of Victorian Prostitutes in York*, Cambridge, 1979; J. R. Walkowitz, *Prostitution and Victorian Society: Women, Class and the State*, London, 1980; A. J. Engel, '"Immoral intentions": University of Oxford and the problem of prostitution, 1827-1914', *Victorian Studies*, XXIII, 1979/80.
28 Sigsworth and Wyke, 'A study of Victorian prostitution', pp. 78-80.
29 Henriques, *Prostitution and Society*, III, pp. 79-80; Mayhew, *London Labour and London Poor*, IV, p. 267; Bloch, *Sexual Life in England*, pp. 102-7; L. Radzinowicz, *A History of English Criminal Law and its Administration since 1750*, II, Cambridge, 1956, pp. 287, 297-301. The Manchester figure was 1,500, and Glasgow 1,800.
30 Walkowitz, *Prostitution and Victorian Society*, pp. 77-8, in a chapter, 'The making of an outcast group: prostitutes and working women in nineteenth-century Plymouth and Southampton', which previously appeared in M. Vicinus, (ed.), *A Widening sphere; Changing Roles of Victorian Women*, Bloomington, Ind., 1977, pp. 72-93; Ellis, *Studies in the Psychology of Sex*, VI, p. 255. For the proportion of servants, see F. B. Smith 'Sexuality in Britain, 1800-1900', *University of Newcastle Historical Journal*, New South Wales, II, 1974, pp. 22; J.L. Newton, M. P. Ryan and J. R. Walkovitz (eds), *Sex and Class in Women's History: Essays from 'Feminist Studies'*, London, 1983, pp. 17-71, and 114-15, (J. R. Gillis, 'Servants, sexual relations and the risks of illegitimacy in London, 1801-1900'); and the next reference.
31 *Select Committee of the House of Lords on the Protection of Young Girls: Report with*

Minutes of Evidence, 1882: C. 344, Accounts & Papers, XIII, reprinted in *Crime and Punishment: Juvenile Offenders*, V, *Sessions 1881-96*, Irish University Press series of British Parliamentary Papers, Shannon, 1970, pp. 487-586.

32 P. Gay, *The Bourgeois Experience*, II: *The Tender Passion*, London, 1986, p. 387. *Select Committee of the House of Lords on the Protection of Young Girls: Report* explained the increase in juvenile prostitution thus: 'a vicious demand for young girls; over – crowding in dwellings, and immorality arising therefrom; want of parental control, and in many cases parental example, profligacy, and immoral treatment; residence, in some cases, in brothels; the example and encouragement of girls slightly older, and the sight of the dress and money, which their immoral habits have enabled them to obtain; the state of the streets in which little girls are allowed to run about, and become accustomed to the sight of open profligacy; and sometimes the contamination with vicious girls in [industrial] schools', p. 490. See also V. and B. Bullough, *Women and Prostitution: a Social History*, New York 1987, pp. 292-307.

33 Bristow, *Vice and Vigilance*, pp. 53, 97; Henriques, *Prostitution and Society*, III, pp. 125, 231. For clandestine marriages, see D. Hudson, *Munby: Man of Two worlds: the Life and Diaries of Arthur J. Munby, 1828-1910*, London, 1972; and Ackerley, *My Father and Myself*.

34 Finnegan, *Poverty and Prostitution*, p. 81; Trudgill, 'Prostitution and paterfamilias', p. 693; Bloch, *Sexual Life in England*, pp. 96-107;Ryan, *Prostitution in London*, pp. 183-7; 'Walter', *My Secret Life*, II, p. 2074; League of Nations, *Report of the Special Body of Experts on the Traffic in Women and Children* (C.52. M.52. 1927. IV), part II, Evidence, p. 89; G. S. Haight, 'Male chastity in the nineteenth century', *Contemporary Review*, 219, 1971, pp. 252-61; Radzinowicz, *History of English Criminal Law*, III, p. 17, n. 13; F.B.Smith, *The People's Health, 1830-1910*, London, 1979, p. 303; PRO, CAB. 128/27/CC(54) 11/12 (24 Feb. 1954.)

35 Acton, *Prostitution*, p. 185; S. and B. Webb, *Prevention of Destitution*, London, 1911, pp. 299, 306; Mayhew, *London Labour and London Poor*, I, 1861, p. 477; T. C. Smout, 'Aspects of sexual behaviour in Scotland', in A. A. MacLaren (ed.), *Social Class in Scotland*, London, 1976, pp. 59-60; Finnegan, *Poverty and Prostitution*, p. 81; Bristow, *Vice and Vigilance*, p. 91; 'Walter' complained that the lower classes all began to copulate at fourteen, and it was very hard for a gentleman to find a virgin (I, p. 1036).

36 Flexner, *Prostitution in Europe*, p. 31; Ryan *Prostitution in London*, pp. 148-50; I. Bloch, *The Sexual Life of our Time in its Relation to Modern Civilisation*, trans. M. E. Paul, London, 1908, pp. 313, 517; [Anon.], *Sins of the Cities of the Plain: or the Recollections of a Mary-Ann*, London, 1881, I, p. 90; P. Coleman, *Christian Attitudes to Homosexuality*, London, 1980, pp. 152-7; [Ashbee], I, *Index*, p. 25, and II, *Centuria Librorum Absconditorum*, London, 1879, p. 414.

37 K. Chesney, *The Victorian Underworld*, London, 1970, ch. 10: 'Prostitution', pp. 327-9; *Crime and Punishment: Juvenile Offenders*, op. cit., note 31 above, V, pp. 83-4, Evidence of C. E. H. Vincent, Director of Criminal Investigations, paras. 646, and 654; H. M. Schueller and R. L. Peters (eds), *The Letters of John Addington Symonds*, Detroit, 1969, III, p. 813, (to E. Carpenter, 5 February 1893); P. Grosskurth, *John Addington Symonds: a Biography*, London, 1964, pp. 98, 178; and *idem* (ed.), *Memoirs of John Addington Symonds*, pp. 254-5.

38 Walkovitz, *Prostitution and Victorian Society*, p. 86 ff; P. M. McHugh, *Prostitution and Victorian Social Reform*, London, 1980; R. T. Shannon, 'Better free than healthy', *Times Literary Supplement*, 25 July 1980, p. 852; F. B. Smith, 'Ethics and disease in the later nineteenth century: the Contagious Diseases Acts', *Historical Studies*, XV, 1971; A. R. Skelley, *The Victorian Army at Home, 1859-99*, London, 1977, pp. 53-8; M. Trustram, '"Distasteful and derogatory"? Examining Victorian soldiers for venereal disease', in the *Sexual Dynamics of History* (London Feminist History Group), 1983, pp. 154-64.

39 Smith, 'Sexuality in Britain', p. 29; Bristow, *Vice and Vigilance*, p. 101 ff; D. Gorham, 'The "Maiden Tribute of Modern Babylon" re-examined: child prostitution and the idea of childhood in late-Victorian England', *Victorian Studies*, XXI, 1977/78; N. Annan, 'The rise of the cult of homosexuality', unpublished paper delivered at the

University of Tampa, Florida, 1974, quoted by kind permission of Lord Annan. Stone, *Family, Sex and Marriage*, p. 680, is, of course, astray in his chronology when he suggests a slowly rising 'permissive tide' among the middle classes beginning in the 1870s, and it is said he intends to correct this in a second edition.

40 Grosskurth, *John Addington Symonds*, p. 283.
41 Chesney, *Victorian Underworld*, p. 364.
42 F. B. Smith, 'Labouchère's Amendment to the Criminal Law Amendment Bill', *Historical Studies*, XVII, 1976; Coleman, *Christian Attitudes to Homosexuality*, p. 140-4; Weeks, *Sex, Politics and Society*, p. 85.
43 *Pall Mall Gazette*, XLV, 21 May 1887; B. Scott, *A State Iniquity*, London, 1890, p. 23; E. B. van Heyningen, 'The social evil in the Cape Colony, 1868-1902: prostitution and the CD Acts', *Journal of Southern African Studies*, X, 1984.
44 D. J. Pivar, *Purity Crusade, Sexual Morality and Social Control, 1868-1900* [in America], Westport, Conn., 1973, pp. 104, 141-3; League of Nations, *Advisory Commission for the Protection and Welfare of Children and Young People: Age of Marriage and Consent* (C.P.E. 90/1, 1927); Gorham, 'The "Maiden Tribute of Modern Babylon" re-examined', pp. 353-79.
45 M. R. D. Foot (ed.), *The Gladstone Diaries*, I, *1825-32*, London, 1968, pp. xl, 269, 285, 351; as a teenager in the 1830s 'Walter' was also worried about it: *My Secret Life*, I, p. 55. The best historical study of attitudes to masturbation is Hare, 'Masturbatory insanity'; see also R. A. Spitz, 'Authority and masturbation', *Psychoanalytic Quarterly*, XXI, 1952; R. H. MacDonald, 'The frightful consequences of onanism: notes on the history of a delusion', *Journal of History of Ideas*, XXVIII, 1967, 423-41; Szasz, *Manufacture of Madness*, pp. 180-206; R. P. Neuman, 'Masturbation, madness and modern concepts for childhood and adolescence', *Journal of Social History*, VIII, 1975.
46 Smith, 'Sexuality in Britain', pp. 28-9; A. N. Gilbert, 'Masturbation and insanity: Henry Maudsley and the ideology of sexual repression', *Albion*, XII, 1980; W. Acton, *Functions and Disorders of the Reproductive Organs*, London, 1857, p. 61; Honey, *Tom Brown's Universe*, pp. 167-70; Bristow, *Vice and Vigilance*, pp. 132-3.
47 D. Newsome, *A History of Wellington College, 1859-1959*, London, 1959, pp. 166-70; Anstruther, *Oscar Browning*, pp. 5-6; see also S. P. B. Mais, *A Schoolmaster's Diary*, London, 1918, pp. 152-3, (re 1911); Honey, *Tom Brown's Universe*, pp 167-213. For Mrs Warre-Cornish's remark, see W. Blunt, *Married to a Single Life: an Autobiography*, I: *1901-38*, Salisbury, Wilts, 1983, p. 78.
48 E. L. Gilbert (ed.), *'O Beloved Kids': Rudyard Kipling's Letters to his Children*, London, 1983, p. 127.
49 Weeks, *Sex, Politics and Society*, p. 96 ff; Idem, *Coming Out*, pp. 1-44; R. Jenkyns, *Victorians and Ancient Greece*, London, 1980, pp. 280-93. A Bray, *Homosexuality in Renaissance England*, London, 1982, pp. 135-7, unsuccessfully challenges Weeks on the crucial role he assigns to the nineteenth-century 'construction' of homosexuality.
50 The homosexual community surfaced in the 1960s with a visibility too high for its own good, dangerously opting for a separate, isolated group identity, with too great a willingness to be socially defined by its sexual lifestyle. All this – however understandable in terms of its previous experience of repression – led to inevitable obloquy when the portentous AIDS global pandemic erupted in the 1980s. G. L. Mosse, *Nationalism and Sexuality: Respectability and Abnormal Sexuality in Modern Europe*, New York, 1985, argues that 'homosexuality' was hated as 'the antithesis of bourgeois respectability'.
51 Weeks, *Coming Out*, p. 21; Bloch, *Sexual Life in England*, p. 491; Benson Diary, 86, f. 14 (September 1906).
52 H. M. Hyde, *The Cleveland Street Scandal*, London, 1976; idem, *Oscar Wilde: a Biography*, London, 1976; R. Ellmann, *Oscar Wilde*, London, 1987, pp. 366-68, 411-49.
53 Bristow, *Vice and Vigilance*, pp. 154-6; M. Gilbert, *Churchill's Political Philosophy*, London, 1981, p. 1; R. D. Storch, 'Police control of street prostitution in Victorian London', in D. H. Bayley (ed.) *Police and Society*, London, 1977, pp. 49-72; idem, 'Crime and justice in nineteenth-century England', *History Today*, XXX, 1980, pp. 32-7.

54 Bristow, *Vice and Vigilance*, pp. 44, 213-18; N. St John-Stevas, *Obscenity and the Law*, London, 1956, pp. 79-87. See also B. Williams (ed.), *Obscenity and Film Censorship: an Abridgement of the Williams Report*, Cambridge, 1981; A. W. B. Simpson, *Pornography and Politics; a Look Back to the Williams Committee*, London, 1983, pp. 3-8. With the attempts to define and discuss pornography, the rhetoric of denunciation practised by the literati reaches unparalleled heights of comic absurdity. Andrea Dworkin writes: pornography 'means the graphic depiction of women as vile whores ... pornography *is* violence against women, violence which pervades and distorts every aspect of culture' (*Pornography: Men possessing Women*, London, 1981). D. Holbrook (ed.), *The Case against Pornography*, London, 1972, presents it as enslaving, impoverishing, blocking normal love, 'the stealer of dreams', 'invader of privacy', even as 'the ultimate absurdity'; but out of twenty contributors to this volume, only George Steiner displays any real knowledge of and thoughtfulness about the subject, and he comes to a far less humourless and hysterical conclusion than the others.

55 V. Bailey and S. Blackburn, 'The Punishment of Incest Act, 1908: a case study in law creation', *Criminal Law Review*, 1979, pp. 708-28; A. S. Wohl, 'Sex and the single room: incest among the Victorian working classes', in *The Victorian Family: Structure and Stresses*, London, 1978, pp. 197-216.

56 A. Grimble, *Return to the Islands*, London, 1957, p. 106. The incest taboo is strongest against parent-child relations, and psychoanalysts today are inclined to eliminate sibling relations from the concept of incest: see D. Meltzer, *Sexual States of Mind*, Perthshire, 1973, p. 151.

57 W. Plomer (ed.), *Kilvert's Diary: Selections from the Diary of the Rev. Francis Kilvert, 1870-9*, London, 1960, II, pp. 262-6, 358; and III, pp. 37-8, 208; 'Walter', *My Secret Life*, I, p. 29.; S. M. Ellis (ed.), *The Letters and Memoirs of Sir William Hardman*, London, 1925, pp. 80-1; J. Anderson and E. Swinglehurst, *Victorian and Edwardian Seaside*, London, 1952, pp. 70-3; M. Hiley, *Frank Sutcliffe: Photographer of Whitby*, London, 1974; T. d'Arch Smith, *Love in Earnest: Some Notes on the Lives and Writings of English 'Uranian' Poets from 1889 to 1930*, London, 1970; p. 157, n. 44.

58 G. Raverat, *Period Piece: a Cambridge Childhood*, London, 1952, pp. 109-10; Cambridgeshire County Record Office, Town Council Commons Committee Minutes (6 July 1894, 7 May 1897, 11 November 1910) – I am grateful to the County Archivist, Michael Farrar, for locating these references for me.

59 L. S. E., British Library of Political and Economic Science, Archives, Hugh Dalton Papers, I/14/34 (Diary 1931), quoted by kind permission of the Librarian.

60 Weeks, *Sex, Politics and Society*, p. 23; J. Parr, *Labouring Children: British Immigrant Apprentices to Canada, 1869-1924*, London, 1980, p. 104; there were also complaints by Welsh landladies about evacuated children in the Second World War: see T. E. B. Howarth, *Prospect and Reality, 1945-55*, London, 1985.

61 R. Skidelsky, *John Maynard Keynes*, London, 1983, I, pp. xvii, 87, 109, 120-9, 301; Dalton Papers, I/14/39 (Diary, 17 August 1931), quoted by B. Pimlott, *Hugh Dalton*, London, 1985, p. 198, and I/I/4 (Diary, 24 January 1916), quoted *ibid.*, p. 89. Frank Richards, *Old-Soldier Sahib*, London, 1936, p. 309, says he was told by a police detective that increasing the penalties for homosexual conduct had only stimulated interest in it as an interesting novelty and thus led to its being more widely practised than ever before.

62 J. Richards, '"Passing the love of women": manly love and Victorian society', in J. A. Mangan and J. Walvin (eds.), *Manliness and morality: Middle-Class Masculinity in Britain and America, 1800-1940*, Manchester, 1987, p. 117; d'Arch Smith, *Love in Earnest: Some Notes on the lives and Writings of English 'Uranian' Poets from 1889 to 1930*, London, 1970. B. Taylor, 'Motives for guilt-free pederasty: some literary considerations', *Sociological Review*, XXIV, 1976; for Canon Eyton see *Crockford's Clerical Directory*, 37, London, 1905, and read between the lines.

63 Dean Inge Diary, 34, 29 January 1934: twenty-five years ago, said Archbishop C. G. Lang, clerical delinquency was almost always either debt or drink or women, but now misconduct with boys outnumbered all these three together.

64 Blunt, *Married to a Single Life*, I, esp. pp. 191, 269-70.

65 Honey, *Tom Brown's Universe*, pp. 182-93; R. Jenkyns, *The Victorians and Ancient Greece*, Oxford, 1980, 'Matters of morality', pp. 280-93; S. Paget (ed.), *Henry Scott Holland: Memoir and Letters*, London, 1921, pp. 36, 43, 94-6; Richards, op. cit., note 62 above, pp. 92-122.

66 E. Thompson, *The Life of Charles, Lord Metcalfe*, London, 1937, pp. 21, 101-2, 179.

67 N. Vance, *The Sinews of the Spirit: the Ideal of Christian Manliness in Victorian Literature and Religious Thought*, Cambridge, 1985; 'The ideal of manliness' in B. Simon and I. Bradley (eds.), *The Victorian Public School: Studies in the Development of an Educational Institution*, London, 1975, pp. 115-28.

68 D. Newsome, *Godliness and Good Learning: Four Studies on a Victorian Ideal*, London, 1961, p. 216. For the growth of the public schools, see T. W. Bamford, *Rise of the Public Schools: a Study of Boys' Public Boarding Schools in England and Wales since 1837*, London, 1966; and R. Wilkinson, *The Prefects: British Leadership and the Public School Tradition*, Oxford, 1964.

69 J. A. Mangan, *Athleticism in the Victorian and Edwardian Public School: the Emergence and Consolidation of an Educational Ideology*, Cambridge, 1981; *idem*, *Games Ethic and Imperialism: Aspects of the Diffusion of an Ideal*, London, 1986. See also S. Collini, 'The idea of "character" in Victorian political thought', *Transactions of the Royal Historical Society*, 5th series, 35, 1985, pp. 45-9. Lord Cromer wanted to recruit for Egyptian and Sudanese administration young men educated in 'school spirit': 'a lad in whom the sense of individual effort and personal responsibility has been fostered naturally becomes *capax imperii*. In the free atmosphere in which his boyhood is passed, he learns a number of lessons which stands him in good stead in after life as one of an imperial race', quoted in M. W. Daly, *Empire on the Nile: the Anglo-Egyptian Sudan, 1898-1934*, Cambridge, 1986, p. 85.

70 Mangan, *Games Ethic*, pp. 34-5; A. Grimble, *A Pattern of Islands*, London, 1952, p. 52, for the efficacy of cricket.

71 R. S. S. Baden-Powell, *Scouting for Boys: a Handbook for Instruction in Good Citizenship*, London, 1908, pp. 309-15; J. Springhall, 'Baden-Powell and the Scout movement before 1920: citizen training or soldiers of the future?', and A. Summers, 'Scouts, Guides, and VADs: a note in reply to Allen Warren', *English Historical Review*, CII, 1987, pp. 934-47: these articles effectively refute A. Warren, 'Sir R. Baden-Powell, the Scout movement and citizen training in Great Britain, 1900-20', *ibid.*, CI, 1986; see also J. Springhall, *Youth, Empire and Society: British Youth Movements, 1883-1940*, London, 1977.

72 J. M. MacKenzie, 'The imperial pioneer and hunter and the British masculine stereotype in late Victorian and Edwardian times', in Mangan and Walvin (eds), *Manliness and Morality*, pp. 177-8, formulates 'something approaching a cultural frontier thesis for British attitudes to masculinity', in which the feedback from frontier into scouting is of particular importance. See also J. M. MacKenzie,, *Propaganda and Empire: the Manipulation of British Public Opinion, 1880-1960*, Manchester, 1984, pp. 243-47.

73 B. B. Gilbert, *The Evolution of National Insurance in Great Britain: the Origins of the Welfare State*, London, 1966, pp. 61-93, 121; Baden-Powell, *Scouting for Boys*, 208-9.

74 A. Davin, 'Imperialism and motherhood', *History Workshop Journal*, V, 1978, pp. 9-65, esp. pp. 11, 43-9; Weeks, *Sex, Politics and Society*, pp. 122-37; P. B. Rich, *Race and Empire in British Politics*, Cambridge, 1986, pp. 68-9.

75 R. R. James, *Rosebery: a Biography of the 5th Earl of Rosebery*, London, 1963, pp. 419-20; R. Hyam, 'Winston Churchill before 1914', *Historical Journal*, XII, 1969, pp. 168-9; G. R. Searle, *The Quest for National Efficiency: a Study of British Politics and Political Thought, 1895-1914*, London, 1971, p. 225; J. Springhall, *Coming of Age: Adolescence in Britain, 1860-1960*, Dublin, 1986, pp. 45-6.

76 R. Burton, *Love, War and Fancy: the Customs and Manners of the East from the Writings on 'The Arabian Nights'*, ed. K. Walker, London, 1964, p. 106; J. F. C. Harrison, *The Second Coming: Popular Millenarianism, 1780-1850*, London, 1979, pp. 140-3: John Wroe (1782-1863), a sub-Southcottian false prophet, underwent public circumcision in Yorkshire in 1824 and tried to make it part of his severely ascetic

programme for his followers.

77 D. Steinberg, *Sexuality of Christ in Renaissance Art*, 1984, appendix. Paintings of the Circumcision itself, of course, depict only the preparatory moment.

78 L. Crompton, *Byron and Greek love: Homophobia in Nineteenth-Century England*, California, 1985, p. 143.

79 'Walter', *My Secret Life*, I, p. 15, 27-9, 35, 43, 958-9; and II, pp. 2133, 2143-9.

80 [Anon.], *Memoirs of a Voluptuary*, London, 1908, II, p. 56; *The Pearl*, III (The Oyster), p. 176.

81 P. C. Remondino, *History of Circumcision*, popular ed., Philadelphia, 1891, p. 186; *British Medical Journal*, 1892, I, pp. 391-2. There is nothing to suggest that Bulwer Lytton in 1871 conceived his *Vril-ya*, the coming master-race, to be circumcised, despite Remondino's speculation (*The Coming Race*, London, 1871).

82 J. Hutchinson, *Archives of Surgery*, London, II, 1891, pp. 15, 267-9; and IV, 1893, no. clxi.

83 *British Medical Journal*, 1891, I, pp. 860, 1078; 1894, I, pp. 1034-4; 1895, I, pp. 291-2; 1899, II, pp. 84-5; 1903, II, p. 448; *Lancet*, 1891, I, p. 1386; Smith, *The People's Health*, pp. 298-9.

84 *British Medical Journal*, 1901, II, pp. 939, 1023-4; 1902, II, pp. 271-2; 1907, I, pp. 1409-12; *Lancet*, 1907, I, p. 593.

85 *British Medical Journal*, 1901, II, pp. 939, 1023-4; Davin, 'Imperialism and motherhood', pp. 14-18; J. M. Winter, *The Great War and the British People*, London, 1986, pp. 15-16. The British royal family employed a Jewish *mohel* as late as the end of 1948.

86 *British Medical Journal*, 1899 II, pp; 84-5; 1965, II/i, p. 419; I. Bloch, *The Sexual Life of Our Time in its Relation to Modern Civilisation*, trans. M. Eden Paul, London, 1908, p. 376; A. Edwardes, *The Rape of India: a Biography of Robert Clive and a Sexual History of the Conquest of Hindustan*, New York, 1966, pp. 16-21, 299.

87 Barker-Benfield, 'The spermatic economy', op. cit., note 3 above, p. 369, n. 121. A major American textbook on paediatrics, L. E. Holt, *Diseases of Infancy and Childhood*, New York, 1897, 11th ed, 1940, recommended circumcision 'because of the moral effect'. Already by the end of the 1890s an equation was being made in America between 'uncircumcised' and 'uncivilised': see S. C. Miller, *'Benevolent Assimilation': the American Conquest of the Philippines, 1899-1903*, Yale, NH, 1982, p. 75.

88 V. W. Turner, *Essays on the Ritual of Social Relations*, ed. M. Gluckman, London, 1962, p. 173; K. E. and J. Paige, *The Politics of Reproductive Ritual*, California, 1981, pp. 9-18, 122-5, 148-54, 263-7; Maurice Bloch, *From Blessing to Violence: History and Ideology in the Circumcision Ritual of the Merina of Madagascar*, Cambridge, 1986.

89 A further suggestion has been canvassed: that circumcision was a reaction to a 'general erosion of male supremacy at the turn of the century'. Some early feminists specifically advocated a 'sex-strike' on the Lysistrata model, as part of a 'mass campaign by women to control and set limits to male sexual behaviour'; see L. Coveney *et al*, *the Sexuality Papers: Male Sexuality and the Social Control of Women*, London, 1984, ch. I and p. 50; S. Jeffreys in *The Sexual Dynamics of History*, pp. 179-80. This is connected expressly to circumcision by Barker-Benfield, *Horrors of the Half-Known Life*, p. 189; but, of course, an American explanation will need more than the Indian and Jewish factors which seem sufficient in the British case.

90 D. Gairdner, 'The fate of the foreskin: a study of circumcision', *British Medical Journal*, 1949, II, pp. 1433-7; D. MacCarthy, J. W. B. Douglas and C. Mogford, 'Circumcision in a natural sample of four-year-old children', *ibid*, 1952 (4 October); T. E. Osmond, 'Is routine circumcision advisable?', *Journal of Royal Army Medical Corps*, 99, 1953, p. 254.

91 J. P. Blandy, 'Circumcision', *British Journal of Hospital Medicine*, 1968, pp. 551-3; this article reflects the post-imperial orthodoxy, discouraging infant circumcision as unnecessary and potentially dangerous. The British anti-prepucial prejudice thus lasted for barely two generations. Circumcision lingered much longer in America, where it was estimated that at the beginning of the 1970s more than ninety per cent of Americans were circumcised at birth, and eighty per cent if Canadians were included: see R. Chartham, *Advice to Men*, London, 1971, p. 98. B. Spock, *Baby and*

Child Care continued to recommend it until the late 1960s (pp. 154-5). It is a curious fact that outside the traditional circumcising communities (Jewish, Muslim, Melanesian, Amerindian and some African) the only Westerners to adopt it as a common practice were the English-speaking peoples.

D

CHAPTER FOUR

Empire and sexual opportunity

Empire of the senses

What men call gallantry, and gods adultery,
Is much more common where the climate's sultry . . .
Love rules the camp, the court, the grove – for love
Is heaven, and heaven is love. [Byron, *Don Juan*]

Since recent research has indicated that the amount and range of sexual
opportunity available in Britain, at least before the Purity Campaign of
the 1880s, was greater than has hitherto been supposed, it probably
follows that many young Victorians going overseas expected to indulge
in casual sex as a routine ingredient of life. Moreover, empire unques-
tionably gave them an enlarged field of opportunity. Greater space and
privacy were often available; inhibitions relaxed. European standards
might be held irrelevant. Abstinence was represented as unhealthy in a
hot climate. Boredom could constitute an irresistible imperative. The
Indian army conveniently arranged for prostitutes. Local girls would
offer themselves; or boys, especially in Ceylon.[1] The white man's status
put him in a strong position to get his way. As Bucknill reported to the
government in 1906, 'of course the lascivious-minded man of European
race can always, in any part of the world, find means of gratifying his
wishes'.[2] The expatriate was, in fact, *more* likely to resort to prostitution
overseas simply because the non-European prostitute was often a much
more attractive proposition than her British counterpart. The best Asian
prostitutes were amusingly playful hostesses. By contrast, British whores
were invariably nasty, dirty and coarse, drawn from deprived backgrounds. In India and Japan, prostitution was a more honourable estate,
and not furtively conducted. Asian prostitutes were likely to be higher
up the social scale, educated and with a proper training for their art.
Captain Edward Sellon, writing of India in the years 1834 to 1844,
praised the cleanliness, the sumptuous dress, the temperance, the
ability to sing and entertain that he had encountered in high-caste Indian
courtesans:

I now commenced a regular course of fucking with native women. They understand in perfection all the arts and wiles of love, are capable of gratifying any tastes, and in face and figure they are unsurpassed by any women in the world. . . It is impossible to describe the enjoyment I experienced in the arms of these syrens. I have had English, French, German and Polish women of all grades of society since, but never, never did they bear a comparison with those salacious, succulent houris of the far [sic] East.[3]

Similarly, in an address to the Anthropological Society of London in the late 1860s, Dr J. Shortt declared the dancing-girls of South India attractive enough to 'meet the admiration of the greatest *connoisseur*'. A generation later, an army officer told Havelock Ellis that he had known perhaps sixty prostitutes, of whom the Japanese were easily the best: clean, charming, beautiful and taking an intelligent interest.[4]

The easy opportunities, the separation from family ties and moral pressures, the fact that syphilis was rife in foreign parts and the knowledge that diagnosis and treatment of venereal disease could be readily concealed from loved ones, make it hardly surprising that venereal disease was always more of a problem abroad than at home, and that the differential between venereal disease rates in the services at home and abroad reflected a more intensive and risky resort to prostitutes overseas, even at a relatively late date. The quinquennial figures for 1921-26 show that the incidence of venereal disease in the army at home was forty per thousand. In Egypt it was 103 per thousand, in Malta 105, in India 110, in Ceylon 184, in South China 169 and in North China 333 per thousand. For the navy (1928 figures) the incidence was eighty-two per thousand at home; for Africa, the Mediterranean and West Indian stations it was 156, for India and Ceylon 204, and for the China station 304. The places of highest risk to the sailor were Shanghai, Yokohama and Singapore, where the combination of numerous multi-racial brothels and lack of alternative entertainment in port proved lethal.[5] Of course, not all venereal disease among sailors was spread by female harlots: it was also acquired *inter se*, so to speak. Churchill's description of the navy as founded upon 'Nelson, rum, buggery and the lash' was not just a good phrase. And evidence from the quarterdeck in the 1790s suggests that only *indiscriminate* mutual masturbation was frowned upon among cadets. Nevertheless, encounters with Muslims tended to the carrying of things further.[6]

Running the Victorian empire would probably have been intolerable without resort to sexual relaxation. The historian has to remember the *misery* of empire: the heat and the dust, the incessant rain and monotonous food, the inertia and the loneliness, the lack of amusement and intellectual stimulus. There were no cars, no radios, sometimes not even enough white neighbours to make up a proper game of tennis or bridge. Sir Robert Hart, running the Chinese customs administration, separated from his wife for years on end, felt this isolation acutely: 'I am utterly *alone* and have not a single *friend* or *confidant* – man, woman or child. . . there are *spasms of loneliness* which hit hard.' Before his marriage he had had a Chinese mistress, who bore him three children.[7] Speaking for European administrators in Malaya, Richard Winstedt (schools inspector and Director of Education, 1916) reflected that it was hardly any surprise that the white exile in the out-stations took to himself 'one of the complaisant, amusing, good-tempered and good-mannered daughters of the East'. Those who did not do so tended to get mental troubles. In thirty-two years in Malaya, he personally knew fourteen Europeans who shot themselves: all had been of sound mind when they went out.[8] As far as Africa was concerned, Joyce Cary wrote as a district officer in Nigeria in 1917 that he could perfectly well appreciate why his French counterparts took local mistresses, and could equally understand 'the queer cases out here of fellows drinking themselves to death, or getting homicidal mania, or breaking down nervously into neurotic wrecks in the back-bush by themselves'. When Cary wrote this he had already had four months without conversing with another white person, but, being newly married (though unaccompanied by his wife) and a keen reader, he reckoned he knew how to guard against nerves, drink and idleness.[9] Language barriers and other cultural impediments to relationships sometimes led Europeans into sexual intimacy with non-Europeans almost as an act of baffled despair. E. M. Forster wrote in 1921 (in a sexual confession only recently published) that an Indian youth he was having intercourse with was a 'goose': 'what relation beyond carnality could one establish with such people?'[10]

It could well be thought that empire exercised a corrupting influence. It certainly unfroze restraint, and produced some imaginative feedback. It can hardly be an accident that all the classics of British erotic literature were written by men who were widely travelled inside and especially outside Europe. John Cleland, the author of *Fanny Hill, or the Memoirs of a Woman of Pleasure* (1748-49), had been a consul at Smyrna and spent thirteen years in the legal department of the East India Company at Bombay, becoming well versed in oriental ways and thought.[11] The anonymous but identified author of the *Romance of Lust* (4 vols, 1873-76) knew India and Japan well, and died in India in 1879. 'Walter' of *My Secret Life* had been to every country in Europe, together with visits to Russia, America (where he certainly had sex with Amerindian women), Egypt and possibly Lebanon. Among the writers of the major unpublished erotica, Captain Searight had saturation experience as an Indian Army officer, and Sir Edmund Backhouse was a professor in Peking.

H. S. Ashbee, erotic bibliographer extraordinary, had travelled in India, China, Japan, Egypt, Tunis and America.[12] 'Imperial' settings enabled writers to treat love and marriage much more frankly than would otherwise have been possible. Hence the instructive contrast between the experience of Kipling and Hardy. *Plain Tales from the Hills* (1888) was readily accepted despite 'strong' themes, while *Jude the Obscure* (1895) was burned by the Bishop of Wakefield and banned by W. H. Smith's.[13]

To return to the main line of argument, there seems every reason to take seriously the allegations of the anonymous contributor to the *Pall Mall Gazette* in 1887 who argued that empire was inconsistent with morality. He suggested that about 500,000 people 'maintained' British relations with the empire: servicemen, officials, travellers, clerks. They were usually unaccompanied by women, and the great majority (basically as a consequence of deferred marriage) fell to the 'level of the immoral heathen', forming 'immoral relations with natives', coming to regard English morality as a local English institution, to be left behind 'along with Crosse & Blackwell's pickles or Keen's mustard, the corresponding substitutes abroad being better adapted to local conditions'. He complained that these servants of empire could cap the Sermon on the Mount with quotations from the 'Kama Shastra', and were beginning to think 'like Burton and his appalling footnotes'. Alternatively some, out of duty, controlled themselves on posting, and then spent furloughs of uninterrupted debauchery in London, where they were not under observation. 'The empire was a Moloch, created by men not of a moral class' (he instanced Wellesley, Wellington, Nelson, Palmerston and, surprisingly, Dalhousie); 'Purity' was to them an invention of Arnold of Rugby (actually it was not), and a sickly plant. At every turn he saw 'the necessity, the universality, and the eternity of sexual vice assumed as the basis of action and legislation'. The result was the creation of a heathen, ribald sensual class of Britons absolutely unbound by convention. The editor could offer little by way of disagreement on this subject of 'deep and painful interest', merely observing that incontinence, like bloodshed, was perhaps now tending to diminish in the empire; and anyway, strictly speaking, the evils were due to trade rather than empire (a false distinction, as we now know), because only a quarter of the half-million were 'State-employed'.[14]

Let us now look at sexual opportunity in some different types of imperial situation, both formal and informal, in an attempt to see how sexual interaction underpinned the operative structures of British expansion. But, first, a preliminary observation.

In many ways what happened in the empire was an extension of what had been pioneered in the Mediterranean. Byron's first trip to Greece was deliberately undertaken to get some pederastic experience, which he and his undergraduate friends had often talked about at Trinity College, Cambridge. His second trip may have been necessitated by an actual indiscretion. Byron's eroticism was nothing if not erudite. His letters home from Greece and Turkey in 1807-10 to a sympathetic friend referred to 'plen. & optabil. coit.', later abbreviated to 'pl & opt c' ('plenum et optabilem coitum' was the expression Eumolpus used in the *Satyricon*). Eventually Byron became tired of it, 'the last thing I could be tired of'. In Smyrna he regularly frequented the Turkish baths, which he described as 'marble palace[s] of sherbet and sodomy'.[15] Later travellers in search of sex fastened upon Naples, Capri and Sicily. Capri was traditionally renowned for an open sexual permissiveness and the complaisancy of its beautiful women and boys. Particularly after the laws relating to male sexuality diverged so dramatically in Britain and Italy at the end of the nineteenth century, and after the Oscar Wilde trials, in the next ten years a steady flow of British literati found it a congenial haven: Somerset Maugham and E. F. Benson, Lord Alfred Douglas and Norman Douglas. Capri also attracted notorious Euro-pederasts such as Fritz Krupp, the German industrialist, and Baron Fersen, his French equivalent. In Sicily pilgrimages were made to Baron von Gloeden, who photographed three generations of nude Sicilian boys, and could show pictures of several sets of grandfathers, fathers and sons all at the age of fifteen.[16]

Plantations, trading posts and mining compounds

Many are the men, of every rank, quality, and degree, who would much rather riot in these goatish embraces [with Negro women], than share the pure and lawful bliss derived from matrimonial, mutual love. [Edward Long, *History of Jamaica*, 1774]

Plantations. According to Edward Long, British men were all too prone to make unions with black women in the West Indies, not from any shortage of white women (although there were twice as many white men as white women in eighteenth-century Jamaica), nor even from the supposed burdens and expenses of marriage, but from the sexual attrac-tiveness of black flesh. He hinted – and he was not alone – that the judgement of many planters was swayed by their concubines. There is some corroboration for these views, though they are not necessarily typical, or even, as far as preference goes, correct. In the eighteenth century, the West Indies do seem to have been a kind of sexual paradise for young European men: it was almost customary for white men of every social rank (but especially of the lower classes) to sleep with black women. Coloured mistresses were kept openly, and the practice was integral to West Indian life. Informal liaisons were common even for married proprietors and their teenage sons. It was not considered reprehensible for a young white to begin his sex life by seducing a slave woman. Samuel Taylor, the richest early-Victorian planter in Jamaica, had several estates – with a family on each. According to Green, 'sexual licence was among the most distinctive characteristics of British Caribbean society'.[17]

Whatever the theoretical objections to the work of Gilberto Freyre on Brazilian slavery, there has been ample support for his general dictum that 'there is no slavery without sexual depravity'. On all plantations, whether worked by slaves or indentured labourers (but especially the former), there was obvious sexual exploitation. [18] Women were likely to be victims of the system. According to Jordan, the sexual leitmotiv of race relations on plantations was emphasised and sustained by a simple fact of everyday life: the slaves were in fact semi-nude, a circumstance which strengthened the sexual undertones in daily contact. It was common practice in the American South for boys of up to fourteen or fifteen years to wait at dinner clad only in a shirt which did not always cover what were optimistically called their 'private parts'.[19] (There were similar reports from South Africa c. 1800.) A study of the Arab plantations of Zanzibar concludes that 'sexual subordination was often an important dimension of slavery', while miscegenation was 'normal and accepted'.[20] The Dutch East India Company in South Africa had a slave lodge at Cape Town which was the leading brothel of the area and highly visible: 'slavery, poverty and prostitution were largely synonymous'.[21] Some other writers, notably Genovese, while not questioning the exploitation that went on, warn against viewing plantations as harems. He argues that the blacks could and did resist, and some women practised steady concubinage with whites, valuing it as conferring status and advantages on their offspring (though this did not extend to manumission in South Africa). In 1860 perhaps only 20 per cent or less of the Afro-American population had white blood, though the proportion became much higher thereafter.[22]

Abolitionists certainly exaggerated the situation, but a clear libidinous pattern is inherent in slavery everywhere. The stark fact was that a slave-master had absolute rights over his slaves and could appropriate his sexual assets. Slaves had no unequivocal right except to be alive. In Brazilian courts it was often successfully argued that in general 'masters cannot commit crimes against their slaves'. Even a slave-holder who was a known molester of young black girls could not be punished: H. F. Pontes was acquitted for raping a twelve-year-old in 1883, and an appeal court decided in his favour in 1884. In short, rape was legal while slavery existed. Even at best, the female slave had little control over her sex life, though often masters did see the sense of acknowledging the validity of slave marriages.[23]

Many of slavery's objectionable features have been shown to resurface in indentured labour systems from India and the Pacific Islands in the nineteenth century – a 'new system of slavery' for men and of prostitution for women. The women accompanying Indian labourers were not uniformly of low character; the number of prostitutes among them has been exaggerated, but indentured life made them less 'moral'. On the tea and sugar plantations of Assam and Ceylon, Mauritius and Fiji, Guiana and Trinidad, many planters exercised a droit de seigneur, though there were also some long-term relationships. A serious strike occurred on a Guiana plantation in 1904 because the manager and his overseers were having 'immoral relations' with the women. At the same time on another estate belonging to the same company, there was much resentment over the manager's allowing one of his overseers to live openly with the Creole wife of an estate coolie. The government were embarrassed at the publicity but took no decisive action. From Fiji in 1913 it was reported that the morality of an estate compared unfavourably with that of an Indian village.[24] In Fiji, the Government of India stipulated that there should be forty females to every hundred males emigrating. But the law did *not* stipulate the maintenance of this proportion on the plantations, and imbalance led to serious problems. A wife was difficult to get, harder to keep, and Indians were reluctant to marry non-Indians. Murders were sometimes on account of 'sexual jealousy' (the official term) – most of the victims were women. Between 1890 and 1919 twenty-eight indentured men and sixty-eight indentured women were murdered in Fiji. In Mauritius, the stipulated proportion was thirty-three women to a hundred men. There was sex exploitation by planters, overseers and sirdars. In 1865 thirteen members of a plantation gang killed their master because of 'jealousy or other kindred feelings in regard to women'. On all plantations, suicide was a common form of protest against the traumas of the system, of which sexual abuse was a symptom.[25]

Indian leaders were convinced that the indenture system condemned their women to prostitution, and this was a major reason why they objected to it. Some Melanesian contract labourers told their anthropologist that they had been passive partners to white plantation overseers.[26] In 1914 Tamils went on strike in Malaya, demanding, among other things, an end to the molestation of female labourers. In Ceylon, many nineteenth-century writers referred to young girls being offered to planters by villagers, but in the 1870s it was noted that unions with Tamil or Sinhalese women were not as frequent as formerly. Edward

Carpenter recorded that in Ceylon he met a tea planter from Assam who was walking out hand-in-hand with boys and youths in Kandy. Planters, Carpenter observed, found their isolated lives very dreary, and it was not correct for them to associate too closely with their own employees (domestic servants were a different matter, however); but 'Ajax' wrote to him from Assam that he got very fond of his coolies and was 'quite attached to some'.[27]

Frontier trading posts also articulated regular patterns of sexual interaction, whether under the Royal African Company in the eighteenth century, or the East India Company in India and on the China coast to the 1830s, where recruits were contractually prevented from marrying during their first five-year term.[28]

The classic case, however, was that of the Hudson's Bay Company. The Canadian fur trade produced a large-scale, long-persisting experience of honourable and recognised interracial marriage *à la façon du pays*. It was taken seriously and brought happiness to both sides. Indians were accustomed to establish friendship bonds with strangers by the loan of women. Almost all Indian societies practised this 'sexual hospitality', and none of them understood celibacy. These marriages were within the context of the Indian moral code, which sanctioned such liaisons provided only that they were based on consent and not secrecy. From the European point of view, as Richard White put it in 1749, 'the Indians were a sensible people, and agreed their women should be made use of'.[29] The pleasures of family life did much to reconcile Europeans to isolation and monotony. The women were important functionaries in the fur trade, as intermediaries, interpreters and preparers of pelts. They had vital skills in making snowshoes and drying skins, preserving food and snaring small game. They were guides and negotiators. Such marriage was also a 'cheap form of scalp insurance', as well as giving access to Indian society. The unions were more Indian than European in form. Children mostly had Indian names and grew up as Indians. The wives got status and some of the comforts of living at company forts, and the system tended to ameliorate their lot. In short, there were advantages for both sides.[30]

The Hudson's Bay Company would have preferred celibacy in its employees, but this proved impossible. The governors and chief factors of the company took the lead in forming these unions. Quite a number took to polygyny too, but it did not develop significantly. By the mid-eighteenth century it was an established practice for a governor to take an Indian wife. Celibacy had to go finally because the company wanted to attract the highly-prized French Canadian voyageurs into their service. In the Montreal-based North West Company, inheritors of the French fur trade from 1763, country marriage was officially sanctioned and had spread much lower down, although the French took a definite stand against polygyny. By the 1820s practically all company officers, and many of the lower-ranked employees too, had made native marriage alliances. Some had wives in Britain. The company was anxious to avoid any cause of dispute with the Amerindians by insisting that men made provision for their offspring. By 1800 the wills of officers and servants showed a conscientious provision for their families: evidence indeed of a definite growth of real family ties. Nevertheless, the company was worried by the expense of having to maintain cast-off wives after employees had returned to Britain. The founding of the Red River Settlement in the early 1800s enabled many fur traders to keep their families on after retirement. But it also became a source of marriage to mixed-blood women, and thus a final discouragement to unions with Indians. As in India in the eighteenth century (see chapter 5), there was a shift in Canada from taking Indian wives to taking those of mixed blood created by liaisons in earlier generations. Thus in the early nineteenth century the mixed-blood wife seemed an ideal partner. Residual relations with Indian women were of an increasingly casual kind henceforth.[31]

James Douglas made a perceptive comment c. 1830:

> There is indeed no living with comfort in this country until a person has forgot the great world and has his tastes and character formed on the current standard of the stage.... To any other being... the vapid monotony of an inland trading post would be perfectly unsufferable, while habit makes it familiar to us, softened as it is by the many tender ties, which find a way to the heart.[32]

There were numerous examples of lasting, devoted and faithful relationships between white men and mixed-blood wives. Even those who came out and at first refused all offers gave way in the face of loneliness and the attractiveness of the girls. (According to James Isham in the 1740s, Cree maidens were most enticing: 'very frisky when young and ... well shap'd ... their eyes large and grey yet lively and sparkling and very bewitchen ...'.)[33] In the nineteenth century an early form of civil marriage developed. Chief factors who were Justices of the Peace could conduct marriages from 1836, and all chief factors from 1845.

In 1821 George Simpson officially recommended such connections, especially in new areas. 'Connubial alliances are the best security we can have of the goodwill of the Natives. I have therefore recommended the gentlemen to form connections with the principal families immediately on their arrival, which is no difficult matter . . .'. Simpson was a very successful officer with the Hudson's Bay Company, becoming a wealthy governor-in-chief of Rupert's Land in 1839 and gaining a knighthood.

'The little emperor of the plains', as he was known, exercised a strong influence on European social life there for four decades until 1860. Even before he arrived in North America he had fathered at least two bastards in Scotland, so he was not the man to ignore the easy opportunities of the fur trade. He had five children by four women in the 1820s; thereafter he tried to keep his new British wife with him, but it was not a happy or successful experiment. Simpson disparagingly referred to his 'bits of brown' (or copper), his 'commodities' or 'articles', upon whom he would 'settle his bollocks' or in whom he would 'deposit a little of my spawn'. (It also has to be said that he was a possessive and tyrannical husband.) Once in authority, he was always nervous about the unrestrained lust of the younger men in the business. Even the arrival of two washerwomen at York Factory worried him, and he ordered that the 'young bucks' should be kept away from them ('otherwise we shall have more fucking than washing').[34] Simpson, on the whole, took a sour view of any entanglements with Indian women. He did not understand the traditional custom and was unusually lax in his relationships. The way in which he and his friend McTavish cast off their Indian women shocked and even disgusted the old Canada hands. McKenzie, the governor of Red River, and McGillivray in the North West, followed their example. The presence of their European wives also generated a lot of ill feeling. This further shattered the norms and tended to reinforce metropolitan attitudes, which made native women appear less desirable as marriage partners. Simpson and McTavish, once married, also cut themselves off from those with mixed-blood wives. From the mid-1830s it became fashionable to have a European wife. By now distinct changes were under way, although country marriages outside Red River were by no means finished. From the mid-nineteenth century the custom was, however, falling into disrepute.[35]

Missionaries played their part in this change. The country marriage contained all the elements of European marriage except the blessing of the Church. A conflict was inevitable between the new evangelical missionaries of the nineteenth century and the Indians: the missionaries believed it was 'living in sin', while the Indians believed it was legal and honourable. Missionaries regarded such marriages as a denial of the authority of the Church. Simpson was keen to drive moralising missionaries off his patch. The Rev. John West, in seizing on exceptions rather than the rule, encountered much resentment, and did not last as long as chaplain of Red River, while the first missionary in Saskatchewan, the Rev. James Evans, was recalled by the Wesleyans in the mid-1840s when Simpson alleged sexual misconduct against him. (Evans may well not have been guilty, but scandalous allegations always wrecked a missionary's career.) If it came to court, judges were more sympathetic than missionaries to local custom, though some of the Catholic missionaries took a more sensible attitude. The Protestant attitude, however, made it inevitable that these marriages would die out with painful repercussions. Instead of stable unions, native women were reduced to the status of temporary mistresses and even prostitutes.[36] Victorian values had inexorably asserted themselves by the 1870s. As Glyndwr Williams writes, 'the contact of races, the mixture of blood, the exchange of skills and customs, which had marked the fur trade from its earliest days, were fading fast'.[37]

Very little has yet been written about male sexual relationships among the fur traders. These were institutionalised among Indians, and Europeans are almost certain to have got involved in them. Jennifer Brown notes that teenage apprentices could have 'surrogate father relationships with older men', strengthening the integration of the trading posts.[38]

Mining compounds in southern Africa from the later nineteenth century show much more clearly how 'closed' situations led to same-sex solutions among the Bantu, causing some passing alarm to missionaries and the imperial authorities, but seldom to mine management. In the earliest days of the migrant labour system, boys were brought in to fag or do 'women's work' in the compounds. They acted, in their hundreds, as cooks, cleaners and bed-warmers, doing the washing and making the tea. Some were so small that they were obviously incapable of mining work, and their surrogate female role (sometimes institutionalised by payment of *lobola*, bridewealth) quickly shaded off into a high incidence of sodomy or quasi-sodomy. Technically it was *hlo bongo* (Zulu) or *metsha* (Xhosa) – intra-crural intercourse – which was more commonly practised under this system of *nkotshane* (Shangaan; literally 'dirty young wives', thus 'boy wives', pejorative).[39] Traditional marriage was aped; gender was dismissed as only a minor inconvenience. As this system of 'mine marriage' developed, the very small boys disappeared, and the partners were aged between their mid-teens and mid-twenties (at which point they would then take boys of their own). These young men were paid well: they could expect to double their wages and receive generous presents of clothing and bicycles. They were often expected to look feminine and remain passive; they could wear false breasts but were expected not to ejaculate. The whole system was governed by clear and conventional rules. It was fun, familiar and safe – for both parties. To the boys it brought financial reward; to the men status, often reinforcing the seniority system of 'boss boys' ('team leaders' or senior black workers in the mine).

Mine workers had access to 'town women' living in nearby townships or on farms, who were available as mistresses or prostitutes (*nongogos*), but generally 'we loved our boys more'. The fear of venereal disease was a powerful and widely expressed reason for preferring 'mine marriage', which continued until recent times. It was most common among Mozambicans, who were on long contracts of one to two years and who had come a considerable distance from home. Deference to elders was maintained. Masculinity was not compromised. Partners were never taken back home, although old relationships might be resumed on renewed mining contracts. Young men became 'wives' in the mines in order to earn the money to become husbands at home. Mine marriage was thus a function of migrancy in the gold-mining labour system, and a means of reinforcing African resistance to proletarianisation. Wherever migrancy decreased and proletarianisation increased in southern Africa, so *nkotshane* receded.[40]

In South Africa, women were not allowed into compounds. In Rhodesia, the *chibaro* labour system did permit the presence of women. This did little to reduce the incidence of *nkotshane*, and only added further problems, such as the use of young girls born to the compound camp followers. The services of the women were also disputed, and venereal disease began to affect productivity. The government and mining companies therefore decided in the 1920s to introduce a system of regulated prostitution. Another point to notice is that *chibaro* paid such low wages that some labourers were obliged to sleep with each other in a shared blanket.[41]

Chinese labour on the Witwatersrand was the subject of a bitter anti-slavery campaign in Britain. Among the objections to it were fears that it was leading to an explosion of sodomy among the gold tips. A thorough investigation was conducted for the government in 1906 by J. A. S. Bucknill (Commissioner of Patents in the Transvaal). Since the subject was the 'unmentionable' his report was never published, but many of the witnesses showed a remarkable knowledge of Chinese and African sexual practices. The Rev. F. Alexander and a busybody called Mr Leopold Luyt had made charges about the fearful scale of the problem, alleging that the Chinese were teaching sodomy to the blacks. These charges, Bucknill concluded, were all grossly exaggerated. Chinese sexual conduct was not flagrant or a public scandal, and not like the 'bare-faced harlotry of Johannesburg'; mostly the Chinese did what they did in secret in disused mineshafts. Syphilis of the rectum seemed practically unknown among them. Perhaps six or seven per cent of the Chinese labourers were 'bugger-boys' (*t'utzu*), most of them actors or barbers of low social rank ('acting and immorality go hand-in-hand... all actors are very lewd fellows'). Bucknill concluded, 'I have been unable to satisfy myself that there is any great or alarming prevalence of this vice on the Rand.' The Medical Officer of Health for the Rand even thought there was less sodomy among the Chinese than there was in London for a corresponding number of males. On the other hand, one particularly well-informed witness was convinced that some of the Chinese were carrying on with 'very little Kaffir piccanins on the veld'. Everyone agreed, however, that the Chinese were not teaching sodomy to the Africans, since it was already common among the Shangaan and other east-coasters, as well as among those from Zambesia and Lake Malawi, though the Zulu, Swazi, Sotho and Xhosa were not involved. Some five or six Chinese theatres were closed down in the compounds and a few dozen catamites were repatriated. The government could not be said to have overreacted. It emerged, incidentally, that Portuguese soldiers and police were enthusiastic participants in the *nkotshane* system.[42]

Convict settlements, mission stations and settler communities

No individual can truly represent the riot and dissipation, and licentious-ness and immorality, which pervaded every part of this settlement . . . (1798)

Drunkenness and whoredom are the two sins to which the unguarded missionary is most exposed, and particularly the latter sin amongst the heathen (1829). [Rev. Samuel Marsden, senior chaplain, New South Wales]

Convict settlements. In Manning Clark's famous description, early Australia (New South Wales and Victoria) was a 'cold, broken and unnatural form of society'. Only about ten per cent of the first convicts were women. In all, some 25,000 women were sent out as convicts, compared with 163,000 men. The ratio of women to men was never more than one to ten among convicts, and perhaps averages out at one to seven over the whole period of transportation. About forty-seven per cent of the women were Irish. The immorality of the convict settle-ments was notorious. Prostitution was as old as the colony and not confined to any particular area. Even in the 1820s, for a woman to become a concubine instead of a prostitute was considered an improve-ment in morals. Prostitution offered female convicts one of their rare chances of employment and one of their few hopes of saving enough money to buy a passage back to Britain.[43] The Rev. Samuel Marsden described early Australia as 'a dreadful society for whoredom and all kinds of crimes'. As senior chaplain, Marsden drew attention to the fact that licentiousness spread from the top downwards, with most magis-trates keeping convict mistresses, and he denounced the outrages of officialdom against convict women. He deserves credit for that. But Marsden also drew up a 'female register' in 1806, which classified all women (except a few widows) as either 'married' or 'concubine' (395:1,035). The basis of this classification was tendentious, to say the least. Marsden recognised as legal only Church of England marriage. With extraordinary bigotry even for an Evangelical, he registered all Catholics and Jews as automatically 'concubines', and the longest and most respectable relationships were thus condemned. Moreover, many common-law marriages, however irregular in theory, may have been admirably stable in fact. Marsden's figures were nevertheless widely accepted without question and have led to the painting of a worse picture than may be justified. The stereotype of women convicts as all in effect prostitutes (though very few had been convicted as such) emerged in part perhaps out of an ignorance of working-class habits. (It is surprising that Marsden was not more aware of this, being the son of a Yorkshire butcher-and-weaver and nephew of a farmer-cum-black-smith, to whom he had once been apprenticed). Sexuality was fairly visible in working-class communities at home, and prostitution re-garded as just another kind of job. So there was a confusion, perhaps, in Australia of working-class mores with convict vices. The extent of licentiousness thus remains in doubt. All contemporary observers, how-ever, over a long period, said prostitution was rife, so perhaps it was. The government investigator, J. T. Bigge, normally a careful observer, described c. 1820 the 'disordered, unruly and licentious appearance of the women', resorting to 'indiscriminate prostitution', at the Parramatta female 'convict factory'. In 1838 the Molesworth Committee claimed that convict women were 'all of them, with scarcely an exception, drunken and abandoned prostitutes'. It is, however, important to remember that not all early Australian white women were convicts. By 1828 only a quarter of them were convicts, while a quarter of them were free immigrants, with roughly another quarter freed ex-convicts and the rest native-born Australians.[44]

Notoriously few sex offences of any kind came to court in early Australia, least of all the sodomy ones. All historians are agreed, however, that sex between men flourished in the convict settlements, even if it did not leave much definite evidence.[45] Indeed, one of the most striking features of the convict system was the opportunity it provided for sex between men and boys. Sodomy was believed by several well-informed observers (W. B. Ullathorne, H. P. Fry, John Frost) to be 'the prevailing crime' at mid-century in Van Diemen's Land and Norfolk Island. 'Deeply rooted and extensively practised . . . so easy to arrange and so difficult to detect', this offence (in theory warranting the death penalty at home) was treated as less serious than pipe-smoking. While merciless floggings were imposed for petty misdemeanours, the local authorities turned a blind eye to sodomy, even when it was vicious in character. There was a reluctance to prosecute for sodomy when the penalty was death. Where legal action could not be avoided, offenders were often merely charged with 'disorderly conduct'. Under Russell's 'probation' system of 1840 the problem became more obvious from the concentration of young offenders. Each probation station now became riddled with it. John Frost believed that it was 'almost impossible for a good-looking youth to be sent to any of these places without falling victim to this hellish system, for if other means fail, he will be forced'. Thousands of boys, he warned, were annually being sent 'to a fate worse than death'. The reformatory at Point Puer at Port Arthur, the penal settlement of Van Diemen's Land, was particularly notorious. In Marcus Clarke's words, 'all degrees and grades of juvenile vice grinned, in untamable wickedness'. Governor Eardley-Wilmot was sacked by Secretary of State W. E. Gladstone in 1846 partly because of his inability to solve the problem or hush it up.[46]

A full-scale parliamentary inquiry was undertaken in 1846-47. Not all the material gathered was printed. What was published was sufficiently unequivocal. Sodomy 'prevailed' at Norfolk Island, was 'bad enough' at Cockatoo Island, but 'not so prevalent' at Moreton Bay, where the men had access to coloured women. Bishop Ullathorne reckoned that two-thirds of Norfolk Island was implicated. Several reasons conspired to promote sodomy. The big barracks, housing two hundred men, were without lights or supervision at night. In some places the men slept 'almost in one continuous bed', lightly clad in the warm climate, or huddled together in the winter cold. Boys sold themselves for tobacco or boots. Some sexual associations were acknowledged almost as 'marriages', a source of rare jealousy and intrigue. According to the Roman Catholic Bishop of Hobart Town, the Rt Rev. R. W. Wilson, boys of sixteen were assiduously corrupted at Norfolk Island, being pursued for months with bribes of tobacco and so on. He agreed that some 'couples' spoke of being 'married', and if one of them went to a secondary gaol his partner would 'commit some crime' in order to join him. Capt. A. Maconochie (superintendent of Norfolk Island, 1840-44) confirmed this: when he arrived, he said, some of the men were assuming female names and dress. It was 'grievously common', perhaps inseparable from the conditions of barrack life. But sodomy was also practised in the bush. According to A. C. Stonor (Crown solicitor in Van Diemen's Land, 1842-47), there were almost 'as many chances by day as by night'. The men were well fed and lightly worked. They could not be watched all the time and they could easily disappear for a while for sexual activity.[47] A veritable sexual tyranny was sustained by overseers, who would not report such small proportion of offences as they discovered, and who were anyway frequently involved themselves. This emerges from one of the few authentic accounts of male convict sex (as opposed to moralising investigation and polemic) – Thomas Cook's *The Exile's Lamentation: Memoirs of Transportation*. Cook said he knew of only two overseers who did not practise sodomy. As a group they were dominant men who did not take kindly to refusal. No doubt for some men and boys a loving sexual relationship was possible in the convict settlements, and could have been the only redeeming feature of their depressing lives. However, it is clear that this was no pederastic paradise; a lot of sexual coercion and sadistic humiliation was taking place.[48]

Mission stations. As pioneers on the moving frontier of European expansion in the early nineteenth century, missionaries quite often ran into trouble, especially in the South Pacific. Some of the early London Missionary Society missionaries in Tahiti slept with Tahitian women. Some defected from the mission for Tahitian or Tongan women, among them B. Broomhall, T. Lewis and G. Vason, the latter taking several wives. Sex was pressed upon the missionaries. Mostly they resisted, but their children often did not, finding the pervasive sensuousness of the South Seas most enjoyable. Missionaries soon aimed to send their offspring back to Britain for their education, in order to reduce their 'premature' exposure to sex.[49]

There were sexual problems to trouble the founder of the Church Missionary Society New Zealand mission (1814), Samuel Marsden. At the Bay of Islands in the 1820s, he found the Rev. Thomas Kendall had been living for some years openly with a native girl, Tungaroa, the daughter of a Maori chief. Kendall confessed his fornication but denied its seriousness: 'where is there a female of my own nation who can charge me with a lascivious look?' – an imperial double standard indeed. Kendall was a schoolteacher, put in charge of the New Zealand mission. He acquired a considerable knowledge of Maori customs. Marsden believed that 'by prying into the obscene customs and notions of the natives with a vitiated curiosity, his own mind had become so polluted too'. His ideas became 'very heathenish', 'his natural corruptions excited, and his passions inflamed, by which means he fell into their vices'. Despite the good work Kendall had done, Marsden felt sure he had to remove him in 1823: 'he was very immoral and too fond of spirits, which led him into other sins. He was so far lost to all religious feelings that ... he would contend that the civilisation of the young women was promoted by their living as prostitutes on board the whalers.' Despite having his wife and eight children with him, Kendall could not keep away from Tungaroa, causing great distress to his family. As if all this were not enough, he made two further mistakes. He sold muskets and powder to the Maoris, and he struck a Maori. The elders complained of his violent temper to Marsden, who was himself appalled at the lack of personal respect shown to so well-mannered a people.[50]

Then there was the awful fate of the Rev. Mr. Yate, a missionary in New Zealand from 1828. Yate was a brilliant evangelical publicist for the mission but he was dismissed and sent home in disgrace in 1837. His downfall came as a result of a return trip to New Zealand when he had had unguarded liaisons with two sailors, Edwin Denison and Dick Deck [sic]. It then emerged that he had been sexually active with many of his young male converts, perhaps fifty to a hundred of them. Piripi Tohi testified to mutual masturbation, Samuel Kohe to intracrural intercourse, Pehi to fellatio for a pound of tobacco. Since there was no evidence of anal penetration, there was no legal case against Yate, and he argued (as any good Buddhist monk would have done) that only adultery with a woman was a sin. His colleagues knew God did not agree, and, to avoid divine retribution, burnt all his property and shot his horse.[51]

Bishop John Richardson Selwyn's Melanesian Mission operated in the New Hebrides, the Santa Cruz Group and the Solomons; its base was in Auckland, which it was hoped would become an antipodean Lindisfarne. Although the mission was held in high regard by the Victorians, partly because it was sanctified by the martyrdom of Bishop John Coleridge Patteson in 1871, its modus operandi was fraught with sexual temptation. An essential part of the technique was to tour the islands recruiting and gathering Melanesian boys for education and training away from home. Some missionaries enjoyed this task too much. In 1874 Charles H. Brooke was dismissed after over-exploiting his solitary visits to Mboli in the Solomons. In the late nineteenth century adolescent sex was 'rampant' at St Barnabas, Norfolk Island. Thirteen Melanesian teachers were suspended for their sexual behaviour in 1899 alone. And in the 1890s three white missionaries were sacked: A. E. Forrest, Arthur Brittain and C. G. D. Browne. Forrest was the most painful case. He had given excellent service, but had been sexually involved with so many boys that the bishop thought the whole mission at Santa Cruz was ruined. Forrest's defence was that the Islanders did not think his conduct wrong. 'If so,' argued Bishop Wilson, 'his work during the nine years he has been there has been worth nothing.' Moreover, Forrest refused to disappear into penitent obscurity, but remained at Santa Cruz as an independent trader, liberally practising 'gross indecency' up to the point of imprisonment in 1901. He then created a further sensation by escaping; he resumed his activities until he committed suicide in 1908, being remembered among the locals as the white man hounded to death by vindictive Christians. There was another round of problems in the late 1920s. E. N. Wilton, assistant Bishop of Northern Melanesia, was compelled to resign in 1929, after only one year in office, because of allegations of sexual misconduct. This was followed in 1931 by the dramatic resignation of the bishop himself, F. M. Molyneux, because of whispered homosexual accusations.[52]

Meanwhile in Papua New Guinea, the Anglican mission suffered resignations over women in the late 1890s and early 1900s. Missionaries complained about digger morals, but the diggers retorted that the mission stations were the worst. The Bishop of North Queensland in 1913-47, J. O. Feetham, was indiscreetly eloquent in public about delightful Papuan youths, who seemed to him to combine the character of St John with the physique of Apollo.[53]

In Africa, the missionary had fewer temptations to face than in the Pacific Islands. Nevertheless, there was a young transgressor missionary bishop of the Orange Free State, Edward Twells, who fled back to Britain in 1870 to escape a sodomy charge and never held any benefice again before his death thirty years later.[54] And there were a number of eccentrics who aroused a good deal of suspicion and occasionally disgust. Skertchly reported in 1874 that the house of the Wesleyan mission in Dahomey under the Rev. Peter Bernasko had for twenty years been the most notorious brothel on the coast, especially since Bernasko had had sole charge of it from 1863. Bernasko traded in palm oil, got very drunk, neglected his mission, fathered a dozen children, and prostituted his elder daughters. Shortly after arriving in Kenya in 1902 to join the King's African Rifles, Meinertzhagen discovered three Italian White Fathers with the Kikuyu at Tusu, doing a 'roaring trade in enticing boys and girls to the mission', there to live a most immoral life: 'they are certainly not "white", but doubtless will soon be fathers'. With them was an Englishman called Smith, who had slept with at least seven girls, saying they could not be true Christians until they had slept with a Christian.[55]

Mission stations certainly produced a crop of plausible excuses for unchastity. Perhaps the most ambivalent and controversial eccentric in the African episcopate was Canon W. V. Lucas, first Bishop of Masasi, 1926-44, who was responsible for pioneering (several years earlier) a Christian *jando* or initiation ceremony for boys in their early teens. It was a seriously thought-out attempt to formulate a syncretist rite, but the combination of circumcision and confirmation was rejected by most other missionaries as 'little better than an orgy', although, as Ranger points out, the local people liked it. Lucas (without a hint of irony) claimed that 'a wonderful opportunity is given in this way to the Christian priest of getting into real personal touch with his boys.' He put 700 boys through this rewarding ritual, but had no plans to extend it to girls. Clitoridectomy posed problems too daunting even for a High

Anglican bishop.

Of course, the behaviour of almost all Victorian missionaries was entirely orthodox, and interracial marriage for themselves was unthinkable – at least after about 1810, that is. J. T. Van der Kemp of the London Missionary Society at Bethelsdorp from 1803 did not set a trend by marrying the daughter of a Malagasy slave woman. As a group, Victorian missionaries were firmly on the side of chastity. For that very reason they seldom got much support from expatriate whites.[56]

Settler communities. In the early days sexual conventions even in the most Europeanised colonies were often fairly relaxed. Canada was a good place for an emigrant paterfamilias, remarked Sir Francis Bond Head in the 1830s: within a year he would 'find all his sons will be *free* and all his daughters *confined'*. In frontier colonies like Natal, things could be very indecorous. But life in colonies was both pioneering and provincial, exotic and conformist, and there was a steadily increasing pressure towards conformity – often accompanied, though, by deeply prurient interest in deviation.[57]

Servants were exploited, just as they were at home. In South Africa, Africans believed that black maids in European houses would be seduced by their employers. The police superintendent of Durban in 1903 agreed, alleging that not more than ten per cent of black girls who came to towns looking for work 'escaped ruin' at the hands of white seducers. This is why from 1897 there was an increase in the employment of Zulu houseboys and male nursemaids by white householders. Despite the occasional 'black peril' scare, and an undercurrent of continuous apprehension, these blacks rarely abused their often intimate domestic responsibilities. The pattern was very similar in the Rhodesias, where white wives experienced virtually no sexual trouble with their black servants.[58] Yet all the southern and central African colonies legislated in the first years of this century to prevent intercourse between white women and African men. Under the Southern Rhodesian Immorality Act (1903) differential treatment was patent. A white prostitute accepting a black customer would get two years' imprisonment, while the African male got five years'. The law was designed to protect white women but not black. Despite the fact that sexual relationships between white men and black women were much more common, there was little public disapproval of them.[59] Similarly, the Europeans in 1926 in Papua New Guinea cynically imposed the death penalty for the rape, and even the attempted rape, of a white woman by a black man, with life imprisonment for indecent assault; but black women got no such protection from European men. Interestingly, the legislation was largely symbolic: there had been no preceding case of rape of a white woman.[60]

In every colony, wherever the unmarried white man found himself isolated, liaisons with local women were common in the nineteenth century. Among some white traders and hunters there was 'a partial equation of frontier life . . . with sexual freedom and indulgence . . . a no-man's land in terms of moral conduct'.[61] In the early nineteenth century there was sexual interaction with the indigenous peoples of New Zealand, Australia and South Africa, including the *trekboer* regions.[62] When Cape Colony came under British rule in 1807, perhaps ten per cent of whites were married to non-whites (probably including Asians and Coloureds); under three per cent of Cape marriages were to pure-blooded Africans, even less in rural areas. But while marriage was not frequent, and intermarriage already in decline, miscegenation was still quite high. It has been calculated that the percentage of non-white blood in today's Afrikaner community is perhaps seven per cent.[63]

Later in the century there was fairly widespread concubinage in central Africa. Not all government officers in Africa kept concubines, but some undoubtedly did, especially in the lonelier districts. The situation in Kenya and in Northern Rhodesia had to be investigated from 1908 to 1910, and the government realised that many administrative officers were still involved in concubinage. This is discussed in chapter 7. A few committed the ultimate sin and 'went native'. J. E. Stephenson, an administrator in Northern Rhodesia under the British South Africa Company, is often quoted as an example, in fact wrongly. Stephenson had already taken an Ngoni wife before becoming a 'native commissioner' in 1901. After objections to his bringing his young son on a visit to the district commissioner, he resigned in 1906 and settled in a remote valley. The company tried to persuade him to change his mind, but he disagreed with official policy in general and objected to pressure to give up his African family. He was an able administrator, who 'might have risen to be governor'. It was his pioneering that opened up the area which was to become the Copperbelt, where he built 180 miles of road under official contract. This was no casual 'going native' or indiscriminate abandonment of white values. He took his books with him, he grew oranges in the bush, he acted as safari guide for European tourists and, when war broke out in 1914, he left to fight for Britain. Although ostracised from white women's society, he had no difficulty in maintaining all necessary contact with government officials. He had more than one African wife, and eight children, and as 'Chirupula' was much respected by local Africans.[64]

Virtually the only brothels in central Africa at this time were in Salisbury (Harare), where in 1910 there were nine houses with twenty to thirty women; this was at a time when there were only about 400 unmarried white male residents. Prostitution in colonial Salisbury was

[107]

defended as a lesser evil than 'going native'. Unfortunately the 'red light' district was precisely on the funeral route to the city cemetery, and thus attracted a lot of unfavourable comment.[65]

The presence of colonial society always imposed the need for discretion, as gossip was rife. But, however stifling colonial society became, there was often a convenient safety-valve near by, usually provided by the Portuguese. From the Rhodesias, help was at hand in Beira and Lourenço Marques; from Hong Kong, it was in Macao, where the early European traders kept their weekend mistresses; from India, there was Goa, to say nothing of Rangoon or Port Said, or a Himalayan hill station, where even English women could refuse to conform to Victorian stereotypes. Port Said, Singapore and Macao were intercontinental sex capitals and initiation centres for whites new to empire. Before 1914 a young man's first experience of the East might well be in a brothel in one of these cities. By the 1930s every street in Macao is said to have had one.[66] Burma had the reputation of being a marvellous place for 'rest and recreation'. The girls were cheap and sensuous. If the army had any doubts about their cleanliness, then an officer could burn their huts and restock with Japanese. Even into the twentieth century (and despite some official attempt to curtail it), W. N. Willis (an investigator who had lived there) believed that ninety per cent of the British in Burma took temporary mistresses. A special school was founded in Rangoon to educate children with European fathers.[67]

There was nothing at all comparable in British Africa, however. (Francophone Africa was different.) It was essentially all a matter of 'social distance'. As a high-minded but nervous imperial ruling class emerged, and where fairly close-knit white communities were established, with white wives as regular participants and moral guardians, the practice of concubinage waned. As the following chapter will show, this happened in India from the 1860s, in the wake of the steamships and the Suez Canal. The memsahibs and their reformed menfolk also brought big changes to Ceylon, South Africa and New Zealand by 1900, though not as yet to Burma or tropical Africa. Black mistresses disappeared in central Africa, however, as the Zambian Copperbelt was opened up in the 1920s.[68] The early Europeans in Fiji had taken concubines with chiefly compliance, but this did not survive the 'Rush' of settlers and speculators, accompanied by white women, from the late 1860s and early 1870s; in the late 1870s the Secretary of the Land Commission was dismissed for marrying a Fijian woman – but offered reinstatement in the colonial service when she died.[69] The longer a place remained unexposed to the scrutiny of the memsahibs and the reformed officials the longer would persist the traditional solution to the problems of loneliness and sexual deprivation. Sarawak was probably the last bastion of concubinage: even into the 1950s something of the old ways seems to have survived.

Things were fairly free-and-easy in Malaya, until the 1930s at any rate. In the proto-Malay civil service, C. F. Bozzolo was a founding father of the administration: an impeccable and popular governor of Upper Perak for many years, he had a harem said to be of dimensions befitting a patriarch. His successor, Hubert Berkeley, kept up the tradition. Indeed, he embellished it, press-ganging into his harem some girls from the local orphanage, which he raided. Even in 1908 Berkeley could offer a recruit a 'sleeping dictionary' of quality – a Malay schoolmistress. In 1911 only twenty per cent of European men in Malaya were married. Planters (apart from the few proprietary ones) needed their company's permission to marry, and many never did. Every village in the Federated Malay States, if it was big enough to have a post office, had its brothel, in which most of the girls were Japanese. In very small towns without a rest house, the brothel doubled as a hotel for Europeans, and these brothels were in regular use. Sir Malcolm Watson, who was well placed to know (being a malariologist in constant touch with planters and officials), estimated that ninety per cent of Europeans in out-stations had Asian mistresses in the 1890s. The young journalist R. H. Bruce Lockhart in the early 1920s had no difficulty at all in living with a well-born Malayan girl for several months while working on a rubber plantation. It was still a recognised custom. These plantation concubines were often Muslims divorced for barrenness, who subsequently purged themselves by a pilgrimage to Mecca.[70]

Opinions vary, as they usually do, about the extent of same-sex activity indulged in by European men: in Malaya it has been put as high as two-thirds, and this option certainly presented itself more overtly than it did in Africa. There was a major scandal in the 1930s when the diary of a professional 'Chinese catamite' fell into the hands of the police, resulting in an official inquiry and the disgrace of 'several prominent persons'. The press was forbidden to report the case. There were some speedy deportations, and the two men left behind both committed suicide. Purcell heard about this; he also knew of a civil servant who lived incestuously with his sister on a remote station, of a baronet who ditched his family in order to elope to Siam with a Chinese girl, and of certain Johore planters who indulged in wife swapping. He himself had a temporary mistress in Canton in the 1920s.[71] Any contact between white women and Malayan men was, however, an extremely sensitive issue. In the mid-1950s it was alleged that a number of British service wives, particularly in Kuala Lumpur, were engaged in 'illicit relations' with Asians, frequently shopkeepers and landlords to whom they owed money. Although the Secretary of State for the Colonies categorically denied in public this state of affairs, the allegation was in fact true. The Commander-in-Chief is on official record as testifying to the accuracy of the reports, and as demanding better married quarters as the solution.[72]

An examination of what happened sexually over a long period in a wide range of imperial situations – labour plantations and trading posts, convict settlements and mining compounds, mission stations and settler communities – has suggested not only a striking contrast with the restrictions of opportunity in Britain itself (even before the advent of the Purity movement), but also a number of similarities between these various forms of imperial organisation overseas. Everywhere there was a natural resort to native women so long as this was not interdicted. Everywhere there was bisexual indulgence in same-sex solutions if opportunity presented itself. The next step in developing the argument of this study will be to see if these generalisations are applicable to the most important imperial situation of all, the empire in India.

Notes

1 J. G. Butcher, *The British in Malaya, 1880-1941: the Social History of a European Community in South-East Asia*, Kuala Lumpur, 1979, p. 196; F. Yeats-Brown, *Bengal Lancer*, London, 1930, pp. 37-8, 49-50; A. Swinson and D. Scott (eds.), *The Memoirs of Pte Waterfield, Soldier in 32nd Foot, 1842-57*, London, 1968, *passim*, which shows what a problem alcoholism was. For seductive boys in Ceylon, see ch. 2, n. 34. V. L. Bullough (*Sexual Variance in Society and History*, New York, 1976, p. 576) was one of the first serious scholars to make the point that Europeans revelled in the sexual opportunities of India: 'Sex life in India apparently had considerable influence on British attitudes, and India provided a haven for those unable to conform to staid British practices. In fact, the whole relationship of colonial countries to Western European masters is comparatively unexplored, and when it is explored, I believe it will be demonstrated that the alternative sexual styles available were a source of attraction to many.' At the time of writing he was able to support this contention by reference only to F. M. Brodie's biography of Sir Richard Burton, *The Devil Drives*, London, 1967; and Allen Edwardes's *Rape of India*, which we now know to be fraudulent (see ch. 2, n. 22).

2 PRO, CO 537/540/38767 (Supplementary secret correspondence), op. cit., note 42 below, comment by Bucknill on the evidence of E. C. Mayers, 7 September 1906.

3 Quoted in [Ashbee], I, *Index*, pp. 379-81, from E. Sellon, *The Ups and Downs of Life*, London, 1867, p. 42; see also F. Henriques, *Prostitution and Society*, I: *Primitive, Classical and Oriental*, London, 1962, pp. 189-91.

4 H. Ellis, *Studies in the Psychology of Sex*, III: *Analysis of the Sexual Impulse*, Philadelphia, 1922, p. 314. See below, p. 133.

5 League of Nations, *Traffic in Women and Children: Advisory Commission for Protection and Welfare of Children and Young People. Licensed Houses*, Appendix: 'Brief survey of . . . VD and prostitution in Great Britain and the Empire', C.T.F.E. 336(2), 1929, p. 80.

6 M. Davidson, *The World, the Flesh and Myself*, London, 1962, p. 282; A. Friendly, *Beaufort of the Admiralty: the Life of Sir Francis Beaufort, 1774-1857*, London, 1977, p. 55; A. N. Gilbert, 'Buggery and the British Navy, 1700-1861', *Journal of Social History*, X, 1976; J. R. Walkovitz, *Prostitution and Victorian Society*, London, 1980, p. 108; J. S. Stavorinus, *Voyages to the East Indies*, I: *1768-71*, London, 1798, repr. 1969,

p. 45.

7 J. K. Fairbank *et al.* (eds.), *The I.G. in Peking: Letters of Robert Hart, 1858-1951,* Harvard, 1975, II, p. 1078 (8 August 1896); see also S. Sneade Brown, *Home Letters written from India, 1828-41,* London, 1878, pp. 14-17.

8 R. Winstedt, *Start from Alif: Count from One, an Autobiographical Mémoire,* Kuala Lumpur, 1969, pp. 17-18, 102-4.

9 M. Crowder, *Revolt in Bussa: a Study of British 'Native Administration' in Nigerian Borgu, 1902-35,* London, 1973, p. 168; see also S. Leith-Ross, *Stepping-Stones: Memoirs of Colonial Nigeria, 1907-60,* ed. M. Crowder, London, 1983.

10 E. M. Forster, *Hill of Devi, and Other Indian Writings,* Abinger edn, ed. E. Heine, London, 1983, 'Kanaya', p. 323.

11 R. Trumbach, 'London's sodomites: homosexual behaviour and western culture in the eighteenth century', *Journal of Social History,* XI, 1977, pp. 13-14; W. H. Epstein, *John Cleland: Images of a Life,* London, 1974, pp. 68-71; I. Bloch, *Sexual Life in England,* London, 1903, p. 533.

12 [Ashbee] III, *Catena Librorum Tacendorum,* pp. 93-4, 183-9; 'Walter', *My Secret Life,* lii (intro. by G. Legman), I, p. 273, and II, p. 2074; H. R. Trevor-Roper, *A Hidden Life: the Enigma of Sir Edmund Backhouse,* London, 1976, pp. 245-9. For erotic literature in general, see P. J. Kearney, *The Private Case: an Annotated Bibliography of the Private Case Erotica Collection in the British (Museum) Library,* London, 1981. It is necessary to defend the inclusion of the *Romance of Lust* in this select company, in view of the derisive strictures of S. Marcus (*The Other Victorians,* London, 1966, pp. 274-7), who harps on the inferior fourth volume; however, it is hardly surprising that after several hundred pages of intensive sexual descriptions the work tails off; in general Marcus is too high-minded and patronising about erotic literature, and does not appear to be particularly well read in it.

13 N. St John-Stevas, *Obscenity and the Law,* London, 1956, p. 77.

14 *Pall Mall Gazette,* XLV, pp. 2-3 (19 May 1887), 'Is Empire consistent with morality? No!', by a Public Servant.

15 L. Crompton, *Byron and Greek Love: Homophobia in Nineteenth-Century England,* California, 1985, pp. 127-61. The first British governor of Ceylon, Frederick North (1798-1805), the youngest son of Lord North, became Chancellor of the Ionian University on Corfu, where he donned classical dress and adopted customs and practices in accord with his unmarried philhellenism: see H. A. J. Hulugalle, *British Governors of Ceylon,* Colombo, 1963, p. 10.

16 J. Pemble, *The Mediterranian Passion: Victorians and Edwardians in the South,* London, 1987; R. Peyrefitte, *Exile of Capri,* trans. 1961; J. Money, *Capri, Island of Pleasure,* London, 1986. Disraeli apparently came back from the Mediterranean with venereal disease: see R. Blake, *Disraeli's Grand Tour: the Holy Land, 1830-1,* London, 1982, pp. 20-24, 102.

17 [Edward Long], *History of Jamaica,* London, 1774, II, pp. 327-32; F. Henriques, *Prostitution and Society,* II: *Prostitution in Europe and the New World,* London, 1963, pp. 200-3, 254; Beth Day, *Sexual Life between Blacks and Whites: the Roots of Racism,* London, 1974 pp. 49-52; W. A. Green, *British Slave Emancipation in the Sugar Colonies and the Great Experiment, 1830-65,* London, 1976, pp. 20-2; see also R. S. Dunn, *Sugar and Slavery: Rise of the Planter Class in the English West Indies, 1642-1713,* London, 1973, pp., 252-5.

18 G. Freyre, *The Masters and the Slaves: a Study in the Development of Brazilian Civilisation,* New York, 1946, p. 323. R. W. Fogel and S. L. Engerman (*Time on the Cross: the Economics of American Negro Slavery,* London, 1974, I, p. 126 ff) challenge the Freyre picture, but their argument is not wholly convincing, I think.

19 W. D. Jordan, *White over Black: American Attitudes towards the Negro, 1550-1812,* Chapel Hill, NC, 1968, pp. 136-7, 161-2; D. B. Davies, *The Problem of Slavery in Western Culture,* Cornell, NY, 1966, pp. 273-7, and n. 27.

20 F. Cooper, *Plantation Slavery on the East Coast of Africa,* Yale, NH, 1977, pp. 17, 35, 195-9; C. C. Robertson and M. A. Klein (eds.), *Women and Slavery in Africa,* Wisconsin, 1983, esp. pp. 87-8, 137-8.

21 R. Ross, 'Oppression, sexuality and slavery at the Cape of Good Hope', *Historical Reflections*, VI, 1979; R. Elphick and R. Shell, 'Intergroup relations, 1652-1795', in R. Elphick and H. Giliomee (eds.), *The Shaping of South African Society, 1652-1820*, London, 1979.

22 E. D. Genovese, *Roll, Jordan, Roll! – the World the Slaves made*, London, 1975, pp. 413-31.

23 H. Brogan, *Longman's History of the U.S.A.*, London, 1986, p. 291; R. E. Conrad, *Children of God's Fire: a Documentary History of Black Slavery in Brazil*, Princeton, NJ, 1983, pp. 273-81.

24 H. Tinker, *A New System of Slavery: the Export of Indian Indentured Labour Overseas, 1830-1920*, London, 1974, pp. 5, 11, 205, 221-2, 341, 362-3.

25 K. Saunders (ed.), *Indentured Labour in the British Empire, 1834-1920*, London, 1984, pp. 98, 107, 148-9, 163; *Workers in Bondage: the Origins and Bases of Unfree Labour in Queensland, 1824-1916*, Queensland, 1982. B. V. Lal challenges the tendency to harp on sexual jealousy as a cause of all troubles on the plantations of Fiji: see 'Kunti's cry: indentured women on Fiji's plantations', *Indian Economic and Social History Review*, XXII, 1985, pp. 56-71; and 'Veil of dishonour: sexual jealousy and suicide in Fiji's plantations', *Journal of Pacific History*, XX, 1985, pp. 135-55.

26 W. Davenport, 'Sexual patterns and their regulation in a society of the S. W. Pacific', in F. A. Beach (ed.), *Sex and Behaviour*, New York, 1965, p. 201.

27 Butcher, *British in Malaya*, p. 266, n. 55; E. F. C. Ludowyk, *The Modern History of Ceylon*, New York, 1966, pp. 110-11; E. Carpenter, *From Adam's Peak to Elephanta*, London, 2nd ed., 1910, pp. 23, 75-81.

28 A. J. Barker, *The African Link: British Attitudes to the Negro in the Era of the Atlantic Slave Trade*, London, 1978, pp. 121-6; G. Woodcock, *The British in the Far East*, London, 1969, pp. 162-7.

29 S. Van Kirk, '"The custom of the country": an examination of fur trade marriage practices', in L. H. Thomas (ed.), *Essays on Western History in Honour of L. G. Thomas*, Alberta, 1976, pp. 49-68, esp. p. 50; idem, *'Many Tender Ties': Women in Fur Trade Society in Western Canada, 1670-1870*, Winnepeg, 1980; idem, 'Women of the fur trade', *The Beaver: Magazine of the North* (Winnepeg), 303/3, 1972, pp. 4-21.

30 Glyndwr Williams, 'The Hudson's Bay Company and the fur trade, 1670-1870, *The Beaver*, 314/2, 1983, pp. 69-77.

31 Jennifer S. H. Brown, *Strangers in Blood: Fur Trade Company Families in Indian Country*, Vancouver 1980; P. C. Newman, *Company of Adventurers*, I, Ontario, 1985.

32 Van Kirk, '"The custom of the country"', p. 59.

33 *Ibid.*, p. 50.

34 J. S. Galbraith, *The Little Emperor: Governor Simpson of the Hudson's Bay Company*, Toronto, 1976, pp. 61-71.

35 M. W. Campbell, *McGillivray, Lord of the North-West*, Toronto, 1967, pp. 55-9; Van Kirk, 'Women of the fur trade'.

36 E. R. Young, *Apostle of the North: Rev. James Evans*, London, 1899, p. 233; Van Kirk, '"The custom of the country"', p. 60.

37 Williams, 'The Hudson's Bay Company and the fur trade', p. 77.

38 Brown, *Strangers in Blood*, p. 33.

39 CO 537/542/9752, Confidential enquiry before J. Glen Leary (Resident Magistrate, Zeerust) and H. M. Taberer (Native Affairs Dept.) into alleged prevalence of unnatural vice among the Natives in the mines of the Witwatersrand, January 1907.

40 T. Dunbar Moodie, 'Migrancy and male sexuality on the South African gold mines', *Journal of Southern African Studies*, XIV, 1988, pp. 228-56; C. van Onselen, *Studies in the Social and Economic History of the Witwatersrand, 1886-1914*, London, 1982, II: *New Nineveh*, 'Regiment of the hills', pp. 179-87. The argument of H. Junod (*The Life of a South African Tribe*, London, 2nd ed., 1926, I: *Social Life*, pp. 97-8, 492-5) that 'unnatural vice was taught to the South African Bantus by men of a foreign race', will not stand up as a generalisation – nor will the contention of Gann and Duignan in *Rulers of British Africa*, pp. 240-2, that homosexual activity was not condoned in tribal Africa: see C. S. Ford and F. A. Beach, *Patterns of Sexual Behaviour*, London, 1952, pp. 136-9.

41 C. van Onselen, 'Chibaro': African Mine Labour in Southern Rhodesia, 1900-33, London, 1976, esp. pp. 174-82 ('Sex in the service of industry and the state').

42 CO 537/540/38767, Chinese Coolies: allegations respecting immorality, including Report of Enquiry held by J. A. S. Bucknill into certain allegations as to the prevalence of unnatural vice and other immorality amongst the Chinese Indentured Labourers employed on the mines of the Witwatersrand 20 September, 1906, together with Memorandum on the prevalence of unnatural vice among Chinese Indentured Labourers on the Witwatersrand, August, 1906, by the Superintendent of Foreign Labour; despatch of Lord Selborne to the Secretary of State, 10 October, 1906, and minute by H. W. Just, October, 1906. See also R. Hyam, Elgin and Churchill at the Colonial Office, 1905-08, London, 1968, p. 88.

43 C. M. H. Clark, A History of Australia, I: From the Earliest Times to the Age of Macquarie, Melbourne, 1962, pp. 235-59; J. W. C. Cumes, Their Chastity was not too rigid: Leisure Times in early Australia, Melbourne, 1979, esp. pp. 6-7, 27-36, 87-91, 215-19; M. Dixson, The Real Matilda: Women and Identity in Australia, 1788-1975, London, 1976, esp. pp. 115-54; M. B. Macintyre, 'Recent Australian feminist historiography', History Workshop Journal, V, 1978, pp. 98-110.

44 A. T. Yarwood, Samuel Marsden: the Great Survivor, Melbourne, 1977, pp. 53-4, 75, 120, 139, 248; R. Hughes, The Fatal Shore: a History of Transportation of Convicts to Australia, 1787-1868, London, 1987, pp. 244-7; Dixson, The Real Matilda, pp. 122, 136; Portia Robinson, The Hatch and Brood of Time: a Study of the First Generation of Native-born White Australians, 1788-1828, I, Melbourne, 1985, pp. 16-17, 66-84.

45 M. Sturma, Vice in a Vicious Society: Crime and Convicts in Mid-Nineteenth-Century New South Wales, Queensland, 1983, esp. pp. 97-8.

46 M. Ryan, Prostitution in London, with a Comparative View of that in Paris and New York, London, 1839, pp. 22-9 (Report of Rev. Dr [W. B.] Ullathorne, [R.C.] Vicar-General of Australian Colonies); H. P. Fry, A System of Penal Discipline, London, 1850, pp. 186-90; John Frost, A Letter to the People of Great Britain and Ireland on Transportation: showing the Effects of Irresponsible Power on the Physical and Moral Conditions of Convicts [1857]; Marcus Clarke, For the Term of his Natural Life, 1929 ed. Sydney, pp. 352-6.

47 Select Committee of the House of Lords on Juvenile Offenders and Transportation: C.447, and C.534, 1847, Accounts and Papers, VII, reprinted in Crime and Punishment: Juvenile Offenders, I, Session 1847, Irish UP series of British Parliamentary Papers, Shannon, 1970, esp. pp. 125-6, 461-75, 510-44.

48 Ibid., p. 524; Hughes, The Fatal Shore, pp. 264-72; A. G. L. Shaw (ed.), Thomas Cook: the Exile's Lamentation: Memoir of Transportation, Sydney, 1978.

49 N. Gunson, Messengers of Grace: Evangelical Missionaries in the South Seas, 1797-1860, Melbourne, 1978.

50 Yarwood, Samuel Marsden, pp. 242-3, 272-5; J. R. Elder (ed.), The Letters and Journals of Samuel Marsden, 1765-1838, Dunedin, 1932, pp. 331, 346-53, 394-7, 415-20.

51 J. Binney, 'Whatever happened to poor Mr Yate?'. New Zealand Journal of History, IX, 1975; E. Ramsden, Marsden and the Missions: Prelude to Waitangi, Sydney, 1936, ch. 2: 'Downfall of Rev. William Yate', pp. 20-44; B. Wannan, Very Strange Tales: the Turbulent Times of Samuel Marsden, London, 1963, pp. 163-9.

52 D. Hilliard, God's Gentlemen: a History of the Melanesian Mission, 1849-1942, Queensland, 1978.

53 D. Wetherell, Reluctant Mission: the Anglican Church in Papua New Guinea, 1891-1942, Queensland, 1977, pp. 67, 140-2, 233, 238, 297.

54 Crockford's Clerical Directory, 1870, London, 1870: J. R. de S. Honey, Tom Brown's Universe: Development of the Victorian Public School, London, 1977, p. 190.

55 J. A. Skertchly, Dahomey as it is, London, 1874, pp. 49-50; R. Meinertzhagen, Kenya Diary, 1902-06, Edinburgh, 1957, pp. 13, 34.

56 T. O. Ranger, 'Missionary adaptation of African religious institutions: the Masasi case', in T. O. Ranger and I. N. Kimambo (eds.), Historical Study of African Religion, London, 1972; W. V. Lucas, Christianity and Native Rites [1949], pp. 46-52; idem, 'Educational value of initiatory rites', International Review of Missions, XVI, 1927; L.

Harries, 'Bishop Lucas and the Masasi experiment', *ibid.*, XXXIV, 1945; C. P. Groves, *Planting of Christianity in Africa*, London, 1958, IV, p. 216; Junod, *Life of a South African Tribe*, I, p. 524. For Van der Kemp see R. Elphick and H. Giliomee (eds.), *The Shaping of South African Society 1652-1820*, London, 1979, p. 226.

57　John Murray Papers, Sir Francis Bond Head to John Murray II, 20 August, 1838. (I owe this reference to Dr Ged Martin.) For Natal see N. Etherington, 'Natal's black rape scares of the 1870s', *Journal of Southern African Studies*, XV, 1988, pp. 42-3.

58　C. van Onselen, *Studies in the Social and Economic History of the Witwatersrand*, II: 'Witches of suburbia: domestic service on the Witwatersrand, 1890-1914', London, 1982; D. Kirkwood, 'Settler wives in Southern Rhodesia', ch. 9, in H. Callan and S. A. S. Ardener (eds.), *The Incorporated Wife*, London, 1984, p. 158.

59　CO 417/372/19101, and 30517 (Bechuanaland and Rhodesia, 1903); R. Blake, *A History of Rhodesia*, London, 1977, pp. 158-9.

60　A. Inglis, *The White Women's Protection Ordinance: Sexual Anxiety and Politics in Papua*, Sussex, 1975.

61　H. A. C. Cairns, *Prelude to Imperialism: British Reactions to Central African Society, 1840-90*, London, 1965, pp. 53-7.

62　M. P. K. Sorrenson, in *Oxford History of New Zealand*, ed. W. H. Oliver, Oxford, 1981, pp. 169-70; Elphick and Giliomee (eds.), *Shaping of South African Society*, pp. 127-35, 372-84; C. D. Rowley, *Destruction of Aboriginal Society*, I, Canberra, 1970, pp. 122, 144; G. W. Martin, *Episodes of Old Canberra*, London, 1978; F. Henriques, *Children of Caliban: Miscegenation*, London, 1974.

63　W. M. Freund, 'Race in social structure of South Africa, 1652-1836', *Race and Class*, XVIII, 1976, pp. 53-67; R. Ross, *Adam Kok's Griquas*, Cambridge, 1976, p. 4; the key work, apparently, is J. A. Heese, *Die herkoms van die Afrikaner, 1652-1867*, 1971.

64　K. S. Rukavina, *Jungle Pathfinder: the Biography of 'Chirupula' Stephenson*, London, 1951; Gann and Duignan, *Rulers of British Africa*, p. 226, give a different account, but cite no references.

65　CO 417/491/8747 (British South Africa Company, 1910), Company meeting, 17 March, 1910 and annexures; CO 417/493/29462, W. H. Milton to Secretary of the Company, 12 August, 1910.

66　G. Woodcock, *The British in the Far East*, London, 1969, pp. 162-9, 197-8; S. O'Callaghan, *The Yellow Slave Trade: a Survey of Traffic in Women and Children in the Far East*, London, 1968, pp. 51-5; J. Beeching, *Chinese Opium Wars*, London, 1975, p. 32.

67　For Japanese prostitution in Burma see B. Farwell, *For Queen and Country*, London, 1981, p. 226; Frank Richards, *Old-Soldier Sahib*, London, 1936, pp. 303-4; A. Mackirdy and W. N. Willis, *White Slave Market*, London, 1913, pp. 247-9.

68　Blake, *History of Rhodesia*, pp. 279-80; R. Hall, *Zambia: the High Price of Principles*, London, 1969, p. 116.

69　C. Knapman, *White Women in Fiji, 1835-1930: the Ruin of Empire? . . .*, Sydney, 1986, pp. 136-41, 173; C. Ralston, 'The pattern of race relations in nineteenth-century Pacific Port towns', *Journal of pacific History*, V, 1970, pp. 39-60.

70　J. de Vere Allen, 'The Malayan Civil Service, 1874-1941', *Comparative Studies in Society and History*, XII, 1970; Butcher, *British in Malaya*, esp. ch. 8; 'European men and Asian women'; R. Winstedt, *Start from Alif*, pp. 17-18; R. H. Bruce Lockhart, *Return to Malaya*, London, 1936.

71　Purcell, *Memoirs of a Malayan Official*, pp. 249-51; Woodcock, *British in the Far East*, p. 217.

72　CO 859/548 (Social service original correspondence), Malaya, 1954-56.

CHAPTER FIVE

The sexual life of the Raj

From bibi to memsahib

The rule which forbade women to be taken to provinces or foreign countries was salutary. A female entourage stimulates extravagance in peacetime and timidity in war... Women are not only frail and easily tired. Relax control, and they become ferocious, ambitious schemers, circulating among the soldiers, ordering company-commanders about. . . The wives attract every rascal in a province. [Tacitus, *Annals* III, 33, speech by Caecina Severus]

Bibi is a Hindustani word meaning 'high-class woman', which in Hobson-Jobson 'Anglo-Indian' parlance came to mean native mistress. Colloquially the *bibi* was spoken of as a 'sleeping dictionary', though the linguistic competence of the British in India was never much improved, and all mixed-blood Eurasians became English-speaking. The initial pattern in all early European empires tended towards intermarriage with local women. The keeping of mistresses was not uncommon in eighteenth-century Britain itself. So the keeping of a mistress in British India became a well-established practice by the later eighteenth century, defended as increasing the knowledge of Indian affairs. Some officers recommended it quite openly, and the pattern was set at the highest level. Job Charnock (d. 1693), founder of Calcutta, had three children by the Hindu mistress he had rescued from a suttee funeral pyre. George Dick (Governor of Bombay in the 1790s) kept a Maratha woman, allowing her to parade about the streets ostentatiously; she was accused of tyranny, corruption and even of spying on behalf of Maratha pirates. Sir David Ochterlony (the Resident of Delhi, 1803-25) apparently had thirteen mistresses among Indian ladies. Even so respectable a figure as Lord Teignmouth, Governor-General (1793-98) and a British and Foreign Bible Society founder, had such a liaison.[1] Col. James Skinner (1778-1841), founder of the crack regiment 'Skinner's Horse', was said to have had a harem of fourteen wives, though the family hotly denied there were ever more than seven; eighty children claimed him as their father.[2]

Lower down the social scale, too, many of the British in India formally married Hindu women or (preferably) half-Indians, known as Anglo-Indians, or in Victorian times as Eurasians. It is estimated that ninety per cent of the British in India by the mid-eighteenth century made such marriages, but there is a great deal of uncertainty about this. In the biographies of the period the phrase 'is thought to have married an Anglo-Indian' occurs with maddening frequency. The marriages of Dupleix, Warren Hastings (as regards his first wife, Mary Buchanan, in 1756), and William Grant all fall into this uncertain category. What is hard fact is that the directors of the East India Company on 8 April 1778 declared that because of the importance of soldiers' marrying Indian women in Madras, they were 'content to encourage at some expense' such marriages, making a christening present of five rupees for every child of a rank-soldier baptised. In other words, a deliberate policy of intermarriage was encouraged by the company, in the interests of building up the army. The Anglo-Indians were thus a vital bulwark of the growth of company power in the early stages of territorial expansion. Moreover, Warren Hastings as Governor-General (1774-85) headed essentially a cosmopolitan society in which reciprocal entertainments between Indians and the British were common. In the 1790s, however, these policies went into reverse. Governor-General Cornwallis purged the administration and widened the social gulf. Wellesley stopped entertaining Indians at Government House. Anglo-Indians were prohibited in 1791 from holding civil or military office with the company. (The exclusion lasted for two generations.) They were disqualified from the army as combatants. There were massive discharges in 1795. By 1808 none was left in the British army. This reversal was a hard blow for the Anglo-Indian community. The most obvious alternative employment was to join the armies of Indian princes, but they eventually found their true vocation with the coming of the railways, which to a considerable extent were built and then run by Anglo-Indians. The size of the community stabilised and became endogamous. (From 1835 the company would not, in any case, allow intermarriage.) By the mid-twentieth century the Anglo-Indians numbered some 300,000.[3]

What caused this major change of attitude in the 1790s – a change that set the British on a sharply diverging line from other European empires? The sudden increase in the 'Christian invasion' of India by Protestant and mainly Evangelical missionaries, signified by the appointment of David Brown in 1786 as first of the famous 'five pious chaplains', is certain to have contributed to a tighter morality in European society in Calcutta.[4] Wellesley's determination to put British rule in India on a permanent basis, properly staffed by well-trained administrators, also increased the distance between ruler and ruled. He disapproved of open

concubinage with Indian women, and expressly founded Fort William
College as an antidote to the temptation of 'habitual indolence, dissipation and licentious indulgence', the 'peculiar depravity' and endemic
corruption of Indian life. David Brown was put in charge.[5] The principal
cause of the reverse, however, appears to have been part of the reaction
to the uprising in the Caribbean island of Santo Domingo after 1791. The
shock waves generated by the unprecedented explosion against white
rule there reverberated around the world. Santo Domingo was a French
possession, not only the wealthiest colony of its size in the world but the
most productive part of the West Indies, with a population of 30,000
whites (a very large community even by the standards of twentieth-
century settler colonies), 30,000 half-castes and half a million black
slaves. Tens of thousands died in the next ten years. The independent
republic of Haiti – the first ex-European colonial successor-state in the
Third World – was declared in 1804. Dessalines, its founder, in 1805
ordered the massacre of all whites except priests and doctors. These
shattering events had a definite bearing on the British decision to start
thinking seriously about winding up the slave trade. And in India too
there were fears that the British might be driven out by Indians officered
by Anglo-Indians.[6]

Nevertheless, although intermarriage was virtually at an end by the
beginning of the nineteenth century, the *bibi* still held her place.
Metcalfe (acting Governor-General 1835-36) had three Eurasian sons
between 1809 and 1817 by an Indian woman he had met at the court of
Ranjit Singh. He never made an European marriage.[7] Anglo-Indian
women were frequently of outstanding beauty. Samuel Sneade Brown,
a magistrate in the Indian Civil Service in the 1830s, noted that many
soldiers attached themselves to attractive Indian women – which he
thought a great deal more moral than a destructive round of dissipation.
The women were not at all like shameless British prostitutes (as those
at home might suppose). Indeed, they were most affectionate:

> I have observed that those who have lived with a native woman for any
> length of time never marry a European. . . so amusingly playful, so anxious
> to oblige and please, that a person after being accustomed to their society
> shrinks from the idea of encountering the whims or yielding to the fancies
> of an Englishwoman.[8]

Sir Richard Burton would have agreed heartily. Whilst in the Indian
army for seven years after 1842 he had at least three love affairs, none of
them with a European. He had a mistress in Baroda. 'I found every officer
in the corps more or less provided with one of these helpmates. We boys
naturally followed suit . . . I had a fine opportunity of studying the pros
and cons of the Búbú.' He believed, incidentally, that Indian women did

not love European men, being contemptuous of their sexual haste and clumsiness. As late as 1858 the future Sir Garnet Wolseley confessed to his mother that he was managing to console himself with an attractive 'Eastern princess', who answered 'all the purposes of a wife without any of the bother'; he had no wish to be caught in European marriage by 'some bitch' unless she were an heiress.[9]

From the 1860s however, it became increasingly shameful for an officer, civil or military, to live in a state which had been normal in previous generations, with part of his bungalow set aside for the *bibi*. Two reasons for this are commonly suggested: the double advent of the Mutiny and of the memsahib. The Indian Mutiny–Rebellion of 1857 obviously placed new barriers between British and Indians. Herbert Edwardes asked, 'How is one ever to work again for the good of natives?' Viceroy Canning believed that sympathy for Indians 'has changed to a general feeling of repugnance'.[10] In the post-Mutiny period, and partly as a strategic response to it, there was a massive surge of railway-building. Together with improvements in steamships and the opening of the Suez Canal in 1869, communications between Britain and India were thus transformed.[11] Getting home on leave, or despatching wives back for confinement, or children for their education, became almost too regular, too certain, too easy. More women came out to India, not all of them yet married. Annually a 'cargo of young damsels' (Lady Falkland's term), popularly known as the 'fishing fleet', came out to India at the beginning of the cold season actually in search of husbands. (Those who failed were unkindly known as the 'returned empties'.)[12] In various ways the larger presence of Englishwomen from mid-century is often held to have widened the distance between Indians and their rulers. Ballhatchet suggests three possible generalisations:

> As wives they hastened the disappearance of the Indian mistress. As hostesses they fostered the development of exclusive social groups in every civil station. As women they were thought by Englishmen to be in need of protection from lascivious Indians.[13]

Likewise, Ingram sees the formation of the pukka sahib code as essentially following upon the Mutiny, and critically dependent for its success on the increasing number of wives in the hill stations. Hill stations were the stronghold of the mems. (As Amy Baker wrote in 1931, 'Up in the hills young men are rare; down in the plains young women are rare. Young men are spoiled in the hills and lost in the plains.') Chasing after respectable women was increasingly disparaged as 'poodle-faking'.[14]

Few groups of women have been so negatively described as the memsahibs. It has long been said that the biggest mistake the British made in India was to bring their women out, thus making it impossible to meet Indians as friends. New standards of racial prejudice were, it was said, imposed by hostesses drawing intricate distinctions between shades of colour, as the memsahibs elaborated an imperial social etiquette. They combined an exhaustive knowledge of precedence within European society with a lamentable ignorance of anything outside it. (Orwell commented on 'the dull, incurious eyes of the memsahib'.) Moping and sickly, narrowly intolerant, vindictive to the locals, despotic and abusive to their servants, usually bored, invariably gossiping viciously, prone to extra-marital affairs, cruelly insensitive to Indian women and hopelessly insulated from them – such is the memsahib stereotype. Even their hobbies were said to be trivial: all they did was play bridge and flirt. Neatly enclosed in their European vacuum, most of them rarely spoke to any Indians except their servants, and few of them ever travelled even five miles into the surrounding countryside.[15]

This picture is probably not wholly wrong, though a historian today who did not reject its cruder variants would lack all credibility. It is, after all, not very difficult to suggest that there must be something fundamentally wrong with it, since it embodies a major contradiction. How can it be that the impact of the memsahib was so profound if she had such minimal contact with Indians? The truth of the matter is that if the mems contributed to racial exclusiveness it was because they were by their very presence meant to do so. Their presence was encouraged by Whitehall in the belief that the services they provided would offset the monetary costs. Their purpose was to provide a self-contained society for white men. Their own direct contacts were indeed actually too limited to have much effect, except at the elite level. The memsahib's function was political: to maintain 'civilised standards', especially sexual standards, and to contain the temptations of the male. 'Social distance' between ruler and ruled was the policy, especially after the Mutiny, and the memsahibs were its instrument. Men defined the rules and regulated the memsahibs' roles, and saw to it that they largely restricted their activities to the European community.

The ideal wife was seen quite simply as a calm, self-denying helpmate. It would make no sense at all if she antagonised the servants. She was to be a good-humoured employer, a gracious and hospitable hostess and an occasional secretarial assistant. She provided her husband with a stable environment, guaranteed his physical and psychological health, represented 'home' standards and reduced the tensions in the European community. As repositories of the folklore, by transmitting advice and support to newcomers, the memsahibs were important links in maintaining the structure of white rule. Flower arranging, supervising servants, gardening and motherhood were their principal occupations,

[119]

E

together with going to church and the club. But some of them did step outside these narrow confines, turning to voluntary and charitable good works, even on behalf of Asian (and later African) women: such things as Women's Institutes, postnatal clinics, Red Cross, Young Women's Christian Association and Girl Guides. It remains true, however, that this work did not usually take them unaccompanied much beyond their familiar white enclaves. The reason was sexual fear of the supposedly lascivious Indian. (These fears were almost certainly much exaggerated: few Indian men found white women as attractive as their own.) There was a further constraint in that officials mostly disliked their wives doing voluntary work with Asians and Africans. They felt it to be interference, a transgression of their proper gender roles. And so it was all too easy for wives to become obsessed with protocol when they had so few opportunities to get to grips with anything more important.

Thus there are many reasons why the memsahib was as she was. Her limitations were largely imposed upon her. Many were neither idle nor inept, and performed their roles effectively, remaining pleasant and well-balanced people. Only a few turned into 'dragons', bitter, intolerant and status-obsessed. The stereotype propagated by novelists undoubtedly existed, but such women were in a minority, regarded by other mems as failures whom they disliked and recoiled from.[16]

The requirements of ruling the Raj seemed to demand ever more aloofness between ruler and ruled as the nineteenth century wore on. In Viceroy Curzon's 1890s cosmology the Indian princes formed a peculiar threat to 'social distance'. Racial, social and sexual jealousies were involved here. He failed to stop the marriage of the Maharaja of Patiala to Miss Florry Bryan; the Raja of Jind secretly married a Dutch or German woman. Curzon did manage to prevent the Raja of Pudukkottai from going to Queen Victoria's funeral – in case he found a white woman in London to marry. When Secretary of State for India (1895-1903) Lord George Hamilton complained that Curzon in thus trying to restrict their European travels was treating Indian princes too much like schoolboys, Curzon retorted that this was precisely what the princes were. He was relieved that the coronation of Edward VII passed off without any of the sepoys seducing Cockney maids. In Burma in the 1890s there was a half-hearted attack on concubinage.[17]

A great deal more could be said on all these matters, but most of it has already been put forward by Ballhatchet in *Race, Sex and Class under the Raj*, to which the reader is referred. For the purpose of the present analysis the salient point to grasp is this: that within a period of little more than a hundred years the sexual scene for British officials in India had changed radically. If in the eighteenth century this was characterised by an active rate of overt sexual intimacy with Indians, by the twentieth century the predominant atmosphere was one of physical aloofness and suppressed eroticism.

Two features of sexual life under the Raj by the twentieth century stand out. One was the impossibility of privacy. As Kipling observed, 'everything in a man's private life is public property in India'. This was a real brake on any activity which the European community would not condone. Most big cities contained two or three Europeans, usually of low social class, who had 'gone native', but they disappeared utterly without trace. The other feature was the unreality to which expatriate emotional life became reduced. Ingram points to the widening gap between appearance and reality, and the stress which could result when individuals tried to bridge it. Europeans in India could flirt outrageously, but they must not fall in love or marry. Paul Scott has written of Englishmen in India who buried their emotions so deep that they 'turned into statues'.[18] This was not, however, true of one important group, the officers and men of the British Indian Army.

The Indian army and the 'lal bazar'

'We'll have all the fun that's going, we will have food and drink and expeditions and parties of pleasure, but what we will not have is sex. . . No sex with the other Cadets, because even at Bangalore they'll draw the line at that. No sex with white women even if readily available, because British women in India are, by and large, idle, conceited, pampered and promoted far above their proper class. They are therefore even more prone than most of their sex to interference and malice, and are to be avoided at any cost. And no sex with native women, if only because they stink'.

'What about half-castes? I'm told they're very appetising.'

'So they may be. But they probably have the pox and they certainly have mothers who chew betel nut.'

[Simon Raven, *Shadows on the Grass*, p. 114, recalling 1946]

In the nineteenth century, marriage in the army below the rank of major was the exception. By 1871 a third of officers were married, but fewer than two per cent of those under the age of twenty-four were. The informal rule was 'subalterns cannot marry, captains may marry, majors should marry, colonels must marry'. A man might be well into his thirties before he became a captain. Marriage allowances were not, in any case, paid until the age of thirty, and quotas were in force. Not unusually only twelve per cent of a regiment overall was allowed to marry, and only six to ten per cent of privates could have their wives in barracks. An unknown number of privates married without permission, but were then treated as single. An unmarried soldiery was thought more efficient.[19] Early in the nineteenth century, officers overseas often maintained mistresses, while the other ranks created havoc in the taverns and brothels of any town available to them. (A French nunnery was opened in the Montreal brothel district in the 1840s in an attempt to quieten down the British garrison.)[20]

The general position in the Indian army had been for a long time much as John Masters described it for the 1930s:

> It is useless to pretend that our life was a normal one. Ours was a one-sexed society, with the women hanging on to the edges. . . In India there was always an unnatural tension, . . . and every man who pursued the physical aim of sexual relief was in danger of developing a cynical hardness and lack of sympathy. . . Of those who tried sublimation, some chased polo balls and some chased partridge, some buried themselves in their work, and all became unmitigated nuisances. . . And some took up the most unlikely hobbies, and some went to diseased harlots . . . and some married in haste, only to worry over who was now seducing their wives in the hill stations where they had seduced so many other people's wives. And a few homosexuals followed their secret star with comparative comfort in that large and easy-going country . . .[21]

In earlier times (according to Colour Sergeant Calladine of the 19th Foot, stationed in Ceylon) a private or NCO could apply for written leave from the officer of his company to sleep out of barracks. When Calladine's regiment left Colombo after twenty-five years in 1820, a great crowd of Sinhalese women saw them off, some of them with three or four children by soldiers of the regiment.[22] But by the end of the 1850s the taking of mistresses in India and Ceylon was in decline, and venereal disease was becoming a serious problem. Especially worrying was the health of the army in the Mutiny districts, where efficiency was essential. The first army lock hospitals were established at Lucknow and Mian Mir (near Lahore). The problem was this. The British army represented 'the scum of the earth, enlisted for drink'. However harsh Wellington's verdict, even in 1914 Flexner described it as an army 'recruited from the adventurous and derelict',[23] while Sir George White (Commander-in-Chief in India, 1888) remarked that 'our soldiers come from a class upon which the prudential motives operating against immoral conduct have little effect'. As many army officers pointed out, the army had on hand a lot of young, unmarried men, fitter and better fed than their mates outside. Leisure was really a choice between lying idly on a barrack bunk, perhaps for eighteen hours a day (for going out in the sun or masturbating were both believed to drive one mad), drinking oneself silly in the canteen, or going to a prostitute (and risking the clap).[24]

There was also a dilemma for the authorities. To increase the marriage quotas would be expensive, because it would mean paying more allowances and building extra married quarters. To allow men out into the unregulated and often dirty brothels ('sand rags') of the cities and villages would increase venereal disease and trouble with the locals, especially if Tommy were drunk. To exclude prostitutes might turn cantonments into replicas of Sodom and Gomorrah. As Viceroy Elgin put it in 1894, this was really their trump card in defence of 'regimental brothels'; no prostitutes meant 'even more deplorable evils . . . there is already an increase in unnatural crimes'.[25] The general army view was that continence was impossible, and the dominant consideration in India was the preservation of the soldier's health, for he was an enormously costly import.

Thus between the mid-1850s and 1888 a system was in operation under which regulated prostitution was available in seventy-five cantonments where the Indian army was stationed (including six in Burma and one in Ceylon). (See fig. 1.) The aim was to keep the women free from disease. Under the system, Indian prostitutes were admitted to the cantonments, to the *lal bazar* (the red-light brothel area of the regimental lines), after medical examination and registration. They remained subject to periodical checks, and by 1865 lock hospitals (not so punitive in their regime as in Britain) were available in all cantonments to treat prostitutes suffering from venereal disease. They were grouped in their own houses, caravanserai-style, with a superintendent paid from cantonment funds, but they were free to move, and their conditions were not significantly different from the tens of thousands of other Indian residents serving the army's every need. In Lucknow the brothel was a substantial building with fifty-five rooms. There was no theoretical proportion of prostitutes to the number of soldiers: it was left entirely to the operation of supply and demand. But it seems that the number of prostitutes in a large cantonment (at least in three of the principal ones, Ambala, Mirat and Lucknow) varied from sixty to 110 at any one time, according to the seasonal total of soldiers stationed there. The maximum average complement of British troops at one of these cantonments would be about 3,750; in other words, on average about one prostitute to forty-four men. The women were supposed to be reserved for white use. Obstacles were placed on their receiving Indian clients, but many military police appear to have done no more than make sure the prostitutes were not seen to consort with Indians (in effect, this meant that Indians could use them while the whites were on morning parade). Indian clients were kept out of the more strictly regimental lines, but the cantonment was a big place, and there were other, cheaper (four- to six-anna) prostitutes in the general bazar and at a greater distance from the regimental lines. When the regiment travelled, the whole supporting

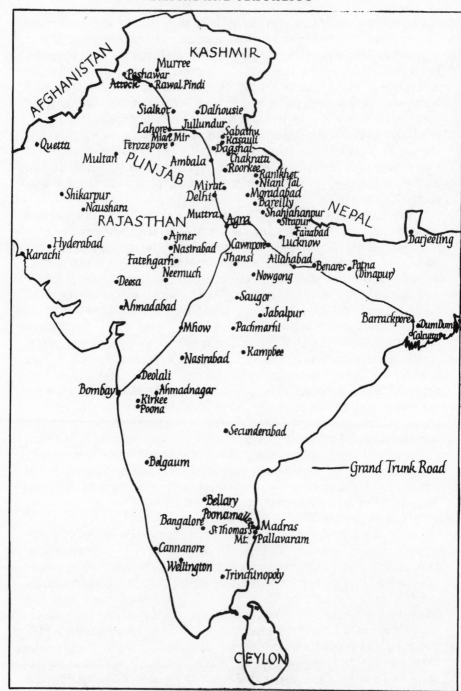

Figure 1 'Regimental brothels' in India, *c.* 1888

bazar marched too, the prostitutes along with the cooks, the ginger-pop makers, the barbers and dhobis.

The organisation did not seem particularly shocking to its defenders. The British had not brought prostitution to India; they had, they believed, only incorporated and regulated part of an old and honourably established business. Few of the girls appeared to be younger than fifteen. The regimental prostitute earned comparatively good money (one rupee per session, often enough) and was not generally ill-treated. With a recognised status, she could enlist the help of the military police in enforcing payment, and she could complain to the authorities. Admittedly she stood at some risk from drunken clients after pay-day or at Christmas, but the soldiers were not normally unkind. The officers recognised that it was important to try to ensure a sufficient number of women who were moderately young and sufficiently attractive, for otherwise the men would seek out unregulated women.[26] There was a notorious demand from the medical officer at Faizabad for the prostitutes there to be urgently replaced by 'others who are younger and better-looking'.[27]

Evidence can occasionally be supplemented from unofficial sources. Frank Richards, a private in the Indian army between 1902 and 1909, recorded a vivid vignette of the brothel or 'rag' at Agra. There were thirty or forty Indian girls aged twelve to thirty for the garrison of 1,500 white men. The brothel was open from 12.00 noon to 11.00 p.m. It was 'generally accepted' that a healthy young man in India could not keep away from women, though Richards knew a number who did, and he admired them. It was impossible, he said, to walk out of barracks without being offered 'jiggy-jig'. Much emphasis was laid on washing afterwards, in order to avoid venereal disease: hot water was provided in a small lavatory in the street. At Agra the 'rag' was right opposite the Protestant church, and it was possible to stand in the road and hear both the preacher and the cries of the soliciting girls. Small boys of six to nine years ran errands and acted as punkah wallahs: 'wicked little devils' they were, and 'very knowledgeable about sex'. Truly the soldiers of the King-Emperor at Agra were in a different world from the barracks at Colchester. Richards also mentioned that at Curzon's durbar a half-caste prostitute aged fifty announced her retirement after thirty-six years and kept open free house for five hours. Enormous numbers paid their farewell respects.[28]

Inevitably the whole system got caught up in the wake of the anti-Contagious Diseases Acts campaign at home. By 1888 criticism was strong enough for the Indian cantonment arrangements to be officially suspended.[29] Many of their main features in practice went on unchanged, however, as two formidable American lady 'Purity' investigators (Mrs E. W. Andrew and Dr K. Bushnell) discovered in 1892–93 and in 1899–1900. Lock hospitals continued under the sanitised name of 'voluntary venereal hospitals'. The critics had not fully understood the position, anyway. The government's special committee on the working of the system (comprising Denzil Ibbetson of the Indian Civil Service, Surgeon-Colonel Cleghorn and Maulvi Sami-ullah Khan) emphatically rejected the picture suggested by its opponents:

> of trembling groups of miserable women, . . . their scanty earnings limited by authority, and accompanied by constant brutality . . . released from their confinement only in order to be subjected to the unspeakable indignity of personal examination . . . condemned to drag on a hopeless life of abject poverty and degradation, of shame, and self-abhorrence, of futile yearnings for escape, till fading charms cause their rejection as articles no longer serviceable . . . For such a picture . . . we find no shadow of foundation.[30]

The regulated system had not, on the other hand, produced any dramatic reduction in venereal disease, but suspension at once made matters lamentably worse. (See fig. 2.) Between 1889 and 1892 about half the British soldiers in Bengal were treated for venereal disease; officially the rate was 522.3 per thousand. Maybe venereal disease was loosely defined, and some of the 'syphilis' cases might have been no more than festering abrasions caused by 'impure coition' (that is, fellatio) in a hot climate. Even so, the British soldier was certainly more vulnerable to venereal disease than his Indian counterpart, who was more likely to be married. Perhaps this was in part also because he had more money to squander, or was more careless when drunk, or less canny in spotting female symptoms, or perhaps he simply maintained his uncircumcised equipment badly.[31]

At all events, in 1895 Secretary of State Lord George Hamilton wanted to bring back the old regulated precautions. Viceroy Elgin, with his habitual good sense and foresight, warned that this might eventually only produce another swing of the Purity pendulum, with the backlash overturning all that they had gained. He therefore suggested simply restarting a voluntary venereal disease examination, taking powers to expel diseased prostitutes from cantonments and, while they were in hospital, stopping the pay of men who had become infected. Such penalisation, he hoped, might restraint the troops and at the same time remove the reproach that the authorities punished only the Indian women. The War Office refused to adopt this, largely from anxiety lest it encourage men to conceal their infections. The new rules actually adopted in 1897 were as follows: no special registration of prostitutes (apart from that required for all inhabitants of cantonments); girls not to be allowed to live in the regimental bazar, only in the main bazar (*sadr*

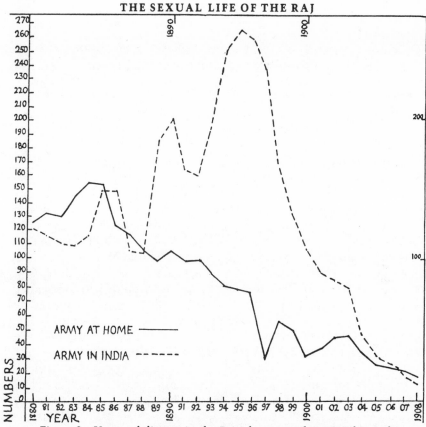

Figure 2   Venereal disease in the British army at home and in India:
admissions per thousand for syphilis 1880-1908
Source: Flexner, *Prostitution in Europe,* pp. 374-5

bazar), where most of them already were by then; and venereal disease
to be compulsorily treated like any other contagious disease. Improved
recreational facilities were also recommended. Some gratifying decline
in venereal disease seemed to result. But 'regimental brothels' persisted
into the twentieth century. Essentially the army outwitted the civilian
objectors and Purity-mongers. The situation only really changed as
recreation became diversified.[32]

Two versions of army promiscuity

He fell on the carpet and kissed my feet, praying for mercy... He had been
such a goose – . . .

What relation beyond carnality could one establish with such people?
[E. M. Forster, 'Kanaya', 1922]

[127]

Two sexual confessions by Indian army officers from the early twentieth century survive.[33] One, in manuscript form, is by Captain Kenneth Searight; the other, published as one of Havelock Ellis's case histories, is by an officer known only as 'G.R.'.

On the voyage from Port Said to India in 1912, E. M. Forster and G. Lowes Dickinson met and subsequently travelled with Kenneth Searight, who had a considerable impact on them. He interested them as a 'young Byronic officer' (Queen's Own Royal West Kent Regiment) who was finding India an easy field for his unabashed pederasty. Lowes Dickinson recorded that Searight was 'writing an autobiography of which he showed us parts, in a style which also seemed to belong to Byron – not good, I suppose, but curiously moving'. Forster and Dickinson then stayed with him for a couple of days in Peshawar.[34] The manuscript they saw had by 1917, when Searight left India, become an extended poem of 2,706 lines in rhymed couplets entitled 'The Furnace: an autobiography in which is set forth the secret diversions of a paiderast'. It occupied 137 pages of a 600-leaved volume which he called 'Paidikion', mostly filled with erotic stories about boys, all written up in a hand of attractive but almost obsessive neatness, and embellished with a dozen or so studio nude photographs by van Gloeden and others. After Searight's death the volume perhaps passed into the possession of C. K. Ogden, an acquaintance with a common interest in artificial languages and the like. (Ogden invented 'Basic' English, and Searight a neutral language which he called Sona.) It was allegedly rescued later by a keen-eyed professional bookseller who paid half-a-crown for it from a remainder stall in the Charing Cross Road. Since this sort of confessional diary rarely escapes destruction as a result of the qualms of its author (or his family), its survival is little short of doubly miraculous.[35]

Searight's 'Paidikion' is a document of intensely felt eroticism, and it contains a record of .encounters systematically made in a way which would have delighted the heart of Kinsey. At the back is an incomplete six-page table, headed 'Paidiology', which lists 129 boys who were Searight's sexual partners between 1897 and 1917. It has columns giving their name and age, the place of encounter, the year, their race, and 'references' – that is, the sexual acts performed. These are represented by thirty-three different symbols, ingeniously built up on a system of quasi-anatomical pictograms. Finally there is an unheaded column of figures, which presumably records the number of orgasms per partner. The average age is monitored page by page and works out at just over fifteen. Ages range from seven to twenty-eight. Almost all his partners were Indian boys, but those over nineteen were exclusively British. He seems to have favoured boys between twelve and fourteen. Although the presence of pubic hair was almost essential to him, eleven of them were ten or younger. The youngest he had anal intercourse with was a nine-year-old Pathan; mostly with the younger boys he practised what he called 'intercrural coitus'. In no time at all he was allowing his partners full reciprocal rights, and mutual anal intercourse was the usual mode, together with fellatio. Analingus began in 1913, but did not feature regularly for another two years. He tried out mutual flagellation with a thirteen-year-old Pathan boy in 1915 but did not repeat the experiment. Towards the end of his Indian days he began to introduce into the programme mutual micturition and urolagnia. Simultaneously with increasing experimentation there was a steady tendency for promiscuity to increase. The number of new partners was two in 1910, ten in 1911, seventeen in 1912, seven in 1913, twenty in 1914, twenty-three in 1915, fourteen in 1916, and twenty-eight in 1917. The number of orgasms per partner averaged 12.3, but appears to drop from twenty-nine with the first twenty partners to five in 1917: a further index of increasing promiscuity. The highest number of orgasms with individuals were all achieved with Pathans aged thirteen and fourteen between 1912 and 1915: ninety-six in one case, ninety-three in another, eighty-two in another, seventy-three in yet another. In addition there were six other partners in the age-group twelve to fifteen with whom he had more than thirty orgasms. In other words, he had many young friends on a fairly regular basis. There were, however, some sixty-three boys with whom he had three orgasms or fewer, half the total number of partners. These may be regarded as casual contacts. Invariably the boys – Mahmud, Abdul, Umar, Mazuffar and the rest – came to his bungalow. Only occasionally did two of them come together.[36]

It all began in Bengal in 1909 when Searight was twenty-six, stationed at Darjeeling. Things took off dramatically when he was posted to Peshawar in 1911. From there he explored a wide area of the Punjab and Rajasthan, helped after 1914 by his post as a railway transport officer. He visited Karachi, Lahore, Cherat, Simla and Bombay and made contacts in all of them. The difference between the 'mild Hindu' and the fierce Pathan immediately struck him:

> I groaned: the boy's untamed ferocity
> So different to the young Bengali's love,
> Filled me with anguish. . .

In 1917 he was transferred to Bangalore, where his sex life was for a time highly active. Later that year his regiment was posted to Iraq, and the record stops. We may be sure, however, that his activities did not, surrounded as he was by the complaisant canoe-boys and dancing-boys of the Mesopotamian marshlands who so entranced Thesiger.

At first Searight was excited by oriental skin-colour:

... my rod of ivory between the mons
Of buttocks fashioned out of gleaming bronze.

But there would 'come a time when I would long for English whiteness'.
He had eleven British young men as partners. They had names like Cyril,
Fred, Jack, Douglas and Herbert. 'Better than all eastern catamites' was
a young artilleryman who 'took me, his senior officer, by storm'. It was,
then, perhaps not surprising that he had some of his most enjoyable
encounters on leave in 1912, travelling to Port Said, Sicily, Naples and
London. There was sex in every port. Cairo produced a memorable
sixteen-year-old German boy prostitute. Naples, and especially its bath-
houses, he found more than satisfactory:

Paiderastic love in flame unchecked
Is what these Neapolitans expect.

And then it was home to pick up a horseguard in Hyde Park.

All the while Searight was experimenting with writing erotic tales. It
is pretty clear that he used his activities with Indian boys to fuel his
fantasies about white schoolboys, whom he would have preferred. This
reached its ultimate expression in a tale called 'Simla' about three
teenagers from Christ Church School in the hill station, breaking with
the narrator many sexual taboos (especially coprolagnia) 'in the midst of
her vast proprieties'. However, his own listing shows only three *Indian*
boys (Ali, Ghulam and Shirkur) seduced in Simla. All the while, too,
Searight remained an ardent narcissistic masturbator before the mirror.
He never attempted even the most casual contact with any women,
whom he thoroughly despised.

What is perhaps of principal interest to us in all this is the way in
which India acted as the safe and effective catalyst or displacement
channel for the pursuit of his dangerous interests in a way that had never
been possible in Britain itself. At school in Charterhouse he had sexual
contact with one boy only, when they were both fourteen. They loved
one another fervently, cautiously trying out 'intercrural' movement as
well as mutual masturbation. In his late teens Searight performed the
same acts once with his crammer's son. His first more intensive
experience appears to have been a single session with a nineteen-year-
old Piccadilly rent-boy. Three sexual partners is hardly excessive sexual
experience for a twenty-six-year-old soldier setting sail for India. His real
initiation into the potentialities of sex came – typically for servants of
the empire – in Cairo; then, he

thus encouraged at once began
To explore the amorous realms of Hindustan.

In Bengal it was pleasant but not particularly easy. It was the Pathans who took him to a problem-free paradise where all inhibitions were dissolved:

> And now the scene shifted and I passed
> From sensuous Bengal to fierce Peshawar
> An Asiatic stronghold where each flower
> Of boyhood planted in its restless soil
> Is – *ipso facto* – ready to despoil
> (Or be despoiled by) someone else; the yarn
> Indeed so has it that the young Pathan
> Thinks it peculiar if you would pass
> Him by without some reference to his arse.
> Each boy of certain age will let on hire
> His charms to indiscriminate desire,
> To wholesale Buggery and perverse letches. . .
> To get a boy was easier than to pick
> The flowers by the wayside; for as quick
> As one went out another one came in. . .
> Scarce passed a night but I in rapturous joy
> Indulged in mutual sodomy, the boy
> Fierce-eyed, entrancing. . .
> And when his luscious bottom-hole would brim
> Full of my impoured essences, we'd change
> The role of firing point (but not the range)
> Until his catapult, e'er strongly charged,
> The target with a hail of sperm enlarged.
> Then half an hour . . . and back again I'd come
> To plunge my weapon in his drenching bum. . .[37]

Like Searight's, G. R.'s account[38] terminates in his mid-thirties, when he was unmarried, but still in India; his interests were much less literary. He enjoyed plenty of sport and exercise, especially pig-sticking and polo. He drank a lot. On religion he described himself as 'a convinced and militant rationalist'. His schoolboy experiences were more extensive than Searight's, but, unlike him, he nevertheless made an effective transition to interest in women. He went to a small private school when he was eleven, practising fellatio there on several occasions. At public school (not named) he used to 'like kissing and hugging the smaller boys', and he soon became 'thoroughly initiated' into the school's habitual system of ejaculating while lying on top of other boys in bed. On leaving school he went to Germany, where he visited two women prostitutes when he was seventeen, and got soft chancre. He occasionally went with prostitutes while at a crammer back in England. His first coitus with a girl who was not a prostitute took place when he was twenty-two. Soon afterwards he contracted syphilis. He was treated – and circumcised[39] – in a private hospital. At about this time a brother officer made advances to him which he refused, but he was surprised to learn the officer was not alone in the regiment in his predilections.[40]

It was in South Africa that G.R. first really began to enjoy coitus, 'and on going to India continued to do so'. Sexually from now on he thought of nothing else, reducing his masturbation to about once in three weeks. He went to brothels wherever they were available: Durban, Cape Town, Colombo, Bombay. At one time he preferred black women to white, but, as with Searight, the underlying preference was for white skin and intimate conversation. In G.R.'s circle it was common practice to have heterosexual orgies in company with brother officers. On one occasion he ordered six women to his bungalow in order to celebrate his birthday by making a present of them to five of his friends after dinner.

Shortly after the South African War he 'fell violently in love with a young brother officer', who would not respond. After several years, when it was time for a long leave in Britain, he went home by way of Japan, taking in the women of the eastern ports until he contracted gonorrhoea in the Tokyo *yoshiwara* or brothel quarter (the Edwardian equivalent of breaking a leg on a ski-ing holiday, or, as he put it, 'depriving himself of the pleasure of trying several new races on the way in consequence'). On his return to India he impregnated a married European woman with whom he was in love. When she left India his luck seemed to run out again, and, with the exception of one 'black' partner, he had no regular connection with any woman for two years. But a young officer went to bed with him in 'a frenzy of passion and surprise'. They developed a continuing sexual relationship, this partner telling G.R. that he had had similar experiences with three other officers of the regiment, as well as several others on the same station. Once G.R. performed with him the night after going to bed with a girl he had met at a ball. 'In the hot weather that followed I had one orgy in Bombay which lasted three weeks.' He 'started with a Greek and a Pole and finished up with a Japanese, two brother officers accompanying me'. Then followed another spell in his lonely bungalow. Recalling the old adage 'women for breeding, boys for pleasure, and melons for sheer delight', he found melon or papaya 'most satisfactory' for masturbation. The 'opportune arrival of a fairly good-looking punkah woman', however, put an end to this form of enjoyment. Going home for his next leave, he visited the Japanese prostitutes of Bombay. In Britain he looked up his former love, and became involved with half-a-dozen other women, all but one of them married.

Five things are striking about this testimony. One is the unequivocal evidence of bisexual behaviour in the Indian army. Then there is the constant and casually accepted encounter with venereal disease. Another is the preference (which he shared with Searight) for European partners, reinforced, if anything, by taking full advantage of the opportunity of Indian contacts:

> I naturally prefer to satisfy myself with a woman, a friend and a lady of my own class; but in the absence of the best I gladly take the next best available, down the scale from a lady for who I do not care, to prostitutes of all classes and colours, men, boys and animals, melons and masturbation.

Fourthly, G.R. believed the application of Indian love-making techniques was an especial liberation for British women. He claimed to have opened the eyes of several of them sexually. Many, he thought, previously were 'slow at producing orgasm', even if they had orgasms at all, but they gratefully learned an intense response to cunnilingus. (He was not a boastful man; he admitted, for example, that with a strange woman he often experienced difficulty in maintaining his erection at the moment of penetration.) Finally, G. R. was a genuine connoisseur of non-European prostitutes, and constructed a well-informed hierarchical ladder of erotic delight:

> Of the prostitutes I have known, perhaps sixty in number, the Japanese easily taken the palm. They are scrupulously clean, have charming manners and beautiful bodies, and take an intelligent interest in the proceedings. Also they are not always thinking about the money. Perhaps the Kashmiris come next, though the Chinese run them very close. Some of the more expensive London women are bearable, but they are such harlots! The white women of the East are insupportable, and small wonder, for they consist of the dregs of the European and American markets. My list comprises English, French, German, Italian, Spanish-American, American, Bengali, Punjabi, Kashmiri, Kaffir, Singhalese, Tamil, Burmese, Malay, Japanese, Chinese, Greek and Pole.[41]

The testimonies of Searight and G.R. provide vivid case studies of British behaviour in India. Although they may not be typical, they indicate in a vital way the range of sexual possibilities which could be pursued uninhibitedly and with impunity within the formal empire well into the twentieth century, at least within the army. The evidence of the pervasive significance of prostitution for the British Indian army alerts the historian to what may be a central feature of the expansion of Europe as a whole. It is appropriate at this point to widen the analysis of its sexual dynamics by looking at the phenomenon of world wide prostitution, not only in Africa but also in the informal empire, especially in Latin America. The Chinese and Japanese forms of overseas prostitution will also need to be considered.

Notes

1 P. Nightingale, *Trade and Empire in Western India, 1784-1806*, Cambridge, 1970, p. 28; M. E. Yapp, *Strategies of British India: Britain, Iran and Afghanistan, 1798-1850*, Oxford, 1980, esp. p. 185; P. Woodruff, *The Men who ruled India: the Guardians*, London, 1954, I, pp. 269, 383; F. Henriques, *Children of Caliban: Miscegenation*, London, 1974. See also D. Wright, 'English memsahibs in Persia', *History Today*, 30, 1980, pp. 7-13.

2 D. Holman, *Sikander Sahib: the Life of Col. James Skinner, 1778-1841*, London, 1961, pp. 160-1.

3 F. Anthony, *Britain's Betrayal in India: the Story of the Anglo-Indian Community*, Bombay, 1969; K. Ballhatchet, *Race, Sex and Class under the Raj: Imperial Attitudes and Policies and their Critics, 1793-1905*, London, 1980, pp. 96-9; T. G. P. Spear, *The Nabobs: a Study of the Social Life of the English in Eighteenth-Century India*, Oxford, 1932.

4 S. Neill, *A History of Christianity in India, 1707-1858*, Cambridge, 1985, pp. 144-6, 255-6; C. Simeon (ed.), *Memorial Sketches of the Rev. David Brown*, London, 1816.

5 C. A. Bayly, *Indian Society and the Making of the British Empire*, New Cambridge History of India, II/1, Cambridge, 1988, p. 83; and *idem*, *Imperial Meridian: the British Empire and the World, 1780-1830*, London, 1989, pp. 115, 142-50; R. R. Pearce (ed.), *Memoirs and Correspondence of Richard, Marquess of Wellesley*, London, 1846, II, p. 215.

6 D. Geggus, 'British opinion and the emergence of Haiti, 1791-1805', in J. Walvin (ed.), *Slavery and British Society, 1776-1846*, London, 1982, p. 123-49, esp. p. 126; Ballhatchet, *Race, Sex and Class*, p. 98; Anthony, *Britain's Betrayal*, p. 17.

7 E. Thompson, *Life of Charles, Lord Metcalfe*, London, 1937, pp. 2, 101-2.

8 S. Sneade Brown, *Home Letters written from India. . . 1828-41*, London, 1878, p. 17.

9 F. M. Brodie, *The Devil Drives: a Life of Sir Richard Burton*, London, 1971 ed., pp. 55-9; J. H. Lehmann, *All Sir Garnet: a Life of Field-Marshal Lord Wolseley*, London, 1964, p. 60.

10 Lady [E. S.] Edwardes, *Memorials of the Life and Letters of Herbert B. Edwardes*, London, 1886, II, p. 50; T. R. Metcalf, *The Aftermath of Revolt: India, 1857-70*, Princeton, NJ, 1965.

11 D. A. Farnie, *East and West of Suez: the Suez Canal in History, 1854-1956*, London, 1969, p. 30; W. J. Macpherson, 'Investment in Indian railways, 1845-75', *Economic History Review*, VIII, 1955, pp. 177-86.

12 J. K. Stanford, *Ladies in the Sun: the Memsahibs' India, 1790-1860*, London, 1962, pp. 3, 127-37; C. Allen (ed.), *Plain Tales from the Raj: Images of British India in the Twentieth Century*, London, 1975, pp. 161-2.

13 Ballhatchet, *Race, Sex and Class*, p. 5.

14 E. Ingram, 'The "Raj" as daydream: the Pukka Sahib as Henty hero in Simla, Chandrapore and Kyauktada', in G. Martel (ed.), *Studies in Imperial History in Honour of A. P. Thornton,*, London, 1986, p. 163; Allen, *Plain Tales from the Raj*, p. 152.

15 A. J. Greenberger, *The British Image of India: a Study in the Literature of Imperialism, 1880-1960*, Oxford, 1969, p. 105; Stanford, *Ladies in the Sun*; see also P. D. Curtin, *The Two Jamaicas: the Role of Ideas, 1830-65*, Harvard, MA, 1955, p. 175; George Orwell, *Burmese days*.

16 H. Callan and S. Ardener (eds.), *The Incorporated Wife*, London, 1984, esp. ch. 10: B. Gartnell, 'Colonial wives: villains or victims?'; and ch. 11: J. Brownfoot, 'Memsahibs in Colonial Malaya'. Margaret MacMillan, *Women of the Raj*, London, 1988. See also C. Knapman, *White Women in Fiji, 1835-1930: the Ruin of Empire? . . .*, Sydney, 1986.

17 Ballhatchet, *Race, Sex and Class*, pp. 112-22, and, for Burma, pp. 144-55.

18 R. Kipling, *Plain Tales from the Hills*, London, 1900 ed., p. 181; Ingram, 'The "Raj" as daydream', p. 164, 175.

19 R. C. B. Bristow, *Memoirs of the British Raj: a Soldier in India*, London, 1974, pp. 65-6; P. Mason, *A Matter of Honour: an Account of the Indian Army, its Officers and Men*, London, 1974, pp. 367-9; M. Trustram, *Women of the Regiment: Marriage and the*

Victorian Army, Cambridge, 1984, pp. 30-1. The situation was not dissimilar in the Indian police: see M. Wynne (ed.), *On Honourable Terms: the Memoirs of Some Indian Police Officers, 1915-48*, London, 1985, pp. 237-8.

20 E. K. Senior, *British Regulars in Montreal: an Imperial Garrison, 1832-54*, Montreal, 1981, pp. 148-9.

21 John Masters, *Bugles and a Tiger*, London, 1956, pp. 153-4.

22 M. L. Ferrar (ed.), *The Diary of Colour-Sgt George Calladine, 19th Foot, 1793-1837*, London, 1922, pp. 72-7; G. Powell, *The Kandyan Wars: the British Army in Ceylon, 1803-18*, London, 1973, p. 274. Calladine may also have had sexual experience with other men: see *Diary*, pp. 43-4.

23 A. Flexner, *Prostitution in Europe*, London, 1914, p. 371. 'Lock' hospitals were so called from the French *logues* = bandages, because the original lock or venereal disease hospital in Britain was in Southwark on the site of an old lazar house for lepers, who were kept under the restraint of 'bandages' (J. Walkovitz, *Prostitution and Victorian society*, Cambridge, 1980, p. 59).

24 Ballhatchet, *Race, Sex and Class*, p. 81. What follows is based also on *Report of the Committee . . . into the Indian Cantonments . . . with regard to Prostitution and the Treatment of Venereal Diseases* (C. 7148: Accounts and Papers, LXIV, 1893); see also F. Henriques, *Prostitution and Society*, I: *Primitive, Classical and Oriental*, London, 1962, ch. 5, pp. 204-40.

25 India Office Library, 9th Earl of Elgin Viceroyalty Papers, MSS. Eur. F. 84/12, Elgin to Secretary of State Fowler, 22 May 1894.

26 *Report of the Committee . . . into the Indian cantonments*, p. 64; *House of Commons Debates, 3rd series*, 326, cc. 1187-90 (15 June 1888).

27 Ballhatchet, *Race, Sex and Class*, p. 58: *Parliamentary Debates, 3rd series, Commons*, 326, cc. 1187-90, quoting Major-General E. F. Chapman's memo. of 17 June 1886, p. 64.

28 F. Richards, *Old-Soldier Sahib*, London, 1936, pp. 76-7, 109-10, 197-202; see also C. Deveureux, *Vénus in India, or Love Adventures in Hindustan*, Brussels, 1889, I, p. 74; A. Swinson and D. Scott (eds), *Memoirs of Pte Waterfield, 32nd Foot*, London, 1968, p. 108.

29 M. Trustram, '"Distasteful and derogatory"? Examining Victorian soldiers for venereal disease', in *The Sexual Dynamics of History*, London, 1983, pp. 154-64.

30 *Report of the Committee . . . Indian Cantonments*, p. 273.

31 Ballhatchet, *Race, Sex and Class*, pp. 25, 83. Dr Breitenstein in 1895 compared 15,000 indigenous circumcised soldiers in the army of the Netherlands Indies (Java) with 18,000 uncircumcised European soldiers living side by side, and concluded that venereal disease was much higher among the uncircumcised; 41 per cent (including 4.1 per cent with syphilis) as compared with 16 per cent among the circumcised locals (0.8 per cent with syphilis): see I. Bloch, *Sexual Life of our Time*, trans. M. E. Paul, London, 1908, p. 376. See ch. 3 above, p. 77.

32 Elgin Viceroyalty Papers, F. 84/15, Elgin to Secretary of State Hamilton, 10 May 1897; Ballhatchet, *Race, Sex and Class*, pp. 94-5.

33 For the nineteenth century, two autobiographical accounts of erotic life were published by Indian army officers, but I do not feel able to use them as case studies: (1) Captain C. Deveureux, *Vénus in India, or Love Adventures in Hindustan*, Brussels, 1889, 2 vols, which I believe introduces fantasy elements (seducing the Colonel's teenage daughters after shooing off an Afghan who was buggering one of them?); unaccountably, 'R. S. Reade', *Registrum Librorum Eroticum*, London, 1936, II, p. 347, gives the date of this volume as 1858, which does not fit the internal evidence of the text; and (2) Captain Edward Sellon, *The Ups and Downs of Life: My Life. . . a Veritable History*, London, 1867, which I have not been able to find (there is no copy in the British Library); there are descriptions of it, however, in I. Bloch, *Sexual Life in England, Past and Present*, trans. W. H. Forstern, London, [1939], pp. 569-78, and in P. Fraxi [H. S. Ashbee], *Index Librorum Prohibitorum*, London, 1877, pp. 379-96, both of which quote extensive extracts. Ashbee says it portrays his career truthfully enough, with only a little colouring; Bloch describes it as true autobiography, a highly erotic book, about half of which is about India, his love affairs with European women, or preferably

Indians. Sellon (1818-66) became an army cadet at sixteen, and then spent ten years in India. Back in England he married in 1844, and promptly seduced his fourteen-year-old maid. Various other escapades followed, until he shot himself. He wrote seriously on Indian culture, for example, *Annotations on the Sacred Writings of the Hindus*, 1865, which discusses Indian religious prostitution (see Fraxi, pp. 74-5); he also translated several erotic books.

34 P. M. Furbank, *E. M. Forster: a Life*, I: 1879-1914, London, 1978, pp. 224, 231-2; D. Proctor (ed.), *Autobiography of C. Lowes Dickinson*, London, 1973, pp. 178-9; Forster, *The Hill of Devi, and other Indian Writings*. Furbank argues (II, pp. 35-51) that a visit to Egypt in 1917-19 made Forster sexually 'more active'; however, I incline to think that the way for this was at least strongly prepared by his encounters with Searight. *Maurice* was begun shortly after his return from India, again very possibly under the influence of Searight: see p. xi of intro. to Abinger ed. of *A Passage to India*, London, 1978, ed. O. Stallybrass.

35 [K. Searight], 'Paidikion', I, 'An autobiography, or the book of Hyakinthos and Narkissos', pp. 250-387, 'The Furnace: an autobiography, in which is set forth the secret diversions of a paiderast', unpublished manuscript, [c 1917]. See also T. Hammond, '"Paidikion": a paiderastic manuscript', *International Journal of Greek Love*, I, New York, 1966, pp. 28-37, for a full bibliographical analysis. Although there are fantasy elements in many parts of this volume, 'The Furnace' appears to be uncontaminated: there is no 'pornographic' exaggeration (for example, penis size is described strictly in accordance with ordinary norms, see. p. 79).

36 'Paidikion', pp. 560-6.

37 *Ibid*, 'The Furnace', lines 1490 ff. The survival of this account is perhaps particularly valuable in correcting the stereotype that Europeans found their pederastic experiences at the courts of Indian princes (such as Ranjit Singh and Tipu Sultan, or J. R. Ackerley with the Maharaja of "Chhokrapur" – see *Hindoo Holiday*, London, 1932); clearly a much wider range of options presented itself.

38 H. Ellis, *Studies in the Psychology of Sex*, III: *Analysis of the Sexual Impulse*, Philadelphia, 1903 and 1922; Appendix B, History No. XIII, pp. 306-15, by 'G.R.'.

39 This gives us a useful cross-reference to the discussion on p. 77 above.

40 Specific evidence of homo-eroticism between European men in India is not easy to come by, but there is corroboration for G.R.'s account in H. J. Wale, *Sword and Surplice, or Thirty Years' Reminiscences of the Army and the Church: an Autobiography*, London, 1880, p. 103, speaking of India in about 1845: 'There were two officers I knew who lived together, like Saul and Jonathan, pleasant in their lives'; when one of them had to go home the other 'became inconsolable . . . [and] was found hidden among some bushes in the compound crying like a child.' For corroborative evidence of heterosexual orgies in India, see 'Walter', *My Secret Life*, I, p. 33, which records a cousin, a young army officer in India, reporting the 'buying' of virgin Indian girls and having three at one time.

41 Ellis, *Studies in the Psychology of Sex*, III, p. 314.

CHAPTER SIX

Prostitution and Purity

Poverty and prostitution

... I lived in a luxurious home until I was sixteen, and then for years after that had the easy life that immoral living brings, and I just cannot be moral enough to see where drudgery is better than a life of lazy vice. [Maimie Pinzer of Philadelphia to Mrs Fanny Howe, 9 December 1910 (*The Maimie Papers*, ed. R. Rosen and S. Davidson, New York, 1977, p. 4).]

Prostitution is an emotive subject. The historian, however, must treat it as a service industry like any other, subject to the laws of demand and run by entrepreneurs.[1] However sordid the basic framework, it would be hypocritical not to recognise that pimps and madams sometimes conducted themselves with business flair and a certain style, and that prostitutes (even from deprived backgrounds) could become both sensuous and successful. The debate about the causes and nature of prostitution goes back more than a century. My reading of this debate is that there is no simple correlation between poverty and prostitution. (And even if there were, it would not altogether explain such awkward phenomena as child prostitution.) To insist on economic determinism in prostitution – women as 'victims of social and economic circumstances beyond their control' – not only has no warrant in the evidence (like all forms of economic determinism in history, indeed) but is now historiographically outmoded.[2] The whole tendency of mainstream historical explanation today, and particularly in the empire field – where even erstwhile neo-Marxists have been quietly recanting – shows a retreat from purely economic explanations in favour of comprehensively embracing wider perspectives of motivation, integrating economic and non-economic interpretations.

We touched on this briefly in discussing Victorian prostitution, finding plenty of evidence to support the emphasis which Professor Gay gives to 'the lure of prostitution'. There is more. In America in 1858 Dr W. Sanger believed that a good half of New York prostitutes entered the profession attracted by the way of life, by the need to combat loneliness:

many were immigrants. In the first fifteen years of this century, it has been estimated, they were earning between $50 and $400 a week. A study of French prostitution by Desprès in 1883 simply rejected as untrue the proposition that 'poverty engenders prostitution'.[3] In Japan a lady investigator concluded in 1916 that for many girls prostitution was a matter of preference, 'because they can eat good food, wear soft kimonos, and make money while leading a sedate life'. She also reported that many, though not all, *karayuki* (overseas prostitutes) returned home to Japan with large fortunes and were treated with respect.[4] Some research for the Kinsey Institute published in the 1960s, and sampling 175 prostitutes, also stressed the ease, the fun, the sensuality of the life and the monetary rewards as motives for taking it up. Again, in Manila *c.* 1950, many of the prostitutes apprehended in police raids on brothels turned out to be college students from well-to-do families.[5]

This is not to say that the lot of a prostitute was not often a hard one. Of course it was. As a global phenomenon, however, we can attempt to distinguish broadly two types of prostitution. These I shall call *contractual* and *non-contractual* prostitution. The latter was basically the Western form, contractual the Eastern. Non-contractual prostitution in turn may be either *entrepreneurial* or *subsistence* prostitution; that is, organised or unorganised, with prostitutes subdivided into 'known' prostitutes and 'clandestines'. The latter operated independently, and were more likely driven to it as a means of survival rather than of making money (unlike their more professional sisters, run by entrepreneurs). These forms were more benign than contractual prostitution, which often enough approximated to quasi-slavery. It is important not to make generalisations about prostitution which take no account of these differences. In any case, within these broad categories, the forms of prostitution were numerous. They included brothel inmates, prostitutes run by pimps (with access to brothel premises), loners using their own homes, temple prostitutes, amateur clandestines. Some women were chosen inside brothels, others sat in windows or verandahs, others walked the streets. In nineteenth-century London the most common system was for street-walkers to pick up men and take them to lodging rooms, which frequently had coffee shops attached. (These were known as accommodation houses.)[6] The Eastern forms of prostitution more or less eliminated street-walking. The most notorious and cynical alternative was the cages of Bombay's red-light district.[7]

In the Western forms of prostitution as they operated in British colonies, including surrogate offshoot forms in African countries, some women got status and reward out of prostitution and could do well from it financially. In Africa, John Iliffe observes, 'prostitution was certainly not a one-way ticket to poverty'.[8] In Nairobi, for example, Luise White has shown how prostitution was a major vehicle of 'upwardly mobile achievement' for black women, producing higher sources of income for them than the average male African labourer could command. She finds that European clients (contrary to stereotype) were often generous to them, and that prostitutes became the first African women to own property and buy or build their own urban homes.[9] In Tanganyika, too, it has been shown by Nick Westcott that prostitution was the most lucrative employment open to African women. During the Second World War both demand and supply increased rapidly. The better class of prostitute could earn more than a docker or clerk, while the ordinary African often had inferior accommodation. Many of the women acted as ayahs (nursemaids) by day. Some prostitutes were among the most educated and affluent citizens of Dar es Salaam. Prostitution there was well organised. The red-light district was almost exclusively dominated by Haya women. Their *grande madame* later became the leading light of TANU in Dar. Haya women were famous as prostitutes throughout East Africa. Eroticism was highly valued among the Buhaya; but more importantly these women freed themselves from male domination and moved out of their villages, both processes being encouraged by missionaries, by education and the Western idea of 'equality of the sexes'.[10]

Recent studies of prostitutes in Western Australia and South Australia also emphasise the positive self-image many prostitutes held of themselves, and reject the old stereotypes about 'pariah sisterhoods of shame'. Here, too, prostitution emerges as allowing economic opportunity to women, many of whom were attracted by the freer life style and regarded it as a reasonable way of making a living. In Perth in the 1930s it was standard practice for prostitutes to get one week off in four, to have their housework done for them and their food provided, earning £5 a week – while a waitress or a servant got £2 a week and only two weeks' holiday a year. As in Nairobi and Dar es Salaam, so in Perth, 'throughout the period 1895 to 1939 it was more profitable for women to sell their sex than their labour'.[11]

It is, however, entirely probable that the situation in small towns, as opposed to large cities, was altogether less favourable, and may well present, worldwide, a picture of hardship.[12] Those who chose prostitution as an actual means of making money were outnumbered by those who were driven to it by poverty, as a means of survival. The tendency in Africa was for subsistence clandestine prostitution to increase, especially in the twentieth century, although the abolition of slavery had often thrown young girls defenceless into prostitution. Perhaps the most appalling growth in modern subsistence prostitution took place in Addis Ababa, which suffered the double misfortune of having an exceptionally high proportion of women and being subject to Italian occupation. In the thirty years after 1938 the number of prostitutes in the Ethiopian capital appears to have increased from under 2,000 to about 80,000. Some forty per cent of them gave unemployment as the cause of their entering prostitution while thirty per cent blamed divorce. Street-walking was more common. Lagos and other coastal towns in Nigeria were by the 1940s the cause of serious concern for child prostitution, with girls being distributed to Liberia and the Gold Coast; but the extent was unknown. By the 1970s, too, there were more prostitutes in Nairobi, and they were not earning as much as their predecessors; they also included a far greater number of young girls. Everywhere in Africa, as urbanisation expanded, the number of prostitutes tended to increase, thus reducing individual earnings.[13]

Chinese and Japanese prostitution operated mainly on a contractual basis. In Japan, girls were often sold into prostitution. Most of the *karayuki* came from northern Kyūshū, which was among the most impoverished regions of Japan. The general roots of it were in rural poverty, the traditional devaluation of girls and the demand of Japanese men both at home and abroad for Japanese prostitutes. The illegalisation of infanticide by the Meiji regime only increased the number of daughters going into prostitution, another example of the way in which the adoption of Western ways so often unwittingly led to an increase in prostitution.[14] In China, also, poverty, natural calamities (famine and flood), revolts, and ignorance fed the stream of prostitution. Most prostitutes were illiterate. Some children were sold into prostitution in order to buy opium for the parents. Chinese prostitution was based on the traditional and ancient system of *mui tsai* (literally 'little younger sisters', a polite euphemism for servants), supposedly an au pair arrangement with a patron. Originally an honourable form of child adoption, *mui tsai* developed into a harsh system of female domestic service, where the girl was bought by her employer: she had no wages and was not free to leave until she was eighteen. She was not normally sexually abused in a family, but the system lent itself to recruiting for prostitution.[15] Prostitutes were of three main types: (1) *sold*, with the brothel keeper taking all the earnings of his 'adopted daughters'; (2) *pawned*, working off a debt contracted on behalf of parents or guardians, receiving board and lodging and half their wages, the other half being used to pay off the debt; and (3) *volunteers*, who worked under similar arrangements but without a debt to pay off. Some were tricked into it by promises of marriage, others were sold when young, and a not inconsiderable number were actually born in brothels.[16] Brothel owners were usually members of secret societies, and the atmosphere could be cruel and unpleasant.[17] William Pickering's unpublished report (1885) on Chinese prostitution in Malaya concluded that the sale of small girls was 'exceedingly common'. They were resold too. He discovered that 'there is a great deal of traffic in young girls going on, and that a large proportion of inmates of brothels are really slaves'. Some estimates said the proportion was eighty per cent.[18]

In general, Chinese men were well organised for sexual gratification. Although the Chinese people as a whole in the nineteenth century were rather strait-laced, they had an atavistic inheritance from an earlier, more libertarian pre-Ch'ing era. 'The chosen people of debauchery', Richard Burton called them. Even he was rather shocked by the extraordinary range of their erotic artifices and artefacts. Footbinding appalled all Westerners. Shanghai had over 40,000 prostitutes (including clandestines) c. 1900. In leading brothel towns like Tientsin, brothels existed in five different grades, with a complicated system of taxation, and there were thirty-five Tientsin male brothels housing 800 boys.[19] Sex between males was especially characteristic of China north of the Yellow River, where some towns were notorious for their actors, barbers and bath-house attendants; indeed, any man from Tientsin was automatically assumed to practise anal intercourse. In China, the availability of small boys was regular enough for it to be the subject of an annual warning to the populace by the superintendent of trade at Canton: do not indulge the Western barbarians with all our best favours. But the authorities were fighting a losing battle, not least against the demand factor, and Europeans were increasingly welcomed in the boy brothels.[20]

In other parts of the world, too, indigenous boy prostitution was common. Boy brothels were well established in Naples, as well as in Cairo and Karachi. Pederasty was endemic among the Persians, the Sikhs and the Pathans, and was elevated into an integral part of Afghanistan culture in the form of the *batsha* troupes of dancing boys. In the early nineteenth century there were reckoned to be more male prostitutes in Constantinople than females. The phenomenon appears to have been a response to demand.[21] So, the existence of this sub-branch of prostitution is a useful gloss on the interpretation of prostitution as a whole, a further reminder of the dangers of assuming that all prostitution is fuelled only by poverty.

Since the expansion of Britain was global, and since an essential part of its cosmoplastic activity was moving so many labourers about the world, the demand for prostitutes had to be met on a world-wide basis. This calls for an examination of the international networks of prostitution, in both the Atlantic and Pacific regions.

White slavery and international prostitution

> They keep on going [to Buenos Aires] as if they expected to find gold in the streets. Out of my houses alone, I lost fifteen girls in four months. It must be as good as they say, because they don't come back. [European brothel keeper, quoted in *Report of the Special Body of Experts on the Traffic in Women and Children*, 1927]

It was often alleged in the mid-nineteenth century that there was a 'white slave' traffic in under-age British girls to the Continent. T. W. Snagge's investigations for the period 1871–79 enabled him to name at least thirty-three girls taken to northern France, Belgium and Holland, mostly aged seventeen or eighteen; three of them were fifteen, one was fourteen, but there was none younger. W. T. Stead, a northern Nonconformist, rapidly promoted editor of the *Pall Mall Gazette*, took up the issues of child prostitution and age of consent, and by a journalistic stunt in 1885 proved it was possible to buy a thirteen-year-old virgin and get her away to Paris. (The girl's name was Eliza Armstrong.) His exaggerated and distorted articles for his paper were reprinted as *The Maiden Tribute of Modern Babylon*. Stead ended up in gaol for three months. He was slightly mad. Inevitably his motives were mixed: one woman who met him said, 'He exudes semen through the skin.' His investigative journalism had some part in raising the age of consent to sixteen in 1885, and thereafter little was heard of 'white slavery' emanating from Britain.[22]

The European white slave traffic was but a sub-branch of a more general phenomenon, as the League of Nations recognised by renaming it the 'traffic in women and children'. In this international prostitution Britain was essentially a customer rather than a supplier. Unlike the French, British empire-builders never took their own prostitutes with them. Their presence was thought to be bad for prestige. Indeed, any British prostitute found in India or elsewhere was sent home. International prostitution was fed by the French, the Italians, and Central European Jews (especially from Poland), together with some Russians. Above all, there were the Chinese and Japanese. Indians and Filipinos were not significantly involved in this movement.

Japanese brothels were renowned the world over for their excellent management, technical proficiency, cleanliness and quietness. Even as late as 1930 Japan maintained 11,154 licensed brothels in 541 different quarters (*yoshiwara*, after the Tokyo prototype), including those in the Japanese empire. In Japan itself there were 50,056 prostitutes. The Japanese maintained a vast network of prostitution extending from Kyūshū, north to Siberia and south to Cape Town, with Singapore, Mauritius and Australia as major termini. Queensland and the eastern goldfields of Western Australia were operated on quite a scale: well over 200 Japanese prostitutes were working in Australia in 1896, about half of them in Queensland. The principal Japanese trafficker, Muraoka Iheiji Jiden, claimed to have superintended the smuggling of 3,222 women from Japan to Singapore, and often thence to Mauritius and Australia (some pardonable exaggeration probably has to be allowed for).[23]

Enormous problems were created for the imperial authorities by the diaspora of Chinese labourers, unaccompanied by their womenfolk, and freed from restraints, over a wide area. Colonies had to accommodate alien customs with no basis in English law. Overseas, the Chinese had prostitutes wherever there were Chinese men at work, for even at home there was tacit approval of prostitution. During the early 1930s there were 6,000 Chinese 'known' prostitutes in Malaya, 4,000 in Hong Kong, 1,000 in Macao and 1,000 in Thailand. There were 2,600 registered brothels in Hong Kong. The Chinese did a not inconsiderable trade in little girls to the United States. There was also a definite and long-standing trade in small boys to Indonesia. Ti-chou troupes of young Chinese boy actors contained some exquisitely expert anal technicians, and their tours among overseas Chinese communities caused considerable excitement and trouble, especially in Thailand, Malaya and Sumatra. When in the 1930s the British authorities decided to ban Chinese theatricals in Malaya, there was such an outcry from the Ti-chou community that they were forced into a compromise whereby the boy actors would still be allowed to perform but were to be recruited locally and not imported.[24]

The principal problem for British administrators, however, was posed by orthodox Chinese brothels in Malaya and Hong Kong. William Pickering (Protector of Chinese) calculated that in 1883 there were 235 brothels in Singapore, housing 2,400 licensed prostitutes, catering for a population of 55,000 Chinese men; of these prostitutes all but 300 were also available to Europeans. Since there were ten Chinese men to every one Chinese woman in Malaya, and since Chinese men so famously knew how to take care of sexual needs without women anyway, Pickering concluded that it would be pointless, even undesirable, to check free (that is, uncoerced) prostitution, though he realised that this advice was as 'unEnglish, unChristian and abnormal as the situation itself'. The Chinese Protectorate was set up to check the worst abuses, such as kidnapping. In Malaya in 1894 there were 587 registered brothels containing 4,514 Chinese, 450 Japanese, eighty-one Malay, and fifty other known prostitutes of various origins. (With keepers and servants the total number of inmates came to 6,596.) In addition there was Singapore, which alone had 246 brothels in 1894 with 1,871 registered prostitutes; Penang had 103 houses with 981 inmates. By 1899 the

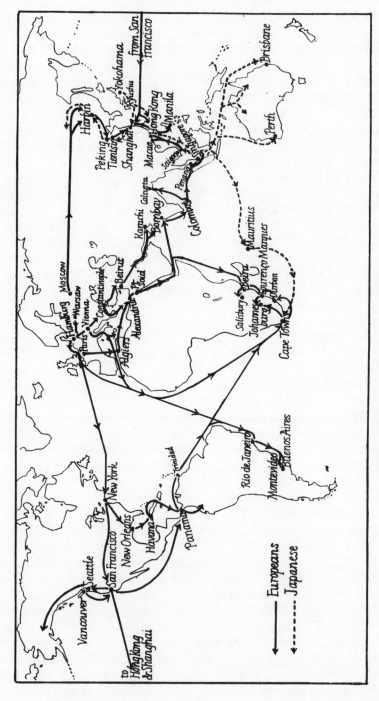

Figure 3   Main prostitution networks, c. 1914

figures had increased still further. Singapore had 311 brothels (236 Chinese, forty-eight Japanese, ten European, nine Tamil and eight Malay houses) in the recognised red-light district, with 861 Chinese, 294 Japanese, thirty-seven European, thirteen Tamil and twenty-eight Malay known prostitutes. Also, there were about half a dozen male brothels in Singapore with about a dozen inmates, half of which were reserved for the Chinese. In Penang by 1899 there were 736 Chinese registered prostitutes, seventy-one Japanese and eighty-six Indians. By the twentieth century British government policy in Malaya, as in India, was directed towards the abolition of compulsory registration and inspection. In Hong Kong, the emphasis was on control of *mui tsai*.[25]

In the geography of white slavery the main route was from Europe to Latin America, especially to Brazil, Argentina and Uruguay. Buenos Aires was something of an international Mecca or Golconda magnet. But there was also a major supply line running to North Africa, Egypt and Constantinople (and taking in Greece on the way). This line, especially after the opening of the Suez Canal in 1869, led on to Bombay, Colombo, Singapore, Saigon, Hong Kong and Shanghai. From Hong Kong and Shanghai there was a further forward extension by rail to Harbin in Manchuria, or by sea to Manila in the Philippines. The Russians had their own export line (for unemployable Siberian peasants), to Manchuria and north China, focusing upon the frontier town of Harbin (the centre of railway construction in the region). In 1932 Harbin had a population of 100,000 Russians and contained nine licensed brothels. Most of the 2,000 white prostitutes in Shanghai c. 1900 were Russians. There were also Russian women in Peking and Tientsin. The Italians had a direct line to the goldfields of Western Australia. As the Witwatersrand mines developed, Johannesburg was brought on to the international vice circuit, partly from New York and partly via the Suez Canal. New York was always a major city in the network, with a westward supply line via San Francisco to Hong Kong and Shanghai, and further branches to Singapore or to the Philippines. The southern route from New York linked up Texas, New Orleans ('the greatest brothel city of all time'), Cuba, Panama and ultimately Cape Town and Johannesburg.[26] (See fig. 3.)

Perhaps one of the most surprising features of the European section of the international prostitution network was the extent to which Jews were induced 'to eat the bread of infamy, and take the wages of shame'. Arthur Moro, an officer in the London Jewish Association for the Protection of Girls and Women, lamented in 1903, 'We have positive evidence that to almost all parts of North and South Africa, to India, China, Japan, Philippine Islands, North and South America and also to many of the countries in Europe, Yiddish-speaking Jews are maintaining

[145]

a regular flow of Jewesses, trafficked solely for the purpose of prostitution.' The roots of this phenomenon, spreading to five continents, were
in destitution, discrimination, persecution, massive migrations and
urbanisation in Central Europe, with a weakening of traditional controls
in towns. To put it in perspective, however: there were more French
prostitutes in Paris than there were Jewish harlots in all the world, and
the French were also heavily represented in a global diaspora embracing
Buenos Aires, the Rand and Manchuria.[27]

The organisers of this international traffic were officially regarded
with extreme disgust, but they were by any standard remarkably
resourceful entrepreneurs. Husband-and-wife teams were typical, the
one a pimp (or *souteneur*, or 'boy', as they called themselves), the other
a brothel madam. They lived peripatetic lives, and passed on their know-
how to their sons and daughters. Whole families from the Polish
underworld were involved – for example the Stanger sisters, one procuring in Europe, one running a brothel in Port Arthur, another operating
in Tientsin. Sadie Solomon was one of the best-travelled figures in the
New York underworld, having run brothels in Johannesburg, Brazil,
Buenos Aires, Panama, Texas and Vancouver by 1914, when she was said
to be worth $50,000. Nathan Spieler gave up pretzel-baking to run
brothels in Shanghai, Constantinople, Bombay and Singapore, and he
was known in the Philippines too. The big-time players had nicknames
which resonated within several continents: 'Sadie the Afrikaner', 'Ever-
ready Rita' and 'Jenny the Factory' are self-explanatory sobriquets. In
Argentina, after two sons of a rabbi had apparently had difficulty getting
a Jewish burial for their father because they were well-known pimps, a
chartered burial society was set up with its own cemetery for those
excluded from the Ashkenazi cemetery on grounds of uncleanness. By
the 1920s this had evolved into the Zwi Magdal Society, a pimps'
fraternity controlling a thousand brothels and 3,000 girls.

By such enterprise did prostitution thrive. The outstanding characteristics of these sexual entrepreneurs were their mobility, their readiness
to diversify and their ruthless professionalism. Movement was essential
to the whole business. Customers needed new faces, and so the maintenance of a chain of brothels along a well-established passing-on route
was essential. There was no formal direction; just a world-wide camar-
aderie of pimps and women constantly on the move. The League of
Nations investigating team in the 1920s bumped into the same pimps
in Buenos Aires, Cairo, Paris, Warsaw and Antwerp. Pimps were well
informed about each other's movements. Many made regular recruiting
trips to Europe, sometimes as many as five times a year, probably
bringing back no more than one girl at a time (to avoid attracting
suspicion). In 1913 the Polish authorities even claimed that traffickers

convened annually for a sort of trade fair in Warsaw. The enterprising George Cuirassier swooped into South Africa to meet the extra demand created by the Boer War, having already operated in France, Manchuria, Argentina, Mexico and the United States. Such men always knew where the big events were, whether it was races in a Mexican border town attracting 100,000 Americans a day or a gymnastic gala in Geneva. Then there was their willingness to take on sidelines. They sold 'pornography' to potential customers and cocaine to weary women. They posed for sexual pictures, or perhaps entered into partnership with a sex photographer. Some were involved in smuggling. They were patient in outwitting the authorities. Making detours was a regular device to reduce the risk of immigration scrutiny – money could always be made en route. They obtained false marriage certificates, went through pseudo-marriage ceremonies, even actual marriage ceremonies. They regularly ordered reinforcements by telegraph. Their professionalism was particularly geared to getting 'green' girls (the raw newcomers) and training them in anal and oral practices. This constituted the vital breakthrough into the 'big time', because a prostitute expert in these refinements could receive up to forty men a day, as compared with six to eight men serviced by straightforward intercourse. Moreover, the tariff was higher, and so a prostitute who had extended her range in this way was reckoned to be worth more than half a dozen ordinary prostitutes.[28]

The League of Nations inquiry held between 1924 and 1927 visited twenty-eight countries and 112 cities and conducted 6,500 interviews. It confirmed that Latin America was the major destination for white prostitutes. The proportion of foreign women in Brazilian brothels was eighty per cent; in Montevideo it was forty-two per cent and in Argentina seventy-five per cent. Buenos Aires had 4,500 foreign prostitutes; there were 585 known brothels. Perhaps a quarter of its prostitutes were French – certainly the largest single group. A clear majority of *all* European prostitutes exported ended up in Argentina. Turning to North Africa, in Alexandria there were 670 brothels in 1923, with 1,356 known prostitutes: one-third were French, and over forty per cent foreign. Algeria had 580 European prostitutes, and Tunisia 115. In both countries the winter tourist season imposed an increased demand. Some houses were operated in conjunction with brothels in Marseilles and Paris, the telegraph again being a vital adjunct to the conduct of business.[29] The parallel inquiry into the situation in the East, covering the whole area from Beirut to Tokyo, was conducted in 1930-32. It came up with the following figures. In Calcutta there were twenty-five French prostitutes, ten Russian, one Italian, one Greek and one Australian. There were twenty whites in Hong Kong (half of them French), twenty in Bombay (mostly Jews), fifteen in Shanghai (including five Americans and three

Australians), ten or more in the Philippines (plus 122 Japanese) and twenty-three in Colombo. Colombo provided the League with its best proof of boy-prostitution (involving Tamil teenagers working in the docks), but nowhere could they uncover much evidence of any substantial *traffic* in boys.[30]

Thus the international diffusion of European prostitutes was remarkably wide at its heyday in the late nineteenth and early twentieth centuries. Years ago Frank Thistlethwaite demonstrated the extraordinary seasonal movements of nineteenth-century European migratory labourers around the Atlantic basin: the 'proletarian globe-trotters', such as the coal-miners and house-painters who divided their time annually between Scotland and America. These had their counterparts working around the Pacific rim, the gold-miners and canal-diggers who moved freely throughout the world as opportunity occurred. The migratory patterns he described have become part of the standard evidence for the vitality of nineteenth-century European expansion, especially when put in the context of the western management of the movement of indentured labourers (Indian, Chinese and Pacific Islanders) throughout the world. To this picture must now be added peripatetic prostitution, the migration of pimps and prostitutes along connected chains of brothels encircling the globe. There was an elaborate informal organisation, efficiently run on the best entrepreneurial lines. The nodal distributive points were Buenos Aires, New York, Alexandria, Constantinople, Hong Kong and Shanghai. The whole international network relied heavily on technological advance: on condoms, cables and canals (Suez and Panama). Southern Africa would not have been brought so quickly on to the network but for the Suez Canal and the railway link from Lourenço Marques to Johannesburg (1895). This soon brought 750 Jewish prostitutes to the region. About a third of the girls were French (the red-light district of Johannesburg was called Frenchfontein), and a fifth of them were German. There were at least 133 brothels in Johannesburg by 1896, and probably a similar number in Cape Town. Most of the inmates were white. Johannesburg's connection to the international network also owed something to the exodus from New York brothels during the police clean-up campaign of 1892-95. By 1909 Smuts was launching his own purge, and broke the hold of the immigrant vice merchants. Prostitution in South Africa reverted once more to its indigenous base. Reversal of the trend towards turning the whole world into the white man's brothel had begun.[31]

The Purity Campaign

We know no spectacle so ridiculous as the British public in one of its periodical fits of morality . . . Once in six or seven years our virtue becomes outrageous... We must make a stand against vice... We reflect very complacently on our own severity , and compare with great pride the high standard of morals established in England with the Parisian laxity. [Lord Macaulay, 'Moore's Life of Byron', June 1830, *Literary and Historical Essays contributed to the Edinburgh Review*]

The twentieth-century international campaign to control prostitution and trafficking was essentially British-inspired: a transmutation on to the world stage of the country's parochial attitudes, which the governments of the rest of the world were curiously ready to accept. The first attempt to close down indigenous brothels would seem to have been that of General Sir Charles Napier, worried in 1845 about the 'corrupting' effect on his troops of the boy brothels of Karachi, which Richard Burton minutely investigated for him.[32] This attempted closure was not actually successful, because the local amirs were keen to keep the system going. League of Nations investigators reported in 1932 that 'a certain amount of homosexual prostitution of young Indian boys' existed in Karachi, many of them said to have venereal disease.[33]

Official reaction against sexual opportunism began in earnest with the Purity Campaign launched in 1869 by Josephine Butler, which was perhaps bound to be exported overseas. We have already noted the struggles in the 1880s and 1890s between public opinion, the Purity people and the government, on the one side, and the medico-military-imperial establishment on the other. The British government officially set its face against regulated prostitution ('reglementation') in any form, and decided that the empire must conform. This policy was reaffirmed by the Colonial Office Advisory Committee on Social Hygiene, whose final report was issued under Lord Balfour of Burleigh as chairman, in 1929.[34] Meanwhile, the tolerated brothels of Colombo had already been closed in 1912, and Lady Lugard had begun (but apparently did not pursue) a clean-up campaign in Hong Kong.[35] The Contagious Diseases Acts in South Africa were repealed in 1919.

Other Powers were moving, too. The Netherlands closed its Indonesian tolerated brothels in 1911 and abolished regulated prostitution in 1913.[36] The Meiji government in Japan was from the beginning worried about the incompatibility between a westernising image and its easy traditional sexual patterns. It soon made changes. In Tokyo from 1871 labourers were required to wear more than a loincloth: 'Do not be laughed at by [prudish] foreigners.' Legal prostitution was modified by reglementation: the government reformed the sale of girls, introduced weekly medical inspection for prostitutes, taxed the brothels and introduced police surveillance. By the end of the nineteenth century the number of domestic Japanese brothels was already beginning to decline. From 1888 the Japanese were considering an end to licensed prostitution altogether. Worried about the effect on their international prestige, the recall of the overseas legions of sensuality was decreed in 1921. Japanese prostitution in Australia had, however, already been dealt a mortal blow by the 'white Australia' policy, in particular the Immigration Restriction Act of 1901.[37]

The profound interest evoked by the Purity Campaign in Britain was meanwhile projected directly into the international arena. In 1889 there was a London congress on the 'white slave traffic'. In Paris in 1904 a dozen European countries came to an international agreement to combat the traffic. In 1910 a similar convention declared procuring to be an offence. The League of Nations inherited this emerging pattern of international co-operation. A 1921 convention raised the age of protection in trafficking to twenty-one, and extended it to boys. Attention was also turned to checking pornography ('a moral pest of which all civilised countries wish to be rid', according to the British delegation). In 1933 an international convention made procuration an offence even for a consenting adult female. Meanwhile individual countries were under pressure to abolish regulated prostitution. The League was convinced that the mere existence of tolerated brothels encouraged the growth of prostitution. By 1937 all Anglo-Saxon countries were taking a tough stand on this, and so was the Netherlands. The licensed brothels of Hong Kong were being closed from 1934. The French, the Portuguese, the Japanese and the Thais, however, were regulationist, but Japan seemed to be moving towards full abolition, and possibly Indo-China was, too. China was already prohibitionist in principles but not rigorous in its application.[38]

Sexual patterns had been considerably affected by the First World War. The networks of international prostitution were thrown into confusion, perhaps never quite fully to recover before the League of Nations moved into action against them. War increased the employment opportunities for women, with some consequent reduction in the numbers entering prostitution. Increasing availability of birth control and changing attitudes at home led to an increase in premarital intercourse, and thus to a reduction in the demand for prostitutes. Venereal disease had dramatically declined through better treatment, and perhaps a decrease in virulence. In any case, the Purity Campaign was successful in persuading large sections of society that sex should be kept to a minimum.[39] After the war, plans for an enlarged Singapore naval base provided an urgent additional reason for getting rid of regulated prostitution in Malaya. Brothels were tolerated throughout Malaya until 1927, and voluntary Chinese prostitutes continued to be admitted. But between 1927 and 1930 there was a transitional period during which the entry of avowed prostitutes was stopped. In 1929 brothels were made illegal throughout the Straits Settlements, and in the Federated Malay States in 1931. Also in 1929, the British government insisted on registration of all *mui tsai*, but progress towards abolition was slow.[40] The effect of international pressure was felt even in China. *Mui tsai* were emancipated in 1927, and in 1928 the Chinese launched a pilot scheme for scrapping tolerated brothels in Nanking. The last licensed brothel in Shanghai was shut in 1934.[41] Somehow, and despite Montgomery's efforts, Egypt escaped the big clean-up. Reformist plans of 1935 went into abeyance when the Second World War broke out, whereupon British troops had their last large-scale experience of oriental sex.[42]

War always tends to increase sexual activity, because of the general heightening of nervous tensions, and because (as Victor Purcell put it) 'the beauties of the fleshpots made a wonderful contrast to the horrors and absurdities of war'. Thus, as in every other war, the incidence of venereal disease increased between 1939 and 1945; the only difference was that there were concomitant big increases in successful treatment. Problems were particularly acute in the Italian campaign, 1943-45, and, outside Europe, in the West Indies, with a large influx of American personnel. Once again the differential rates for home and overseas service should be noted. In the Royal Air Force the incidence of venereal disease abroad was almost double what it was at home; and in the British army in India more than six times as high as in the United Kingdom stations.[43] In the war in the Far East, the effects of the international Purity Campaign were reversed as prostitution was restored by the Japanese in the conquered areas of Asia. The Japanese military authorities, worried about the prospects of an orgy of rape, organised matters closely in alliance with civilian contractors. Need was calculated on the basis of one prostitute to forty men, so more than 80,000 women were drafted into prostitution, a great many of them from Korea.[44]

The end of the Second World War revived the morality of the interwar years and took it a stage further. The Holocaust and the establishment of Israel removed the Jews from international prostitution. The American occupation of Japan led to the abolition of mixed nude public bathing there and the destruction of whole warehouses of erotic material. Licensed prostitution in Japan was finally abolished in 1957. The Japanese were, however, extremely fortunate in not being occupied by the even more prudish British.[45] Communists everywhere were puritanical. Mao Tse-tung closed the unregulated brothels of Shanghai in 1954. Inmates dispersed to Macao, Taiwan and Hong Kong. Shanghai's

F

persistent boy brothels (still patronised by Europeans) were a principal cause of the affront which prostitution gave to Communist ideology.[46] Similarly, the accession to power of Dr Machel in Mozambique closed off another sexual outlet for Europeans some twenty years later.[47] The Vietnam wars caused an unexpected sexual explosion, a disgraceful finale to sexual exploitation by Western Powers, especially the Americans.[48] As empires came to an end, some newly independent regimes initially saw a future in sexually-motivated tourism: hence Fanon's famous dictum that the first thing an independent elite did was to 'set up its country as the brothel of Europe'. (He instanced Morocco, Mexico, Brazil and Cuba, but on a smaller scale support for such a thesis could for a while be seen everywhere from Manzini in Swaziland to Manila in the Philippines.)[49] But such proceedings also in the end succumbed to the backlash of puritanical international interdiction. Sun City, Bophuthatswana, might become the exception which proves the rule, but is more likely to go the way of all flesh.

Did Josephine Butler and the *Pall Mall Gazette* ever guess that their Purity Campaign was destined within a century to leave its mark on the whole world? Many people's essentially harmless pleasures are now penalised, prostitution is widely frowned upon, and in Britain and America even family photographs are being monitored. For most parts of the world these are recent and not necessarily desirable developments. Yet there remain some real but untackled sexual issues. There are in the West vital but unresolved problems concerning, for example, young people or public figures. For adolescents, appropriate and acceptable forms of sexuality have yet to be evolved. For politicians and other leaders, the proper relationship between private life and public morality has still to be sensibly agreed. In these matters Britain has made no significant official changes or progress in a hundred years, and has instead meanwhile merely exported to the international community the fearful intolerance and neurotic frustration which Purity exacts as the price of its adoption.

It is perhaps doubtful whether the British Purity movement could ever have achieved such universal influence but for the fact that it synchronised with the need of the imperial authorities for a more serious and respectable administration of its enlarged formal responsibilities from the end of the nineteenth century. The task of the next chapter will therefore be to demonstrate in more detail the crucial victories of Purity in the Edwardian African empire. In doing so, we shall adjust the focus of our investigation rather considerably by putting under the microscope for the first time the well-documented world of metropolitan policy-making and parliamentary debate. It will be possible to see in precise terms how Whitehall and Westminster imposed their moral views on hitherto free-wheeling servants of imperial administration in Africa, making a massive and indeed revolutionary intrusion of public authority into the private lives of official classes overseas.

Notes

1 H. Ellis, *Studies in the Psychology of Sex*, IV: *Sex in Relation to Society*, Philadelphia, 1910 and 1921, ch. vii: 'Prostitution'.
2 M. Berger, 'Imperialism and sexual exploitation: a review article', *Journal of Imperial and Commonwealth History*, XVII, 1988.
3 D. J. Pivar, *Purity Crusade, Sexual Morality and Social Control, 1868-1900*, Westport, Conn., 1973, p. 23; V. and B. Bullough, *Women and Prostitution: a Social History*, New York, 1987, p. 245; R. Rosen and S. Davidson (eds), *The Maimie Papers*, New York, 1977, p. xxviii.
4 M. Hane, *Peasants, Rebels and Outcastes: the Underside of Modern Japan*, New York, 1982, pp. 207-8, quoting Koyama, *Taisho Daizasshi*, pp. 202-3.
5 PRO, CO 859/550, article on White Slave Trade, November, 1953; V. and B. Bullough, *Women and Prostitution*, pp. 292-309.
6 K. Chesney, *The Victorian Underworld*, London, 1970, p. 336; H. Mayhew, *London Labour and the London Poor*, IV, 1862, p. 257.
7 F. Henriques, *Prostitution and Society*, I: *Primitive, Classical and Oriental*, London, 1962, p. 229.
8 J. Iliffe, *The African Poor: a History*, Cambridge, 1987, pp. 183-5.
9 L. White, 'A history of prostitution in Nairobi, Kenya, c. 1900-1952', unpublished PhD thesis, Cambridge, 1984; 'Prostitution, identity and class consciousness in Nairobi during World War II', *Signs: a Journal of Women in Culture and Society*, XI, 1986, pp. 255-73.
10 N. J. Westcott, 'The impact of the Second World War on Tanganyika, 1939-49', unpublished PhD thesis, Cambridge, 1982, pp. 291-3.
11 R. Davidson, '"As good a bloody woman as any other woman . . .": prostitutes in Western Australia, 1895-1939', in P. Crawford (ed.), *Exploring Women's Past: Essays in Social History*, London, 1984, pp. 171-201.
12 A. M. Butler, *Daughters of Joy, Sisters of Misery: Prostitutes in the American West, 1865-90*, Illinois, 1985; and review by N. L. Shumsky in *Journal of Social History*, XX, 1986, p. 395.
13 Iliffe, *African Poor*, p. 185; CO 859/224/5, Nigeria: Colonial Annual Reports, 1946 and 1947.
14 Kane, *Peasants, Rebels and Outcastes*, p. 209-19.
15 League of Nations, *Traffic in Women and Children: Conference of Central Authorities in Eastern countries at Bandoeng, February 1937*, minutes of meetings, pp. 11-12 (C.476. M.318. 1937. IV); C0 859/552, Mui tsai in Hong Kong; R. Heussler, *British Rule in Malaya: the Malayan Civil Service and its Predecessors, 1867-1942*, Oxford, 1981, pp. 163-4.
16 V. Purcell, *The Memoirs of a Malayan Official*, London, 1965, pp. 163-4.
17 W. Blythe, *Impact of Chinese Secret Societies in Malaya*, Oxford, 1969, pp. 204-14.
18 CO 273/121/13612 (Straits Settlements), W. A. Pickering, annual report (1882) on Chinese Protectorate, Singapore and Penang (12 April 1883), and minute by C. P. Lucas, 15 August 1885.
19 R. Gulik, *Sex Life in Ancient China*, Leiden, 1961; R. F. Burton (ed.), *A Plain and Literal Translation of the Arabian Nights . . . The Book of the Thousand Nights and a Night . . .*, London, 1885-6, X: 'Terminal essay', p. 238; V. W. Ng, 'Ideology and sexuality: rape laws in Qing China', *Journal of Asian Studies*, 46, 1987, pp. 57-70. For footbinding see J. K. Fairbank, *The Great Chinese Revolution, 1800-1985*, New York, 1986, pp. 68-73; and H. S. Levy, *Chinese Footbinding: the History of a Curious Erotic Custom*, New

York, 1966. Footbinding was a painful deforming process, an amazing piece of 'physio-psycho-sociological engineering', which spread to all ranks of society. The preferred length of a woman's foot was three inches, and feet could be reckoned more important than facial beauty. The small foot, thus rendered highly sensitive by the compacting together of nerve-endings, could be sucked. It was believed to tighten the vagina, and to increase female erogenousness by fifty per cent.

20 CO 537/540/38767, Memorandum on prevalence of unnatural crime among Chinese indentured labourers on the Witwatersrand, by the Superintendent of Foreign Labour (August 1906), and evidence of J. E. Cooke (Chinese Interpreter to the Government), etc; M. Beurdeley *et al., The Clouds and the Rain: the Art of Love in China*, Fribourg, 1969, pp. 159-68; F. Wakeman, *Strangers at the Gate: Social Disorder in South China, 1839-61*, London, 1966, p. 55.

21 D. Drew and J. Drake, *Boys for Sale: a Sociological Study of Boy Prostitution*, New York, 1969; J. A. St John, *Egypt and Mohammed Ali: or, Travels in the Valley of the Nile*, London, 1834, II, pp. 323-4; J. Berque, *Egypt: Imperialism and Revolution*, trans. J. Stewart, 1972, p. 89; A. Edwardes, *Jewel in the Lotus: Historical Survey of the Sexual Culture of the East*, London, 1961, pp. 216-48. An important recent survey of child prostitution is *Canada: Report of the Special Committee on Pornography and Prostitution*, 2 vols, Ottawa, 1985, which suggests to me that the extraordinary range of practices required of young prostitutes is such that money alone would not be a sufficient incentive.

22 D. Gorham, 'The "Maiden Tribute of Modern Babylon" re-examined: child prostitution and the idea of childhood in late-Victorian England', *Victorian Studies*, XXI, 1977/ 8, pp. 353-79; R. Pearsall, *The Worm in the Bud: the World of Victorian Sexuality*, London, 1969, pp. 367-77; *Select Committee of the House of Lords on the Protection of Young Girls: Report with Minutes of Evidence (1881)*: C. 448, Accounts and Papers, IX, reprinted in *Crime and Punishment: Juvenile Offenders*, V: *Sessions 1881-96* (Irish UP series of British Parliamentary Papers, Shannon, 1970), p. 141: Report by T. W. Snagge on traffic in English girls for immoral purposes in foreign towns.

23 League of Nations, *Report of Commission of Enquiry into the Traffic in Women and Children in the Far East* (C.849. M.393. 1932. IV), pp. 103-4); Henriques, *Prostitution and Society*, III, pp. 295-306; D. C. S. Sissons, '"Karayuki-san": Japanese prostitutes in Australia, 1887-1916', *Historical Studies*, XVII, 1977, nos. 68 and 69, in two parts. A British official, R. Winstedt (who was less impressed with Japanese prostitutes than most Westerners), described then as 'very clean little people, these dutiful daughters of Japan, who sell their frog-like Degas bodies in order to maintain impoverished parents' (*Start from Alif: Count from One, an Autobiographical Mémoire*, Kuala Lumpur, 1969, p. 52).

24 League of Nations, *op. cit.,* note 15 above, pp. 11-12, 23, 33; *op. cit.,* note 23 above, pp. 135-46; *Annual Reports* (C.825. M.282. 1925. IV).

25 CO 273/121/13612, Pickering, Annual Report (1882) on Chinese Protectorate, Singapore and Penang, 12 April 1883; CO 273/197/18487, report by G. T. Hare (Acting Assistant Protector of Chinese) on brothels in Straits Settlements and Protected Native States, 12 September 1894; CO 273/258/30403, report by A. H. Capper (Acting Protector of Chinese) on the working of the Women and Children's Protection Ordinance XIII of 1899. See also E. Sadka, *The Protected Malay States, 1874-95*, Kuala Lumpur, 1968, p. 311, n1. On the organisation of Chinese prostitution, see Purcell, *Memoirs*, pp. 163-4; R. N. Jackson, *Pickering: Protector of Chinese*, Kuala Lumpur, 1965, pp. 92-9; Blythe, *Impact of Chinese Secret Societies*, pp. 204, 245, 307; C. M. Turnbull, *A History of Singapore, 1819-1975*, Kuala Lumpur, 1977, pp. 87-8. For prostitution in Hong Kong see H. Lethbridge, *Hong Kong: Stability and Change, a Collection of Essays*, Hong Kong, 1978, ch. iv: 'The Po Leung Kuk' [Society for the Protection of Women and Girls], pp. 71-103.

26 League of Nations, *Reports on Traffic in Women and Children* (1923-37), esp. *Report of the Special Body of Experts on Traffic in Women and Children* (C.52. M.52. 1927. IV); and, for the Russians, *Commission of Enquiry into Traffic in Women and Children in the Far East* (C.849. M.393. 1932. IV), pp. 30-6, 143-6. See also C. Terrot, *The Maiden*

Tribute: a Study of the White Slave Traffic of the Nineteenth Century, London, 1959; H. Wilson Harris, *Human Merchandise: a Study of the International Traffic in Women*, London, 1928; A. Mackirdy and W. N. Willis, *The White Slave Market*, London, 1912; J. Marchant, *The Master Problem*, London, 1917.

27 E. J. Bristow, *Prostitution and Prejudice: the Jewish Fight against White Slavery, 1870-1939*, Dublin, 1982.

28 This paragraph is based on the sources cited in notes 26 and 27 above; for the point about 'refinements' of the trade, see *Report on Traffic in Women and Children*, 1927, part II: *Evidence*, p. 18.

29 *Ibid.*, pp. 12-13, 59-60, 75-9, 182-3.

30 League of Nations, *op. cit.*, note 23 above, pp. 21-2; and, for Ceylon, p. 378. For follow-up reports from Ceylon see *Summary of Annual Reports for 1934/35*, p. 21, (C.88. M.32. 1936. IV), etc.

31 C. van Onselen, *Studies in Social and Economic History of the Witwatersrand*, I: *New Babylon*, London, 1982, 'Prostitutes and proletarians', pp. 102-62. See also W. Nasson's chapter in P. Warwick (ed.), *The South African War, 1899-1902*, London, 1982, pp. 132-3.

32 F. M. Brodie, *The Devil Drives: a Life of Sir Richard Burton*, London, 1971 ed., pp. 76-99.

33 League of Nations, *op. cit.*, note 23 above, p. 344.

34 CO 273/544/52032, *Final Report of Advisory Committee on Social Hygiene*, 1928, which was well received in the Colonial Office.

35 N. J. Miners, *Hong Kong under Imperial Rule, 1912-4*, Hong Kong, 1988; Mackirdy and Willis, *The White Slave Market*, p. 80.

36 League of Nations, *op. cit.*, note 23 above, p. 378; *op. cit.*, note 15 above, minutes of meetings, p. 46; Mackirdy and Willis, *White Slave Market*, p. 80; E. B. van Heyningen, 'The social evil in the Cape Colony, 1868-1902: Prostitution and the CD Acts', *Journal of Southern African Studies*, X, 1984, p. 194.

37 Sissons, '"Karayuki-san": Japanese prostitutes in Australia', part II, pp. 474 ff; D. Sladen and N. Lorimer, *More Queer things about Japan*, London, 1904, appendix: 'The Yoshiwara from within', pp. 457-83); G. B. Sansom, *The Western World and Japan: a Study in Interaction of European and Asiatic Cultures*, London, 1950, p. 385.

38 League of Nations, *op. cit.*, note 15 above, p. 49 (C.516, M.357, 1937. IV); *Suppression of . . . Traffic in Obscene Publications* (C.734. M.299. 1923. IV); Miners, *Hong Kong under Imperial Rule*.

39 Bristow, *Prostitution and Prejudice*, p. 320-22; *idem, Vice and Vigilance*, p. 147; J. Weeks, *Sex, Politics and Society*, London, 1981, pp. 207-9.

40 CO 273/543/52032, Cmd. 2501, 1925, *First Report of the Advisory Committee on Social Hygiene* (W. Ormsby-Gore); Purcell, *Memoirs*, pp. 163-4; *idem, The Chinese in South-East Asia*, 2nd ed., Oxford, 1965, p. 274; R. Bruce Lockhart, *Return to Malaya*, London, 1936, pp. 121-4; Lethbridge, *Hong Kong*, p. 94; Miners, *Hong Kong under Imperial Rule*, pp. 153-90.

41 League of Nations, *op. cit.* note 15 above, pp. 35,48.

42 Henriques, *Prostitution and Society*, III, pp. 293-4; K. Kishtany, *The Prostitute in Progressive Literature*, London, 1982, pp. 100-1. Surprisingly, Montgomery was quite indulgent towards a modicum of what he jokingly called 'horizontal relaxation'; what he objected to (1931-33) was the dangerous excesses inspired by Cairo, especially the homosexual and pornographic temptations: See N. Hamilton, *Monty*, London, 1973, I, pp. 234-5: and B. Montgomery, *A Field-Marshal in the Family*, London, 1973, p. 215.

43 J. Costello, *Love, Sex and War: Changing Values, 1939-45*, London, 1985; *Official Medical History of World War Two*: W. F. Mellor (ed.), *Casualties and Medical Statistics*, London, 1972, pp. 15, 119, 330, 526, 536; A. S. MacNalty (ed.), *The Civilian Health and Medical Services*, London, 1955, I, pp. 114-24; Purcell, *Memoirs*, p. 32; CO 859/105/5 (1943-4).

44 Hane, *Peasants, Rebels and Outcastes*, p. 219; L. Allen, *Burma: the Longest War, 1941-45*, London, 1984, pp. 590-99: 'Sex on the battlefield'.

45 N. Braybrooke (ed.), *Letters of J. R. Ackerley*, London, 1975, p. 196, quoting the opinion

of C. R. Boxer; J. van de Wettering, *Empty Mirror: Experiences in a Japanese Zen Monastery*, London, 1973, p. 46; S. O'Callaghan, *Yellow Slave Trade: a Survey; Traffic in Women and Children in the Far East*, London, 1968, p. 84; V. Bullough, *Sexual Variance in Society and History*, New York, 1976, p. 682.

46 O'Callaghan, *Yellow Slave Trade*, p. 15; T. Terzani, *Behind the Forbidden Door: Travels in China*, London, 1986, describes the process in Peking's 237 brothels (with 1,000 prostitutes) in 1950, when the girls were taken off to labour camps for 're-education', and there were hundreds of arrests.

47 R. Blake, *History of Rhodesia*, London, 1977, p. 280.

48 S. Brownmiller, *Against our Will: Men, Women and Rape*, London, 1975, pp. 87-93; C. Enloe, *Does Khaki become you? The Militarisation of Women's Lives*, London, 1983, pp. 33-5.

49 F. Fanon, *The Wretched of the Earth*, 1961, trans. C. Farrington, London, 1965, p. 125; J. Ennew, *The Sexual Exploitation of Children*, Cambridge, 1986, ch. 5; L. Davis, *The Philippines: People, Poverty and Politics*, London, 1987, ch. 4: 'Prostitution', pp. 99-124.

CHAPTER SEVEN

Chastity and the Colonial Service

An Edwardian revolution

Gravely improper conduct of this nature has at times been the cause of serious trouble among native populations, and must be strenuously condemned on that account; but an objection even more serious from the standpoint of the Government lies in the fact that it is not possible for any member of the administration to countenance such practices without lowering himself in the eyes of the natives, and diminishing his authority to an extent which will seriously impair his capacity for useful work in the Service in which it is his duty to set an honourable example to all with whom he comes into contact. [Lord Crewe's Circular on concubinage (1909), Enclosure 'A']

In 1909 a sexual directive was issued to members of the Colonial Service which for the first time laid down a general rule to discourage concubinage, warning of the severe penalties that could be expected.[1] This change of official attitude was one of the few tangible elements differentiating the post-Edwardian empire from what had gone before. Even more remarkably, perhaps, it marked a vivid divergence from official French policy in West Africa. Concubinage, in fact, was deliberately encouraged by French empire-builders as the easiest, pleasantest and surest means of gallicising West Africa. 'A temporary union with a well-chosen native woman' was recommended by L. G. Binger (Director of African Affairs, Colonial Ministry) in 1902. It was defended as a necessary part of the French 'colonial moral code', as being as desirable for the health and hygiene, discipline and prestige of the French official as it was for his imperial authority and linguistic competence.[2] How striking is the contrast! The British authorities decided on a completely opposite policy, condemning concubinage as an 'injurious and dangerous' evil. The Crewe Circular (variously known as the 'morals despatch', the 'immoral relations memo' or the 'concubine circular') warned new recruits of the 'disgrace and official ruin which will certainly follow' should they enter into 'arrangements of concubinage with girls or women belonging to the native populations'; the warning to those already in post, however, was less explicit.

And yet at the beginning of the twentieth century, although concubinage was no longer the custom in India and the white dominions, it was still widely practised in certain parts of the empire by members of the British colonial services, as well as by white traders, railway engineers and unmarried settlers. It was common in Burma, Malaya and Sarawak, in Kenya and Uganda, in Nyasaland, Northern and Southern Rhodesia, in the Gold Coast and other parts of West Africa. In the lonelier districts it was probably the norm for bachelors. There were occasional reports of 'veritable harems of native women' being maintained by high-ranking officials, from the Ghansi district of western Bechuanaland to Upper Perak in Malaya. Missionaries made regular protests about it from Mashonaland and Swaziland to Papua and Borneo. The attitudes of authority varied. The Brookes in Sarawak actively encouraged concubinage and discouraged white wives. Sir Hugh Clifford was sympathetic to it in Malaya and wrote novels about it. By contrast, Sir Harry Johnston was repelled by the way it was regularly practised in Uganda in the 1890s by the 'best and most hard-working' officials, and he was not the only administrator who condemned concubinage as demoralising and undesirable. Certainly, too, that was the view taken in Burma in the 1890s by the Lieutenant-Governor: 'What cannot be done in England ought to be equally impossible in Burma': a revolutionary doctrine indeed.[3] The Colonial Office's unwritten rule at this time was, however, that moral issues and a man's private life did not concern the government so long as they did not cause a public scandal; a blind eye was officially turned to concubinage. Provided there was no interference with married women, many officials believed it did no harm to relations with African societies. In the Sudan, on the other hand, a strict requirement for continence was in force from the beginning.

As the twentieth century opened, the two polar opposites in imperial practice were in Sarawak and Sudan. In Sarawak, although James Brooke had reservations about over-familiarity with the local women, his private secretary (1848-55), B. Spenser St John, took a proselytising interest in them, declaring quite openly, 'I want to amalgamate races', and he influenced several young men to follow his example by keeping native mistresses. Charles Brooke likewise had a number of liaisons with Sarawak women before he became raja in 1873, and had a son. By then concubinage was extremely common. 'I can never believe', he said, that 'conventional modes of etiquette can remain stable in the East, where flesh and blood are so different.' He tolerated casual relations, but was less happy about permanent marriage arrangements which conferred status on native women.[4]After the death of his Eurasian wife, Hugh Low had a Sarawak concubine (he was Colonial Secretary at

Labuan before joining the Malayan Civil Service as a Resident in 1876).[5]

In Sudan, the most striking characteristic of the Political Service established in 1899 was its high moral code, its consistent practice of sexual restraint. This, as one of its members put it, was a regime so free of scandal as to be in itself scandalous.[6] The tone was set from the beginning by Sir Reginald and Lady Wingate, who were happily married.[7] The received picture is, however, almost too good to be true. Two small caveats may be entered. First, it is possible that down to 1924 (but not after that), one medical officer at least was still advising newcomers that there was no objection to temporary marriage with Sudanese women, provided it was in an out-district. But although some were tempted, few gave in. This was a service of high achievers, seriously committed to their careers and their civilising mission in Africa. They were acutely aware of the threat to their impartiality as magistrates and administrators if they contracted local marriage alliances, which would automatically draw them into the interests of Sudanese in-laws. This was a major constraint.[8] Second, sodomy in northern Sudan (but not in the south) was practically a national Sudanese pastime, and it is almost inconceivable that one or two officials did not get discreetly co-opted. But there is no hard evidence, and no scandal ever developed.[9]

Why then did British imperial authorities turn so unexpectedly and so decisively against concubinage in 1909, and extend the Sudanese model to the empire as a whole? Broadly speaking, the answer lies in the convergence of two reformist programmes operating at different levels of British society. The more general of these was the energetic Purity Campaign launched in the mid-1880s, establishing a comprehensive code for the enthronement of sexual restraint, and attacking promiscuity and prostitution. This campaign was certainly in part concerned to maintain an 'imperial race', and the more specific programme of 'colonial reform', directed at the empire-elite, was a natural offshoot. Ballhatchet has shown how it came to be believed that 'the social distance between the official elite and the people had to be preserved' in India. Ranger has explained the desperate official need, with the coming of formal rule, to turn European activity in Africa away from the 'tatty, squalid, rough and inefficient' towards a more respectable, ordered and convincing rulership. A proper imperial ruling class, it was thought, had to be brought into being: benevolent, but more aloof and conformist than its *ad hoc* heterogeneous prototype, with its often colourful and even outrageous characters. Under the new recruiting procedures adopted by the Colonial Office after 1900, graduates were preferred, and over a third of British governors were to be sons of Anglican clergymen.[10] Nevertheless, although sexual respectability appealed to many in its hierarchy, the Colonial Office had not *planned* a vigorous assault upon concubinage, if only because this would in many areas have led to the dismissal of a great many officers. Lord Crewe as Secretary of State was forced to act in 1909 faster and more forcibly than intended, mainly as the result of the unwelcome publicity given to the activities of a particular offender in Kenya. He was called Silberrad, and his case was the catalyst in the genesis of the Crewe Circular. It was to prove a decisive turning-point in the way the empire was run.

The Silberrad case and the Crewe Circular

A slight deterioration in mental or moral tone is inevitable to anyone in close grips with savage Africa, but the government does not help in the least or even consider the dangerous conditions of isolation. [R. Meinertzhagen, *Kenya Diary*, p. 219]

Perhaps the standards of white officers, civil and military, were nowhere as dubious as they were in the newly formed British East Africa Protectorate (Kenya).[11] Arriving at Nairobi in 1902 to join the King's African Rifles, Richard Meinertzhagen discovered that his brother officers were mostly

regimental rejects and heavily in debt; one drinks like a fish, one prefers boys to women and is not ashamed. On arrival here I was amazed and shocked to find that they all brought their native women into mess; the talk centres round sex and money and is always connected with some type of pornography... Nearly every man in Nairobi is a railway official. Every one of them keeps a native girl, usually a Masai, and there is a regular trade in these girls with the local Masai villages. If a man tires of his girl he goes to the village (*minyatta*) and gets a new one, or in several cases as many as three girls. And my brother officers are no exception.

Meinertzhagen also referred later to a civil administrative officer who committed suicide after forcing a regimental bugler-boy to commit 'an act of indecency'; and to another (W. Mayes) who had installed half a dozen Nandi concubines in his house after deserting his wife in Mauritius. In northern Nyanza province there was a district commissioner who, it was alleged, 'combined tax collection with rape'.[12]

Hubert Silberrad was an assistant district commissioner at Nyeri, near Fort Hall in central Kenya. Not much is known about his background. He was educated at Wren's School, and studied engineering at technical college. After working with the Imperial British East Africa Company, he took up his post at Nyeri in May 1903. He acquired two local girls from his colleague, C. W. I. Haywood, who left to be promoted to district commissioner at Kisumu in April 1905. The girls were called

Niambura and Wameisa. Haywood had paid forty goats in bridewealth for each of them. Both girls had apparently lived happily with Haywood, but Wameisa, who was still no more than twelve, was reluctant to be passed on to Silberrad, while Niambura came to live with him in return for a monthly wage. A third girl, aged twelve or thirteen, whose name was Niakayena, was passed to Silberrad by her husband, Mugalla, an askari (African policeman). Mugalla subsequently disputed her custody with Silberrad. In February 1908 they scuffled together at Silberrad's kitchen door, and Silberrad locked up the askari in the guardroom for a night, on grounds of insubordination. At this point Silberrad was descended upon by two outraged neighbours, Mr and Mrs W.S. Routledge. They took Niakayena and Niambura away from Silberrad, and Routledge reported the matter to the Governor, riding four days in the rains to Nairobi in order to do so. Routledge was a settler who had lived in Nyeri for six years, enjoying the sport and claiming to study African life and interests; he was an Oxford graduate, but at best a self-styled anthropologist. More obviously, he was a Purity-minded, interfering busybody, who appeared to be jealous of Silberrad's authority. It was also unfortunate for Silberrad that the askari, Mugalla, was an uncircumcised Maasai, and, as a result, peculiarly touchy about his sex life.

The Governor, Sir James Hayes Sadler, took the unusual step of ordering a private investigation by Judge Barth. This was held between 25 and 29 March 1908, and the judge reported on 13 April. The allegations seemed to be substantially true, but in Haywood's case uncomplicated and not particularly shocking. The judge was inclined to believe Wameisa's evidence that she went reluctantly to Silberrad but had consented to do so. Silberrad may have thought she came to him willingly enough, but it was dangerous for an officer to assume there was no difficulty just because there was no disobedience. He considered that Silberrad was unjustified in taking the askari's girl in circumstances that amounted to poaching. There was, however, no evidence that Silberrad had purchased or corrupted any of the girls. The most serious aspect of the case was his action over the askari, for the dispute between them had very obviously brought the administration into disrepute. The matter then went before the Executive Council, which (rejecting Wameisa's plea of unwillingness) recommended by two to one that Silberrad should lose one year's seniority and not be put in charge of a district for two years. Haywood was severely admonished by the Governor, after which he returned to duty. (He apparently remained in post until 1914.)

Hayes Sadler, who had served in the Indian Army until 1899, knew about demi-official circulars condemning open concubinage in Burma, and in May 1908 caused a similar admonition to be circulated in Kenya. This stated that 'morals apart', such proceedings tended to lower the

British name, were incompatible with an officer's position and prestige and were 'in every way detrimental to the interests of good government'. Such lax behaviour must be ended, and any further cases would be 'severely dealt with and may entail serious consequences'. He hoped this threat would check a practice 'which there is now reason to believe is more general than was supposed'. His personal recommendation in the case was that Silberrad should be degraded to the bottom of the list of assistant district commissioners. (Silberrad was actually head of the list of twenty-eight officers for promotion.)[13]

The case went to the Legal and General Department of the Colonial Office and not to the East African desk. The first principal minute was written by T. C. Macnaghten on 26 June 1908. He believed that the Governor's suggested punishment was too severe and would ruin Silberrad's career. Even the Executive Council's recommendation seemed harsh. It would be more appropriate to censure him and merely pass him over twice for promotion. Macnaghten understood that there were many officers in Kenya who had lived more loosely than Silberrad and Haywood, and it was hard that they should have been made scapegoats. The treatment of the askari was certainly awkward and discreditable. The Governor, he felt, was right to warn administrative personnel of the possibility of dismissal in future cases. Macnaghten was well aware that important issues of future policy were now forced upon the Colonial Office. The existing state of affairs 'could not be tolerated indefinitely'. In the old days it 'was not unnatural that a loose morality should be common', and perhaps only a small percentage of unmarried white officials had abstained entirely from concubinage. But now things were changing rapidly. Africans were 'emerging from savagery, and a better class of white official is being introduced'. It was time for a general ruling to be laid down. But he hoped that specific cases 'may be leniently dealt with – at any rate for a good many years to come'.

Macnaghten's minute anticipated quite accurately the reaction of senior officials. To Sir Francis Hopwood (Permanent Under-Secretary) and H. B. Cox (Legal Assistant Under-Secretary) it was a 'nasty and delicate' business. The general question unhappily and acutely arising was 'whether the fact that an officer keeps a black mistress is in itself a scandal requiring the attention of the government'. Barefaced promiscuity, such as maintaining several women simultaneously in different places, could not be tolerated, and the Governor's steps to raise the standard of morals among white officers in Kenya must be supported. But they should proceed carefully, since no previous indications of official disapproval had been given. To discourage concubinage in future, a general circular should be issued, but officers ought not to be threatened: rather, an appeal should be made to their sense of propriety and good conduct. These conclusions were arrived at rather reluctantly, and the officials' distaste for Routledge's actions was reinforced by his demand (made direct to the Secretary of State) that Silberrad's punishment should be a deterrent to others. Routledge said that if he was not satisfied with the government's decision, he would, 'as representing the public', see that the whole matter was revealed to Parliament and the press. The office was thoroughly indignant at this threat, especially since it was now known that Routledge had himself almost certainly followed local custom and had intercourse with African girls before his marriage. It was also obvious that Routledge had a grudge against Silberrad, who had had to take official action against him on liquor charges involving his Maasai workers and porters. Routledge's importunate demands were counterproductive. The fact that he was 'disposed to be nasty' in public was probably one of the considerations which led Crewe not to adopt the Governor's tough punishment proposals, but to accept instead the Executive Council's more moderate recommendation that Silberrad should lose one year's seniority (from April 1908), and not be put in charge of a district for two years. Meanwhile, Silberrad was to take five months' leave (three months on full pay and two months on three-quarters). In conveying these decisions to Silberrad on 30 July 1908 the Secretary of State emphasised his condemnation of the aggravating offence of Silberrad's being involved in an altercation with a black subordinate over a girl, for this was a clear example of how concubinage could bring the government service into disrepute.Crewe told the Governor that his conduct of the affair was generally approved, but he rejected Routledge's claim to be treated as 'representing the public'. Unfortunately, the Governor (while not disagreeing in principle) had promised to keep Routledge informed of the outcome of the Silberrad case. This gave Routledge the chance to stir up further trouble later.[14]

The Colonial Office asked the India Office for a copy of the Burmese circular to which Hayes Sadler had drawn attention, and did not begin any drafting of its own until this had been received at the end of November. (The Indian bureaucracy took five months to disgorge the information.) In the meantime, Silberrad took his leave, and had the good sense or good fortune to get married in England. He then returned to Kenya as assistant district commissioner at Kiambu, only some fifty miles from Nyeri, his previous posting. This was a mistake, and the move was to be strongly criticised.[15]

The egregious Routledge (to say nothing of Mrs Routledge) felt that Silberrad was getting off the hook altogether too lightly. And so he employed his ultimate weapon by writing to The Times, portentously signing himself 'W. Scoresby Routledge, M. A. (Christ Church, Oxon.), Erichsen Prizeman, University College Hospital (Lond.)'. His letter was published on 3 December 1908. In it, Routledge denounced the government for not acting severely enough to check the 'abuses' in Kenya or stop the 'demoralisation' of African women by British officials. He 'named' Hubert Silberrad in full and revealed the details of his case. He protested that Silberrad's punishment was 'utterly insufficient'. And since the Colonial Office was proposing only to 'discourage' concubinage, the issue was 'Whether the representatives of the Crown are to be allowed to withdraw ignorant girls, committed to their charge, from the well-defined lines of tribal life, and to lead them into courses of which the inevitable tendency is to end on the streets of Nairobi.' Was not this calculated 'adversely to affect the power and influence' of British administration?

Officials reacted angrily. Routledge had (as they feared) hurled his publicity bombshell, and had done so knowing not only that these sexual transactions were 'exceedingly common' in Kenya, but also that Silberrad was trying to make a fresh start through marriage. The letter made use of accurate quotations from Judge Barth's report, but how had Routledge managed to see it? The letter was 'dangerously clever', full of 'venomous personal malice' and 'monstrous cruelty'; it could *not* have been written purely in the public interest. The reference to 'the streets of Nairobi' Macnaghten regarded as 'a wilful attempt on the part of a man who must know better to hoodwink the uninformed members of the British Public into supposing that Mr Silberrad's offence is as bad as that of a man who commits a similar offence with a young girl in England, and that he has been the cause of a similar social and moral downfall'. He regarded Sir Harry Johnston's opinion as extremely pertinent: that almost every girl in east-central Africa ceased to be a virgin well before puberty. Two days after *The Times* letter, Crewe recorded his opinion, opening with a gloomy reflection that perhaps they were about to witness one of Lord Macaulay's 'periodical fits of morality':

> We are all agreed that conduct of this kind is not merely morally reprehensible (which is not directly our affair), but disadvantageous to the public service. . . The whole subject is very properly one for admonition, and where necessary for censure, with a view to its becoming the standard of opinion in the Service that these connections are degrading. But we cannot hope to eradicate the trouble entirely.

Crewe could see no essential difference from any other 'offence against morals of its class'. It therefore did not seem to him a case for a vindictive punishment or for ruining Silberrad's career. He distrusted Routledge's motives. It was 'very "strong" indeed' to give Silberrad's name to the press, when he could have withheld it, and this procedure 'would make me personally decline Mr. Routledge's acquaintance'.[16]

The interest of Members of Parliament was immediately aroused by Routledge's thundering exposure. Colonel J. E. B. Seely (as Parliamentary Under-Secretary) had to make a Commons Statement on 7 December, based on Crewe's minute and drafted by Hopwood. This defended the punishment as sufficiently severe, involving Silberrad in considerable pecuniary loss. Seely also announced that the government was going to warn all members of the Colonial Service that such actions were 'damaging and unworthy' and could lead to the 'gravest consequences' as a penalty. Although this statement got the House generally into a fair humour, some Members of Parliament remained agitated, and soon afterwards a deputation confronted Seely in his room. This consisted of Sir Clement Hill (formerly Superintendent of African Protectorates at the Foreign Office), Mr. H. Pike Pease, Sir G. Scott Robertson (a former Indian administrator) and Josiah Wedgwood (then much interested in African affairs). Some members of the deputation maintained that there was evidence of a general laxity in the administration of the East Africa Protectorate. Sir Clement Hill denied this, and no immediate action was contemplated, but Seely agreed to show the deputation advance copies of the proposed circular. Seely felt he had survived the parliamentary ordeal pretty well, but prompt action was necessary: 'feeling was very strong in all parts of the House, and the Prime Minister informed me that he was much concerned; the danger of the situation is that in this matter what one may call the high – official – disciplinary – Tory mind makes common cause with the humanitarian – pro-native – Liberal mind...'. Seely was thus now convinced (despite the misgivings of Hopwood, Cox and Antrobus) that a warning on the lines of the Burmese circular should be automatically presented to all personnel in the colonies most affected, and that this was essential in fairness to officers. He agreed with Macnaghten that it would otherwise be unjust to deal severely with future cases. He also thought that such action would not be represented as vindictive self-righteousness or 'unctuous rectitude', because such confidential instructions had from time to time been given in the older dependencies in the past, and been extraordinarily effective; as a result, concubinage by officials was now almost at an end in India, South Africa and New Zealand. His advisers were in full agreement that officers in Africa obviously needed instruction: like Haywood, they seemed to regard government resentment of their conduct as an unwarranted interference merely on moral grounds. As Macnaghten observed, Haywood 'does not seem to have the slightest idea that such practices are more detestable from the point of view of the Service than they are from the point of view of morals: that interference with native women has even led to risings in the past and might do so again', though admittedly the Silberrad case had not evoked African protest.[17]

[165]

For more than a week, the energies of the Colonial Office were much absorbed by this issue. Seely and Crewe each wrote several minutes which were as long as any written by either of them about anything. Crewe made his decision on 12 December. The difficulty as he saw it was in 'launching by surprise against the whole Colonial Service, young and old, married and unmarried, a thunderbolt forged for reasons of which they will have heard nothing, to the effect that if they engage in relations with native women they run the risk of being dismissed'. He proposed to get out of this difficulty by issuing two different circulars, with a covering letter instructing governors on their use. A drastic circular would warn new recruits of severe treatment, but a more general circular would be issued to all officers already in the service. This would impress on them the danger and scandal to the public service, but it would not contain threats of dismissal. The principle of the drastic circular might, however, if necessary be applied at any time to any officer. Macnaghten now set to work to draft the circulars. In front of him was the text of Lieutenant-Governor Sir Frederick Fryer's demi-official Burmese Minute (1903), which consolidated the substance of earlier confidential circulars issued in Burma. None of its phrasing was in fact copied.[18]

Ministers continued to face criticism throughout December. On 11 December, Mrs Routledge had an interview with Colonel Seely. She complained that the severity of Silberrad's punishment had not been increased, repeating the objection to Haywood's being let off with a reprimand. Seely replied that it would be especially inequitable to increase Silberrad's penalty after all the adverse publicity, and without new facts being adduced. And he reminded Mrs Routledge that Haywood had been exonerated of all serious charges, and had in fact been doubly reprimanded, by the Governor and by the Secretary of State. Next day, the office was agitated over an article in the *Spectator* entitled 'A canker in imperial administration', which also took the line that Silberrad's punishment was inadequate and Seely's Commons statement unsatisfactory. The empire would be ruined if officials exercised their powers to gratify their animal passions (the argument ran); the accepted standard in East Africa was lower than in the empire as a whole, and had reached a point of peril. The administrative personnel was unsatisfactory, and the blame really lay with the government for paying such low salaries. The article concluded with a suggestion that someone like Sir George Goldie should head a commission of inquiry.

Officials thought that the article made some reasonable points, even if it was unfair in the particular case of Silberrad. After all, they reflected, he had only acted in accordance with the common local custom of officials and he had not used force; the object of the punishment decided upon was to be severe without marring his future efficiency or breaking his spirit. It was true, they agreed, that the administration was substandard: it had been created in a hurry, and some unsatisfactory people were taken over from the Imperial British East Africa Company, Silberrad among them. Many of them had now been got rid of, but, as Antrobus observed, it was impracticable to make a clean sweep of every unsatisfactory official. The Treasury was indeed paying less than the Colonial Office had repeatedly urged; and small salaries (about £250 a year for an assistant district commissioner) were a genuine hardship, discouraging marriage. An inquiry into concubinage was clearly impracticable, however. It was bound to be unsavoury, and there was the problem also of what evidence would be admissible. Would it extract confessions, or demand denunciations from colleagues? Hopwood said they should stick to the policy of issuing a circular, and not be unduly rattled by newspaper criticism. Crewe summed up their reaction to the *Spectator* article:

> There are several unsatisfactory features in the administration of British East Africa. . . But I do not propose that the Congregation of the Holy Office should institute a special enquiry into the British East Africa morals. We must try to elevate the general standard by sending good men there in all ranks. This is particularly necessary from the presence of a population of settlers, whose standard in all cases cannot be high.[19]

The Times carried several letters commenting on the Silberrad case, together with an editorial on 26 December. This emphasised that Seely's statement had by no means entirely disposed of public anxiety, 'which will demand some definite assurance that such offences will in future be rigorously put down'. There was some exchange as to whether or not an African girl was 'ready for marriage' at twelve. Some correspondents asserted that 'the honour of Britain' was at stake, but a former administrative officer, writing anonymously, thought Silberrad's punishment was too severe.T. F. Victor Buxton (heir to the baronetcy) contributed the most forceful of the letters (9 January 1909), strongly urging much greater governmental stringency in dealing with such problems. Public servants, he wrote, could not divest themselves of the prestige attaching to their office; 'if therefore we are to rise to our responsibilities as an Imperial race – if we are not to bring grievous discredit upon the Christianity we profess – it is essential that those who represent us abroad should be clean-living men, whose conduct may command the respect of the peoples they govern'. This went right to the heart of the issues of the Silberrad case as perceived by the British 'establishment'. The Colonial Office sent him a copy of the draft circular, which he thought admirable. In the interest of dampening down simmering agitation, Seely also sent copies to other *Times* correspondents.

Macnaghten had submitted his drafts on 16 December. They expressly dealt with concubinage and not with occasional 'illicit acts'. Antrobus saw no good reason for distinguishing between new and serving officers by having two different warnings, but Crewe insisted that this was necessary. It was decided to issue the circular overseas, and not at home, in case it fell into the hands of the parents of recruits and horrified them. A lot of attention was paid to eliminating any impression that the government regarded the morality of its servants as generally questionable. On the whole, Macnaghten's drafts were approved, the principal amendments being to the annexes, where Hopwood made a number of changes. At a late stage of drafting, Crewe decided to remove the requirement on governors to *report* cases (following the Burma precedent), merely asking them instead to 'make it the subject of official action'. Considerable thought was given to the question of exactly which colonies and protectorates should receive the circular. It would obviously be a bad blunder to send it to the West Indies, Mauritius and the Seychelles, where black and white regularly lived together and intermarried, and it was not in fact sent to them. Antrobus held that it was irrelevant to Ceylon and Hong Kong, but he was over-ruled. (On receiving it, however, the Governor of Ceylon protested his certainty that no civil servant there now lived in concubinage with local women; the Colonial Office had to agree that he need not issue the circular in Ceylon.) The circular was never intended for places not thought to be affected, or for those areas not under the direct responsibility of the Crown. It was thus not sent to Malta, Gibraltar, Sarawak, the Federated Malay States, South Africa (including the High Commission Territories), or North-western and North-eastern Rhodesia (which were under the British South Africa Company).[20] How the government tackled the Rhodesian situation will be discussed in the following section.

Crewe finalised the wording on 3 January, and the circular was published on 11 January 1909. It had no heading, but a file for possible replies was opened with the title 'Immoral relations with native women'. Each recipient colony was sent enough copies of Annex 'B' to distribute to all its serving white officers, together with several years' supply of the sterner Annex 'A', which was to be handed to newcomers, and to such old-timers as seemed seriously in need of special exhortation. When supplies ran out, the Colonial Office would arrange for reprinting. With the single exception of Sir Henry McCallum's protest from Ceylon, no replies or comments appear to have been received.[21]

The Silberrad case was again raised in the House of Commons on 27 July 1909, during the Colonial Office part of the Supply debate. The main speakers were H. J. Wilson, who had attacked the Indian Contagious Diseases Acts in 1888 and planned to outlaw all fornication, and Josiah

Wedgwood, who called for 'less leniency' and 'more reprobation' from the Colonial Office over concubinage. Alfred Lyttelton (as a former Colonial Secretary) uttered caustic remarks about deplorable, reprehensible, miserable weakness on the part of the government: it was monstrous, he said, to pride ourselves about keeping natives from drink if we did not stop this sort of thing, and Joe Chamberlain would never have allowed it. Seely's defence was the familiar one that they could not dismiss Silberrad, because he had been given no previous warning of this possibility; but he had been effectively punished, and it was anyway only an 'isolated' offence. The circular was a positive and 'very stern' warning; the phrase 'grave consequences' in his statement would be read as meaning 'end of career'.[22]

Many critics felt Silberrad had been re-employed too near to the scene of his offence, and he was transferred to Nyasaland in July 1909 as a '2nd grade Resident'. There he remained until 1923, his career irretrievably stuck. Silberrad was the victim of domestic Purity pressures and the supposed requirements of racial prestige. It is worth emphasising that the pressure for action against him and others like him was political. Missionary comment was decidedly muted. A short and ambivalent editorial note in the *Church Missionary Review* conceded that Routledge had served 'the honour of the ruling race in Africa' by his unsavoury revelations, but concentrated on urging readers to remember the better side of the 'white intrusion', such as the work of the medical missions.[23]

How effective was the 'immoral relations' circular? The problem did not disappear all at once. In Kenya in 1929 the Kikuyu Central Association listed concubinage as one of its grievances and demanded action to stop it. This had the Governor's wholehearted support. Wide and varied enquiries had, however, led him to conclude it was rare, and open examples of it unknown, so legislation was, he thought, unnecessary even if practicable. Kenyatta was assured that the government would certainly act against it, but 'happily the practice is comparatively uncommon, and the general opinion of European settlers was strongly against it', so 'the evil would be best combated by public opinion'.[24] More generally in Africa, Crewe's action can hardly have been said to have been welcomed at the time. Some respectable married men were furious at being presented with it. Few governors ever wanted to impose it actively. Guggisberg of the Gold Coast, for example, wrote in 1927: 'In my view, while I expect Heads of Department to set an example to, and to advise their juniors, it is not advisable to pry too closely into the lives of officers so long as they do their work efficiently and do not cause a scandal.'[25] Nevertheless, so unequivocal a directive could not possibly be ignored, and concubinage was generally eliminated in African colonies by the mid-1920s, except in the remote outstations. (As late as 1927 in Wajir, with the King's African Rifles, Brian Montgomery was offered a Somali *bibi*, or 'sleeping dictionary'.) Some dismissals for 'immorality' occurred even in Papua in the five years before 1914.[26] Malayan officers showed a marked decline in the resort to concubinage in the decade after 1909: and, according to J. G. Butcher, by 1928 it was certainly practised by less than ten per cent of them and may have been down to two per cent. Several officers married their Malayan mistresses. In the opinion of the Secretary for Chinese Affairs (1922) the circular had not only deterred officers in Malaya from concubinage, but also from resort to 'known' brothels. European residential segregation and the increasing presence of white wives in the colonies were important factors in changing sexual patterns, and it is therefore difficult to make precise statements about the continuing significance of Crewe's circular in bringing about the demise of concubinage. To deny its impact would be wrong, but it was not issued in a vacuum and its application was not universal. The issue of the circular did not reactivate the earlier (rather half-hearted) discouragement of concubinage in Burma. No dismissals were being made there. The weight of public, and therefore of official, concern was clearly concentrated on Africa. It never applied to Sarawak, where concubinage continued to flourish until the end of Brooke rule in 1946, and possibly even beyond.[27]

It was from Sarawak that Denis Garson wrote in 1948, eulogising its 'delightful relationship of races': 'It is impressive the way the Administrative staff mix with the people, though I suspect that its origins would not earn the commendation of moralists or of the author of the famous confidential despatch on morals.' The point was, he felt, that 'the good here must not be lost – the ease of race relations. . .'. He greatly feared that the new generation of memsahibs would only impose their small-minded standards in Sarawak 'as they had done to the detriment of India and Malaya and elsewhere'. Some members of the Colonial Office hierarchy were thus certainly aware that the stiff and aloof social relations of the twentieth-century empire, partly promoted by the Crewe Circular, were often a disaster.[28] To some, the end of concubinage was a matter of regret, but not very deeply so: Margery Perham doubted whether most Britons in the 1930s actually wanted that kind of 'un-English' intimacy with Africans.[29] However, the equivocal nature of the whole debate comes out strongly in the Rhodesian case, where the principles of the Crewe Circular were rapidly applied once the Colonial Office had got the Purity bit firmly between its bureaucratic teeth.

Rhodesian scandals

A man should, whatever happens, keep to his own caste, race, and breed. Let the White go to the White and the Black to the Black. Then, whatever trouble falls is in the ordinary course of things – neither sudden, alien, nor unexpected. [Rudyard Kipling, 'Beyond the Pale', in *Plain Tales from the Hills*]

A theme of significance in the history of imperial administration is the difference of perception between the Colonial Office and the field administrators. The latter have often taken the standpoint of short-term expediency with an eye to their own convenience, resenting the imposition of long-term imperial principles and policies. At the beginning of the twentieth century nowhere was this divergence more marked than in differing local and metropolitan outlooks upon sexual indulgence. On this issue the Colonial Office principles emerged by the end of the Edwardian era a clear winner, which was by no means always the case in other areas of dispute.

In the spring of 1903 the conduct of T.A. Raikes, Assistant Native Commissioner for North Mazoe district, Mashonaland, in Southern Rhodesia, was the subject of official inquiry by W. S. Taberer, the acting Chief Native Administrator of Mashonaland. Thomas Raikes had kept three African women, following what he took to be, in the euphemism of the time, 'a commonsense view with regard to health'. He employed an African called Sombrero to go round the kraals looking for attractive girls. He had a particular request for Juma, whom he had seen at a big dance, but she was not willing. Raikes then told Sombrero to call in her father, and threatened to arrest him. Juma was afraid of being beaten, so she went to sleep with Raikes for about two months, until Raikes agreed to let her go. Although he had said he would pay *lobola* (bridewealth), he never did. He offered payment direct to the mother, who objected. He was very angry about that and refused to give the girl anything for having slept with him. Sombrero was then asked to find an alternative girl. After two refusals, Raikes gave Sombrero a rifle in order to fetch another woman. She also refused, rejecting a first-instalment gift. Nevertheless, Raikes insisted, knowing she had previously lived with a white man, and sent Sombrero back for her. Her father was reluctant but afraid, and gave his permission when *lobola* was promised. She stayed with Raikes three and a half months, until he sent her away once her father began 'giving himself too much importance' by demanding *lobola*. After her departure, Raikes refused to leave her alone; threatening to kill any husband she took, he had intercourse with her again, for which he paid four shillings. Thereafter, she was adamant in her refusal ever to see him again. Sombrero was accordingly despatched once more. By now he had a local reputation as 'the boy that goes to the various kraals taking girls to Mr Raikes'. Kabotso, whom Raikes wanted, managed to avoid him through pleading illness, but after her recovery, hearing he still wanted her, she ran off into Angola. Sombrero was then sent to a dance to seek out a girl conforming to the type his master fancied. Armed with a rifle, he found a willing girl, but, on the return journey, she was tragically shot, accidentally, by Sombrero's assistant. The assistant was carrying the rifle, and he panicked, fearing a lion attack. Raikes called Sombrero a fool and made him pay compensation to the dead girl's family, but did not report her death. He was reluctant to pay Sombrero for six months' abortive work as his pimp, giving him a hut tax token instead. Finally, Raikes was offered as his third concubine a young girl who slept with him for six weeks until he was suspended, although at first he had objected that she was too small; she was probably not more than sixteen.

Raikes's more or less formalised concubinage arrangements were not the whole story. Several witnesses told how he went to kraals and took liberties with messengers' wives, patting their breasts, opening their legs, 'examining their private parts', and generally playing 'disgusting tricks with them'. Sometimes the women were laid across his knees for mutual fondling. He rewarded them with bars of soap, except for one whose breasts he complained were too small. One of these married women told the inquiry, 'I thought he had the right to do what he liked, as he is the Native Commissioner here'. Raikes denied there was any indecency: 'I have always treated these people as children. I have chafed them and played with them but I have never had any evil design . . . towards them.' One girl reported that her boyfriend was fined ten shillings (plus three months' loss of messenger's salary) for sleeping with her, because Raikes wanted her himself. The inquiry interviewed several women who had refused to go with Raikes. They all said they had told him they did not want him because he was a white man, and that he should marry a white woman.[30]

The Administrator of Southern Rhodesia, W. H. Milton, was prepared to give Raikes a chance in some other department after he had been severely reprimanded and removed from native affairs. Raikes, he argued, was a young man of good intelligence who had done useful work: 'young, active and clever, but seems cursed with an unruly member'. Appealing to the High Commissioner, Lord Milner, he pointed out that Raikes was the son of the late well-known Postmaster-General (1886-91), Henry Raikes, the Member of Parliament for Cambridge University. (The family were ardent churchmen, and young Raikes a graduate of Trinity Hall, Cambridge, with a Second in Classics.)[31] Although he had narrowly failed the Indian Civil Service examination, he was 'just the class of young man we have been anxious to keep'. For the sake of his family and career, Milner recommended that the 'lewd offender' be let off as lightly as the circumstances allowed.[32]

The Colonial Office would have none of it. Whilst the Raikes inquiry was proceeding, another official had been sacked. He was G. H. McCulloch, Native Commissioner of Magundi district, Southern Rhodesia, formerly an assistant magistrate at Enkeldoorn in Mashonaland. He paid £15 and some blankets as *lobola* for Senwa; there was a brief cohabitation with her in April 1903, until a couple of weeks later he learned that she was already married. Apparently he had been tricked by the paramount chief Chisunga, the 'father' as he believed. It turned out, however, that Chisunga had practically stolen her from her husband and then taken *lobola* for her from McCulloch. McCulloch denied any dishonesty or meanness, bullying or abuse of his position, directly or indirectly – but he could not deny that he had paid *lobola* for a concubine. He belonged to the 'old and inferior' type the administration was trying to weed out, and he was dismissed.[33]

As a consequence, the Colonial Office did not see how they could possibly merely let Raikes off with a reprimand, since his behaviour was incomparably the worse of the two. And especially so if his education were taken into account; as G.V.Fiddes minuted: 'We look to these men to set a higher standard, and we ought to have no mercy on them when they fail us in this respect.' More generally, he added, 'the simple and cast-iron rule should be that any white man having connection with, or behaving indecently to, any black woman will be at once fired out of the service.' Secretary of State Joseph Chamberlain needed little persuading: 'If Native Commissioners behave in this way to Natives they will bring white administration into contempt. Mr Raikes and Mr McCulloch must both go, and I can give no encouragement whatever to the idea of employing them again.' Some civil servants may have queried the thesis that concubinage was invariably bad for prestige, but the tendency to leniency so marked in officials on the spot was firmly rejected by those in Whitehall.[34]

The dismissal of two officers was a deterrent. No further scandals were reported from Southern Rhodesia. In Northern Rhodesia, however, the situation remained unchecked until 1909-10, when the sexual activities of three men attracted attention: C. J. Macnamara, R. L. Harrison and R. A. Osborne.

Macnamara, Native Commissioner of Guimbi sub-district in North-western Rhodesia, admitted concubinage with an African woman from December 1906 until September 1907. He was dismissed in April 1910. There were other alleged irregularities in his official conduct too (such as flogging), but it was the concubinage which caused his downfall. Harrison was Native Commissioner of Mkusi sub-district, also in

North-western Rhodesia. Charges were brought against him by Mr. G. Graham that he was using his official position to procure African women against their will. Harrison admitted concubinage with several women in 1907, but said it was with their full consent; in any case, he had now given the practice up. A large number of witnesses was called, and inquiry failed to establish any coercion; in several cases, intercourse was denied by the women. There was clearly no impropriety subsequent to 1907. Harrison married a European woman in 1908, and started a family. The High Commissioner, now Lord Selborne, felt that in view of this, Harrison's past conduct, though 'most reprehensible', should be condoned and the offender allowed to retain his appointment. Reluctantly, the Secretary of State agreed: in view of the marriage, a written 'severe reprimand' should be given and the case closed. But Crewe was uneasy. Was it certain no coercion (with Harrison's knowledge and consent) had been used? When an official of this rank 'makes known his wish to a native woman or instructs a servant to procure such a woman for him, he must be aware that the element of coercion, cannot, in the necessary circumstances of the case, be entirely eliminated'. It was a pertinent comment. The whole story Crewe found discreditable, and if concubinage had continued to the present, he would certainly have had Harrison dismissed .[35]

The Osborne case was much the most significant of the three dealt with in 1909-10. R. A. Osborne was a Native Department official at Luwingu in North-eastern Rhodesia. In 1909 he took as concubine Kasonde, daughter of Kasonka. Just before he was due for leave, at the end of the year, he dismissed her for misconduct with his cook, Jeremiah, though both of them strenuously denied adultery. Failing to find Kasonde in Jeremiah's hut, Osborne, enraged, turned out all Jeremiah's goods and chattels and burned them. Next morning he returned to beat Jeremiah with twenty strokes. A few days later he beat him again, ten strokes this time. Finally, he fined the cook thirty shillings, to be deducted from pay and given to Kasonka as compensation for being 'disgraced by his daughter'. Osborne was unable to deny the substance of the allegations, and he was suspended on half-pay from December 1909. L. A. Wallace, the acting Administrator of North-western Rhodesia, found that his qualifications and services were well spoken of, so he recommended that Osborne should be retained in British South Africa Company service, but in a more subordinate position. The board of the company recognised that Osborne had punished his cook excessively for the gratification of a private revenge, 'being involved in conduct resulting in your irregular life becoming a public scandal'. However, they represented to the Secretary of State 'the difficulties and temptations attached to Mr Osborne's isolated position amongst the natives', and stressed the excellent reports they had received on his character and ability; and they hoped he could be allowed to vindicate himself by continuing in their employ.[36]

Once again the Colonial Office took issue with the local administrators. In the eyes of the Colonial Office this was a grosser abuse of position than Macnamara's, and it could scarcely be dealt with more leniently. The case of Raikes and his 'unruly member' was invoked as a precedent. Some officials thought it in some respects worse than the earlier scandal. They held that it would be a mistake to abandon their principle of dismissal established in 1903. Meddling with black women must mean dismissal and nothing short of it. The argument of 'special temptations' struck them as nonsense. Sexual temptation was the worst that any man who undertook tropical service was obliged to meet and overcome, 'but it was an *ordinary* temptation'. In any event, it was irrelevant in Osborne's case, where the trouble was not his temptations but his temper. H. M. Lambert noted that it was, of course, 'easy to compound for sins we are inclined to by damning those we have no mind to', but 'however invidious severity may be I think we should in these cases be, as Mr Chamberlain was, inflexible'. White rule depended on 'moral power', he added: such proceedings 'destroy the very basis on which the authority of Government rests'; the leniency of local officials must be resisted. The Office view was unanimous. Osborne would have to go. Lord Crewe agreed. He went.[37]

Colonel J. E. B. Seely, the Parliamentary Under-Secretary, who himself had had a liaison with a Maori lady, did, however, introduce a more sympathetic note into the office discussion. Because concubinage was obviously so 'exceedingly common' in the lonelier districts of North-eastern Rhodesia, to dismiss men for it could lead to the loss of 'a great many officers'. They ought to recruit more married men, make British possessions healthier, and assist with passages and free quarters for wives where it was possible for white women to live. He was convinced that concubinage arose out of loneliness and the absence of wives. Accordingly, the government must be prepared to spend more money on salaries and travel allowances so as to make it easier for married men to be in the Colonial Service. Crewe accepted that there was much to be said in favour of increasing the number of married officers, 'but the real difficulty is that isolated posts at which temptation may be strongest to the officers are just those at which life is most difficult for a white woman'. For the moment his main concern was to get the British South Africa Company to adopt the serious view of concubinage being taken by the Colonial Office.[38]

The Crewe Circular of 1909 was now in effect applied to the Rhodesias and the High Commission Territories (the Bechuanaland Protectorate, Basutoland and Swaziland). A circular about 'sexual relations between officials and native women' (dated 14 June 1910) was issued by the High Commissioner. It explained that there had been 'certain recent flagrant cases' of concubinage; the difficulties of service in isolated districts were acknowledged, but 'grave concern' was expressed over 'the growing evil which must result . . . and consequent dangers to sound and healthy administration'. Younger men especially must be warned: 'proved misconduct with native women will inevitably be followed by serious consequences'.[39]

This uncompromising directive drew a heated response from Judge L. P. Beaufort, the acting Administrator of North-eastern Rhodesia (who had investigated Osborne). The circular, he said, was unjust and inexpedient. He feared the possibility that Africans might blackmail Europeans. He believed too rigid a surveillance of concubinage could only lead to the establishment of prostitution as an alternative. Indiscriminate promiscuity and abuse of power were of, course, wrong and degrading, but he held concubinage with one woman only, 'maintained with constancy and decently veiled', to be quite different. It was unjust to condemn it before it gave rise to trouble or scandal. Very often the best administrators, those most qualified to deal with African questions, were the men who had had youthful experience of concubinage and had emerged from it to become good husbands and effective officers. Beaufort urged the need to be sympathetic to young men suddenly called to solitary life in the tropical wilds. Concubinage kept the young officer sane, gave him a knowledge of the language, enabled him to get warning of planned crimes or uprisings. 'It has been of material comfort and advantage to many a lonely European; it is not in the least degrading to the women of this country nor the least likely in itself to give rise to native trouble.' Often indeed it had saved officials from the contempt and suspicion with which Africans viewed those living and eating alone.

These arguments – regarded as old-fashioned at best, foreign at worst – received no support from Viscount Gladstone as High Commissioner. He could understand the temptations but would not modify his attitude, believing concubinage 'had repeatedly been the source of grave scandal in the past', incompatible with prestige.[40]

Beaufort's rearguard action was, however, taken seriously in the Colonial Office, if only to dispose of the argument once and for all. The Secretary of State sought the opinion of C. B. Sanby, who had had long experience of these problems overseas. He came to a balanced conclusion between the divergent metropolitan and local perceptions. On the one hand he rejected the view that concubinage was incompatible with prestige; on the other he insisted the scandals must stop. Africans, he argued, saw Europeans in a detached way as a different order of being, 'as we should regard Martians as different, not inferior or superior'. Concubinage they viewed with 'tolerant indifference':

> So long as there is no interference with married women, the acquisition of a native wife, twenty wives, no wife, or a motor-bicycle, or an ice-machine would provoke in a native the same amount of respect, or contempt, or astonishment or indifference. I have seen a Governor receive the messengers of a Paramount Chief in his shirt-sleeves, and while engaged in pulling a motor-bicycle to pieces: he might have filled Government House ten times over with concubines and not excited in the native mind a tithe of the contempt for the British administration that was aroused by this very innocent, though very thoughtless action.

Sandby did not, however, accept Beaufort's arguments about the supposed benefits of concubinage, except in so far as it did perhaps assist the preservation of sanity and forestall the spread of prostitution. It was not necessary for the language. For one useful warning of trouble there were a hundred untrue reports. A concubine did not make a more comfortable home for an official than a good servant would. Concubinage was self-limiting, perhaps, since African women were mostly unattractive to look at. No doubt it was degrading, but drink was a much more serious problem. Sandby urged the office to understand that desk-wallahs simply could not realise the power of the temptations. These could not, in fact, be realised by anyone 'who has not been actually exposed to them'. In conclusion, he argued that to satisfy home opinion and meet local needs, they needed to establish two things: (1) 'open scandal, of whatever nature, will meet with instant and severe punishment', and (2) administrators who will not put this into effect will themselves be removed. He was, however, opposed to any attempt to enquire into the details of private life. It would be possible to weed out officers to such an extent that only those who had never made a mistake were left, 'and he who never makes a mistake makes nothing else'.[41]

Lewis Harcourt, now the Secretary of State, agreed sympathetically with most of this – as well he might, considering his own predilections – but the salient point was, he believed, the need to 'recognise the exigencies and prejudices of Parliamentary Government'. It was obvious that parliamentary and public opinion generally would not allow a more lax position to be taken up. The circular must therefore stand. As in the Silberrad case in Kenya, the Rhodesian discussions again threw up doubts as to whether or not the hard line on concubinage was actually required by any African demand for it. There was general agreement in the office that it was not. The decisive factor was always metropolitan puritanical insistence, backed by bureaucratic preoccupation with prestige and social distance.[42]

During the course of these intensive Rhodesian investigations and discussions, a considerable number of further scandalous allegations were flying about. Missionaries in Swaziland sought to enlist the aid of the government in checking concubinage there. It was undoubtedly practised widely among European settlers and traders, but, having satisfied themselves that no officials were involved – most of them indeed were married – the Colonial Office declined to pursue the matter.[43] Then from North-western Rhodesia in 1910 came luridly sweeping allegations against officials in general, and R. E. Codrington, a former Administrator of North-eastern (1900-06) and North-western Rhodesia (1907-08), in particular. These were made by C. N. B. Venables, a planter at Kafue in North-western Rhodesia, who admitted having himself taken a concubine in 1906. He did not think it inherently degrading, but its 'almost universal' practice amongst unmarried officials was 'an unpleasant feature' of white rule throughout Central Africa, especially when some officials indiscriminately maintained several women all over their districts: Codrington, for example, he accused of having had a 'plurality of concubines' in the principal towns. The authorities refused to pursue this allegation, since Codrington had recently died in office , and there was no point in upsetting his relatives. It seems likely that the charge as formulated was untrue, although Codrington's relations with African women were far from non-existent. The Colonial Office chose to believe that in general the picture painted by Venables was grossly exaggerated, but they were in any case confident that they had now by their circulars taken decisive action which would put an end to concubinage in the colonial services.[44]

Among all the scandals in the various east and central African territories described in this chapter two stand out from the rest: the cases of Raikes and Osborne. The lubriciousness of the one and the vindictiveness of the other are indefensible. Quite clearly they overstepped the mark. It is important to see these two scandals in perspective. They are not typical. Harrison, Codrington, McCulloch, Haywood, even Silberrad, are much more representative of the normal behaviour of officials who took concubines in Africa: they had two or three steady relationships and conducted them for the most part quietly and without trouble. In none of these cases was there any evidence that African authorities raised objections. Indeed, despite some vague and tendentious official assertion to the contrary, the privately organised practice of concubinage of itself never produced any confrontations with African peoples. Accordingly, it has little positive bearing on race relations as a whole – that is to say, on African perceptions of white man's rule. The imposition of the sterner morality by the Edwardian Colonial Office was mainly in the interests of more efficient administration. It did not want its officers messing about with women in the kraals; it wanted them to collect more taxes. The Colonial Office's only concern was with its own administrators. Rulers of empire seldom wanted to add to their problems by attacking indigenous customs other than slavery. Bentinck's abolition of suttee in India *c.* 1830 was exceptional. Thus it came about that the principal clashes of European and Afro-Asian cultural values were produced, not by government, but by missionaries, whose activities were not infrequently looked upon by government with disapproval. Nevertheless, the Protestant missionary movement was a quintessential feature of British expansion, and one which displayed considerable anxiety about indigenous sexualities.

Notes

1 R. Hyam, 'Concubinage and the Colonial Service: the Crewe Circular (1909)', *Journal of Imperial and Commonwealth History*, XIV, 1986, pp 170-86; the full text of the circular is given on pp. 182-4.

2 J. D. Hargreaves (ed.), *France and West Africa: an Anthology of Historical Documents*, London, 1969, pp. 206-9, 'Colonisation through the bed': Dr Barot, *Guide pratique de l'Européen dans l'Afrique Occidentale* (1902), intro. and pp. 328-31. See also M. Perham, *West African Passage: a Journey through Nigeria, Chad and the Cameroons, 1931-32*, ed. A. H. M. Kirk-Greene, London, 1983, pp. 133-4, 140, 179.

3 R. Oliver, *Sir Harry Johnston and the Scramble for Africa*, London, 1957, p. 316; C. J. Edwards, *The Rev. John White of Mashonaland*, London, 1935, p. 51. K. Ballhatchet, *Race, Sex and Class under the Raj: Imperial Attitudes and Policies and their Critics, 1793-1905*, London, 1980, pp. 145-55, gives a full discussion of concubinage in Burma, 1888-1903. In the Gold Coast, the colonial secretary at Accra issued in March 1907 a circular letter on his own authority (and unknown to the Colonial Office), threatening those who kept concubines with being reported to the Secretary of State (see L. H. Gann and P. Duignan, *Rulers of British Africa, 1870-1914*, Stanford, 1978, pp. 386-7, n. 55). For West Africa generally, see K. Little, *African Women in Towns*, London, 1973, pp. 117-19.

4 R. H. W. Reece, 'A "suitable population": Charles Brooke and race-mixing in Sarawak', *Itinerario*, IX, Leiden, 1985, pp. 67-112. The old system was at an end by the early 1950s, although intermarriage remained very common, and High Commissioner Malcolm MacDonald was a frequent visitor to an Iban longhouse.

5 R. Heussler, *British Rule in Malaya: the Malayan Civil Service and its Predecessors, 1867-1942*, Oxford, 1981, p. 58: J. de Vere Allen, 'The Malayan Civil Service, 1874-1941', *Comparative Studies in Society and History*, XII, 1970.

6 R. O. Collins and F. M. Deng (eds), *The British in the Sudan, 1898-1956: the Sweetness and the Sorrow*, London, 1984, ch. 7, by F. M. Deng, pp. 226-8.

7 R. Wingate, *Wingate of the Sudan: Sir Reginald Wingate*, London, 1955, p. 257; R. O. Collins, 'The Sudan Political Service: a portrait of the "imperialists"', *African Affairs*, 71, 1972, pp. 293-303, esp. p. 300.

8 Collins and Deng, *British in the Sudan*, esp. pp. 91-2; K. D. D. Henderson, *Set under Authority: being a Portrait of the Life of the British District Officer in the Sudan, 1898-1955*, Somerset, 1987, pp. 27-8.

9 Collins and Deng, *British in the Sudan*, p. 56. A. Hollinghurst's novel, *The Swimming-pool Library*, London, 1988, suggests the possibility of an intense erotic appreciation of Sudanese males by some Sudan civil servants, but it was admiration at a distance.

10 Ballhatchet, *Race, Sex, and Class under the Raj*, p. 164; T. O. Ranger, 'The invention of tradition in colonial Africa', in E. Hobsbawm and T. O. Ranger, (eds), *The Invention*

of Tradition, London, 1983, p. 215; I. F. Nicolson and C. A. Hughes, 'A provenance of proconsuls: British colonial governors, 1900-60', *Journal of Imperial and Commonwealth History*, IV, 1975, p. 200.

11 H. A. C. Cairns, *Prelude to Imperialism: British Reactions to Central African Society, 1840-90*, London, 1965, pp. 53-7; Gann and Duignan, *Rulers of British Africa*, pp. 226, 240-3.

12 R. Meinertzhagen, *Kenya Diary, 1902-06*, Edinburgh, 1957, pp. 9-13, 148, 176.

13 PRO, CO 533/44/21793 and 46/33653.

14 CO 533/44/21793 and 56/25633.

15 CO 533/48/45971 and 49/30560.

16 CO 533/52/44293 and 51/44448.

17 *Parliamentary Debates, 4th series, Commons,* 198, cc. 68-73; minute by Seely, 8 December 1908, CO 533/52/45005 (the key file on the circular).

18 CO 533/52/45005. The Burmese circulars remained demi-official, because it was felt specific formal rules would become public knowledge and only draw unwelcome attention to the situation. The India Office reported that the circulars had 'unfortunately' led some officers to marry their mistresses, and the only really effective way of extinguishing concubinage seemed to be through 'the more general presence of English ladies and the social pressures exerted by them' (CO 533/49/43627).

19 Minute, 21 December 1908, CO 533/52/45714 and 45715.

20 CO 533/52/45005; CO 854/168; CO 54/723/6285 (Ceylon). The recipient colonies and protectorates were: Fiji, Western Pacific, East Africa Protectorate, Nyasaland Protectorate, Somali Protectorate, Uganda Protectorate, Gambia, Gold Coast, Northern Nigeria, Southern Nigeria, Sierra Leone, [Ceylon], Hong Kong, Straits Settlements, Weihaiwei.

21 CO 862/15/190-91 (Replies to circular despatches). As to Ceylon, R. E. Stubbs remained sceptical: if the report from McCallum was true, 'things are better than they were a few years ago. You will remember the case of the Engineer who was considered "socially impossible" because he used to play cricket with his half-caste bastards – the objection being not that they were bastards or half-castes, or, altogether, that he played cricket with them, but that he did so on ground adjoining the Lawn Tennis Club's courts' (minute, 23 December 1909, CO 54/723/6285).

22 *Parliamentary Debates, 5th series, Commons,* VIII, cc. 1031-38, 1048, 1067-69, 1077-80, 1119-28.

23 *Church Missionary Review,* LX, January 1909, p. 61, editorial notes: 'The honour of the ruling race in Africa'.

24 CO 533/384/9/29 and 41 (1929-30).

25 CO 96/670/X4049 (Gold Coast, 1927); H. Kuklick, *The Imperial Bureaucrat: the Colonial Administrative Service in the Gold Coast, 1920-39*, Stanford, 1979, pp. 122-30.

26 C. Allen, (ed.), *Tales from the Dark Continent*, London, 1980 ed., p. 18; A. Inglis, *The White Women's Protection Ordinance: Sexual Anxiety and Politics in Papua*, Sussex, 1975, pp. 15-16. Fulani virgins were still on offer in Northern Nigeria in the mid-1930s: see Stanhope White, *'Dan Bana': Memoirs of a Nigerian Official*, London, 1966, p. 11.

27 J. G. Butcher, *The British in Malaya, 1880-1941: the Social History of a European Community in Colonial South-East Asia*, Kuala Lumpur, 1979, pp. 206-12. See also R. Winstedt, *Start from Alif: Count from One; An Autobiographical Mémoire*, Kuala Lumpur, 1969, pp. 17-18; V. Purcell, *The Memoirs of a Malayan Official*, London, 1965, pp. 297-8; A. Mackirdy and W. N. Willis, *The White Slave Market*, London 1912, p. 249; C. Allen (ed.), *Tales from the South China Seas: Images of the British in South-East Asia in the Twentieth Century*, London, 1984 ed., pp. 151-2.

28 Magdalene College Archives, Group F: A. D. Garson Diaries (1947-57), I, pp. 77-78 (22 January 1948), quoted by kind permission of the Master and Fellows of Magdalene College, Cambridge. Garson was Head of Training, Appointments, Transfers and Promotions, 1948-62.

29 Perham, *West African Passage*, p. 140 (24 February 1932).

30 CO 417/372/32474 (Bechuanaland and Rhodesia), report by W. S. Taberer, 30 April 1903.

31 *The Historical Register of the University of Cambridge . . . to 1910*, Cambridge, 1917, p. 677. Raikes got a 2:3 – a class which no longer exists.
32 CO 417/372/32474: W. H. Milton to Lord Milner, 19 June 1903; Milner to Secretary of State, 4 August 1903.
33 CO 417/372/32473.
34 CO 417/372/32474, minutes by G. V. Fiddes (3 September 1903), F. Graham (24 September), H. W. Just (28 September and 24 October), and Joseph Chamberlain (29 September 1903).
35 CO 417/491/10550 (British South Africa Company, 1910); CO 879/104 (Confidential Print, 1911): Africa (S) 948, Further correspondence (1910) *re* German South-West Africa Protectorate, Bechuanaland Protectorate and Rhodesia, nos. 67-69, 72, 96, 123; Lord Crewe to Lord Gladstone, 13 August 1910 (20932 and 32415).
36 CO 417/491/10367, British South Africa Company board meeting, 23 March 1910, and annexures 12-18.
37 CO 417/491/12506, minutes by H. Lambert (29 April 1910), H. W. Just (29 April), Sir Francis Hopwood (29 April), Colonel Seely (1 May), and Lord Crewe (3 May 1910); CO 879/104, African (S), 948, nos. 60 and 63.
38 CO 417/482/13936 and 483/19358. The impression remained that the government was 'against' marriage. 'Marriage was regarded in the same light as prohibition, communism and cat-worship – conditions known to prevail in certain impossible areas of the planet, but unworthy of rational discussion': E. F. G. Haig, *Nigerian Sketches*, London, 1931, pp. 22-3.
39 CO 879/104, African (S) 947, no 172; CO 417/488/21797.
40 *Ibid.*, no 285 (38728/1910), L. P. Beaufort to High Commissioner, 4 October 1910; Lord Gladstone to Beaufort, 14 November 1910.
41 CO 417/484/38728, minute by C. B. Sandby, 12 January 1911.
42 *Ibid.*, minutes by W. Robinson (12 January 1911), H. W. Just (12 January), Colonel Seely (16 January), and Lewis Harcourt (16 January 1911).
43 CO 417/469/16451 (Swaziland, 1909) Bishop of Zululand to High Commissioner, 26 March 1909, Lord Selborne to Bishop Wilmot, 1 April 1909, C. N. Rodwell to Bishop Wilmot, 21 April 1909; CO 417/502, R. T. Coryndon to Lord Gladstone, 24 April 1911, Lord Gladstone to Secretary of State, 21 October 1911; CO 417/509/21588 (Swaziland, 1911).
44 CO 417/493/38589 (British South Africa Company, 1910), C. N. B. Venables to C. N. Rodwell, 11 May 1910, L. A. Wallace to Lord Gladstone, 30 September 1910; minute by Lambert, 23 December 1910.

CHAPTER EIGHT

Missionary confrontations

The problem of polygyny

Man is by nature polygamic whereas woman as a rule is monogamic, and polyandrous only when tired of her lover. For the man, as has been truly said, loves the woman, but the love of the woman is for the love of the man. [Richard Burton, 'Terminal Essay' on *The Arabian Nights*].

Throughout the world missionaries objected to an immense range of traditional attitudes and activities quite apart from obvious targets like slavery, infanticide, cannibalism, suttee, and footbinding. Nudity and long hair were regarded as indecent, tattooing as degrading, polygyny as adulterous, bridewealth (*lobola*) as little better than the buying and selling of wives, anal intercourse as unnatural and an abomination, conventional courtship intimacies as disgusting, drumming and dancing as lascivious, initiation ceremonies as immoral if not obscene, female circumcision (and in the early days male circumcision, too) as wrong. Some early-Victorian missionaries even thought living in round houses rather than square ones was somehow uncivilised. It has already been seen above how Protestant missionaries attacked intermarriage in the Canadian fur trade from the 1830s. In some societies, especially in the South Pacific, almost the entire range of social amusements and communal activities became interdicted. Victorian missionaries seldom stopped to enquire what structural function the practices they objected to so often performed in ensuring the cohesion of traditional societies.[1]

Almost all pre-literate communities organised their interpersonal relations with strict rules, carefully regulated and pragmatically based. Nowhere was sexual licence as such actually condoned or promoted. The rules of personal conduct were often minutely differentiated in Africa, as for example, in the different ways of treating mother's brother and father's brother – in these contexts an undifferentiated European term like 'uncle' seemed extraordinarily crude. Sloppy notions like 'love' had little place. Few traditional societies shared the western reverence either for monosexuality or for romantic love. As C. S. Lewis once observed, 'the notion of romantic love has erected impassible barriers between us and the classical past or the oriental present'. An Mfengu elder, trying in 1883 to explain to a white man's commission of inquiry why his people were finding it so difficult to cope with European intrusion, declared: 'It is all this thing called love. We do not understand it at all. This thing called love has been introduced' – and everything had begun to go wrong.[2] The principal aim of traditional African marriage was the production of children, not personal happiness.

Missionaries completely misunderstood bridewealth. African marriage was a contract between families rather than one between individuals 'in love'. *Lobola* (to use the Bantu term) gave a number of the wife's relatives a material stake in the continuation of the marriage: if the marriage broke up, the wife's relations would have to give back cattle to the husband's family. It thus performed a useful social function, legalising and stabilising the marriage. It was not a brideprice but rather a marriage insurance. It also conferred legitimacy on children and ensured their membership of the father's clan by compensating the bride's family. But the most central and persistent objection of missionaries was to polygyny, together with its attendant complications of polyandry, levirate, sororate and so forth. It was pre-eminently an African problem, practised and admired in almost every African society.[3] Though they realised that African domestic slavery would have to be tackled gradually, missionaries would not tolerate polygyny for a moment. It was to them not just a social evil but 'an offence against the law of God'. Its rejection, writes Ajayi, was the most essential dogma of nineteenth-century Christianity, partly because it was an individualistic religion which wished to strike at the supposedly communal way of life it symbolised. Life in polygamous households seemed at best incomprehensible, at worst the devil's own institution.[4] Livingstone saw only too clearly what a big obstacle the principle of monogamy was to Africans: those who partially knew the gospel, he wrote, 'hate it cordially because of monogamy'.[5] The demand for monogamy was indeed the most serious obstacle to the adoption of Christianity in Africa, especially where it was in competition with Islam.

Again, as with *lobola*, the missionaries had little understanding of polygyny. Its incidence was not, in fact, all that high. In Africa south of the Sahara about thirty-five per cent of all married men were polygynous, having (theoretically) 2.4 wives each. (It was more common in West and South Africa than in East Africa). So nowhere in black Africa was home life for the ordinary man anything like that of a harem. At any one time the majority of African men were monogamous.[6] The possession of 'wives and other cattle' was, however, an important status symbol, and some kings were accumulators of both on a grand scale.

[183]

(Even in the mid-twentieth century the king of Swaziland had 117 wives.) There were, in African terms, sound reasons for polygyny. It promoted useful alliances and kinship (that fundamental cement of all its societies). It tended to ensure the continuation of the family line, minimising the risk of the stigma – indeed calamity – of childlessness. It freed women from constant pregnancies, and ensured widows and children were cared for. It alleviated the deprivation of sexual intercourse, which was taboo during the suckling of children (who were often not weaned for about two to three years). It improved a man's status and chances of high office. It increased a man's labour supply, so guaranteeing food for his family, and enabling a chief to do his entertaining properly, which was his principal obligation to his followers. The Kikuyu had a proverb : 'one wife is a passport to death'. Paradoxically, a plurality of wives was seen as ever more essential in terms of making a successful entry into western economic enterprise. Those who went into cash-cropping for the international market needed the labour supply of additional wives in order to maximise their new profit opportunities. In this way, Christianity came to seem an actual obstacle to the upward mobility which it approved. Much heart-searching resulted.[7]

Mission work in Africa grew rapidly from the 1850s. From the start the issue of polygyny was of central importance, and it remained at the heart of the battle for an African Christianity. The first missionaries in Nigeria evolved the formula that the wives in a polygamous marriage could be baptised if true converts, but no man could be baptised if he retained more than one wife. In 1856, Henry Venn, the Secretary of the Church Missionary Society, decisively supported this formula, ruling that 'a state of polygamy is unlawful within the Church of Christ, even though commenced in ignorance'. A challenge to this position came from Bishop Colenso in Natal, who powerfully argued in 1862 that it was 'unwarranted by the Scriptures, unsanctioned by Apostolic example or authority, condemned by common reason and sense of right and altogether unjustifiable'. But Colenso was condemned as a heretic; his views on polygyny did not prevail, even with the black Bishop of the Niger, Samuel Crowther. In 1888 the Lambeth Conference held firmly (despite minority voices) to Venn's ruling. The Anglican bishops believed the Christian conception of marriage had to be protected despite its unpopularity: 'any immediate and rapid successes which might otherwise have been secured in the mission-field would be dearly purchased by any lowering or confusion of this idea'. This position was endorsed by the Lambeth Conferences of 1908 and 1920. Moreover, the World Missionary Conference at Edinburgh in 1910 was equally emphatic, revealing an almost complete unanimity of opinion that polygamy was 'simply one of the gross evils of heathen society, which, like habitual murder or slavery, must at all costs be ended'.[8]

This, of course, was not at all how Africans saw it. The repudiation of wives caused injustice and distress. Even to convert customary marriages into church marriages was impossible for most ordinary people without great effort and some expense. Government officials often disapproved of missionary policy, not infrequently regarding it as immoral, if not leading to actual immorality. The missionary demand for monogamy certainly had some unexpected and unwelcome results. The restriction to one wife, together with the removal of restraints on the liberty of women which Christianity encouraged, led to the development of prostitution and to an occasional disaster such as the syphilis epidemic in Buganda in 1906. As Schapera concludes for the Kgatla of Bechuanaland, 'as far as the family is concerned, Christianity was the most directly subversive factor'. (In the West Indies, missionary policy on marriage was one of the factors leading to high bastardy rates and, since the baptism of illegitimate children was discouraged, perhaps seventy per cent of West Indians were debarred from church membership.)[9]

In the vast majority of African cases, church marriages in the twentieth century were either preceded or followed by customary marriage. At least half the Christians in Africa never married in church at all. Even among well-established urban westernised populations, Christian marriage had little appeal. In the early twentieth century in Lagos, an average of only fifty Christian unions a year occurred out of a Christian population of 10,000; perhaps only about two-fifths even of the Lagosian elite made Christian marriage work. Christian marriage among Christian Africans was most prevalent in Malawi, but least popular in eastern Uganda, where only about one in eight Christians ever married in church. African independent churches accepted polygyny; although they would have been founded in any case, their membership was certainly expanded by those who were troubled by the missionary stand against polygyny, a stand for which these churches could find no scriptural warrant. Independent churches were thus an extremely attractive option for those who wanted to become Christians but not to submit to monogamy. The move away from church marriage in the 1960s was described as 'fairly massive'. But even in the mid-1950s in rural eastern Buganda, for example, eighty-five per cent of adult Africans were debarred from communion on account of their marital status. As Fr Adrian Hastings concluded caustically in 1973: 'in many places the Church is in a process of excommunicating itself'. Too late it was being realised that missionary effort had contributed to the disintegration of African family life, 'through too negative an appraisal of traditional domestic institutions'.[10]

Insistence on monogamy thus forms a long, difficult backdrop to the missionary penetration of Africa. It is a battle that the missions are not winning in the second half of this century, as they are well aware, although they believe they have to go on trying to uphold it as the proper Christian ideal, involved as it is with 'the equal sanctity of all human beings'.[11] It is against this unspectacular background of smouldering discontent over polygyny that we should view the most dramatic reactions to missionary teaching on sexual matters: the attack on sodomy, which produced the Baganda martyrs in the 1880s, and the attack on clitoridectomy among the Kikuyu, which launched modern political protest in Kenya in the late 1920s.

Buggery in Buganda

'In my opinion', said Iskhomakhos, 'those who are mad about sex cannot be taught to care about anything more than that. It is not easy to discover any hope or concern more pleasurable than a passionate desire for sexual intercourse with boys.' [Xenophon, *Oeconomicus*, 12.13]

Missionaries the world over, whether Catholic or Protestant, have always consistently targeted anal intercourse as one of the first traditional practices to be eliminated. One reason for Christian hostility was the association of sodomy with Islam. Xavier in Japan in the mid-sixteenth century had three principal messages: pray only to God, give up sodomy and stop infanticide. He and his preachers were ridiculed in the streets by incredulous Japanese: 'these are the men who think sodomy is wrong!' It was widely and openly practised among Buddhist monks and at the Tokugawa court. Ricci in Peking only a little later found it everywhere: 'the horrible sin to which everyone here is much given, and about which there seems to be no shame or impediment'.[12] Their Protestant successors were even more opposed to it. In Buganda in the late 1880s confrontation on this issue resulted in the martyrdom of a considerable number of boys and young men at the court of Mwanga (Kabaka, 1884-88, 1889-97).

These Baganda martyrdoms were grouped in three phases. In the first, three Protestant boys from Alexander Mackay's Church Missionary Society entourage were killed in January 1885. In the second, thirty-one boys and young men were burned alive in a mass funeral pyre at Namugongo on 3 June 1886, while their leader, Charles Lwanga, was martyred separately. Of these, thirteen were believed to have been Catholics, thirteen Protestants and five non-Christians, who were probably in the main unbaptised neophytes. In the third phase, an unknown number perished in the mopping-up operation finally concluded on 27 January 1887. In 1964, twenty-two Roman Catholic Baganda martyrs were canonised as saints, of whom thirteen were pages at the Kabaka's court. Seven of them were eighteen or younger, mostly about fifteen or sixteen, though one of them might have been a thirteen-year-old. Of the rest, many were ex-pages.[13]

The Kabaka's court contained about 500 pages, drawn from the best families throughout Buganda. They were, among other things, responsible for the Kabaka's personal safety. Sodomy may or may not have been introduced by the Arab traders, but it was well established at court under Mutesa long before Mwanga's accession. A conventional harem was available, but Mwanga preferred the pages. (From his point of view he was, after all, surrounded by the pick of Buganda's boyhood.) He was totally involved in male sex himself as a boy. At the same time he had been attracted to Christianity, and had begun to receive instruction. However, once it was clear that Christianity meant renouncing anal intercourse – and he checked the point carefully – Mwanga, in angry disbelief, declared it was asking the impossible. He was only eighteen when he succeeded to the throne, and many of his court officials were only a little older than himself, that is, at the peak of their sexual imperiousness. His chancellor (the *katikiro*) was a passionate addict of coitus with boys, which he combined with increasing dislike of Christianity. The martyrdoms of the first phase were triggered off because chancellor Mukasa had selected a particularly attractive boy of about eleven or twelve either for himself or Mwanga, and the boy had refused. In the period following, more and more pages refused sexual overtures under the influence of their majordomo, Joseph Mukasa Balikuddembe, who had become a Christian. He discreetly taught the boys the new religion, convincing them that sodomy was wrong, and making excuses for his converts not to respond to any summons from the Kabaka which looked likely to end in a sex session. It now became a regular occurrence for boys to reject propositions. If Mwanga resented this, it was as nothing compared with the fury of other boy-lovers at court, who began to taunt Mwanga with his lack of control over the pages. The result was the removal and execution of majordomo Joseph, his ostentatious replacement by a Muslim who was an unequivocally proselytising pederast, and the re-establishment of the old sexual hegemony. Sodomy at once came more and more into the open, being freely indulged in, as court officials became determined defiantly to break once and for all the threat of Christian teaching to their way of life. The leadership and protection of the Christian pages was now assumed by Charles Lwanga. He became the principal martyr.[14]

When the storm broke, the court was at Munyonyo. This was little more than a hunting-lodge, serviced only by a comparatively small complement of pages. But for this circumstance, the holocaust would have been much greater in scale. The precipitating incident was the sudden refusal of sodomy by Mwafu, an exceptionally beautiful boy who had become Mwanga's favourite. The Christians were trying to convert Mwafu. This was the last straw. Not only were fresh pages refusing to be drawn into the Kabaka's sex circle because of their acceptance of Christian teaching, but the Christians were now attempting to detach from him even those who were his regular partners. Since Mwafu was the *katikiro*'s son he escaped the wrath to come. But Mwanga was thrown into a paroxysm of rage. He struck and wounded Apolo Kagwa (a future *katikiro*), and demanded a decision from all the pages to hand as to whether or not they would meet his sexual demands. Any one of the martyrs could have saved himself if he had consented to sodomy. There were a few summary decapitations. Before the main executions took place (not on the same day), Baganda chiefs (some of them the fathers of the condemned and recalcitrant boys) were asked for their consent. This apparently, they readily gave: if these boys will not do your bidding, they replied, we will replace them for you with those who will. But they did not approve of any widening of the persecution against Christians in general.[15]

A follow-up persecution outside the court nevertheless took place, but the Kabaka, having spent his anger upon his immediate entourage, left the organisation of this wider operation to the *katikiro*, who used it to settle some old political scores. This part of the persecution was not, however, really systematic. It was easy enough to escape or prevaricate. Some court favourites were pardoned; others had their sentences commuted to castration. Nevertheless, perhaps a hundred youths all told were killed in Buganda. No more Christians died after the last victim in January 1887. Mwanga was satisfied that he had demonstrated who was master.

There have sometimes been attempts to suggest that Mwanga was motivated by objections to Christianity other than those prompted by his sexual frustration. With any historical event it makes sense to distinguish long-term underlying causes from the immediate triggering episodes. It may be true that he was in a general way disappointed by the unwillingness of missionaries tamely to contribute to Bagandan needs as he defined them, for example as to gun supply. The emergence of a competing allegiance at court cannot have been welcome to a despotic king. It may also be the case that he was worried about the threat of a possible foreign take-over, and accordingly was especially anxious to have no kind of rebelliousness at court – but it was not an actual threat at this time. The idea that he might have seen the pages as spies or as politically disloyal seems untenable. The only information passed by them to Europeans concerned details of the murder of Bishop Hannington. The martyrs were remarkable not least for their personal loyalty to the Kabaka. Many of them could have fled when it was obvious they were doomed. Not one of Lwanga's group did. This might, of course, suggest a deliberate and conscious desire for martyrdom, but even if this were a factor for a few of them, it could not possibly have held good for the entire group. Nor is it likely that boys only just into their teens would have been identified as political subversives. Moreover, it is only by recognising the specific sexual causes, both long-term and short-term, of the Kabaka's wrath that it is possible to explain why the persecution was so patchy and incomplete, or why some Christians were rapidly reinstated into highly privileged positions. Ironically some were given so much new power that in 1888 they were able to engineer the so-called 'Christian Revolution' in Buganda.[16]

Mwanga died in exile in the Seychelles in 1903, a baptised Christian, and presumably in expectation of a joyous reunion with the martyrs in heaven.[17]

For the churches, what happened in Buganda in the 1880s was a chastening experience. No one could argue here the Tertullian thesis that the blood of martyrs was the seed of the church. It was thus forty years before missionaries again pushed an African society to the limits of its patience on a sexual issue. The storm then broke in Kenya over clitoridectomy. Although the results were not so dramatic as in Buganda, the Kenyan confrontation was actually more serious. It was one thing to have challenged the practices of a monarch and his court in respect of selected teenage boys, but it proved to be quite another to take on an entire community about the means of bringing its womenfolk to adult status. And as we shall see, missionaries themselves did not agree how to deal with it.

Clitoridectomy in Kenya

It is impossible for a member of the tribe to imagine an initiation without clitoridectomy . . .. The initiation of both sexes is the most important custom among the Gikuyu ... the moral code of the tribe is bound up with this custom and it symbolises the unification of the whole tribal organisation. [Jomo Kenyatta, *Facing Mount Kenya*]

Clitoridectomy is not a precise term. It covers two basic variations: *female circumcision*, which is cutting of the prepuce or hood of the clitoris, and *excision*, which is cutting of the clitoris and of all or part of the labia minora. The latter is much the more common form. It is an African Islamic practice, as well as being performed in more than twenty countries right across the bulge of Africa from Senegal to Somaliland, being especially entrenched in Senegal, Mali, northern Sudan and Somalia, where it was often combined with infibulation (the stitching up of the vaginal orifice until marriage). It is widespread in many parts of French West Africa, and in the area southwards from Egypt to northern Tanzania. Perhaps seventy-four million women in the 1970s were circumcised, though the exact extent of the sexual invasion varied greatly. The Kikuyu practised excision, while their neighbours the Luo did not; so too the Yoruba, Ibo and Hausa in Nigeria, but not the Nupe or Fulani. In Kenya the most drastic cutting occurred among the Chuka, the Wimbe, the Igoji section of the Meru, and the Mathira section of the Kikuyu: here the violent gouging out of the clitoris and surrounding tissues 'left a hole big enough for the insertion of half a golf-ball'. By contrast, Leakey described the traditional Southern Kikuyu operation in fairly innocuous terms: the operator

> parted the *labia majora* and took hold of the clitoris between the thumb and first finger of her left hand. Pulling it forward as much as she could, she cut off a tiny portion of the skin, using a special sharp razor to do so . . . Sometimes the operator also excised a little piece of the *labia minora* on either side of the clitoris.

If the operation was carelessly performed, or if the wound was inadequately tended in the days following, scar tissue formed across the top of the labia minora in the soft area around the birth canal, where normally elastic tissues might be replaced by a rigid ring of hard fibrous tissue. This could result in constriction of the genitalia, making childbirth difficult, dangerous or even impossible without surgical intervention. Moreover, as well as dyspareunia, it might also lead to dysmenorrhoea to say nothing of difficulties with micturition. The problem medically was that it was an operation difficult to limit, and injury to the surrounding areas was hard to avoid.[18]

Clitoridectomy is analogous in intention to male circumcision. In both cases the aim is to achieve sexual differentiation and make clean. The clitoris is perceived as representing the masculine element in a girl, just as the foreskin represents femininity in a boy. Both needed to be removed. It is also widely believed that the clitoris is an aggressive organ, threatening penis and baby alike. Without the operation a woman could not have healthy children, it is said. Moreover, throughout the eastern side of Africa at least, the female genitalia are considered dirty and ugly, so that it is 'done for beauty and cleanliness'. In one sense clitoridectomy is cosmetic surgery. (Without it, 'the two leaves [labia minora] will grow too big and dangle like a male organ'.)

The sociological functions of the operation were profound. Without circumcision women were not adult and not members of society, and therefore not able to marry, nor own property, nor take public office. Without it, too, they were subject to severe psychological pressures as outcasts. Circumcision was the focal point of initiation, and all initiation ceremonies were integral mechanisms for the assertion of tribal unity and loyalty.[19] In societies which practised polygyny and sexual abstinence during prolonged weaning of children, it was reckoned helpful to reduce the sensitivity of the female sexual response. Clitoridectomy could be seen as a means of controlling women's threatening propensities. (With that aim in mind an attempt had been made in the 1860s to introduce it to Britain and America, but it was quickly discredited.)[20]

Missionaries by the twentieth century rather liked male circumcision, in conformity with its new-found widespread acceptance in Britain itself. They had long given up trying to eradicate it in Africa. It had a degree of biblical sanction. Their residual worries about it were purely moral objections to initiation ceremonies. And so sometimes they tried to get it done in infancy and in hospital rather than at puberty and in public. Clitoridectomy was different. They found no virtue in it. Indeed, they often compared it with Hindu suttee and Chinese footbinding and *mui tsai*. The 'brutal and revolting' removal of 'a principal seat' of sexual pleasure, perhaps rendering a woman passive to man, seemed medically unnecessary and indefensible. The operation was inevitably a painful one, but their fundamental objection was moral rather than medical. Missionaries were particularly disturbed by the thought of eleven- or twelve-year-old girls being stripped naked and put through a public initiation ritual which focused attention so unequivocally on their genitals. Even worse, the operation was often accompanied by 'obscene practices' – the operator would perform ceremonial intercourse with her spouse in the presence of the initiates. (The intention was that the initiates should *witness* coitus, but this does not necessarily mean to say they actually had to *watch* it.)[21]

In the early part of the twentieth century – not least as a result of urbanisation – there was an increase in the complications, in the severity of the operation, as untrained and unscrupulous operators got to work in and near towns. (Traditionally they were supposed to serve a seven-year apprenticeship, and they were highly paid, which created a vested interest.) Medical missionaries, of course, tended to see only the cases which had led to complications; often, too, they misjudged the normal extent of the operation by seeing mainly the results of forcible and punitive circumcision. (Some girls were now running off to mission schools in order to try to escape circumcision.) It was virtually impossible for Europeans to judge just how severe the effects of the operation were. The Church of Scotland Mission (CSM) seemed to think complications were almost inevitable. But one medical missionary believed they occurred only in ten per cent of cases; while one private doctor thought the effects were negligible.[22]

Systematic teaching by missionaries in Kenya against clitoridectomy began in 1906, by the controllers of the CSM hospital in Kikuyu, notably by Dr J. W. Arthur, who became head of the mission station there. The first medical missionary at Tumutumu, Dr H. A. Philp, also campaigned against it from 1910. The Americans of the Africa Inland Mission followed from 1914. The Church Missionary Society had no uniform policy, but left individual missionaries to take their own line. By about 1915 all Protestant missionary societies were agreed on its undesirability. (The Catholics, however, held that no question of 'faith or morals' was involved.) In 1916 the Church of Scotland forbade it for African Christians, and introduced discipline (that is, excommunication) regarding it. Many groups of Christian Africans were coming to see that it was undesirable. Missionary pressure on government to do something about it increased steadily. It was always presented as 'sexual mutilation of women'. The Conference of East African Governors discussed the problem in 1926, agreeing that it should not be interfered with, since it was impracticable to suppress something so significant to African opinion; the governors felt, however, that it would be worth trying to persuade tribal leaders to ensure a return to the more ancient and less brutally extensive forms of the operation. They preferred Africans to reform their own practices, and they wanted to keep the government's position neutral.[23]

The issue was forced at the CSM at Tumutumu in 1929, followed shortly afterwards by confrontation at Kikuyu. CSM schoolteachers were asked to sign a declaration renouncing 'sexual mutilation of women', together with membership of the Kikuyu Central Association (KCA) until it stopped 'attacking' the mission on this question. It was, however, one thing to make renunciation of clitoridectomy a religious test, a condition of baptism and church membership (as in 1916); it was quite another to extend it to eligibility for school entry and make it part of teachers' conditions of employment. Dr Arthur sacked all teachers who subscribed to clitoridectomy. This provoked the confrontation. He was mobbed, the Kikuyu ostracised his appointees and disrupted church services; his schools were almost completely boycotted and church attendances were much reduced. The Kikuyu Christians split into *kirore* (abolitionist) and *karinga* (traditionalist) groups. Independent schools were formed by some of the teachers who had left the mission schools.[24]

The CSM's version of these events was that the confrontation was provoked by the politically minded younger Kikuyu: that the mission was attacked by the KCA. No one outside missionary circles agreed with this interpretation, least of all the Colonial Office. Even McGregor Ross, an old friend of Dr Arthur's, believed Arthur was solely to blame, regarding his action as 'a most unwise and deplorable frontal attack'. As late as February 1929, the KCA did not even mention female circumcision among its massive list of grievances presented to the government.[25]

Within a month, ninety per cent of the communicant congregation was lost to the CSM church in Kikuyu, and to the Africa Inland Mission at Kijabe. Other congregations were not affected to such a drastic degree. In the Gospel Missionary Society the largest number suspended was twenty per cent, though its main station at Kambui was totally unaffected. The Church Missionary Society outstations experienced a good deal of trouble, and there was a secession at Embu, where the missionaries took a tough line which led to the closure of thirteen out of thirty-eight schools. Eighteen out of sixty-six teachers left one school, and the Embu congregation fell to twenty out of five hundred. Generally it was the outstations and the schools that bore the brunt of the reaction. The CSM temporarily lost fifty-three per cent of the school roll, the Africa Inland Mission slightly less, the Gospel Mission twenty-five per cent. As the crisis died down, congregations began to return. By the end of 1930 at Tumutumu, only seven per cent of the total baptismal roll was permanently lost to membership, about two hundred names. By the middle of 1931 the CSM at Kikuyu was back to a little over a third of what it had been in September 1929.[26]

It had, however, all been traumatic. Some of the CSM missionaries began talking like Covenanters of old, at least one of them hoping to see KCA leaders hanged.[27] At the height of the crisis, rumours spread among the Africans (sometimes in songs) that the Europeans wished Kikuyu girls not to be circumcised so that they might have them for themselves, and seize their land through marriage with them. Or, as Kenyatta later wrote: 'the overwhelming majority of them believed that it is the secret aim of those who attack this centuries-old custom to disintegrate their social order in order thereby to hasten their Europeanisation'.[28] Some forcible circumcisions were performed. Early in January 1930 came the terrible news of the murder of Miss Hulda Stumpf, a seventy-year-old missionary with the Africa Inland Mission at Kijabe. It is alleged she was raped several times, then viciously circumcised, and that she died from the operation, which led to yet further genital mutilation. The suspects were Mkamba and not Kikuyu, however.[29]

The British government was determined that this murder should not divert them from a cool handling of the dispute. The British response was largely directed by Dr T. Drummond Shiels, the Parliamentary Under-Secretary of the Colonial Office, who was very critical of Dr Arthur's tactlessness, if not actual stupidity, in 'mixing up politics with bad surgery'. Drummond Shiels was especially anxious to dissociate the administration from Dr Arthur. In order to differentiate clearly between them, he demanded Arthur's resignation from the Executive Council – otherwise there was a danger that Arthur would be regarded as the government's agent. Medically, Drummond Shiels believed that clito-ridectomy involved a lot of undesirable scar-tissue, and felt it would be best to abolish it. (Since no effective control would ever be possible, there seemed no point in merely trying to alter procedures to the less harmful methods.) He believed that if the issue had been handled as a medical question, and if efficient practical propaganda by government health officers had been tried, they might well have been on the way to solving the problem. 'I believe that feeling could be sublimated into a willingness for abolition in the interests of the race, if it were properly put.'[30] He saw the Kikuyu leader, Jomo (or Johnstone, as he then was) Kenyatta, on 23 January 1930, confident that he would co-operate in such an approach. Kenyatta indeed said he was sure the Kikuyu would listen if the bad results of excision were explained to them by doctors; what they resented was being told they could not be Christians if circumcised. 'Pulpit denunciations', he added, only made people think something was being taken from them: 'any attempt to coerce my people by *force majeure* will have the very opposite of the desired effect as it causes my people to attach accentuated importance to the maintenance of this custom.'[31]

Government did not want to run foul of the KCA. There were many good reasons for caution on the whole mater. Such an issue could not be decided in Kenya alone, since clitoridectomy was widespread across Africa. (Thirty to forty million circumcised women was the contempo-rary estimate.) Any campaign against it might conceivably result in an uprising, with the attendant possibility of rape, murder and forcible circumcision of white women on isolated farms. It was, in fact, impos-sible to stop a practice which could, if need be, take only a few seconds with a rusty razor blade in a hut. If askaris were charged with enforcing a government prohibition there was a risk that they would use their powers for indiscriminate molestation, which in turn would lead to further trouble. Governor Grigg believed that repression was almost certain to lead to violence and bloodshed. Missionaries, he said, had lost sight of the 'fundamental principle of African development': progress must be slow and gradual. Nor did it seem right to interfere where there was no abuse. As one Colonial Office official put it: we would not propose to make the Jewish rite of male circumcision a penal offence in this country. On the other hand, the government did not want a rift with the missions, who usefully provided schools and, through education, an important 'moral anchorage' for African subjects.[32]

The field administration was told of the government's preference for the milder forms of clitoridectomy. Let it be known, they were instructed, that no girl could be operated on legally against her wish. Africans should understand that there were dangerous effects from *all* forms of the operation. Lord Passfield's directive as Secretary of State was: proceed by education and propaganda, and get the help of native authorities. Propaganda should be extensive, but there should be no general attempt to abolish immediately the milder forms, though these should be included in the propaganda along with warnings about the more serious forms. On the missionary side, the Bishop of Mombasa's pastoral letters to the Church Missionary Society missionaries (1 January 1930 and 12 October 1931) stressed that 'it is quite certain that this circumcision of girls is not in agreement with the commands of Christ'. It harmed the body and was 'also closely associated with many evils that do grievous harm to the soul'. Any member of the Anglican church who permitted or performed it must be 'brought under discipline'. Beyond that, he admitted that the clergy were not agreed. Those, however, who were not in favour of total prohibition 'should at least co-operate to enforce an end to the associated heathen practices', such as its performance in public.[33]

What were the aims of the KCA in making a political issue out of clitoridectomy? By 1928 they were seeking new ways to secure acceptance by and 'incorporation' in the workings and patronage of the colonial state, and to dissociate themselves from the chiefs. Female circumcision suited their purpose well, because it would restore their reputation with the older and more conservative elements in the traditionalist masses, who had been looking rather askance at the doings of these young 'hotheads'. It would help to cut the ground from under the chiefs, who tended to favour the less extensive forms. The aspiring young men – with their commercial ventures – were disenchanted with Christianity, mainly because of its insistence on monogamy. Clitoridectomy did not worry them so much, but it was a useful rallying cry to re-establish their credibility with the traditionalists. It was taken up as the means to another end. It was a bid for wider popular support. And for larger subscriptions.[34]

Drummond Shiels was alert to much of this. The movement for political advancement among the Kikuyu and others, he thought, 'could not be killed by police or missionaries'. It was bound to grow. The government task was to see that it was directed into constitutional channels. With careful handling, the KCA could be brought round. It was no use trying to crush it, and it would be impolitic to let Kenyatta lapse into hostility. 'Something of the nature of the KCA is springing up in most colonies, and must be regarded more or less as a permanent feature which Governments have to reckon with.' Properly treated, 'it would act as a safety valve', which would be very valuable. The Colonial Office felt that the Kikuyu had real grievances, which Kenyatta had presented well; they and he must be taken seriously.[35]

The results of the missionary confrontation were almost entirely counterproductive. In the short run it led to an extremely unpleasant upheaval, which probably increased the incidence of the more extensive forms of clitoridectomy. Maurice Bloch has recently shown, using the example of male infant circumcision among the Merina of Madagascar, how easy it is to manipulate these rituals for political purposes, and especially to increase their scale, elaboration, extensiveness and sense of mass commitment.[36] In the middle term, the campaign against clitoridectomy was a complete failure. From the end of 1930, Kenyatta agreed to help get the children back to the mission schools – on condition there would be no teaching about 'female circumcision'. In the long run, clitoridectomy persisted strongly. It seems to have revived in the 1940s, and the colonial administration felt powerless to act.[37] By the 1960s it was estimated that not less than ninety per cent of women in the villages of Kenya were circumcised, including large numbers of professing Christians. Only in 1982 did President arap Moi move to ban these practices in Kenya, following a major scandal in which fourteen children died following excision. The most important, and immediate, outcome of the 1929/30 crisis was the beginning of the independent schools movement and the foundation of Kikuyu 'separatist' churches. The break with the missions in 1929 later came to seem so crucial to the whole history of Kenya as to be comparable with Henry VIII's breach with the Church of Rome on the great matter of his divorce. Both were seen as 'sexual' confrontations with an alien authority. The independent schools were the focus of Kikuyu political activity for the next twenty years, and, some thought, centres of agitation if not actual subversion.[38]

The outcome of the confrontation over clitoridectomy was a sharp reminder to the pretensions of Protestant missionaries that the customary sexual order in Africa was not lightly to be interfered with, still less derided. For the future, they were to be more circumspect, as the Catholics always had been. Moreover, the sexual controversy helped to trigger off profound changes in the relations between Britain and the Kenyan peoples, notwithstanding the attempts of government to dissociate itself from the quixotic missionary stand. Nor did clitoridectomy's tryst with destiny end there. Because it tends to destroy vaginal sensation, it leads to a high incidence of heterosexual anal intercourse. Thus it was that AIDS first established itself mainly in women in those African communities that practised clitoridectomy and infibulation.

Notes

1   A. Moorehead, *The Fatal Impact: an Account of the Invasion of the South Pacific, 1767-1840*, London, 1966; B. Hutchinson, 'Some social consequences of nineteenth-century missionary activity among the South African Bantu', *Africa*, 27, 1957, pp. 160-75; P. Curtin, *The Two Jamaicas: the Role of Ideas, 1830-65*, Harvard, 1955, p. 169.

2   C. S. Lewis, *The Allegory of Love: a Study in Medieval Tradition*, Oxford, 1951, p. 4; M. Gluckman, *Custom and Conflict in Africa*, Oxford, 1955. p. 98.

3   A. R. Radcliffe-Brown and D. Forde (eds), *African Systems of Kinship and Marriage*, Oxford, 1950; E. E. Evans-Pritchard, *Kinship and Marriage among the Nuer*, Oxford, 1951; L. Mair, *African Marriage and Social Change*, London, 1969.

4   J. F. A. Ajayi, *Christian Missions in Nigeria, 1841-91*, London, 1965, pp. 105-7.

5   I. Schapera (ed.), *Livingstone's Missionary Correspondence, 1841-56*, London, 1961, p. 9.

6   V. R. Dorjahn, 'Polygyny' in W. R. Bascom and M. J. Herskovits (eds), *Continuity and Change in African Cultures*, Chicago, 1959, pp. 103-9.

7   D. W. Throup, 'Clitoridectomy and the Kikuyu Central Association', unpublished seminar paper, Cambridge, 1986; D. Gaitskell, '"Wailing for purity" prayer unions… 1912-40', in S. Marks and R. Rathbone (eds), *Industrialisation and Social Change in South Africa, 1870-1930*, London, 1982, pp. 338-57.

8   A. Hastings, *Christian Marriage in Africa: being a Report commissioned by the Archbishops of Cape Town, Central Africa, Kenya, Tanzania and Uganda*, London, 1973, esp. pp. 12-20, 45-60.

9   H. B. Hansen, *Mission, Church and State in a Colonial Setting: Uganda, 1890-1925*, London, 1984, pp. 260-79; F. B. Welbourn, *East African Rebels*, London, 1961, p. 66; I. Schapera, *Married Life of an African Tribe*, London, 1940, p. 349 (the tribe was the Kgatla of Bechuanaland). For the West Indies see Curtin, *The Two Jamaicas*, p. 169.

10 Hastings, *Christian Marriage in Africa*; K. Mann, *Marrying Well: Marriage, Status and Social Change among the Educated Elite in Colonial Lagos*, Cambridge, 1985, esp. pp. 43-53, 115-18; J. B. Webster, *African Churches among the Yoruba, 1888-1922*, Oxford, 1964, esp. p. 65; *idem*, 'Attitudes and policies of the Yoruba African churches towards polygamy', in C. G. Baëta (ed.), *Christianity in Tropical Africa: Studies presented at a Seminar in Ghana, 1965*, 1968, pp. 224-46.

11 Hastings, *Christian Marriage*; S. Neill, *A History of Christian Missions*, 2nd ed., London, 1986, ed. O. Chadwick, pp. 452-3.

12 G. S. J. Schurhammer, *Francis Xavier: his Life and Times* (trans. M. J. Costelloe), IV: *Japan and China, 1549-52*, Rome, 1982, pp. 77-85, 144, 154-5, 160-2, 259, 287; *idem*, *Shin-tō: the Way of the Gods in Japan, according to the Reports of Japanese Jesuit Missionaries in the Sixteenth and Seventeenth Centuries*, Bonn, 1923, p. 169; H. Dumoulin, *A History of Zen Buddhism*, London, 1963, pp. 199, 309 n.2; D. H. Shiveley, 'Tokugawa Tsunayoshi, the Genroku Shogun', in A. M. Craig and D. H. Shiveley (eds), *Personality in Japanese History*, California, 1970, pp. 97-101; J. D. Spence, *The Memory Palace of Matteo Ricci*, London, 1985, ch. 7: 'The men of Sodom', pp. 201-31.

13 J. P. Thoonen, *Black Martyrs*, London, 1941, revised by J. F. Faupel, *African Holocaust: the Story of the Uganda Martyrs*, London, 1965; review by H. B. Thomas, *Journal of African History*, V, 1964, pp. 150-2. An attempt to list the names of the martyrs is made by H. B. Thomas, 'The Baganda Martyrs, 1885-7', *Uganda Journal*, XV, 1951, pp. 84-91.

14 Faupel, *African Holocaust*; see also R. Oliver, *Missionary Factor in East Africa*, London, 1952 and 1965, pp. 103-5; Neill, *Christian Missions*, pp. 217-18; C. C. Wrigley, 'Christian revolution in Buganda', *Comparative Studies in Society and History*, II, 1959.

15 Faupel, *African Holocaust*; E. Stock, *The History of the Church Missionary Society*, III, 1899, pp. 411-16 – the explanation given here was that the persecution began with *one* page 'who refused to commit a disgraceful sin'. *The Times*, 30 October 1886, merely referred obliquely to Mwanga's 'insolent enmity'.

16 J. A. Rowe, 'The purge of Christians at Mwanga's court', *Journal of African History*, V. 1964, pp. 55-71. M. Twaddle, 'The emergence of politico-religious groupings in late nineteenth-century Buganda', *Journal of African History*, XXIX, 1988, p. 81-92, points out that some ten years earlier *Muslim* pages had been put to death by Mutesa for taking their foreign religion too seriously; he regards the 1886 attack on Christians as being broadened in a similar way into something 'more than just one frustrated individual's campaign for revenge'. However, it is clear that it was *not* just Mwanga who was sexually frustrated at court. See also P. Katumba and F. B. Welbourn, 'Muslim martyrs of Buganda', *Uganda Journal*, XVIII, 1964, pp. 151-63.

17 Stock, *History of the Church Missionary Society*, IV, 1916, p. 86.

18 L. S. B. Leakey, *The Southern Kikuyu before 1903*, London, 1977, I, pp. 620-22; II, p. 523; S. McLean and S. E. Graham, *Female Circumcision, Excision and Infibulation*, Minority Rights Group Report No. 47, London, 2nd ed. 1985; PRO, CO 533/394/10.

19 *Female Circumcision: Memorandum prepared by the Mission Council of the Church of Scotland*, 1931, pp. 1-7 (Kenya National Archives: DC/FH.3/2); J. Kenyatta, *Facing Mount Kenya*, London, 1938, pp. 130-5. There is a PhD thesis which I have not seen: J. Murray, 'The Kikuyu female circumcision controversy', California, 1974.

20 The Victorian operation was pioneered by Dr Isaac Baker Brown between 1858 and 1867, when he was expelled as a Fellow of the Obstetrical Society. His operation was much criticised. He used it mainly to treat 'excessive masturbation', 'nymphomania' and occasionally epilepsy and hysteria. Baker Brown's mistake was not so much the operation itself (which continued to be available until 1872) but the fact that he too often failed to obtain the consent of the husband or even of the patient herself. The operation persisted longer in the United States: to 1904 at least, and perhaps until 1925. See S. M. Edwards, *Female Sexuality and the Law: a Study of the Constructs of Female Sexuality as they inform Statute and Legal Procedure*, Oxford, 1981, pp. 85-90; G. J. Barker-Benfield, *Horrors of the Half-known Life: Male Attitudes towards Women and Sexuality in Nineteenth-Century America*, New York, 1976, p. 96; R. A. Spitz, 'Authority and masturbation', *Psychoanalytic Quarterly*, XXI, 1952, pp. 490-527.

21 Leakey, *Southern Kikuyu*, II, p. 629; McLean and Graham, *Female Circumcision*.

22 CO 533/394/11, memorandum by Director of Medical and Sanitary Services.

23 *Female Circumcision, op. cit*, note 19 above, p. 21.

24 *Ibid.*, p. 38 ff; J. Middleton, in *History of East Africa*, II, (ed. V. T. Harlow and E. M. Chilver), Oxford, 1965, ch. vii, pp. 362-5.

25 CO 533/394/10; CO 533/395/6.

26 G. Hewitt, *The Problems of Success: a History of the Church Missionary Society, 1910-42*, I, London, 1960, pp. 167-70.

27 J. M. Lonsdale, 'European attitudes and African pressures: missions and government in Kenya between the wars', *Race*, X, 1969, p. 149.

28 Kenyatta, *Facing Mount Kenya*, p. 135.

29 CO 533/394/10.

30 *Ibid.*, minute, 23 January, 1930; CO 533/392/11, minute, 21 December 1929.

31 CO 533/394/10; Kenyatta to Secretary of State, 22 January 1930; CO 533/395/6; CO 533/384/9/33.

32 CO 533/394/10 and CO 533/394/11, minutes by A. Stanton, and despatch from Grigg, 30 March 1930; meeting between Governor and deputation, 22 February 1930.

33 *Female Circumcision, op. cit.* note 19 above, Appendix VI; CO 533/407/14.

34 D. W. Throup, 'Clitoridectomy and the Kikuyu Central Association', unpublished seminar paper, Cambridge, 1986, based on reports in the Kenya National Archives, esp. DC/NY/I/3/1, South Nyeri Annual Report, 1929.

35 CO 533/384/9/33, and CO 533/394/10. Colonial Office records reveal fascinating sidelights upon their first encounter with Kenyatta, with comments which prefigure many of the observations made later during the Mau Mau crisis. For example: 'it is hard

to know what Kenyatta is saying to his people, because Kikuyu is so allegorical the meaning to be attached to any phrase is not self-evident'; 'the more we hear about Kenyatta here, the less satisfactory a person he is'; 'he is in touch with those who hold what are known as "extremist views" – Communists certainly, and Indian malcontents'; he is 'a harmless individual when left alone. . . . he has no real influence or importance with his tribe, but is the tool of men not friendly to Britain' (CO 533/384/9/33, and CO 533/395/6, 1929-31).

36 M. Bloch, *From Blessing to Violence: History and Ideology in the Circumcision Ritual of the Merina of Madagascar*, Cambridge, 1986.

37 A white farmer-magistrate, W. Evans, saw a Kikuyu circumcision ceremony *c.* 1944: 'it is the most gruesome ceremony I have ever seen, and I never wish to see it again. . . The whole business was fanatical and diabolical and left me wondering whether we were really getting anywhere with the Africans' (CO 537/7213, W. Evans to Lord Chancellor Jowitt, 26 February 1951).

38 Welbourn, *East African Rebels*, pp. 135-43, 207; F. D. Corfield, *Historical Survey of the Origins and Growth of Mau Mau*, Cmnd, 1030, London, 1960, p. 41; L. S. B. Leakey, *Mau Mau and the Kikuyu*, London, 1952, pp. 89-90.

H

CHAPTER NINE

Conclusion:
race, sex and empire

The problem of the twentieth century is the problem of the color-line, – the relation of the darker to the lighter races of man in Asia and Africa, in America and the islands of the sea. . .

I have seen a land right merry with the sun, where children sing, and rolling hills lie like passioned women wanton with harvest. And there in the King's Highway sat and sits a figure veiled and bowed, by which the traveller's footsteps hasten as they go. On the the tainted air broods fear. Three centuries' thought has been the raising and unveiling of that bowed human heart, and now behold a century new for the duty and the deed. The problem of the Twentieth Century is the problem of the color-line. [W. E. B. Du Bois, *The Souls of Black Folk* (1903), ch. 2, 'Of the dawn of freedom']

How have race relations in the British empire been affected by sexual attitudes and practices?[1] To begin to answer this final question we need to remind ourselves of the chronology. Mid-eighteenth-century metropolitan attitudes towards non-Europeans were not as unfavourable as they were to become. There was an underlying belief in the essential homogeneity of mankind as a whole, a respect for oriental civilisations, some idealisation of the so-called 'noble savage' and but little in the way of specific colour prejudice. (Blacks in Britain were not unpopular in the way Catholic Irish and immigrant Jews were.) These attitudes were only slowly eroded, and in two broad stages. (Unrealistic idealisation soon disappeared.) The erosion of *respect*, which took place roughly between 1790 and 1840, was followed by the erosion of *sympathy* and the growth of prejudice, which mainly occurred between the mid-1850s and the late 1860s. The first signs of change appeared in India in the 1790s, when miscegenation became officially disapproved of, and the Anglo-Indian community was rejected as a possible 'collaborating class'. This decision, as crucial as it was cynical, did the British no credit at all. It was, we argued, largely due to the fears generated by the revolt in Santo Domingo, together with a clearer determination to impose a permanent raj, and the beginning of the Protestant missionary movement with its strongly evangelical motivation.

Disillusionment with non-Europeans accumulated as actual experience grew of trying to govern and convert them. This was a key factor in the hardening of racial attitudes. So too was the galvanic effect of the Industrial Revolution, intensifying the British sense of mastery and superiority, and leading to a devaluation of those societies previously admired for a stability that now seemed mere stagnation. Belief in the *potential* equality of all mankind lingered on well into the nineteenth century, however, to be shattered in the concatenation of wars, revolts and upheavals that marked the decade of imperial crisis between 1857 and 1867. The Indian Mutiny and the Jamaica Uprising were only the most prominent manifestations of what seemed to be almost a general rejection of western influences throughout the globe. Thereafter, pessimism about remoulding the entire world in the British Victorian image was a fundamental characteristic of imperial rule. Instead of trying to 'improve' non-European peoples and raise them in the 'scale of civilisation' , sound administration, paternalist and condescending, now became the order of the day. With the increased scepticism about the capacity of Afro-Asian peoples for constructive change, more reliance came to be placed on white settlers as apparently the most efficient way of bringing about the economic development of underdeveloped regions. Their voices were then stridently added to governmental demands for the maintenance of 'social distance'. In the interests of establishing an unimpeachable imperial ruling elite, close contact between rulers and ruled was progressively reduced everywhere

The chronology of British changing attitudes towards sex fits this general pattern closely. Although intermarriage with non-Europeans was virtually at an end in most of the empire outside the West Indies, Mauritius and (as yet) Hudson's Bay by the close of the first decade of the nineteenth century, interracial sex remained common until the 1860s. While race relations in general were relatively relaxed, sex across the colour-line persisted, but as racial attitudes became more tense and problematic, so these sexual relationships were more and more frowned upon. At home, what are known as Victorian sexual values were, in fact, established only rather late in the day. Relatively robust and forthright eighteenth-century approaches to sexuality persisted a long while beyond their heyday, like slow detumescence after a climax. The 1860s saw the gradual beginnings of effective change, but we have identified the 1880s as the main watershed, the years which witnessed the final repudiation of earlier 'laxity', the enthronement of a flaccid 'respectability', and the inauguration of a fanatical Purity campaign. The result, undoubtedly, was a reduction of sexual opportunity in Britain itself. Almost inevitably, this campaign was extended overseas, not only to the empire (notably, as we have seen, in Kenya and Rhodesia), but eventually to the wider international arena as well. This process was aided after the First World War by the establishment of the League of Nations, which was persuaded by the British Purity-mongers to concern itself with the international prostitution traffic. Right from the start of the 1880s Purity campaign, an attempt had been made to remove organised military prostitution from the cantonments of the Indian army. This was quickly followed by the first rather feeble moves to get officials in Burma to give up their concubines. Neither was successful. The Crewe Circular (1909), forbidding such liaisons to the Colonial Service, was the fruit of a renewed and much fiercer Purity attack on Edwardian scandals. It was an important landmark. By the 1920s the red-light districts of Bombay, Singapore and Hong Kong were all under moralistic scrutiny, although the task of stamping out internationally organised prostitution was an uphill one. Meanwhile, the missionaries were hard at work – harder than ever in some cases – as they had been for a century or more, in trying not just to hold British officials to Christian sexual standards, but to impose them on the rest of the world as well. This campaign, however, received what was to prove a decisive setback with the sexual murder of Miss Stumpf in Kenya in 1930 at the height of the clitoridectomy controversy. Thereafter, the missionary invasion of indigenous sexual practices was forced into a less aggressive gradualism.

So much for the basic framework and larger generalities. What of the views of the ordinary officials and boxwallahs, the men on the spot? It has often been noticed that British administrators admired or felt more at ease with some peoples rather than others. There was, for example, a marked empathy with Muslims, and with so-called 'martial races' such as the Sikhs, which was complemented by a distaste for the 'mild Hindu', pejoratively known as the 'Bengali *babu*'. The approval bestowed on Malays – strictly Malayo-Muslims – amounted (it has been said) to a veritable 'Malayophilia'. Africans seldom seem to have evoked a similar generalised response, however devoted the individual district officer may have become to 'his' people. These racial evaluations were to some extent influenced by sexual attitudes. An administrator was likely to feel more sympathetic to a community if he found their women attractive. Also, there is a whole literature of preferential admiration for sexy Arab boys, spirited Indian youths, and even the occasional faithful African servant. Such sexual preferences were easily projected from the individual on to races as a whole.[2] Probably the British liked those peoples best who most conformed to western values in standards of beauty and behaviour. Certainly, Victorian class and gender stereotypes were transferred into racist ideology.[3] Burmese and Malayo-Muslims satisfied the canons of gentlemanly manliness in a way the Bengalis did not. The latter were regarded as 'effeminate', that is to say unmanly and degenerate, because believed to indulge in sexual relations at much too early an age (child-brides being a particular objection) and to lack the essential 'manly' control of the sexual urges: A. O. Hume (a founder of the Indian National Congress) complained that masturbation was universal among Bengalis and was causing physical deterioration.[4] An official long experienced in the Far East decided that the secret of the liking so many Europeans had for Japan was that '*the girls are charming*'.[5] Most Asian and Polynesian women were indeed notably sexually attractive to white men. We have encountered several examples of men who found European partners insipid fare after their sexual experience with Asians: Burton, Sellon, G. R. and others. By contrast, African, Afro-Caribbean and black American women were much more of an acquired taste. Moreover: 'To no modern race does its women mean so much as to the Negro nor come so near to the fulfilment of its meaning.' So wrote Du Bois, and this black respect for their visibly important womenfolk may have been a further stumbling-block in British evaluation of blacks, as British men inclined rather to regard Muslim purdah favourably. It was a more congenial system, not least because it conveniently removed from them, as outsiders, the ambivalent temptations of availability. Black observers have often remarked the nonchalant attitudes of British men towards their women. Indian women seldom thought much of them as lovers.

One thing is certain. Sex is at the very heart of racism. Racism is not caused simply by sexual apprehensions, and there are many other factors involved, such as fear of the unfamiliar, fear bred by memory of historic conflicts, fear of demographic swamping by the superior numbers of a culture perceived as alien and inferior, fear of disease, fear of economic competition for limited resources – but the peculiarly emotional hostility towards black men which it has so often engendered requires a sexual explanation. From New Orleans to New Guinea, from Barbados to Bulawayo, from Kimberley to Kuala Lumpur, the quintessential taboo to be explained is the white man's formal objection to intimacy between black men and white women. Granting political equality was perceived as giving freedom for black men to go to bed with white women, and in the American south or in southern Africa that stuck in the gullet. By the twentieth century, thirty out of the forty-eight states of the United States of America had laws prohibiting mixed marriages.

In South Africa, one of the first acts of the National Party in government after 1948 was to pass the Prohibition of Mixed Marriages Act (1949). Previously, under the Immorality Act (1927), casual sex between blacks and whites had been illegal; now it became a criminal offence for Europeans to marry non-Europeans. Even the South African parliamentary Opposition agreed mixed marriages were an 'unmitigated evil' with tragic social consequences; in the debates on the Bill, Smuts declared, 'if there is one thing on which all South Africans are agreed, it is this, that racial blood mixture is an evil'. Nevertheless, the new law was largely symbolic, a triumphalist expression of Afrikaner political ascendancy, in formalising apartheid, rather than a reflection of sexual morality as such, for it was not dealing with a serious actual problem. There were fewer than a hundred South African mixed marriages in the mid-1940s, and seldom more than forty-five convictions for interracial sex. The gratuitous new law provoked anger, just as in earlier days recurrent rape scares in South Africa and other settler communities themselves embittered race relations, not least because they had no real sexual foundation, whatever might have been their political undertones.[7] The most famous mixed marriage in the history of the British empire had meanwhile been contracted (in September 1948) between Seretse Khama (heir to the chieftaincy of the Bangwato in Bechuanaland) and Ruth Williams, a London secretary. Their marriage was opposed by almost everyone around them, including the bride's father, an ex-Indian Army officer. Some sections even of British opinion regarded Ruth as no better than a 'filthy white creature', as having done something disgusting, while in South Africa itself the marriage was condemned as not only 'distasteful and disturbing' but as 'striking at the root of white supremacy'. When Ruth arrived in Bechuanaland, the European community tried to ostracise her. Despite these deeply unpropitious circumstances and all the interstate controversy, the marriage was in every way successful, with four healthy children. So why all the frenetic, symbolic and apocalyptic condemnation surrounding mixed marriages?[8]

Sexual fears are obviously capable of manipulation for political ends, such as the maintenance of white control. But sexual fears are not (as has often enough been argued) a mere rationalisation of political and economic fears, and white men were genuinely apprehensive of the erotic competition. Thus in the opinion of many historians of race these sexual worries are 'the ultimate basis of racial antagonism'.[9] Assumptions of an aggressive black sexuality were deeply ingrained in Britain itself and throughout the American and colonial world.[10] Frequently, this has been specifically related to a belief that the black man has a larger penis than the white man and greater sensual staying power. At least from the fifteenth century it was widely put about that the blacks were exceptionally well-equipped (or, in the words of a seventeenth-century traveller, that they had 'large Propagators'). This was probably a scientific commonplace by the eighteenth century, but the notion of the black 'super-penis' only began to assume widespread and obsessional significance in the 1860s as a result of the deterioration of race relations throughout the Anglo-Saxon world, a process especially notable in the increasing segregation and negrophobia of the American South following the end of slavery. Many commentators dismiss this obsession as a myth, as no more than part of the racist paraphernalia and thus automatically discredited; and they argue that there is no essential difference between penis-size in black and white. Unfortunately, they are almost certainly being naive, both physiologically and psychologically. Anatomically, as modern phalloplethysmographical studies have shown, the truth is that the black penis is on average a *little* larger than the white man's. And analytically, whatever the facts, the important thing is what people think is the case. Thus the notion of the black 'super-penis' remains 'a classical instance of the influence of sexual insecurity upon perception':

> Whatever the objective facts of the matter, the belief blended flawlessly with the white man's image of the Negro. If a perceptible anatomical difference did in fact exist, it fortuitously coincided with the already firmly established idea of the negro's special sexuality; it could only have served as striking confirmation of that idea, as salt in the wounds of the white man's envy.

It has thus been further suggested that Amerindians were the subject of less prejudice in the United States because their 'propagators' were (on average) a little *smaller* than those of the whites, and their sex-drives lower.[11] Intermarriage with them was never illegal. Nor was it in New Zealand with the Maoris. Are we then in a position to posit an emerging general theory that penis-length determines whether sexual fears are present or not? Is this the crucial reason why white men got on well with the Maoris? Not really. Professor Sinclair acknowledged that the absence of a feeling of sexual rivalry or jealousy towards Maori males is important in comparatively good race relations in New Zealand. He was unable to suggest an explanation: 'But there is no real or imagined difference in sexual organs or practices to cause jealousy'. Although the negative point is not unimportant, there are more significant reasons for interracial respect, in New Zealand and elsewhere. In the Maori case, these included martial spirit and lighter skin-colour.[12]

If, for whatever reason, white men were anxious to keep black men away from their womenfolk, they (notoriously) imposed no parallel self-denying ordinance on themselves in their relations with black women. 'English colonials were caught in the push and pull of an irreconcilable conflict, between desire and aversion for inter-racial sexual union'; desire (which was biological) and aversion (which was cultural) 'rested on the bedrock fact that white men perceived Negroes as being *both alike and different* from themselves'. And perceived black men as *alike* in wanting white women, yet *different* in being more likely to give satisfaction, in being socially inferior but sexually privileged.[13]

It is essential, of course, to distinguish between sexual objective and sexual object, between aim and actuality: what you would prefer and what you can get. If black and brown flesh had met all white male requirements there would have been little need for the white slave traffic, yet, as we have seen, this was organised on a grand scale. Outside this network the accessible may not have met the ideal, but it was seldom rejected. Blacks may not have represented sexual perfection for white men, but they were – especially in slave plantations – supremely accessible. There may have been some white men who had a genuine preference for black or brown partners, but they were probably not the majority. Mixed-blood women were preferred everywhere from Montreal to Madras. We have more than once noticed in these pages that those who were most promiscuous with non-Europeans would, in fact, have preferred white partners if only they had been available. Some theorists (for example, Stember) would argue that *everyone* prefers a white woman; and that the black man (when the restraints were removed) was all too ready to see interracial intercourse as a revenge for having been so long denied access. There are obvious difficulties with this thesis – it would not seem true of Indians, and perhaps not of the Bantu – but it would indeed explain why it was a mid-Victorian commonplace that if revolts against Europeans broke out they would lead to assaults on white women. (This did not always happen, but in the breakdown of the Belgian Congo in 1960 the rape of European women certainly occurred.)[14]

This is not to say, however, that interracial sex was only a form of glorified rape, inherently cynical and uniformly opportunistic. The example of the Canadian fur trade gives the lie to any such interpretation. Elsewhere, too, sometimes what had begun as casual use ended as affectionate caring. Emotional involvement and real concern have been impressively shown to exist among white masters even within the deeply unpropitious institutionalised exploitation of the slave plantation.[15] Of all forms of sexual interaction between Europeans and non-Europeans this was the one that had the worst effects. As Du Bois wrote:

> The red stain of bastardy, which two centuries of systematic legal defilement of Negro women had stamped upon his race, meant not only the loss of ancient African chastity, but also the hereditary weight of a mass of corruption from white adulterers, threatening almost the obliteration of the Negro home.[16]

There has been a very particular devaluation of black American women, for so long regarded by whites as sluts and mammies, fit only for sex and suckling, scrubbing and skivvying. Sex on the slave plantation was in essence part of a system of gross and indefensible abuse. Black American militants and novelists are prominent among those who regard all black–white sexual relations as inherently exploitative. This is perhaps understandable in an American context, but not necessarily valid for wider application. In other extra-European situations there is a large grey area where matters lack this judgmental certainty. Is it 'exploitation' if the white man is offered 'sexual hospitality' in accordance with traditional custom? Is it exploitation if he negotiates with the father or headman, presents the expected gift and pays the requisite bridewealth for a temporary wife? Is it exploitation if Afghan or Maori women throw themselves at British soldiers or sailors and demand sex?[17] It simply is not true that native women had always to do the bidding of the white man because the structure of power relations in an empire left them no alternative. Most Algerian women in the nineteenth century steadily refused to service Frenchmen even though theirs was a conquered country; and in Indo-China, too, the women were far from complaisant. Officers of the British South Africa Company in Edwardian Rhodesia, such as Raikes (he of the 'unruly member'), certainly found some local women who conveniently believed that as rulers the Europeans had the right to require sexual relations; but equally there were many African women who refused in no uncertain terms to co-operate. When violence erupted as a result of frustrated interracial liaisons in British Africa, this was almost never directed against the women themselves, but against their competing boyfriends or unco-operative fathers. (This is true of the Silberrad case in Kenya, as well as that of Osborne in Rhodesia.) Rape, properly so-called (the use of force), by British administrators in Africa was virtually unknown. In Queensland, Saunders's investigation of Melanesian indentured labour indicates that immigrant women on the plantations were far more likely to be raped by Melanesian men than by Europeans.[18] Some indigenous women, too, were arguably better off by sexual incorporation into the white man's world – the Inuit women married to Canadian fur-traders being the most significant example. Nor should it be forgotten that Europeans were the first to challenge the formidable subjection and mutilation of non-European women: suttee, footbinding, clitoridectomy and the like.

Whatever may be true of the American South and the West Indies, the most common charge against the British empire has not in any case been that of systematic interference with Afro-Asian womenfolk. It has been that white wives blighted racial harmony. This hypothesis of the fatally advancing feminine frontier has never been more forcefully put than by James McAuley, the Australian poet and academic with experience of working in New Guinea from the 1940s. Noting that despite some admirable achievements the 'great enterprise' of European expansion

J

has been widely rejected throughout the world as *sterile*, he asked

> Why? Perhaps the simple answer is: the white woman. While European men went out to Asia and Africa and the Pacific without wife and family, they entered into a different sort of relationship, socially and sexually, with the people. When the white wife came out all was inevitably different ... the white woman is perhaps the real ruin of empires. If New Guinea had become a mulatto society it would be a slatternly, but more colourful and easy-going society, with the minor vices of concubinage and sloth, rather than the major respectable vices of coldheartedness and hypocrisy.[19]

McAuley sympathised with the plight of white women, and his vision of what-might-have-been has a certain appeal. Nevertheless, making the white woman the sole scapegoat for the 'ruin of empires' is repudiated by all historians today, if only because of its unsubtle monocausality. The memsahib was not an independent agent acting in a vacuum. She did what she was told, performed the role required of her. She was part of a general intensifying economic and political grip on the colonial world. It has always been assumed that her attitudes were identical to those of her husband; but we are nowadays more aware of differences of sexual attitude between the sexes, and it is at least plausible to suggest that some women, at any rate, were *less* subject to racial antipathy than white men, not more ('... the old saying is, Black men are pearls in beauteous ladies' eyes').[20]

Blame can also be partially shifted on to their menfolk in that they must bear responsibility for not constructing an adequate framework of friendships with non-European men. (Or, perhaps we should say, abandoning the framework which Warren Hastings had tried to operate in India.)[21] As a result, when sexual union with local mistresses collapsed there was no substitute structure to take its place. The idea that there was ever a golden age in the colonial past when race relations were harmonious is obviously nonsense. Nevertheless, when all the objections have been rehearsed, the idea that memsahibs were at least in part centrally involved in the deterioration of race relations from the 1860s still will not quite go away. For all that the arrival, in numbers, of resident wives, and the development of 'social distance' (or even an actual colour bar) is a contested conjuncture, the timing remains evidence of a remarkable correlation, to say the least. The root explanation may well be that the increasing ambitions and aspirations and defensive aloofness of European settlers and administrators, with aims quite unlike the easy-going beachcombers, adventurers and amateurs who preceded them, were what initiated the change and heightened the political and economic tensions, but that the simultaneous appearance of European women on the scene, as a community, strengthened and consolidated these trends in various places at critical points in time, adding a further discordant element. An insensitive wife in administration could quite inadvertently do a good deal of harm.[22] It certainly remained the official view in Whitehall until 1909 at least that the only sure way to get rid of interracial concubinage was through the more general presence of white women in colonial communities, and the social pressures 'they alone could exert'. The Crewe Circular, however, proved to be a highly effective alternative thereafter. Good race relations in Sarawak continued to be attributed to the absence of the memsahibs, but, of course, the circular was not issued there.[23]

The investigation now concluded has covered a lot of ground through a period of time extending beyond its nineteenth-century core to cover nearly two hundred years. It has examined the British and imperial sexual 'mentalities' and their shifting discourses, both in general terms and as they manifested themselves in groups and individuals throughout the formal and informal empire. Confronted with so much evidence of people's sexual preoccupation, the question naturally arises: what difference did it make? What connection is there between private sexual attitudes and public performance? Although there always are some people prepared to sacrifice career, family and health in pursuit of sexual pleasure, the more usual (and indeed more interesting) strategy is the attempt to maintain a balance between them, keeping private and public life formally separate. Accordingly, involvement in a sexual scandal by no means normally extended to a general degeneration. The fact that Lewis Harcourt was an exhibitionist paedophile, and Montgomery a repressed one, emphatically did not mean they were ineffective in their public duties. Among British African administrators, even those heavily involved in rows over the unpleasanter aspects of concubinage – Silberrad, Raikes and Osborne – were in all other respects regarded as good officers. 'Petticoat influences' on imperial politics and government are hard to find. Parnell was highly unusual amongst politicians in letting his love-life come to dominate him, though Lugard's judgment as a governor seems to have been for a while distorted by his desire to spend more time with his new-found wife. At least since the end of the eighteenth century, nobody allowed concubines the remotest influence on the conduct of affairs.

What about the susceptibility of those attracted to other males? Here the chances of a partner's making an active or direct contribution to decision-taking and policy-making appears to have been even more remote, despite the observation of W. T. Stead in 1902 that the whole history of South Africa might have been different if those who held its imperial destiny in their hands in the 1890s – Rhodes, Milner, Jameson and Beit – had all not been unmarried.[24] But what exactly was he driving at? He surely cannot have been hinting at any 'homosexual conspiracy'; for one thing, the heterosexual credentials of Beit and Milner are fully attested by the former's brazen visits to brothels and the later's prolonged maintenance of a mistress. Perhaps Stead supposed bachelors were more ruthless than husbands and fathers? Or that friendships between the four intensified their mutual resolve to force on the assertion of British supremacy? Or that the emotional attachment Rhodes felt for Jameson blinded him to his defects as an instrument for leading 'the Raid' on the Transvaal in 1895? This last point may have a certain plausibility. If so, it would be an isolated example. For the rest, the male attachments formed by Rhodes were typical of those among the ruling elite in being not between equals; and thus they had no actual bearing on the conduct of their gubernatorial or entrepreneurial activities. The attraction they experienced was so often to youngsters or members of lower social classes. No real influence in the public sphere can possibly be attributed to Rhodes's 'lambs', any more than to Henry Lawrence's 'off-sets', or Raja Brooke's midshipmen 'skylarking over his body', or to Kabaka Mwanga's court catamites – still less to General Gordon's Gravesend urchins in the bath-tub, or Field Marshal Montgomery's small friends on the Swiss ski-slopes. Similarly, mistresses and concubines were not integrated into a man's workaday world. (Taking concubines seriously meant 'going native'.)

Thus all these relationships, with women as much as with boys and youths, were essentially *parergal*: that is to say, they were recreational side-lines, subordinate interests, subsidiary to the main business of life, divergent from the principal characteristics of a public persona. To conceptualise them in this way is not, however, to argue that these relationships were unimportant. They may have had no specific direct impact on public action, but their indirect significance could be subtly fundamental. The careless sensuality of these relationships, often frivolous, adolescent or reckless, was the hidden side of responsibility and maturity, the obverse of achievement and fame won through self-discipline. In the total structure of personality, the parergon, superintending a concealed sexual hobby, can be a major component, perhaps even energising or stabilising the whole. Take away the emotional supports, the mechanisms of relaxation, the occasional secret triumph of sexual exaltation, the photograph beside the camp-bed, and what becomes of the motivation to succeed and even to survive? Particularly in times of hardship, readjustment and loneliness – and that is after all what life on the imperial frontier invariably involved – it is not at all certain that men could function properly as agents of empire without an effective parergon life and all the well-stocked memories that could go with it. In this sense, the sexual aspects of personality do matter. And it does make a difference that the empire provided its servants with the sexual opportunities they might need. Where individual conduct is concerned, beyond some such general conclusions of this sort it is not safe to go. There is no point in descending into the murky realms of reductionist psychobiography which tries to explain too much.

Fortunately, the significance of sexual factors in running the empire, viewed as a general system, is less problematic than in tracing their influence upon individual cases. This study has tried to show how administrators, settlers, soldiers, missionaries and others coped with the utterly alien indigenous approaches to the management of sexuality which they encountered in different parts of the world: how they responded to uninhibited courtship practices, 'natural' sodomy, polygyny, *mui tsai*, clitoridectomy and so forth. We have delineated the outlines of the forms of sexual organisation in a broad spectrum of imperial situations: in tropical plantations (using slaves or indentured labourers), in Australian penal settlements, in trading posts, mining compounds and mission stations, as well as in the Indian Army, Malayan estates and settler communities. Everywhere, sexual opportunity was well to the fore. The thoughts of soldiers and sailors regularly turned to sex as a result in part of the assumption of service authorities that they would inevitably seek out prostitutes. For civilians, in the pioneering days at least, the taking of native mistresses was common. In some places, estimates of ninety per cent have been quoted as conforming to this custom: eighteenth-century West Indies and India, nineteenth-century Burma and even twentieth-century Malaya. Because this was a world-wide empire maintained by sea communications, every journey to and from a posting or contract offered at least the potential of sexual experience. Cabin-boys and deck-stewards had a certain tradition in these matters. It was the sea voyage which – to recall a couple of examples almost at random – brought about the downfall of the Rev. Yate and served to introduce E. M. Forster to Captain Searight. In short, we have found sexual preoccupations overseas to be pervasive, and the empire an unrivalled field for the maximisation of sexual opportunity and the pursuit of sexual variation. For this reason if no other, sexuality was the spearhead of racial contact. And since sex is so fundamental a part of the human sense of what life is all about, and demands an attitude (even if that is only one of a-sexual rejection), it was also a central ingredient of racial fears. These fears were heightened because the British had some reason to doubt their expertise in a field where, compared with many Afro-Asian peoples (who traditionally paid more time and attention to refining sexual performance), their skills were in a somewhat atrophied or latent state.

A principal aim of this book has been to show that it is quite impossible to understand the nature of the British empire, or the dynamics of

British expansion overseas, without taking account of the sexual attitudes and expectations of the men who were in charge. The sexual
structures they encountered or created or adapted have to be built
integrally into the imperial picture if it is to be in any sense a true one.
The empire was as much a system of prostitution networks as it was (in
Kipling's famous phrase) a web of submarine cables. The extraordinary
movement of 'proletarian globe-trotters' and indentured labourers which
the British superintended had its essential parallel in the migration of
pimps and prostitutes, who readily took the whole world as their oyster
every bit as much as missionaries regarded it as their parish. The
brothels of Cairo, Port Said, Bombay and Singapore routinely provided
sexual initiation for young Britons travelling east of Suez. Regimental
brothels were part of the experience of serving in the Indian Army, where
there was a highly favourable ratio of about one prostitute to every forty-
four men. (Compare the 'ideal' ratio aimed at by the Japanese Army
during the Pacific War: one to forty.) There is ample evidence from all
parts of the empire of sexual contact between males. This was, however,
almost entirely opportunistic or the product of circumstance, and
without prejudice to relationships with women. In other words, it was
essentially bisexual. The evidence of the empire suggests a powerful
case for the deconstruction of the idea of homosexuality, which is
merely a recent western concept.

We have seen how some individuals, at all levels of imperial hierar-
chies and organisations, seized their overseas opportunities in ways that
can sometimes only be described as promiscuous. Examples occur among
proconsuls and commanders-in-chief (Clive in India and Macdonald in
Ceylon), through the lesser-ranking governors and consuls (Fitzroy in
Australia, Pottinger in India and South Africa, Codrington and Casement in Africa, Bozzolo and Berkeley in Malaya), right down to ordinary
army officers (Burton, Searight, G. R.) or even missionaries (Kendal and
Yate, Forrest and Twells). No doubt these characters had their analogues
among the traders and box-wallahs, engineers and mechanics. This is a
sector much less well-documented, however, except for incidents where
larger issues became involved, as with Phineas Macintosh in Bechuanal-
and in the 1930s. Nor were literary figures, from Byron and Flaubert to
Rider Haggard and E. M. Forster, immune from the temptation to
explore the sexual opportunities of the overseas world in a way they
could not or would not have done at home. On the other hand, it is important to remember that determination to maximise sexual opportunity was not necessarily typical. The majority probably conducted their
affairs modestly. There were many abstainers, too. Even for those who
resisted the temptations of empire, however, the argument has been
reiterated here that their public performance is incompletely under-

stood, if not actually inexplicable, without some reference to the exigencies of their private lives: the loneliness and frustrations that drove a Lugard or a Montgomery, for instance, or the sexual preoccupations that so vitiated the later leadership of a Wellesley or a Parnell.

Nor was it all a one-way process. Empire may have provided special opportunities, an efflorescence of eroticism, but it also exacted its own imperatives. The demands of an imperial career not infrequently led the rulers of empire into personal restraint and emotional sacrifice for shorter or longer periods, so that the prevailing impression has been one of the bleak prospects for marital happiness at the elite level. Empire caused marital breakdowns, which in turn drove men into more casual liaisons. Moreover, it was the official requirement for disciplined and efficient administration that led to the rewriting of the 'rules of engagement' with native women in India from the 1790s and in Africa in the 1900s. That same requirement also had domestic repercussions, contributing to the reorganisation of the Victorian public schools (which in turn became the models for the grammar schools), to the reformulation of the ideals of masculinity, and even, from the 1890s, to the introduction of circumcision for British middle-class boys.

The approach adopted in this study has been sufficiently chronological to allow these two periods of decision-making to be identified as major turning-points overall. Cornwallis and Wellesley put a stop to the young drunken and licentious John Company employees of the past roaming freely about late eighteenth-century India. Miscegenation was frowned on thereafter, and Anglo-Indians repudiated as a foundation for imperial rule, in the belief that all half-castes inherited the worst characteristics of both races and were potentially subversive. In parallel with these developments, the Protestant missionaries began their fierce reordering of life in the Pacific islands; everywhere they turned against forms of interracial marriage over which they had no control, finally discrediting the Hudson's Bay Company fur trade marriages, and helping to effect the demise of intermarriage in South Africa, too. Although the Indian Mutiny-Rebellion, the increase in the number of army chaplains and the coming of the memsahibs also had their effect in diminishing concubinage in India from the middle of the nineteenth century, changes in the empire as a whole of equal significance with those of the 1790s did not take place until the early years of the twentieth century, when Crewe and Selborne, by ruling definitively against concubinage, and stopping randy district officers roaming the kraals in predatory fashion, performed for African administration a function similar to that of Cornwallis and Wellesley for India. Simultaneously, the Protestant missions were attempting with increasing aggressiveness the reordering of African life by attacking polygyny and other sexual customs, although with less success than their predecessors in the South Pacific. In other words, whenever and wherever imperial rule became *serious*, as in India from the late eighteenth century or Africa from the late nineteenth, British administrative and moral standards were tightened up, Protestant codes of behaviour were asserted more importunately and 'social distance' between rulers and ruled was remorselessly widened. By 1914, in conjunction with the domestic triumph of Purity and prudery, the whole tone of the British empire had become radically different from what it had been only thirty years before. The influence of the memsahibs from the middle of the nineteenth century, while it cannot be eliminated from the account, does not appear to be of the same order of magnitude as these two sets of official decisions a hundred years apart, regulating sexual contact with Indians and Africans respectively. These decisions both significantly altered the way the empire was run, and defined a peculiarly British way of doing things.

In their empire, the French rejected the British assumption that an end to interracial sex was desirable anyway. They continued to encourage concubinage for their administrators. Did this lead to better race relations in the French empire? The French, possessed of a greater sexual self-confidence than the British, felt less need to maintain 'social distance'. They were also more willing to accept (assimilated) blacks as equals, thus perhaps avoiding the worst mistakes of the British, with their disdainful attitudes towards the western-educated (the 'wogs').'We looked upon imitation as parody; they as a compliment' (T. E. Lawrence).[25] As Kirk-Greene observes of the British case: 'The Achilles heel of empire is less likely to have been the stereotype stuffiness of memsahibdom or the ostracisation of miscegenation than the injury, unforgiven and unforgettable, inflicted by the blunt snubbing of an aspirant elite', a process which he believes brought race relations in the twentieth-century British empire to a 'tragic nadir'.[26] In other words, it is not what happened in the bedroom that matters, but what did not take place in the dining-room.

There are, at least in the pre-AIDS era, worse sins in running an empire, as in life, than the sexual ones. Sex in an imperial context does not need to be seen automatically as an act of racial domination. The view that it is such an act is principally only a tendentious extension of the suspect feminist argument that all sex is domination within a power relationship. Yet, as we have seen, the behaviour of a Simpson in Canada or a Raikes in Africa, distasteful as it was, was not violent, and it was not representative. It is important not to exaggerate the level of abuse and exploitation by harping on the nastier scandals. There is no reason why sex cannot be an act of racial conciliation. Though sex cannot of itself enable men to transcend racial barriers, it generates some admiration and affection across them, which is healthy, and which cannot always be dismissed as merely self-interested and prudential. For some British men, an introduction to the unabashed sexuality and erotic variation of the Arab and Asian worlds was a liberation and refreshment, gratefully received. For some, it was the only real contact they had with indigenous peoples. Moreover, though it by no means always does so, sex can sometimes actually mitigate the harshness of race relations. For example, when West Indian sailors came to Liverpool in the First World War, and race riots erupted in 1919, they found that the only thing which stopped life being hell for them was the continuing consolations of sympathetic white women.[27]

Sexual interaction between the British and non-Europeans probably did more long-term good than harm to race relations. Where unreal fears exist – and racial fears mainly are unreal – these are only reduced by being tackled head-on. Intermarriage can surely only contribute in the long run to a more peaceful, unpuritanical and sensible society. Essentially, it is no different from any other kind of marriage: difficult and demanding, and quite likely to go wrong, but it can hardly be argued that the world would be better off without it. Since it is unlikely ever to become common, it is all the more vital that some shared links between racial communities are maintained. Sex is one such link, and one of the more important ones at that. Interracial sex, like all other forms of sex, may be subject to abuses, but to insist that it is thereby rendered fundamentally undesirable is a counsel of despair compounded by a denial of the common humanity of us all. In this sense at least, the world as a whole cannot be said to be worse off for the sexual activity of the British in their empire.[28] More damaging by far has been the willingness of Third World governments to adopt the peculiar Purity laws and conventions of Britain in the 1880s as if they represented ultimate truths about human civilisation. They do not. All they represent, like most other sets of conventions, is a localised cultural perception (or in this case some may think misperception) and, in particular, a puritanical code politically attuned to the supposed needs of ruling a world-wide empire with aloof if benevolent dignity. They are not an appropriate model for a post-imperial world, especially one which, if it is to function in a civilised way, needs to recover some of the simpler truths about human nature that the West has suppressed. With AIDS now portentously upon the scene, the task of making this recovery is a formidable challenge indeed. The problem of the twenty-first century will be the problem not merely of finding the maximum limits of racial integration in society, but also of establishing the minimum requirements of sexual integration in the individual as well.

Notes

1 The literature on race relations is vast. Pioneering studies, still worth reading, include R. Benedict, *Race and Racism*, London, 1943; and P. Mason, *Prospero's Magic: Some Thoughts on Class and Race*, Oxford, 1962. The best of the general theoretical works on racism are M. Banton, *The Idea of Race*, London, 1977; and R. Ross (ed.), *Racism and Colonialism*, Leiden, 1982. On the sexual aspects of racism there is a considerable amount of American writing: the key work is C. H. Stember, *Sexual Racism: the Emotional Barrier to an Integrated Society*, New York, 1976. For the history of race relations in the British empire, the obvious place to start now is P. Fryer, *Black People in the British Empire: an Introduction*, London, 1988. Much of the central historical ground is covered in four works: A. J.Barker, *The African Link: British Attitudes to the Negro in the Era of the Atlantic Slave Trade, 1550-1807*, London, 1978; D. A. Lorimer, *Colour, Class and the Victorians: English Attitudes to the Negro in the Mid-Nineteenth Century*, Leicester, 1978; G. D. Bearce, *British Attitudes towards India, 1784-1858*, Oxford, 1961; and C. Bolt, *Victorian Attitudes to Race*, London, 1971. There is also a lot of background material in V. G. Kiernan, *The Lords of Human Kind: European Attitudes towards the Outside World in the Imperial Age*, London, 1969. For the crucial hardening of racial attitudes in the 1860s, see my *Britain's Imperial Century, 1815-1914*, London, 1976, ch. 3. There is as yet no classic work on the history of race relations in Britain itself, but J. S. Walvin, *Black and White: the Negro and English Society, 1555-1945*, London, 1973, is probably the most useful book to date. Of the recent studies, the most interesting are R. Winks, 'Infrastructure of race contact', in G. Martel (ed.), *Studies in Imperial History in Honour of A. P. Thornton*, London, 1986; and P.B. Rich, *Race and Empire in British Politics*, Cambridge, 1986.

2 A.H. M. Kirk-Greene, 'Colonial administration and race relations: some research reflections and directions', and A. P. A. Busia, 'Miscegenation as metonymy: sexuality and power in the colonial novel', *Ethnic and Racial Studies*, IX, 1986, pp. 275-87, and 360-72.

3 G. L. Mosse, *Nationalism and Sexuality: Respectability and Abnormal Sexuality in Modern Europe*, New York, 1985, pp. 36-37, 140-4; Lorimer, *Colour, Class and the Victorians*, p. 172.

4 M.Sinha, 'Gender and imperialism: colonial policy and the ideology of moral imperialism in late-nineteenth-century Bengal', in M.S. Kimmel (ed.), *Changing Men: New Directions in Research on Men and Masculinity*, California, 1987, pp. 217-31.

5 J. K. Fairbank *et al.* (eds), *The I. G. in Peking: Letters of Robert Hart, 1868-1907*, 2 vols, Harvard, 1975, II, p. 987.

6 W. E. B. Du Bois, 'The damnation of women', *Writings* (Library of America, ed. N. Huggins), New York, 1986, p. 959; C. C. Hernton, *Sex and Racism*, London, 1969, pp. 156-7. On British prejudices in favour of purdah, see T. G. P. Spear, *The Nabobs: a Study of the Social Life of the English in Eighteenth-Century India*, Oxford, 1932, p. 133.

7 Stember, *Sexual Racism*, pp. 4-11, 66, 151-63. A. du Toit, 'Political control and personal morality', in R. Schrire (ed.), *South Africa: Public Policy Perspectives*, Cape Town, 1983, pp. 54-83. C. van Onselen, 'The witches of suburbia', *Studies in the Social and Economic History of the Witwatersrand, 1886-1914*, II: *New Nineveh*, London, 1982. Colonial rape scares were often a reflection of non-specific fears of losing white control in general: see N. Etherington, 'Natal's black rape scares of the 1870s', *Journal of Southern African Studies*, XV, 1988, pp. 36-53.

8 R. Hyam, 'The political consequences of Seretse Khama: Britain, the Bangwato and South Africa, 1948-52', *Historical Journal*, 29, 1988, pp. 921-47.

9 Walvin, *Black and White*, pp. 9, 208-9.

10 D. Reynolds ('The Churchill government and the Black American troops in Britain during World War II', *Transactions of the Royal Historical Society*, 5th series, XXXV, 1985, p. 130) makes this point in discussing official attempts to keep black G. Is. from British civilians. In 1882 it was reported that there was a separate class of brothel for black seamen in Liverpool, although all the prostitutes were white: see *Report of*

House of Lords Select Committee on the Protection of Young Girls, 1882, C. 344, p. 521.

11 W. D. Jordan, *White over Black: American Attitudes towards the Negro, 1550-1812,* Chapel Hill, NC, 1968, pp. 34 and 159, and especially ch. iv; 'Fruits of passion: the dynamics of interracial sex', pp. 136-76. See also Stember, *Sexual Racism,* pp. 57-61; and E. D. Genovese, *Roll, Jordan, roll! – the World the Slaves made,* London, 1975, pp. 428 and 462. Probably there is little actual difference in sexual capacity between black and white man, but blacks paid more attention to cultivating their sexuality.

12 K. Sinclair, 'Why are race relations in New Zealand better than in South Africa, South Australia or South Dakota?', *New Zealand Journal of History,* V, 1971, pp. 121-27.

13 Jordan, *White over Black,* p. 137; Stember, *Sexual Racism,* pp. 197-98.

14 *Ibid.,* pp. 46, 196-210; B. Day, *Sexual Life between Blacks and Whites: the Roots of Racism,* London, 1974, pp. 9 and 196; Lorimer, *Colour, Class and the Victorians,* p. 188. For the Belgian Congo in 1960 see M. Crawford Young, 'Zaire, Rwanda and Burundi', in *Cambridge History of Africa,* VIII; *From c. 1940 to c. 1975,* ed. M. Crowder, Cambridge, 1984, p. 718.

15 Day, *Sexual Life between Blacks and Whites,* pp. 56-60, 87-92, 200-1; Genovese, *Roll, Jordan, roll!,* pp. 415-19.

16 W. E. B. Du Bois, 'The souls of black folk' (1903), ch. I, *Writings* (Library of America), p. 368.

17 A. W. Crosby, *Ecological Imperialism: the Biological Expansion of Europe, 900-1900,* Cambridge, 1986, pp. 231, 242-4.

18 K. Saunders, *Workers in Bondage: the Origins and Bases of Unfree Labour in Queensland, 1824-1916,* Queensland, 1982, p. 106.

19 J. McAuley, *The Grammar of the Real: Selected Prose, 1959-74,* Melbourne, 1975, 'My New Guinea' (1961), pp. 172-73.

20 Shakespeare, *Two Gentlemen of Verona,* V, ii, 11-12; Stember, *Sexual Racism,* 207-9.

21 Spear, *The Nabobs,* pp. 135-8: it was Wellesley who stopped inviting Indians to entertainments at Government House. See also J. G. Taylor, *The Social World of Batavia: European and Eurasian in Dutch Asia,* Wisconsin, 1983, pp. 140-1.

22 C. Ralston, 'The pattern of race relations in nineteenth-century Pacific port towns', *Journal of Pacific History,* V, 1970, pp. 39-60; C. Knapman, *White Women in Fiji, 1835-1930: the Ruin of Empire?. . .,* Sydney, 1986, esp. pp. 136-47; see also H. Callaway, *Gender, Culture and Empire: European women in Colonial Nigeria,* London, 1987.

23 See above, Notes, p. 180, n. 18 and n. 28.

24 W. T. Stead (ed.), *The Last Will and Testament of Cecil John Rhodes. . .and Political and Religious Ideas of the Testator,* 1902. The best discussion of Rhodes's sexuality is R. I. Rotberg (with M. F. Shore), *The Founder: Cecil Rhodes and the Pursuit of Power,* Oxford and New York, 1988, esp. pp. 404-8.

25 T. E. Lawrence, *Seven Pillars of Wisdom: a Triumph,* London, new ed. 1940; Day, *Sexual Life between Blacks and Whites,* pp. 30-1. A black French West Indian, Gaston Monnerville, as President of the French Senate, would automatically have taken over the government if President de Gaulle had died in office, according to F. Henriques, *Children of Caliban: Miscegenation,* London, 1974, who believes this could not have happened in Britain, pp. 155-6.

26 Kirk-Greene, 'Colonial administration and race relations', p. 284.

27 R. May and R. Cohen, 'The interaction between race and colonialism: a case-study of the Liverpool race riots of 1919', *Race and Class,* XVI, 1974, p. 117.

28 I do not know enough about the sexual life of other European empires to make definite comparisons. However, it is my impression that, the French and Dutch perhaps apart, the behaviour of other Europeans was rather more ruthless than the British: see C. R. Boxer, *Mary and Misogyny: Women in Iberian Expansion, 1415-1815,* London, 1975; H. Chevigny, *Russian America: the Great Alaskan Venture, 1741-1867,* London, 1965; H. Ridley, 'Germany in the mirror of its colonial literature', *German Life and Letters,* XXVIII, 1975, pp. 375-86; D. Mack Smith, *Mussolini's Roman Empire,* London, 1976, pp. 112-14. See also V. G. Kiernan, *European Empires from Conquest to Collapse,* London, 1982, p. 162.

BIBLIOGRAPHY

Primary Sources

Unpublished records

Public Record Office

All quotations from Crown Copyright materials by kind permission of the Controller of H. M. Stationery Office.

Ceylon: CO 54/682-6, 723 (1903-09)

Gold Coast: CO 96/624, 654 and 670 (1921-27)

Straits Settlements (Malaya): CO 273/121, 176, 197, 203, 258, 543, 544 (1883-1900, 1927-28)

South Africa (High Commission): CO 417/372, 465-509 (1903-11)

Kenya: CO 533/44-56 (1908-09); 384/9, 392/1 and 10 and 11, 394/ 10 and 11, 395/6, 407/14, 408/3 and 4 (1929-31)

Supplementary secret correspondence: CO 537/410 and 411, 540-2 (1903-07), 7213 (1951).

Circular despatches, secret and confidential: CO 854/168 (1907-15)

Social Service: CO 859/ 11/14, 105/5, 165/1, 224/2 and 5, 548, 550-3 (1939-56).

Replies to circular despatches: CO 862/15 (1909-10)

Confidential Print: CO 879/104 (1910-11)

Private papers

9th Earl of Elgin Viceroyalty Papers, 1894-99 (India Office Library)

F.-M. Lord Roberts Papers, 1903 (National Army Museum)

Hugh Dalton Papers, 1916-51 (London School of Economics, British Library of Political and Economic Science, Archives)

A. C. Benson Diary, 1897-1925 (Magdalene College, Cambridge, Archives, Group F)

A. D. Garson Diary, 1947-57 (Magdalene College, Cambridge, Archives, Group F)

W. R. Inge, Diary, 1907-49 (Magdalene College, Cambridge, Archives, Group F)

Published records

British Parliamentary Papers

1847 C. 447 and C. 534, *Report and Minutes of Evidence of the Select Committee of the House of Lords on Juvenile Offenders and Transportation.*

1881 C. 448, *Report and Minutes of Evidence of the Select Committee of the House of Lords on the Protection of Young Girls*

1882 C. 344, *Report and Minutes of Evidence of the Select Committee of the House of Lords on the Protection of Young Girls*

1893 C. 7148, *Report of the Committee... into the Indian Cantonments... with regard to Prostitution and the Treatment of Venereal Diseases*

1925 Cmd. 2501, *First Report of the Advisory Committee on Social Hygiene*
1930 Cmd. 3424, *Hong Kong: Papers relative to the Mui-Tsai Question, 1929-30*

*League of Nations Papers: Reports on the Traffic in Women, Children
and Obscene Publications* (1923-37)
A. 12. 1935. IV
A. 29. 1927. IV
A. 36. 1923. IV
A. 106. 1926. IV
A. 111. 1925. IV
C. 2. M.2. 1934. IV
C. 28. M.14. 1928
C. 52. M.52. 1927. IV
C. 85. M.12. 1930. IV
C. 88. M.32. 1936. IV
C. 127. M.65. 1935. IV
C. 164. M.40. 1924. IV
C. 164. M.59. 1931. IV
C. 164. M.77. 1932. IV
C. 293(1). 1925. IV
C. 330. M.110. 1925. IV
C. 476. M.318. 1937. IV
C. 516. M.357. 1937. IV
C. 734. M.299. 1923. IV
C. 825. M.282. 1925. IV
C. 849. M.393. 1932. IV
C.P.E. 90(1). 1927
C.T.F.E. 234. 1925
C.T.F.E. 250. 1925
C.T.F.E. 336(2). 1929
C.T.F.E. 365. 1928

Secondary materials

Principal journals consulted

African Affairs
American Historical Review
The Beaver: Magazine of the North
British Medical Journal
Comparative Studies in Society and History
English Historical Review
Ethnic and Racial Studies
Feminist Studies
Historical Journal
Historical Studies

History
History Workshop Journal
International Review of Missions
Journal of African History
Journal of the History of Ideas
Journal of Imperial and Commonwealth History
Journal of Interdisciplinary History
Journal of Social History
Journal of Southern African Studies
The Lancet
New Zealand Journal of History
Past and Present
Race and Class
Transactions of the Royal Historical Society, 5th series
Uganda Journal
Victorian Studies

Select bibliography of modern secondary works

Chapter I: Introduction: Problems and Approaches

Bullough, V. L., *Sexual Variance in Society and History*, New York, 1976.
Ellis, Havelock, *Studies in the Psychology of Sex*, VI: *Sex in Relation to Society*, Philadelphia, 1910, 1921.
Ford, C. S. and Beach, F. A., *Patterns of Sexual Behaviour*, London, 1952, 1965.
Foucault, M., *The History of Sexuality*, I: *An Introduction* (1976), trans. R. Hurley, London, 1979.
Freud, S., *Three Essays on the Theory of Sexuality* (1905), trans. J. Strachey, London, rev. ed. 1962.
Kinsey, A. C., Pomeroy, W. B., and Martin, C. E., *Sexual Behaviour in the Human Male*, Philadelphia and London, 1948; *Sexual Behaviour in the Human Female*, Philadelphia and London, 1953.
Meltzer, D., *Sexual States of Mind*, Perthshire, 1973.
Scruton, R., *Sexual Desire: a Philosophical Investigation*, London, 1986.
Stone, L., *The Family, Sex and Marriage in England, 1500-1800*, London, 1977.
—'Sexuality', in *The Past and the Present Revisited*, London, 1987, ch. 19; repr. from 'Sex in the West', *New Republic*, 3677, 8 July 1985, pp. 25-37.
Trumbach, R., 'London's sodomites: homosexual behaviour and western culture in the eighteenth century', *Journal of Social History*, XI, 1977, pp. 1-33.

Chapter 2: Sexual imperatives

Bence–Jones, M., *Clive of India*, London, 1974.
—, *The Viceroys of India*, London, 1982.
Bourne, K., *Palmerston*, I: *The Early Years, 1784-1841*, London, 1982.
Brodie, F. M., *The Devil Drives: a Life of Sir Richard Burton*, London, 1967, 1971.

Chenevix Trench, C., *Charley Gordon: an Eminent Victorian Reassessed*, London, 1978.

Chitty, S., *The Beast and the Monk: a Life of Charles Kingsley*, London, 1974.

Howarth, T. E. B. (ed.), *Monty at Close Quarters: Recollections of the Man*, London, 1985.

Jeal, T., *Baden-Powell*, London, 1989.

Longford, E., *Wellington*, 2 vols, London, 1969 and 1972.

Lyons, F. S. L., *Charles Stewart Parnell*, London, 1977.

Morison, J. L., *Lawrence of Lucknow, 1806-57: the Life of Sir Henry Lawrence*, London, 1934.

Perham, M., *Lugard*, I: *The Years of Adventure, 1858-98*, London, 1956.

Rotberg, R. I. (with M. F. Shore), *The Founder: Cecil Rhodes and the Pursuit of Power*, Oxford and New York, 1988.

Royle, T., *Death before Dishonour: the True Story of 'Fighting Mac'*, London, 1982.

Shore, M. F., 'Cecil Rhodes and the ego ideal', *journal of Interdisciplinary History*, X, 1979, pp. 249-65.

Singleton-Gates, P., and Girodias, M. (eds.), *The Black Diaries: an Account of Roger Casement's Life and Times*, Paris, 1959.

Tarling, N., *The Burthen, the Risk and the Glory: a Biography of Sir James Brooke*, Kuala Lumpur, 1982.

['Walter'], *My Secret Life*, 2-vol. ed., New York, 1966.

Chapter 3: The British home base

Bristow, E. J., *Vice and Vigilance: Purity Movements in Britain since 1700*, Dublin, 1977.

Crompton, L., *Byron and Greek Love: Homophobia in Nineteenth-Century England*, California and London, 1985.

Davin, A., 'Imperialism and motherhood', *History Workshop Journal*, V, 1978, pp. 9-65.

Gay, P., *The Bourgeois Experience, Victoria to Freud*, I: *The Education of the Senses*, New York and London, 1984; II: *The Tender Passion*, 1986.

Harrison, B., 'Underneath the Victorians', *Victorian Studies*, X, 1967.

Honey, de S., J. R., *Tom Brown's Universe: the Development of the Victorian Public School*, London 1977.

Mangan, J. A., and Walvin, J. (eds.), *Manliness and Morality: Middle-Class Masculinity in Britain and America, 1800-1940*, Manchester, 1987.

Porter, R., 'Mixed feelings: the Enlightenment and sexuality in eighteenth-century Britain', in P.-G. Boucé (ed.), *Sexuality in Eighteenth-Century Britain*, Manchester, 1982, pp. 2-27.

Smith, F. B., 'Ethics and disease in the late-nineteenth century: the Contagious Diseases Acts', *Historical Studies* (Melbourne), XV, 1971, pp. 118-35.

—, 'Sexuality in Britain, 1800-1900', *University of Newcastle Historical Journal* (New South Wales), II, 1974, pp. 19-32.

—, 'Labouchere's Amendment to the Criminal Law Amendment Bill', *Historical Studies*, XVII, 1976, pp. 165-73.

The People's Health, 1830-1910, London, 1979.
—, St John-Stevas, N., *Obscenity and the Law*, London, 1956.
Walkowitz, J. R., *Prostitution and Victorian Society: Women, Class, and the State*, Cambridge, 1980.
Weeks, J. *Coming out: Homosexual Politics in Britain from the Nineteenth Century to the Present*, London, 1977.
—, *Sex, Politics and Society: the Regulation of Sexuality since 1800*, London, 1981.

Chapter 4: Empire and sexual opportunity

Berger, M., 'Imperialism and sexual exploitation: a review article', and R. Hyam, 'A reply', *Journal of Imperial and Commonwealth History*, XVII, 1988, pp. 83-98.
Binney, J., 'Whatever happened to poor Mr Yate?, *New Zealand Journal of History*, IX, 1975, pp. 111-25.
Brown, J. S. H., *Strangers in Blood: Fur Trade Company Families in Indian Country*, Vancouver, 1980.
Butcher, J. G., *The British in Malaya, 1880-1941: the Social History of a European Community in Colonial South-East Asia*, Kuala Lumpur, 1979.
de Vere Allen, J., 'The Malayan Civil Service, 1874-1941', *Comparative Studies in Society and History*, XII, 1970, pp. 149-78.
Dunbar Moody, T., 'Migrancy and male sexuality on the South African gold mines', *Journal of Southern African Studies*, XIV, 1988, pp. 228-56.
Elphick, R., and Giliomee, H. (eds.), *The Shaping of South African society, 1652-1820*, London, 1979, chs. 4 and 10.
Galbraith, J. S., *The Little Emperor: Governor Simpson of the Hudson's Bay Company*, Toronto, 1976.
Green, W. A., *British Slave Emancipation: the Sugar Colonies and the Great Experiment, 1830-65*, London 1976.
Gunson, N., *Messengers of Grace: Evangelical Missionaries in the South Seas, 1797-1860*, Melbourne, 1978.
Hilliard, D., *God's Gentlemen: a History of the Melanesian Mission, 1849-1942*, Queensland, 1978.
Hughes, R., *The Fatal Shore: a History of the Transportation of Convicts to Australia, 1787-1868*, London, 1987.
Inglis, A., *The White Women's Protection Ordinance: Sexual Anxiety and Politics in Papua*, Sussex, 1975.
Purcell, V., *The Memoirs of a Malayan Official*, London, 1965.
Ranger, T. O., 'Missionary adaptation of African religious institutions: the Masasi case', in T. O. Ranger and I. N. Kimambo (eds.), *Historical Study of African Religion, with Special Reference to East and Central Africa*, London, 1972.
Ross, R., 'Oppression, sexuality and slavery at the Cape of Good Hope', *Historical Reflections*, VI, 1979, pp. 421-33.
Saunders, K. (ed.), *Indentured Labour in the British Empire, 1834-1920*, London, 1984.

Tinker, H., 'A New System of Slavery': the Export of Indian Indentured Labour Overseas, 1830-1920, London, 1974.

Van Kirk, S., 'Women of the fur trade', The Beaver: Magazine of the North, (Winnipeg), 303, 1972, pp. 4-21.

van Onselen, C., Studies in the Social and Economic History of the Witwatersrand, 2 vols, London, 1982.

—, 'Chibaro': African Mine Labour in Southern Rhodesia, 1900-33, London, 1976.

Yarwood, A. T., Samuel Marsden: the Great Survivor, Melbourne, 1977.

Chapter 5: The sexual life of the Raj

Allen, C. (ed.), Plain Tales from the Raj: Images of British India in the Twentieth Century, London, 1975.

Anthony, F., Britain's Betrayal: the Story of the Anglo-Indian community, Bombay, 1969.

Ballhatchet, K., Race, Sex and Class under the Raj: Imperial Attitudes and Policies and their Critics, 1793-1905, London, 1980.

Barr, P., The Memsahibs: the Women of Victorian India, London, 1976.

Callan, H., and Ardener, S. (eds.), The Incorporated Wife, London, 1984, chs. 10 and 11.

Ellis, Havelock, Studies in the Psychology of Sex, III: The Analysis of the Sexual Impulse, Philadelphia, 1903, 1922, Appendix B, History no. XIII, pp. 306-15, by 'G.R.'

Hammond, T., '"Paidikion": a paiderastic manuscript', International Journal of Greek Love (New York), I, 1966, pp. 28-37.

Ingram, E., 'The "Raj" as daydream: the Pukka Sahib as Henty hero in Simla, Chandrapore and Kyauktada', in G. Martel (ed.), Studies in Imperial History in Honour of A. P. Thornton, London, 1986.

Kipling, Rudyard, Plain Tales from the Hills, London, 1900 ed.

Richards, F., Old-Soldier Sahib, London, 1936.

Trustram, M., Women of the Regiment: Marriage and the Victorian Army, Cambridge, 1984.

Yeats-Brown, F., Bengal Lancer, London, 1930.

Chapter 6: Prostitution and Purity

Bristow, E. J., Prostitution and Prejudice: the Jewish Fight against White Slavery, 1870-1939, Oxford, 1982.

Davidson, R., '"As good a bloody woman as any other woman...": prostitution in Western Australia, 1985-1939', in P. Crawford (ed.), Exploring Women's Past: Essays in Social History, London, 1984.

Hane, M., Peasants, Rebels and Outcastes: the Underside of Modern Japan, New York, 1982.

Henriques, F., Prostitution and Society, 3 vols. London, 1962, 1963 and 1968.

Iliffe, J., The African Poor: A History, Cambridge, 1987.

Jackson, R. H., Pickering: Protector of Chinese, Kuala Lumpur, 1965.

Lethbridge, H., Hong Kong: Stability and change, a Collection of Essays, Hong

Kong 1978, ch. iv: 'The Po Leung Kuk', pp. 71-103.

O'Callaghan, S., *The Yellow Slave Trade: a Survey of the Traffic in Women and Children in the East*, London, 1968.

Sissons, D. C. S., '"*Karayuki-san*": Japanese prostitutes in Australia, 1887-1916', *Historical Studies*, XVII, 1977, nos. 68 and 69, pp. 323-35, 474-88.

van Heyningen, E. B., 'The social evil in the Cape Colony, 1868-1902: prostitution and the CD Acts', *Journal of Southern African Studies*, X, 1984, pp. 170-94.

White, L., 'A history of prostitution in Nairobi, Kenya, *c.* 1900-52', unpublished PhD thesis, Cambridge, 1984.

Woodcock, G., *The British in the Far East*, London 1969.

Chapter 7: Chastity and the Colonial Service

Allen, C. (ed.), *Tales from the South China Seas: Images of the British in South-East Asia in the Twentieth Century*, London, 1983, 1984.

Cairns, H. A. C., *Prelude to Imperialism: British Reactions to Central African Society, 1840-90*, London, 1965.

Collins, R. O., 'The Sudan Political Service: a portrait of the "imperialists"', *African Affairs*, LXXI, 1972, pp. 292-303.

Collins, R. O., and Deng, F. M. (eds.), *The British in the Sudan, 1898-1956: the Sweetness and the Sorrow*, London, 1984.

Gann, L. H., and Duignan, P., *The Rulers of British Africa, 1870-1914*, Stanford and London, 1978.

Hyam, R., 'Concubinage and the Colonial Service: the Crewe Circular (1909)', *Journal of Imperial and Commonwealth History*, XIV, 1986, pp. 170-86.

Kuklick, H., *The Imperial Bureaucrat: the Colonial Administrative Service in the Gold Coast, 1920-39*, Stanford, 1979.

Meinertzhagen, R., *Kenya Diary, 1902-06*, Edinburgh, 1957.

Reece, R. H. W., 'A "suitable population": Charles Brooke and race-mixing in Sarawak', *Itinerario* (Leiden), IX, 1985, pp. 67-112.

Rukavina, K. S., *Jungle Pathfinder: the Biography of 'Chirupula' Stephenson*, London, 1951.

Winstedt, R., *Start from Alif, Count from One: an Autobiographical Mémoire*, Kuala Lumpur, 1969.

Wraith, R. E., *Guggisberg*, London, 1967.

Chapter 8: Missionary confrontations

Ajayi, J. F. A., *Christian Missions in Nigeria,, 1841-91*, London, 1965.

Faupel, J. F., *African Holocaust: the Story of the Uganda Martyrs*, London, 1965.

Hansen, H. B., *Mission, Church and State in a Colonial Setting: Uganda, 1890-1925*, London, 1984.

Hastings, A., *Christian Marriage in Africa: being a Report commissioned by the Archbishops of Cape Town, Central Africa, Kenya, Tanzania and Uganda*, London, 1973.

Hewitt, G., *The Problems of Success: a History of the Church Missionary Society, 1910-42*, I, London, 1960.

Kenyatta, J., *Facing Mount Kenya*, London, 1938.

Lonsdale, J., 'European attitudes and African pressures: missions and government in Kenya between the wars', *Race*, X, 1969, pp. 141-51.

McLean, S., and Graham, S. E., *Female Circumcision, Excision and Infibulation*, Minority Rights Group Report No. 47, London, 2nd ed., 1985.

Mann, K., *Marrying Well: Marriage, Status and Social Change among the Educated Elite in Colonial Lagos*, Cambridge, 1985.

Middleton, J., 'Changes in African life, 1912-45', in Harlow, V. T., and Chilver, E. M. (eds.), *History of East Africa*, II, Oxford, 1965, ch. vii, pp. 333-94.

Neill, S., *A History of Christian Missions*, 2nd ed. (ed. O. Chadwick), London, 1986.

Rowe, J. A., 'The purge of Christians at Mwanga's court', *Journal of African History*, V, 1964, pp. 55-71.

Webster, J. B., *African Churches among the Yoruba, 1888-1922*, Oxford, 1964.

Chapter 9: Conclusion: race, sex and empire

Busia, A. P. A., 'Miscegenation as metonymy: sexuality and power in the colonial novel', *Ethnic and Racial Studies*, IX, 1986, pp. 360-72 (Special issue in honour of Kenneth Kirkwood).

Etherington, N., 'Natal's black rape scares of the 1870s', *Journal of Southern African Studies*, XV, 1988, pp. 36-53.

Fryer, P., *Black People in the British Empire: an Introduction*, London, 1988.

Jordan, W. D., *White over Black: American Attitudes towards the Negro, 1550-1812*, Chapel Hill, NC, 1968.

Kirk-Greene, A. H. M., 'Colonial administration and race relations: some research reflections and directions', *Ethnic and Racial Studies*, IX, 1986, pp. 275-87 (Special issue in honour of Kenneth Kirkwood).

Knapman, C., *White Women in Fiji, 1835-1930: the Ruin of Empire? . . .*, Sydney, 1986.

Lorimer, D. A., *Colour, Class and the Victorians: English Attitudes to the Negro in the Mid-Nineteenth Century*, Leicester, 1978.

May, R., and Cohen, R., 'The interaction between race and colonialism: a case-study of the Liverpool race riots of 1919', *Race and Class*, XVI, 1974.

Ralston, C., 'The pattern of race relations in nineteenth-century Pacific port towns', *Journal of Pacific History*, V, 1970, pp. 39-60.

Rich, P. B., *Race and Empire in British Politics*, Cambridge, 1986.

Sinclair, K., 'Why are race relations in New Zealand better than in South Africa, South Australia or South Dakota?', *New Zealand Journal of History*, V, 1971, pp. 121-27.

Stember, C. H., *Sexual Racism: the Emotional Barrier to an Integrated Society*, New York, 1976.

GLOSSARY

analingus	licking of the anal orifice
asexual	(biological) absence of sex
a-sexual	lacking interest in sexual activity
askari	African policeman (Swahili)
bibi	Indian mistress
bonze	Buddhist monk
box-wallah	European businessman (derogatory)
chibaro	Rhodesian system of mine labour, seen as servile
clitoridectomy	female circumcision or removal of clitoris
corprolagnia	sexual enjoyment in watching defaecation
coprolalia	use of 'dirty' words as sexual stimulus
coprophilia	sexual use of excrement
dhobi	Indian laundryman
durbar	court; levee
dysmenorrhoea	difficult or painful menstruation
dyspareunia	difficult or painful coitus
fellatio	sucking of the penis
gerontophilia	sexual attraction to the elderly
hlo-bongo	intracrural intercourse (Zulu)
infibulation	stitching of the vagina to prevent intercourse
intracrural	(of intercourse) between the thighs
Kabaka	ruler of Buganda
karayuki	Japanese prostitute working overseas
katikiro	chief minister of Buganda
kraal	African village (cattle enclosure)
lal-bazar	Indian army regimental brothel
levirate	marriage to a man's dead brother's widow
lobola	transaction with wife's family to legitimise marriage (Bantu)
memsahib	European lady in Asia (Anglo-Indian)
mui tsai	Chinese female domestic bond service, often leading to prostitution
necrophilia	sexual attraction to corpses
nkotshane	African practice of young males taking the female role (Shangaan)
nongogo	African prostitute
paedophilia	sexual attraction to prepubertal children
pederasty	sexual activity with pubertal boys
phalloplethysmography	scientific measurement of penis-size
polyandry	marriage of a woman to more than one husband
polygamy	marriage to more than one spouse
polygyny	marriage of a man to more than one wife

[226]

pukka sahib	European man in Asia respected as a 'real gentleman'
punkah-wallah	operator of a cooling-fan
reglementation	system of regulating tolerated prostitution
rent-boy	young male prostitute
scopophilia	sexual desire to see naked bodies
smegma	secretion of the foreskin
sororate	marriage to a man's dead wife's (unmarried) sister
souteneur	pimp living on the earnings of a prostitute
suttee	Hindu widow-burning
sympneumata	limiting sexual activity to prolonged mutual masturbation (usually heterosexual)
urolagnia	sexual use of urination
yoshiwara	Japanese brothel quarter
zoophilia	sexual attraction to animals

INDEX

INDEX